UKCAT is the abbreviated title for the United Kingdom Clinical Aptitude Test published by Pearson. This publication does not contain any real UKCAT questions or test material. It has been devised first and foremost as a source of help in preparing for the challenge of the UKCAT. The questions and advice have been written to help real candidates pass the real test.

HOW TO MASTER THE UKCAT

2nd edition

Over 750 practice questions for the United Kingdom Clinical Aptitude Test

Mike Bryon, Jim Clayden and Chris Tyreman

KoganPage

LONDON PHILADELPHIA NEW DELHI

Whilst the authors have made every effort to ensure that the content of this book is accurate, please note that occasional errors can occur in books of this kind. If you suspect that an error has been made in any of the tests included in this book, please inform the publishers at the address printed below so that it can be corrected at the next reprint.

Publisher's note

Every possible effort has been made to ensure that the information contained in this book is accurate at the time of going to press, and the publishers and authors cannot accept responsibility for any errors or omissions, however caused. No responsibility for loss or damage occasioned to any person acting, or refraining from action, as a result of the material in this publication can be accepted by the editor, the publisher or any of the authors.

First published in Great Britain and the United States in 2009 by Kogan Page Limited as *How to Pass the UKCAT*
Reprinted 2009 (twice)
Second edition published as *How to Master the UKCAT*, 2010

120 Pentonville Road
London N1 9JN
United Kingdom
www.koganpage.com

525 South 4th Street, #241
Philadelphia PA 19147
USA

4737/23 Ansari Road
Daryaganj
New Delhi 110002
India

ISBN 978 0 7494 5690 0
E-ISBN 978 0 7494 5921 5

British Library Cataloguing-in-Publication Data

A CIP record for this book is available from the British Library.

Library of Congress Cataloging-in-Publication Data

Bryon, Mike.
How to master the UKCAT : over 750 practice questions for the United Kingdom clinical aptitude test / Mike Bryon, Jim Clayden, Chris John Tyreman. -- 2nd ed.
p. ; cm.
Rev. ed. of: How to pass the UKCAT / Mike Bryon and Jim Clayden. 2009.
ISBN 978-0-7494-5690-0
1. UK Clinical Aptitude Test--Study guides. I. Clayden, Jim. II. Tyreman, C. J. III. Bryon, Mike. How to pass the UKCAT. IV. Title.
[DNLM: 1. Medicine--Great Britain--Examination Questions. 2. College Admission Test--Great Britain--Examination Questions. W 18.2 B916h 2010]
R838.5.B79 2010
610.76--dc22

2009046645

Typeset by Saxon Graphics Ltd, Derby
Printed and bound in India by Replika Press Pvt Ltd

Contents

1

Use this book to maximize your UKCAT score

If you have been searching for a way to improve your UKCAT score then you have found it. This book provides practice to maximize your chances of getting into medical school with over 800 questions and signposts to thousands more. Use it to get down to some serious score-improving practice. It includes warm up material to assist the candidate who prefers a new challenge to be broken down into its constituent parts, difficult material to help ensure that the practice remains a challenge throughout your programme of revision, and timed, realistic mini-tests to ensure you get right the all-important start in a computer-adaptive test like the UKCAT.

Our aim is simply to provide everything you need to ace the test. We will not spend time discussing why you want to be a doctor or how you might best prepare for medical school. Instead we will focus purely on giving you the practice you need to meet the challenge of the five sub-tests that make up the UKCAT.

You should have carefully studied the very important information provided at www.ukcat.ac.uk. You should be completely familiar with the details regarding the stated purpose of the test, what it attempts to predict and its key features. You should follow the online application process to the letter and regularly check your inbox for e-mails from UKCAT. You should have already downloaded the practice questions and tests. You will realize that the UKCAT is made up of sub-tests of verbal reasoning, decision making, quantitative reasoning, abstract reasoning and non-cognitive analysis. Note that some of the questions in each sub-test may be non-scoring, as they are being trialled for inclusion as scoring items in future tests. You are not given any indication as to which are scoring, so treat every question with the same determination. You should also realize that, like all selection tests, the UKCAT is under almost constant development and so some things may change. You will find a great deal of interesting (soft) information about the UKCAT on forums, for example www.thestudentroom.co.uk. However, take some of the views expressed on these sites with a largish pinch of salt.

The computer-administered test

Be sure to take the time to become entirely familiar with the way in which the UKCAT is administered onscreen. Pay attention to, for example, how to use the onscreen calculator in the qualitative sub-test. Be aware that diagrams on the computer screen can be misleading, especially in the case of geometric shapes, tables and graphs, as the screen can distort the image or the scale or both! The test author is aware of this and will have provided sufficient information to arrive at the answer. Take note of what is said and avoid drawing unnecessary assumptions about the appearance of a diagram, table or graph on the screen. For example, if a shape is described as a cube but on the screen the sides do not all seem quite equal, ignore it and treat the shape as a cube. Equally, if a table or graph says that quantity x is the largest but on the screen it looks as if quantity y is the same or in fact bigger, then take no notice and treat quantity x as the largest.

You need a good UKCAT score

Competition for places at medical, dental and veterinary school and especially at the more prestigious schools is fierce. The score range for the UKCAT is 300–900, with 500–700 being the normal range and 600 being the average mark in each section (note that the non-cognitive paper is scored differently from the other four sub-tests). To ensure that your score supports your application you will generally need an above-average score in each sub-test. However, the averages are based on a very broad range. Some people will get into the school of their choice with lower scores than others. There will not be a minimum score that you have to achieve. The UKCAT is only one of the many assessments used to decide if an applicant is to be offered a place, but it is in your interests to try to maximize each element of your application.

You may also need a well-balanced score

Doing really well in, for example, the quantitative part of the UKCAT will compensate for a weaker performance in the verbal parts of the test, but this compensation needs to be within certain limits. Most schools will prefer candidates who do well across all five sub-tests. The need for a balanced score makes it really important that candidates identify and work to address areas of personal weakness. If you have always found maths difficult but until now have succeeded in spite of it, it is time to correct this. You will feel more confident and will recognize what is behind a question and the significance of the subtle differences in the suggested answers.

Most UKCAT candidates will have strengths and weaknesses, but, if you believe that you have an imbalance that may be seen as too great, make sure you start work early to address it. Everyone can become proficient in the aptitudes examined; it is simply a matter of giving yourself enough time to practise. It takes some candidates longer to reach the required standard in any area of personal challenge, but given hard work and determination everyone can realize it. It can be boring, painful even, but if you have decided to follow a career that requires you to realize a good balanced pass in the UKCAT then you have little alternative but to get down to some serious hard work. Once again, if you are not prepared to put in the hard work to maximize your scores on these tests, then it is likely that medical, dentistry or veterinary school and a related career are not for you.

Practice makes a big difference in UKCAT scores

It is important that you realize that most people who score well in the UKCAT will have worked hard preparing for the test. There is no secret. Studies show that those who put in the most hours do best, whether in sport, music or academic achievement. Above all else, this requires time and especially commitment. Without the latter it is unlikely that you will do very well.

In addition to plain hard slog, there are also some strategies to adopt so that you are not only working harder, but working smarter too.

Adopt a 'no going back' philosophy

Treat every question as a passport to fulfilling your dreams. Adopt the mindset that each question counts, so be sure of every answer before moving on to the next. When practising, resist the temptation of going back and reviewing your answers. In the real test you will not have time to do this, so do not hit the submit button for each answer without a final, brief review.

Manage your time expertly

You need to work quickly through every sub-test. Sometimes you may find it difficult to attempt all the questions in the given time. You should practise answering the questions in this book in an average of 30 seconds per question, so that in the real test you will be able to concentrate on the questions and take your time management for granted. Resist wasting too much time on difficult questions.

Guess intelligently

If you do not know the answer you have little alternative but to guess. Straight guessing offers a 20 per cent chance of getting the right answer, but remember to look at the suggested answers to see if you can rule any out as definitely wrong. If you can, then you will improve your chances of guessing correctly. If the end of the test approaches and you have not attempted all the questions, then, in the last 60 seconds or so, randomly guessing answers to the remaining questions may well secure a couple of extra percentiles.

Make a really good start

In the UKCAT every question counts, but try especially hard to get the first question right in each sub-test, then the first five questions and then all the rest! The opening questions in a computer-administered test are especially significant because these tests are often computer adaptive. This means that the first question will be of the level that the 'average' candidate should get right. The next question will be a bit harder and so on. But, and this is important, you have to get the question right before the program presents you with the harder questions. Keep getting the questions right and you will soon be following along branches into the upper percentiles, rapidly leading to the level that will win you a place at medical school.

Whatever you do, avoid a bad start

A bad start is something you should try to avoid in every test. The early questions in almost all tests are a bit easier than the rest and a bad start means you fail to pick up on these relatively easy marks. A bad start is especially problematic in a computer adaptive test. Get the first few questions wrong and a computer adaptive test will continue to present you with questions at the level that the average candidate gets right and you risk having to play catch up before you can progress onto the upper percentile branches. The adaptive process continues throughout the test, so make every question count and treat every one of them as the opportunity to win a place at medical school.

Key stages in preparing

We each have our preferred method of revising for exams, and your study to date will have made you aware of what you have to do to meet the challenge of the UKCAT. However, if it is some years since you last sat an exam (and there are many mature applicants to medical schools), then the following advice should help you towards a successful UKCAT campaign.

Adopt a winning mindset

Doing well in the UKCAT is not simply a matter of intelligence. It is critical that you realize that to do well you have to try very hard indeed. Weeks before the test you will need to undertake extensive revision; then during the exam you will need to really 'go for it'. After the exam you should feel mentally fatigued. If you don't then you probably failed to apply yourself sufficiently and may not have fully done yourself justice. You may well have to dig deep towards the end of the test session and find the mental strength to keep going; otherwise you risk getting a disappointing score in the last paper because by this stage in the process you felt tired.

It is common to experience feelings of irritation or resentment about having to do a test like the UKCAT, as after all the institutions can see how good you are from, for example, your A level results, school references and so on. If you harbour these kinds of feelings then it is crucial that you put them aside. They can be very counterproductive. Try not to wonder about the validity of the test or how it is used by institutions. What you think of the UKCAT and its predictive value is entirely irrelevant. You need to do well in this test if you are to realize your goal of winning a place in medical, dental or veterinary school. Do well and an important opportunity will become possible. Focus on that goal and put all else aside for a few weeks. You really need to let your determination to do well in the UKCAT take over your life for a while.

Practise a successful exam technique

Some very clever and highly educated people do not do well at tests like the UKCAT. In some cases their training and inclination do not serve them well under the rather artificial conditions and abstract questions of a tightly timed test. This happens when, for example, the candidate thinks too deeply about the question or reads the passages and questions too carefully. Some place too high an emphasis on accuracy at the expense of speed. The outcome is that their test result does not reflect their true ability or their achievements to date. If you are such a person then you may need to develop an approach that involves a slightly greater risk of getting a question wrong for the sake of speed, or you may need to accept the assertions and statements at face value and focus on the immediate task of answering the questions. Work hard on your exam technique and do not rest until you can demonstrate the necessary balance between speed and accuracy.

Equally, if you have not familiarized yourself with the challenge that each of the sub-tests presents before attending on the day, you may underachieve. Be completely sure that you understand each of the five styles of questions involved and what they demand of you. Practice is key to achieving this, so make sure you allow yourself lots of time to develop a winning approach.

Devise and implement an unbeatable study plan

High-scoring candidates in every exam are confident of their abilities. They know what to expect and find that the exam contains few if any surprises. They turn up at the test centre looking forward to the opportunity to demonstrate how good they really are. To make sure you are such a candidate, begin by preparing a study plan well in advance of the test date.

Step 1 Understand each stage of the challenge

Make sure that you know exactly what to expect at each stage of the test. This should include the exact nature of each task and how long you are allowed.

Step 2 Make an honest assessment of your strengths and weaknesses

To prepare thoroughly for any test you should obviously try hard to improve the areas in which you are weakest. You probably already know which part of the UKCAT you would struggle with if you were to take the test tomorrow. You really need to try to go a step further than this and as objectively as possible assess the extent to which your area(s) of personal challenge will let you down. Only then can you ensure that you spend sufficient time addressing the challenge.

Step 3 Plan a programme of practice

Now you need to decide how much time you need to spend preparing for the challenge. A winning plan is likely to involve work over a minimum of two months, twice or preferably three times a week. If English is not your first language, if to date you have accomplished much despite never mastering maths or if you find the rules of English usage a complete enigma, then be prepared to set aside more time than this.

Step 4 Obtain enough practice material

Many candidates facing psychometric tests cannot find sufficient relevant practice material. The 800 practice questions this book contains will ensure you can get down to some serious practice. In the Kogan Page testing series the following titles also contain extra practice questions ideal for including in your UKCAT revision plan:

How to Pass Advanced Numeracy Tests (over 400 questions)
How to Pass Advanced Verbal Reasoning Tests (over 500 questions)
How to Pass Diagrammatic Reasoning Tests (over 300 questions)
How to Pass Graduate Psychometric Tests, 3rd edition (over 500 questions)
Ultimate Psychometric Tests (1,000 questions)
The Graduate Psychometric Test Workbook (realistic practice tests)

If you need further advice on sources of practice then by all means e-mail us at the following address: help@mikebryon.com.

Step 5 Undertake two sorts of practice

First, to get the most from your practice, begin working in a relaxed situation without constraint of time, reviewing examples of questions and working out the answers in order to become familiar with the demands of typical questions. Feel free to review answers and explanations and to refer to textbooks and dictionaries or use a calculator. Each chapter of this book starts with questions for this sort of practice, which we call 'warm up questions'.

Next, and once you are familiar with the challenge of each question type, you should start to practise under realistic test conditions. This involves putting aside the dictionary or calculator and working against the clock without help or interruption. The purpose is to develop a good exam technique and to improve your stamina and endurance. Learn not to spend too long on any one question, and practise educated guessing. Each chapter contains a series of what we have called 'mini-tests' so that you can undertake this very important sort of practice. To get the most out of it, set yourself the personal challenge of trying to beat your last score each time you take a mini-test. You will need to try very hard and take the challenge seriously if you are to succeed in beating your previous best score or getting all the questions right time after time and sufficiently quickly. When you finish a mini-test you should feel satisfied that you are creating a realistic real-test feel.

The questions in the master class sections are harder than you'll find in the real test, but these are not supposed to make you anxious. We are providing them because it is proven that practising on more difficult material will give you the edge in the real test. If you can battle your way through these advanced questions under relaxed conditions, you are likely to do well in the real test answering easier questions when feeling anxious and under pressure.

Answers to, and explanation of, the practice questions are found in Chapter 7.

Things to remember on the day of the test

1. Read through the instructions sent with your invitation to the test centre regarding the conditions, procedures and regulations.
2. The most important thing to take with you when you attend the test centre is suitable ID. For reasons of test security the test administrator will want to be able to confirm that no one is impersonating you and completing the test on your behalf. The most usual forms of ID are a passport, a national ID card or a driving licence. Note that acceptable ID should not have expired and should contain your name (spelt exactly the same as on your test appointment), a recognizable photograph and your signature.

   You may also be required to sign a confidentiality statement and agree to follow the centre's regulations.
3. You will not be allowed to take very much into the test room. They provide you with everything you need or are allowed, including scrap paper for doing rough working. Once again, make sure you have thoroughly read all the information given in order to understand what you can and cannot take with you. You are not allowed any other sort of computer aid or mobile phone in the testing room. A stopwatch is provided on the computer screen.

It would be a big mistake to arrive late for your appointment, so locate the centre and make sure you can find it with time to spare. Aim to arrive at least 30 minutes before your appointment time.

If English is not your first language

The medical school of your choice may require you to pass the TOEF or IELTS as well as UKCAT. The school to which you apply will inform you of their policy.

Some parts of the UKCAT are likely to present a greater challenge to you, so you need to adjust your programme of revision accordingly. For a speaker of English as a second language, the verbal reasoning, decision analysis and non-cognitive analysis questions are likely to prove the most challenging. The quantitative reasoning and abstract reasoning sections should be no more difficult for you than they would be for a native speaker.

Meet the challenge of the UKCAT by starting your programme of review at an early stage and spend time reading quality newspapers and journals, if possible daily. This will help build your vocabulary and improve your proficiency at assimilating the meanings of the complex sentences and sentence structures that occur in the UKCAT. Look up unfamiliar words. Practise writing 70-word reviews of articles found in these publications.

The warm up material found at the start of each chapter of practice questions will be especially useful to a speaker of English as a second language.

If you are planning to sit the UKCAT many years after studying

If it is some or many years since you studied, or more particularly since you sat a multiple-choice exam, then the UKCAT may well present a number of specific hurdles. The first thing to do is to review examples of each type of question and assignment that makes up the UKCAT and make an honest assessment of which of these components represents the greatest challenge. To demonstrate your full potential, well before sitting the test you will need to begin a programme of revision. Start with the aspects of the test that you feel you are least good at.

You may need to set aside a fairly considerable amount of time for revising the demands of the verbal and numerical sub-tests. Aim at 10 hours a week of practice, ideally over a number of months, in order to achieve a good, well-balanced score. Making the necessary commitment will demand discipline and determination. The time spent practising will at times seem tedious and frustrating. For many people, revising for the UKCAT is not what they dream of doing in their spare time. But, if you want to go to medical school and they insist on a good score, you have no real alternative.

Work to redevelop a good exam technique. We cannot emphasize enough that this demands a balance between speed and accuracy. Some very good candidates will need to unlearn a thoughtful, considered approach to issues. Practise answering realistic questions under the pressure of time and, where appropriate, refer to the suggested answers for clues. As it is likely that you will be pushed for time, practise informed guessing, where you can eliminate some of the suggested answers and then guess from those that remain.

On a positive note, practice should afford you a marked improvement in your performance in all tests, particularly perhaps the decision analysis and non-cognitive analysis sub-tests.

If you suffer a disability

If your ability to undertake the UKCAT could be adversely affected by a disability then speak to the school to which you are applying. Seek their advice at an early stage on how your requirements can best be accommodated. Provide full details of your condition and be clear about the special arrangements you require when you register online for the test so that the organizers have time to obtain formal proof if required. There is a version of the UKCAT designed especially for candidates with special needs, and this longer version of the test may be more appropriate for you.

2

Verbal reasoning

For a sizable minority of candidates, tests of verbal reasoning are their worst nightmare. Often these individuals are accomplished in, for example, science or mathematics but they can do little better than realize the norm rating in these common verbal tests. If you are the sort of candidate who will shine in the quantitative reasoning and abstract reasoning tests but fear that you will struggle with the verbal reasoning paper of the UKCAT, now is the time to get down to some serious score-improving practice.

The verbal reasoning sub-test comprises a series of passages followed by questions. Each question is a statement, and your task is to decide if, according to the passage, the statement is true or false or if you cannot tell if it is true or false. Typically these questions require you to comprehend meaning and significance, assess logical strength, identify valid inference, distinguish between a main idea and a subordinate one, recognize the writer's intention and identify a valid summary, interpretation or conclusion.

The subjects of the passages are drawn from a great many fields, such as current affairs, business, science, the environment, economics, history, meteorology, health and education. In fact, expect almost any subject. If you know something of the area, take care not to use your own knowledge. Be especially careful if you know a great deal about the subject or if you believe the passage to be factually incorrect or controversial. You are expected to answer the questions using only the information the passage contains. It is not a test of your general knowledge, your knowledge of the latest findings in the discipline or your political views. So feel completely at ease about answering true to a statement that is true in the very limited context of the passage even if you know that it is false given what you have learnt at university or read in a newspaper that morning.

When publishers of real tests develop an advanced verbal reasoning test they rely on fine distinctions between the suggested answers in order to distinguish between the scores of the large numbers of candidates. These distinctions are much finer than those we draw on a day-to-day basis. As a result, it is common for candidates to feel irritation and complain that these tests are to a large extent arbitrary. And in a way they are, for after all this is not how we use language at work or anywhere else but in the surreal world of tests. This is something you just have to accept and get used to, and with practice you will get to recognize the subtle distinctions being drawn.

Take care not to err too much towards the 'cannot tell' suggested answer by making the mistake of applying too strict or too inflexible a test of proof. Be sure to read the questions as carefully as you read the passage and learn to pick up the many clues provided in the wording of it. For example, if the passage refers to 'a valid argument, inference or premise' or asks 'Is it necessarily the case that...?', apply a strict criterion of proof. However, if the question asks 'Is it reasonable...?', 'On the balance of probability...?', 'Might the author...?', then apply a less strict criterion. You will soon master these subtle differences and gain the necessary confidence to make the correct judgements.

If, when taking lots of time in the relaxed conditions of your home, you find these questions easy, take care that you do not slip into a false sense of security. In the real test you will be pressed for time and may well be suffering from some anxiety. You should aim at undertaking just one careful read of the passage before referring back to it in order to answer the question. Some people find it helps to read the questions before the passage.

There are 180 practice questions in this chapter. They are organized as 60 warm up questions, eight mini-tests and two full-length practice tests. You will find hundreds more verbal reasoning questions and full-length verbal reasoning practice tests ideal for practice for the UKCAT verbal reasoning sub-test in *The Verbal Reasoning Test Workbook, How to Pass Advanced Verbal Reasoning Tests, The Graduate Psychometric Test Workbook* and *How to Pass Graduate Psychometric Tests*, 3rd edition, all published by Kogan Page.

To begin with, the average number of words in each passage is fewer than you might expect in the real UKCAT. This is intentional, as it allows you to improve your verbal reasoning skills. You will find longer passages in the full-length practice timed tests.

Warm up questions

The aim of this practice is to realize the demands of verbal reasoning questions of the type found in the UKCAT so that you feel more confident when answering them. Practise these questions without a time limit and in an informal relaxed situation. This section includes some deliberately hard material, so don't expect to get all the questions right. Refer to the answers and explanations as often as you like, and take time thinking about the question and passage before selecting your answer. Feel free to check the precise meanings of the words you are unsure of in a dictionary or thesaurus. However, remember to use the information in the passage to answer the questions, so if you use a dictionary to check the meaning of a word and a question asks, for example, about the author's intended meaning or how a term or phrase is used then be sure to refer only to the passage in deciding your answer and leave the dictionary aside.

Passage 1

Towns that have become commuter and second-home hotspots are valued for their housing stock, schools and unspoilt civic centres. It is now possible for working families to relocate away from cities without affecting their earning power. Commuting three days a week and working from home the rest has meant that many more people are willing to give up the city life and move to more rural areas to fulfil their dream of homes with gardens and cricket on the green. So many metropolitan dwellers have made the move that property prices in the more popular locations have become amongst the most expensive in the country.

Q1. New technology is the reason why it is possible for working families to relocate without affecting their earning power.

True ☐ False ☐ Cannot tell ☐

Q2. The only reason for these locations becoming so popular is only due to commuting even if for just part of the week.

True ☐ False ☐ Cannot tell ☐

Q3. An idea of an unspoilt civic centre could include, along with cricket on the green, a traditional high street with local shops.

True ☐ False ☐ Cannot tell ☐

Passage 2

Asparagus is a perennial and wild asparagus is found growing in light, well-drained soil across Europe, northern Africa and central Asia. People from all over the world enjoy eating it. The most sought-after domesticated varieties are from Canada and they prefer a soil with a ph of around 6.5. The domesticated varieties grow best in a humus-rich medium and will then each produce around half a kilo of crop. In the spring the plant sends up the spears that if left will open to form new foliage but for the first six weeks of each season these are cut when they are around 10 centimetres tall. After the cutting season the spears are allowed to mature so that the plants can re-establish themselves. The spears of the cultivated varieties are far thicker than those that grow in the wild and the crown (the shallow root ball) much larger, but the flavour of wild asparagus is superior. In the autumn the female plants fruit to produce small inedible berries.

Q4. All asparagus plants like a soil with a ph of 6.5.

True ☐ False ☐ Cannot tell ☐

Q5. It can be inferred from the passage that when the author describes the fruit as inedible he means that humans can't eat it.

True ☐ False ☐ Cannot tell ☐

Q6. Asparagus only grows in Europe, northern Africa and central Asia.

True ☐ False ☐ Cannot tell ☐

Passage 3

When each year an average of 500,000 immigrants entered the country the Home Office calculated that the fiscal benefit of this level of inward migration was £2.5 billion a year. This calculation was used extensively by the government of the day to support their immigration policies. The findings of the Home Office stood out against the findings of other western nations which found the benefits of large-scale inward migration to be so small as to be close to zero. The difference in the findings arose because the Home Office figure was based only on the effect of inward migration on the country's total Gross Domestic Product (GDP), while the other studies measured the effect on GDP per head. However, the Home Office calculation was obviously flawed, and they have since stopped using it, because immigration manifestly increases both the total GDP and the population. While the overall effect of inward migration may be negligible nationally in fiscal terms, the indigenous low paid and low skilled stand to lose out because as a consequence of the inward migration they face greater competition for work. Some employers have much to gain from the improved supply of labour and savings made from not having to train young people.

Q7. It is no longer the case that half a million immigrants enter the country.

True ☐ False ☐ Cannot tell ☐

Q8. The author's intended meaning when he wrote 'However, the Home Office calculation was obviously flawed, and they have since stopped using it, because immigration manifestly increases both the total GDP and the population' would be better served if instead of immigration he wrote inward migration.

True ☐ False ☐ Cannot tell ☐

Q9. There are no clear winners in an economy experiencing large-scale inward migration.

True ☐ False ☐ Cannot tell ☐

Passage 4

Jupiter orbits the sun every 12 years and is five times the distance of Earth from the sun. It is a huge gaseous planet with a rocky core twice the size of Earth and has four principal moons, Io, Europa, Ganymede and Callisto. These moons were first recorded by Galileo in 1609. The outer reaches of our solar system contain three giant gaseous planets, the others being Uranus and Neptune which both lie beyond Jupiter. Uranus takes 84 years to orbit while Neptune takes 165 years. These planets were visited by Voyager space probes between 1979 and 1989 and all were found to have distinctive rings, satellites (or moons) and experience enormous storms in their upper atmospheres identifiable as large white or coloured rotating spots, some of which last for months or even years.

Q10. The huge gaseous planets of the outer reaches of our solar system have rocky cores.

True ☐ False ☐ Cannot tell ☐

Q11. In the passage we can conclude that the words 'huge, giant' and 'moon, satellite' are treated as synonyms.

True ☐ False ☐ Cannot tell ☐

Q12. Of the three gaseous planets Neptune is the furthest from the sun.

True ☐ False ☐ Cannot tell ☐

Passage 5

If anyone was surprised when it eventually weakened it was only because it did not happen sooner. People can live beyond their means for quite some time before they run out of credit and must start to address the accumulated debt. An enormous economy like that of the United States can live beyond its means for years and accumulate an enormous amount of debt before the inevitable happens. The correction occurred when too many of the dollars held by America's creditors were sold. The American central bank responded to the crisis by lowering interest rates which triggered further selling as investors sought higher returns in alternative currencies. The emergent Chinese and Indian economies have also contributed to the weakness of the dollar. Rising living standards in those countries have led to their currencies strengthening. The dollar is trading against the currencies of these fast-developing nations at a much lower historic rate and this is a trend that is bound to continue.

Q13. Even if the US economy was free of debt the dollar would have weakened and remained trading at below the historic rate at least against some of the world's currencies.

True ☐ False ☐ Cannot tell ☐

Q14. What the author meant by the term 'inevitable' is that the US economy would go into recession.

True ☐ False ☐ Cannot tell ☐

Q15. For years people had predicted that the dollar would weaken.

True ☐ False ☐ Cannot tell ☐

Passage 6

The giant wind turbines on the nearby hill supply the community with 8 million kilowatt hours of electricity each year. Several hundred homeowners have erected solar panels on their roofs to provide most of their summer-time hot water needs. Bio-waste is collected for fermentation to produce methane gas which drives a local generator to augment the town's electricity needs when there is insufficient wind to fully power the turbines. Better insulation has cut the fuel requirements of many homes. Local generation in this isolated, rural community has led to saving on the investment cost of additional transmission lines in the national network. Further efficiencies are gained because the local production of power avoids losses to electrical resistance in the long-distance transmission of power.

Q16. The motives for this community's investment in the local generation of its energy needs are rising fuel costs and climate worries.

True ☐ False ☐ Cannot tell ☐

Q17. When the wind is blowing and the sun is shining, locally generated power accounts for most of this community's energy needs.

True ☐ False ☐ Cannot tell ☐

Q18. This isolated rural community is located in a part of the world where the national power network is practically non-existent.

True ☐ False ☐ Cannot tell ☐

Passage 7

The outsourcing of jobs to India from Europe and America has evolved from giving them relatively low-skilled work to passing on highly skilled roles. Multinationals have decreased the number of employees in Europe and America that undertake engineering design, science and software writing and instead now employ tens of thousands of skilled Indian workers in these challenging roles. Some are establishing second headquarters in the country because they have so many senior executives working on key projects there. The shift is in part due to it being easier in India to fill highly skilled, English-speaking positions and because, for the time being anyway, the wages for these roles are notably lower than wages in Europe and America. But it is also because companies want to position their businesses where they believe the future lies. India is one of the world's three biggest pools of highly skilled English-speaking labour and some commentators believe that as many as 30 million European and American skilled jobs are at risk of being moved.

Q19. The case that many more skilled jobs will be moved to India would be strengthened if even more than 30 million European and American jobs were at risk of moving.

True ☐ False ☐ Cannot tell ☐

Q20. Three rationales for the outsourcing to India are portrayed.

True ☐ False ☐ Cannot tell ☐

Q21. The claim that American and European jobs are being lost to India because Indian workers are prepared to work harder than their American and European counterparts can be rebutted.

True ☐ False ☐ Cannot tell ☐

Passage 8

Annually the average household spends on running electrical appliances: £82 on washing and drying, £49 on lighting, £38 on refrigeration of food, a rather wasteful £95 on the wide-screen TV, £17 powering computers, wireless networks and charging phones and, not surprising for the British, £23 on boiling the kettle for all those endless cups of tea. If families were more attentive and for example did not leave unnecessary lights on then they could save a considerable sum of money. Just appliances left unnecessarily on standby are guesstimated to waste £25 a year per household. The typical family's electricity bill could be quite significantly cut if we learnt to use electricity more frugally and became a little more attentive in order to reduce the waste. A trial showed an average saving of £75 a year on electricity bills which should prove a big incentive for most families.

Q22. You can infer that the average household's annual electricity bill (net of taxes etc) is a little over £300 (the sum of all the individual items listed).

True ☐ False ☐ Cannot tell ☐

Q23. The main point of the passage is an account of the saving that could be made if we were more frugal with our use of electrical appliances.

True ☐ False ☐ Cannot tell ☐

Q24. Were we to learn to use electricity more frugally and become a little more attentive in order to reduce the waste, we would hardly notice the difference in terms of the impact on our daily lives.

True ☐ False ☐ Cannot tell ☐

Passage 9

A thing of beauty can completely lack physical form. We find some experiences beautiful despite their lack of physical appearance and we find some theories beautiful despite them being ideas that lack any physical structure. Perfume is the only beauty product that just plays on the emotions. We cannot see a scent and despite its complete lack of visual structure it can have an immediate and intimate effect. We can love or hate a smell for the image it elicits. A smell can evoke memories of an unhappy episode while someone else will identify it as warm and pleasing. We can be moved to describe a scent as beautiful because of the delicate impression or because of its zesty, exciting chemistry. Interestingly a scent can smell different on different people. We can love a scent for the way it smells on others but hate the way it smells on us. The perfume we are provoked into calling beautiful is not something we can objectively decide. Freewill and personal choice play no part in the process.

Q25. Literally beauty is in the eye of the beholder.

True ☐ False ☐ Cannot tell ☐

Q26. In the opening sentence of the passage when it is said that a thing of beauty can completely lack physical form it means that it lacks physical structure.

True ☐ False ☐ Cannot tell ☐

Q27. The passage would be improved if the author wrote 'we can love or hate a smell for the reminiscence it elicits' rather than 'we can love or hate a smell for the image it elicits'.

True ☐ False ☐ Cannot tell ☐

Passage 10

Over $50 billion was spent shopping online last year and it is hardly surprising that criminals want a share of the action. No businessman or woman in his or her right mind would leave a shop unattended, unlocked and without an alarm and most take precautions to protect their virtual shops too but not to the same degree of security. Many businesses do little more than install a firewall and antivirus and anti-spyware software and they believe this is all the security that is required. But the more recent developments in online threats are no longer guaranteed to be excluded by the most commonly available security software. Retailers should take professional advice on the system and consider redirecting all of their inbound and outbound traffic to web security specialists who scan all traffic and block threats. Extra special care needs to be taken with the management of systems involved in the handling of payments by credit cards.

Q28. Online shopping offers the criminal the promise of rich pickings.

True ☐ False ☐ Cannot tell ☐

Q29. Firewalls and antivirus and anti-spyware software are the virtual equivalents of shop assistants, locks and alarms.

True ☐ False ☐ Cannot tell ☐

Q30. The antivirus and anti-spyware software usually updates automatically and so the business owner is led to believe that their security will remain up to date too.

True ☐ False ☐ Cannot tell ☐

Passage 11

As an institution the British public house, usually called a pub, has a very long tradition of selling alcoholic drinks, in particular beer, which people consume on the premises. In recent years, however, profits of British pubs have fallen by 20 per cent and many have reported a further worsening of their financial state since the introduction of a new law and a series of tax increases. The new law involved the banning of smoking in public places and this has led to a marked decrease in pub custom. The increase in taxes involves a series of above-inflation rises in the duty charged on alcohol sold both in pubs and off-licences (the name of licensed premises allowed to sell alcohol for home consumption) that has markedly increased the cost of drinking alcohol. The combined effect of the smoking ban and increase in the alcohol duty are reported to have led to the loss of many jobs in the pub trade.

Q31. The author is opposed to the new laws and the effects they are having on the pub trade and this is evidenced by the last sentence of the passage and the loss of jobs in the pub trade.

True ☐ False ☐ Cannot tell ☐

Q32. It is reasonable to infer that some pubs are operating at a loss or at no profit.

True ☐ False ☐ Cannot tell ☐

Q33. The smoking ban has encouraged traditional pub customers to drink and smoke less.

True ☐ False ☐ Cannot tell ☐

Passage 12

Taking recreational drugs in the privacy of your own home should be no one else's business but your own and yet the government has made it illegal. Millions of law-abiding citizens have used recreational drugs. Studies suggest that some 10 million people have used recreational drugs at some stage of their lives and 2 million use them on a regular and long-term basis. The studies suggest that it's not just young people who are recreational drug users either; most studies find that close to half the long-term users are aged over 24 years of age. Recreational drugs are classified into three categories according to the level of harm they cause. Penalties for possession of class C drugs, the lowest classification, include imprisonment for up to two years and an unlimited fine. Dealing in these drugs can result in imprisonment for up to 14 years. Possession of class A drugs can result in seven years' imprisonment. Cannabis, perhaps the most commonly used recreational drug, is soon to be reclassified as class B from its current classification of class C.

Q34. It is not true to say that people who use recreational drugs are law-abiding citizens.

True ☐ False ☐ Cannot tell ☐

Q35. The author of the passage does not agree that it should be illegal to use recreational drugs in the privacy of your own home.

True ☐ False ☐ Cannot tell ☐

Q36. Dealing in all classes of these drugs can result in imprisonment for up to 14 years.

True ☐ False ☐ Cannot tell ☐

Passage 13

In 1997 a previously long-dormant volcano on the Caribbean island of Montserrat erupted. In just a few minutes a fast-moving lava flow surged down the mountain covering a great swathe including the capital Plymouth. The lava was followed by mud slides and almost the whole of the south of the island was buried in a choking layer of ash. The residents of the capital and the affected parts of the island had been evacuated prior to the eruption. A great many lives were undoubtedly saved but 19 lives were still lost and everyone knew that life there would never be the same again. Twenty years after the eruption only 4,000 of the original population of 12,000 remain.

Q37. Twenty years after the eruption only 4,000 people lived on the island.

True ☐ False ☐ Cannot tell ☐

Q38. The evacuation prior to the eruption averted a disaster.

True ☐ False ☐ Cannot tell ☐

Q39. There must be a mistake in the claim that the eruption occurred in 1997 because this book was published in 2010. Twenty years could not have passed since it was found that 4,000 of the original 12,000 population remain.

True ☐ False ☐ Cannot tell ☐

Passage 14

The early manned missions visited lowlands and plains while the later missions explored highlands. Selecting a suitable site was never going to be easy as even the apparently flattest of locations were found to be on closer inspection potholed from meteorite strikes and plastered with small boulders. The moon is rugged and very mountainous and in the 1960s a number of lunar probes had photographed the moon's surface during close orbit passes and even performed soft landings in the search for suitable sites for the manned missions that were to follow. In 1969 Neil Armstrong and Edwin Aldrin in Apollo 11 made the first ever manned lunar landing. The last manned landing was made in 1972 with Apollo 17.

Q40. The first lunar landing was made in the 1960s.

True ☐ False ☐ Cannot tell ☐

Q41. Apollo 17 visited a mountainous region of the moon.

True ☐ False ☐ Cannot tell ☐

Q42. When referring to a 'suitable site' in the second sentence it means suitable sites for the landing of manned missions.

True ☐ False ☐ Cannot tell ☐

Passage 15

We suffer a suspension of judgement when we hand over a card to purchase something and spend funds that we intended to use for something essential or unintentionally create an unauthorized overdraft. These spur-of-the-moment lapses are more likely to occur when we pay for something electronically or with credit than with hard cash. This is because of a widely held perception that electronic money and credit are somehow not as real or valuable as notes and coins. Retailers play on this emotional weakness with offers of in-store cards and 'buy now play later' deals. But, nowhere is our Achilles' heel exploited more than on the internet where it is impossible to pay with ready money and perhaps the sites that have perfected this form of exploitation are those that offer gambling. The sites regulated by the Gaming Commission have safeguards but the unregulated sites set out to encourage people to stake more to recover their losses and do not provide facilities to allow the gambler to set limits on how much they will fritter.

Q43. We suffer a suspension of judgement when we hand over a card to purchase something.

True ☐ False ☐ Cannot tell ☐

Q44. Electronic money and credit have a lower psychological value than cash in your hand.

True ☐ False ☐ Cannot tell ☐

Q45. Sites unregulated by the Gaming Commission are unlicensed.

True ☐ False ☐ Cannot tell ☐

Passage 16

Poor farmers and poor food-exporting countries have for years suffered the disincentive of low food prices but recently they have seen their returns improve by an average of 20 per cent and this has brought real benefits to communities that rank amongst the poorest in the world. On the other hand, many, many millions of the world's poor are landless and live on $1 a day or less and these people already living in absolute poverty now face famine. Most governments of the poorest food-importing countries are counterbalancing the rapid rises in staple food prices with improved food subsidy programmes. Those that have not are facing domestic food price protests. Already modest educational and health programmes are being squeezed in order to fund these plans.

Q46. Rising food prices weigh more heavily in some places than others.

True ☐ False ☐ Cannot tell ☐

Q47. The main issue in the passage is rising food prices and how they create winners and losers.

True ☐ False ☐ Cannot tell ☐

Q48. Food subsidy programmes are intended to ease the pain of the effect rather than stop the development.

True ☐ False ☐ Cannot tell ☐

Passage 17

The estimated cost to widen both sides of 240 miles of the world's busiest motorway has been priced at a figure higher than the annual gross domestic product (GDP) of one quarter of the world's nations. It is a major construction project but with the same sum of money many of the world's nations fund their entire annual government expenditure, including road building. The rate of inflation for raw materials and therefore for construction is running many times higher than general inflation and given this and the fact that such projects have a record of overrunning their estimates there must exist a real possibility that the scheme will cost even more than the estimate. Construction work has not yet started but the pre-construction phase has begun even if the decision to proceed with the project has still to be made.

Q49. An estimate is not a commitment to spend.

True ☐ False ☐ Cannot tell ☐

Q50. The sum of one quarter of the world's nations' GDP is less than the estimated cost to widen both sides of a length of the world's busiest motorway.

True ☐ False ☐ Cannot tell ☐

Q51. If a road's length is taken to be the distance you can drive on it then the project involves 480 miles of road building.

True ☐ False ☐ Cannot tell ☐

Passage 18

Due to Private Finance Initiatives (PFIs), schools and hospitals are being built that the government would otherwise not be able to afford. PFIs are currently preferred by government over traditional public procurement for the building of schools, hospitals, social housing and prisons. Straight public procurement is notorious for cost overruns and delays while PFI projects rarely suffer either. Another advantage and the most important for the government is that PFIs are what are called off-balance-sheet expenditure. The cost of building is not funded by the government upfront. Instead the private sector pays for the building and the government lease the building from the private owner and guarantee an annual rent. This allows the government to spread out the cost and so PFIs help the Treasury to balance the books.

Q52. Given the advantages of PFI over public procurement it is hard to imagine that public procurement will again be used to fund the building of public buildings.

True ☐ False ☐ Cannot tell ☐

Q53. Even if all initiatives, both PFI and public procurement, suffered the same delay and overspend, government may still prefer the PFI route.

True ☐ False ☐ Cannot tell ☐

Q54. The last sentence would be less open to misinterpretation if it was rewritten to read 'This allows the government to spread out the cost of building and so PFIs help the Treasury to balance the books'.

True ☐ False ☐ Cannot tell ☐

Passage 19

All too often organizations jump onto the real food bandwagon to cynically exploit the public's appetite to know more about where their food comes from and by whom and how it is grown. An example might be a pack of processed meat with a picture on the packaging of a farmhouse, a kind-looking farmer and country scene and yet its content is processed in a factory from meat grown on countless farms and transported from all over the world. The same is sadly true with respect to the rise of responsible tourism. Tourists want a guilt-free holiday and so they prefer to use the services of a tour operator who is contributing to the local community and contributes to rather than distracts from the ecosystem they visit. An example might be a holiday resort that provides the land and building for a school and employs local people in the resort. Visitors to the resort are encouraged to contribute to the running costs of the school and to fund the provision of a meal each day for the children.

Q55. The owners of the holiday resort that provides the land and building for a school for local children is portrayed in the passage as an example of a tour operator who is cynically exploiting our appetite for responsible tourism.

True ☐ False ☐ Cannot tell ☐

Q56. To say that 'organizations jump on the real food bandwagon' is to offer a metaphor.

True ☐ False ☐ Cannot tell ☐

Q57. Tourists do not want to use the services of a tour operator who is contributing to the local community and ecosystem only because they want a guilt-free holiday.

True ☐ False ☐ Cannot tell ☐

Passage 20

The jet stream is a two-mile-high column of wind and in this part of the world it determines the boundary between the Arctic and Atlantic air. When it moves south, much of northern Europe and North America is subjected to cold air and when it moves north, northern Europe and North America enjoy warmer air. In the spring and autumn the jet stream moves much more than at other times of the year and this largely explains why spring and autumn weather in the northern hemisphere can be so changeable. In a matter of a few days the position of the jet stream can fluctuate and warm and possibly wet spring or autumn weather can suddenly be replaced by cold air and dry, clear skies.

Q58. It can be inferred from the information provided that in relative terms Arctic air is cold and Atlantic air is warm.

True ☐ False ☐ Cannot tell ☐

Q59. By 'this part of the world' it implies northern Europe.

True ☐ False ☐ Cannot tell ☐

Q60. If it were in fact untrue that the jet stream was a two-mile-high column of wind then the explanation of why spring and autumn weather in the northern hemisphere is so changeable would be compromised.

True ☐ False ☐ Cannot tell ☐

Eight mini-tests

The next 40 questions of this chapter are organized as eight mini-tests. It is far better to practise little and often when preparing for a test and most people can find a few minutes without distraction to undertake one of these mini-tests. Each contains five multiple-choice questions and you are allowed four minutes in which to attempt them. The first question is of average difficulty and they become progressively harder. This is what you can expect to happen in the real UKCAT. Use these questions to get down to some really serious score-improving practice and be sure of the very best start in your real UKCAT verbal reasoning paper.

Read the first passage and answer the questions that relate to it and, when you have very briefly rechecked your choice, enter your answer in the answer box and move on to the next question. Try to avoid going back to reconsider a previous answer because you will risk wasting precious time, so practise getting the answer right first time and move confidently on to the next question. You will find that each mini-test comprises two passages and each is followed by either two or three questions (always making a total of five).

Put away the dictionary and thesaurus and treat these mini-tests like a real test. Get the most out of this practice by setting yourself the personal challenge of trying to beat or, if you get all five right, match your last score each time you take a mini-test. That way you will create a realistic, real-test feel. You will need to try very hard and take the challenge seriously if you are to really succeed in beating your previous best score or getting five out of five every time. Time management will be critical, so be sure to stick to the four-minute time limit and not spend too long on any one question, and practise making one careful detailed read of the passage to save on time going back to check detail. Keep practising until you consistently get all five questions right. Achieve this and you can take strength from the fact that you are likely to make a very good start in your real UKCAT verbal reasoning paper. The only thing then left to do is to keep up that rate of success through to the end of the real test!

Mini-test 1

Passage 1

The world's population is expected to increase to more than 10 billion by 2050. Having a child in the developed world has a greater environmental impact than having a child in the developing world. Likewise having a large family in the developed world has a far greater environmental impact than having a large family in the developing world. This is because a child born into the developed world is much more likely to go on to have a high carbon dioxide emission lifestyle given that they are more likely to take regular fiights, drive cars, live in a large energy-hungry home and so on. This has led some campaigners to argue that families in the developed world should think far more seriously about the environmental consequences of having children and should elect or be encouraged to have fewer.

Q1. If it were the case that all of the world's future population growth was projected to occur in the developing world and that the population of most developed countries would have fallen if it wasn't for immigration, then the case made for smaller families in the developed world would be weakened.

True ☐ False ☐ Cannot tell ☐

Q2. If families living in the developing world were to have fewer children then they too would make a major cut in their families' future carbon dioxide output.

True ☐ False ☐ Cannot tell ☐

Passage 2

To enjoy a comfortable retirement, many retired people recommend retiring on two-thirds of final salary and around 4 million workers have paid into pension schemes for the bulk of their working lives in order to realize this goal. Those who have contributed to a final salary pension scheme will reach that standard and in fact exceed it when the person's state pension is added to the equation. Those workers who have contributed to a pension scheme that lacks the final salary guarantee and instead depend on the investment value of their total contributions to purchase their pension on retirement are less fortunate. Even when their state pension is included the bulk of these people will retire on an income of around 40 per cent of their final salary. As for the remaining 11 million workers who have made little or no contribution to any other pension scheme than the compulsory state scheme, it is feared that they will find themselves dependent on means-tested benefits.

Q3. Four million workers will reach or exceed the standard where they retire on two-thirds of the final salary.

True ☐ False ☐ Cannot tell ☐

Q4. Workers with pension schemes without the final salary guarantee will have to manage on a lot less than the amount thought to be needed for a secure retirement.

True ☐ False ☐ Cannot tell ☐

Q5. The country to which the passage refers has a total population of 15 million.

True ☐ False ☐ Cannot tell ☐

End of test

Mini-test 2

Passage 1

Twice as many people live till they are 100 in France as in Britain. Yet the two countries have similar sized populations and have diets with similar amounts of fat. In fact life expectancy is considerably better in France from the age of 65 onwards and it seems that lifestyle and diet may have a lot to do with it. Leaving aside the fact that the French probably have the best national health service in the world, statistics suggest that the French remain active longer and consume more units of fruit and vegetables. They also enjoy considerably more glasses of red wine and it seems these differences give rise to far lower levels of death caused by heart disease and this allows significant numbers of people to live until their centenary.

Q1. Four differences are attributed to the reason the French have a far lower level of death caused by heart disease: the best national health service, remaining active, consuming more fruit and vegetables and enjoying more red wine.

True ☐ False ☐ Cannot tell ☐

Q2. Even if twice as many people in France see their centenary it may be that very few people live to see their 100th birthday in either country.

True ☐ False ☐ Cannot tell ☐

Passage 2

Last year's summer was noteworthy for being very wet and very windy and yet neither of these qualities featured in the meteorological service's long-term forecast. We were advised that we could expect a typical summer with above-average temperatures and average or slightly above-average levels of rainfall. There was no mention whatsoever of the widespread flooding that occurred. This raises the question of whether the forecast was wrong and they in principle could have but did not forecast the exceptional weather or whether it is in principle impossible to forecast specific long-term exceptional events. Long-term forecasts are based on baseline averages over an extended period and trends in that baseline are used to build the forecast and predict, for example, if that trend is to continue. If extreme weather is occurring more frequently then it is feasible that the forecast might include the prediction that the frequency of these events will continue to be higher than the historic average.

Q3. It is a mistake to believe that the exceptional can be forecast over the long term.

True ☐ False ☐ Cannot tell ☐

Q4. The summer of 2007 was noteworthy for being very wet and windy.

True ☐ False ☐ Cannot tell ☐

Q5. It is not possible to predict long-term specific weather events such as the flooding last summer.

True ☐ False ☐ Cannot tell ☐

End of test

Mini-test 3

Passage 1

In almost zero gravity and no wind very large droplets of water can form. In normal atmospheric conditions and no wind droplets of around 2 millimetres diameter commonly occur. In normal conditions with wind smaller droplets form and the diameter of those found in a typical summer gale might measure less than one millimetre. In every situation droplets do collide and these combine to form larger droplets that may well survive but air resistance and the relatively weak surface tension of water mean that droplets with a diameter larger than 5 millimetres very quickly break up.

Q1. The claim that giant globules of water cannot form is rebutted by the passage.

True ☐ False ☐ Cannot tell ☐

Q2. Droplets of between 2–5mm only occur in windless conditions.

True ☐ False ☐ Cannot tell ☐

Passage 2

So what is it that decides if a language is to endure or to be threatened with extinction? The number of languages spoken in the world is expected to continue to decrease dramatically but what decides the winners and the losers? Surprisingly some commentators argue that along with languages spoken by very small communities the really 'big' languages like English also face extinction. The case against the small linguistic community is obvious; if there is no one left to speak a language then that language dies. The case against a dominant, apparently all-conquering, language like English is less apparent and is therefore so much more interesting. As more and more of the world speaks English it is inevitable, the argument runs, that it will break up first into dialects and then distinct languages linked only by their common linguistic heritage. This is a controversial point because it goes against the view that dialects need isolation before they can form (without isolation, speech is standardized by the dominant language promulgated through international science, engineering, medicine and business and worldwide printed and digital media and this squeezes out dialects).

Q3. The case made for the extinction of English derives from its worldwide dominance.

True ☐ False ☐ Cannot tell ☐

Q4. The passage does not answer the question asking what decides if a language is to endure or become extinct.

True ☐ False ☐ Cannot tell ☐

Q5. The passage is ambivalent in respect to whether or not English will become extinct.

True ☐ False ☐ Cannot tell ☐

End of test

Mini-test 4

Passage 1

At a university campus in 1971, 23 male volunteers spent two weeks role playing prisoners and guards. The volunteers were upright ordinary 'good' students. The exercise sought to explore the extent to which the external environment influences human behaviour and in particular our potential for evil. Early on in the experiment the guards started subjecting the prisoners to psychological and physical punishments. As the experiment proceeded the punishments got worse. Philip Zimbardo, the originator of the experiment, identified that conformity and anonymity were two of a number of factors that can bring about callous behaviour in otherwise caring people. Anonymity was important because it led the perpetrators to believe that they would not have to answer for their actions. Conformity was significant because it pressurized the more humane guards to adopt the behaviour of their less humane peers. Another of Zimbardo's factors was boredom.

Q1. In this experiment in social psychology there were more prisoners than guards.

True ☐ False ☐ Cannot tell ☐

Q2. It would be wrong to deduce from the passage that women volunteers in the same circumstances would not act callously.

True ☐ False ☐ Cannot tell ☐

Q3. Only two of Philip Zimbardo's factors that can bring about callous behaviour in otherwise caring people are identified.

True ☐ False ☐ Cannot tell ☐

Passage 2

Japan's population is projected to fall from the current almost 130 million to around 90 million by the middle of the next century and this smaller population will be faced with the added challenge that it will be disproportionately elderly. By then Japan's total GDP will be half that of India's and one-fifth the size of China's and Japan will have slipped to being the fifth largest super power in terms of the size of its GDP. Japan's answer to the challenge to its competitiveness is to seek out even greater innovation. It is currently very innovative if you measure it in terms of the number of patents registered and the amount spent on research and development. But in other measures of innovation it does not score so well. When compared to the European Union and the United States of America (currently the economic zones with the largest GDPs) its working practices are considered inflexible and it shuns foreign investment and cultural influences. The latter two are considered important because unless Japan engages in new ways of thinking and changes in worldwide values it is hard to see how it will remain the pioneer of bestselling products to future generations.

Q4. The big question for Japan is how it is to remain competitive.

True ☐ False ☐ Cannot tell ☐

Q5. The tone of the passage suggests that the ability to engage in new ways of thinking can be attributed to India and China.

True ☐ False ☐ Cannot tell ☐

End of test

Mini-test 5

Passage 1

English is spoken as a first language by 400 million people and one in four of the world's population claims to speak elementary English. In an English dictionary the C section contains the second largest number of entries and is the second longest. The S section contains the largest number and the P section is the third largest in terms of entries. One of the shortest sections lists the words beginning with Q but the section with the fewest entries is the W. Italian is spoken by around 60 million people and in an Italian dictionary the sections J, K, Y and W are very short and contain only foreign words used in Italian while the U and Q sections contain the least number of Italian entries. The longest section in the Italian dictionary and the section that contains the most entries is the S section and the next longest is the C section.

Q1. The S section of the Italian and English dictionaries both contain the largest number of entries.

True ☐ False ☐ Cannot tell ☐

Q2. In the English dictionary the S section is the longest.

True ☐ False ☐ Cannot tell ☐

Q3. The Q sections of both English and Italian dictionaries contain close to the fewest number of entries.

True ☐ False ☐ Cannot tell ☐

Passage 2

Andy, Betty, Charles, Diana, Edward, Fay, George, Hope. In an average hurricane season meteorologists in the Atlantic expect to name nine tropical storms. The christening of storms began when weather forecasts were broadcast over shortwave radio and naming them helped mariners to keep track of the weather system. The tradition evolved so that each successive storm was given a name beginning with successive letters of the alphabet. Initially only girls' names were used but later this was changed so that the names alternated from boy to girl names. If a named storm turns out to be particularly savage then the name may be dropped and not used in future years. The same system of naming storms is adopted in the north and south Pacific forecast regions.

Q4. The list of names at the beginning of the passage could be the list of names used in a year that experienced an average hurricane season.

True ☐ False ☐ Cannot tell ☐

Q5. When weather forecasts were broadcast over shortwave radio the storms were only given girls' names.

True ☐ False ☐ Cannot tell ☐

End of test

Mini-test 6

Passage 1

Except for Nepal's, which is the shape of two connected triangles, all modern national flags are rectangular and their colours hark back to the days when flags were extensively used for identification and communication. Nowadays the colour red is intimately associated with nations born from left-wing political movements but at the time of the French revolution the tri-colour (blue, white and red) was the symbol of the fight for freedom and inspired the design of many national flags including, for example, those of the United States of America and the Republic of Ireland. In many instances green stands for Islam (along with the crescent moon) while the cross shape usually signifies a Christian nation. The pan-African movement adopted the colours of the Ethiopian flag (green, yellow and red), the oldest independent African nation, and many African states when they emerged from colonialism adopted these colours.

Q1. The reason given for most flags being rectangular is that in the past they were extensively used for identification and communication.

True ☐ False ☐ Cannot tell ☐

Q2. Despite the fact that it is not, you can infer from the passage that the flag of the Republic of Ireland should be blue, white and red.

True ☐ False ☐ Cannot tell ☐

Q3. Today symbolic designs as well as colours are used to convey meaning and identity on national flags.

True ☐ False ☐ Cannot tell ☐

Passage 2

You can find out so much about people on the internet these days that civil liberty campaigners are arguing for new laws so that people can get back some vestige of control over their personal data. The 1998 Data Protection Act gives us the right to know the personal information companies are holding. But the new threat to personal liberty is quite the opposite – it is the threat of complete strangers finding out our personal details. Undertake an internet search on someone you know with any of the main search engines and you are likely to obtain thousands of results which if trawled through can provide particulars of employment, a work phone number and e-mail address. Find a CV belonging to that person and you will get hold of their home address, date of birth, home telephone number, personal e-mail address and a listing of their educational history and interests. If the person for whom you are searching is active on a social network site or an internet specialist interest forum then you may well be able to identify a database of friends and contacts and by reading recent postings obtain a flavour of their views and preferences. Search the database of a genealogy site and you may well be able to identify generations of family members.

Q4. The threat to personal liberty is no longer one of secrecy and finding out what organizations know about us.

True ☐ False ☐ Cannot tell ☐

Q5. The penultimate sentence of the passage illustrates the sort of things that people post on the internet.

True ☐ False ☐ Cannot tell ☐

End of test

Mini-test 7

Passage 1

Do scientific investigations of our past add to our understanding or do they whittle away at the mystery? Archaeology, carbon dating and DNA analysis have been used to 'disprove' popular explanations of historic events and to claim that supposed historic events could never have taken place.

Q1. An example of the scientific debunking of popular belief is the use of satellite images to locate a fabled, lost city.

True ☐ False ☐ Cannot tell ☐

Q2. Science can play a positive role and rather than be seen to discredit popular belief instead enrich it.

True ☐ False ☐ Cannot tell ☐

Passage 2

In terms of territory Russia is the world's largest country and Canada the second. Between them these huge nations occupy most of the northern part of the northern hemisphere. Both countries include a sizable extent of frozen wilderness. Canada covers the northern part of the North American continent while the Russian federation sits astride the northern parts of Europe and Asia. The two nations both have vast areas of forest and their forestry industries produce a large part of the world's softwood and wood pulp. Both countries hold extensive mineral deposits and the mining of zinc, uranium and nickel in Canada and iron ore, tungsten, gold, silver and diamonds in Russia rank these countries among the world's key producers. Five per cent of Canadian land is suitable for the growing of crops while 10 per cent of Russian land is arable. The majority of Russians live in the temperate, European part of the country while the bulk of Canadians have settled in the clement conditions found within 400 km of the border with their southern neighbour the United States.

Q3. You can infer that Russian arable production is greater than that of Canada.

True ☐ False ☐ Cannot tell ☐

Q4. The second sentence may have been more correct if it read '… the Russian federation covers the northern part of both Europe and Asia' rather than 'sits astride the northern part of Europe and Asia'.

True ☐ False ☐ Cannot tell ☐

Q5. The author of the passage would agree that the polar regions of both countries are relatively sparsely populated.

True ☐ False ☐ Cannot tell ☐

End of test

Mini-test 8

Passage 1

Waves become swell when they leave the area of wind in which they were generated. Long after the wind that created it has stopped blowing, swell can continue to travel for thousands of miles and have a life span dependent on its wave length and the extent of ocean. The longer the wave the faster it travels and given sufficient sea room the longer it continues to travel. Wind can generate waves that travel faster than the wind itself and after a few hours of blowing the wave can be a long way ahead of the wind. At sea the arrival of a swell can be an indication of bad weather to come. If a long low swell arrives and it steadily increases in height then you should prepare for an approaching gale. If the swell remains long and low then it is likely that the wind that generated it is a long way away and you will escape it. Sometimes a swell generated far away crosses the waves generated by another wind. This can lead to a confused and in the extreme a dangerous sea state.

Q1. The views expressed in the passage are a statement of the findings of experimental investigations.

True ☐ False ☐ Cannot tell ☐

Q2. The sentence 'wind can generate waves that travel faster than the wind itself and after a few hours of blowing the wave can be a long way ahead of the wind' would be more correct if it read 'Wind can generate waves that travel faster than the wind itself and after a few hours of blowing the swell can be a long way ahead of the wind.'

True ☐ False ☐ Cannot tell ☐

Passage 2

The world's major religions are Islam, Christianity, Hinduism, Buddhism, Judaism and Sikhism. The oldest is Hinduism which is believed to have been worshipped for at least 5,000 years. Religion provides a sense of community, a shared set of values that shape daily life, a definition of the meaning of life and a set of beliefs as to how the world began and what happens after death. Except for Buddhism the major religions all identify a supreme god and define the way in which followers commune with that god. Religions have sacred texts, for example in Sikhism the text is called the Adi Granth, and religions have revered places for communal worship. In Judaism the synagogue is the place for communal prayer and religious learning. All religion involves ceremony and festivals and observances at points in a religious calendar and at significant stages in the life of its prophet or prophets and the lives of its followers. For example, followers of the Christian faith celebrate baptism, the rite of a person's entry into the faith, and Muslims celebrate important events in the life of the Prophet, including his birthday.

Q3. Providing an explanation of what happens after death is attributed to all major religions except for Buddhism.

True ☐ False ☐ Cannot tell ☐

Q4. The passage is illustrated with specific details from five of the six major religions of the world.

True ☐ False ☐ Cannot tell ☐

Q5. The main theme of the passage is an examination of the ceremonies, festivals and observances of the world's major religions and the lives of the prophet or prophets and the followers.

True ☐ False ☐ Cannot tell ☐

End of test

UKCAT-style timed tests

Hints and tips

This section of the aptitude test is based on English comprehension exercises. It requires a response to text, ie reading a passage of prose and then eliciting facts from it.

The material used for comprehension questions can be quite varied, and the candidate is advised to read widely and to try to evaluate, particularly when reading a newspaper or textbook, what has actually been said. Another hint for preparation is to try to improve your reading speed without detracting from the understanding. The faster you can read, the more time you have for answers.

In the UKCAT you are given passages of prose followed by a statement. You have to decide whether the statement is true, false, or impossible to say (can't tell), based solely on the facts in the passage. The passages can vary in length, with most ranging between approximately 250 and 350 words.

When answering this type of question it is normal practice to read the passage through first, followed by the statement, before scanning back through the passage to find key words or phrases that relate to those of the statement. However, there is insufficient time in the UKCAT to read through the entire passage first, so read the question and then scan through the passage for key words or phrases that fit with the statement. You have three choices:

True: the statement is clearly true, implied or a reasonable conclusion to draw.
False: the statement is clearly untrue, a distortion of the facts or an unreasonable conclusion to draw.
Can't tell: the statement lacks sufficient information to say whether it is true or false with any certainty.

Candidates are sometimes unsure when to use the answer 'can't tell' as opposed to true or false. The following example provides guidelines.

Example: Conservative colours

Most people choose a conservative colour for their new car. According to one motoring organization, 6 out of 10 people prefer silver, blue or red. In contrast, only 1 in 10 people opt for white or green and only 1 in 100 choose turquoise, yellow or pink. Car manufacturers have no desire to buck this trend, and offer up to four shades of silver per model. If you order a silver car it can be ready in a week, whereas a pink one can take up to three months to arrive.

With respect to the colour of new cars:

1.	Most are silver, blue or red.	True
2.	Silver is one of the least popular.	False
3.	Silver is not as popular as blue.	Can't tell
4.	Silver is the most popular.	Can't tell
5.	Silver might be the most popular.	True
6.	Over half are silver, blue or red.	True
7.	Pink is one of the most popular.	False
8.	Pink is not as popular as yellow.	Can't tell
9.	Pink is the least popular.	Can't tell
10.	Pink might be the least popular.	True
11.	A silver car cannot be ready in a week.	False
12.	A pink car will be ready in a week.	Can't tell
13.	A pink car might be ready in a week.	True
14.	A pink car cannot be ready in a week.	False

As a general principle, the answer is 'can't tell' (C) if there is uncertainty arising from the paragraph, ie it is impossible to indicate either true or false. 'Can't tell' is also used when the question introduces new material that is not covered in the paragraph. The answer is likely to be true (T) or false (F) rather than 'can't tell' if the uncertainty arises in the question.

Read the following comprehension passages carefully; then choose whether the statements are true (T), false (F) or can't tell (C).

UKCAT-style verbal reasoning timed tests 1 and 2

(10 sets of four questions in 20 minutes.)

1. Healthy minds (300 words)

Mental health problems are the second-largest cause of people taking time off work, outnumbered only by muscle-related problems like back injuries. Depression and anxiety are the most common problems. Less well-known, less common ailments include bipolar disorder, schizophrenia and paranoia. Stressful life events, suppression of feelings or a difficult family background can lead to neuroses like depression and anxiety. A family history of mental illness or an imbalance in the body's chemicals may be associated with psychoses such as schizophrenia and bipolar disorder (formerly manic depression). The first point of contact with the NHS is usually the doctor's surgery. The patient's GP will try to identify the cause of the problem and treat it. Only 5 per cent of people are referred to a consultant psychiatrist and, of these, many are seen at the outpatient clinic. Psychiatric wards are under the control of a consultant psychiatrist, who works with a team that includes psychiatric nurses, social workers and occupational therapists.

Psychotic illness can be treated with psychotropic drugs that alter mood, perception and behaviour. With neurosis, psychotherapy sessions encourage a person to talk freely about his or her feelings, and to relate to the experiences that lie behind the distressed state. Most people recover completely from mental distress, but some become chronically ill and will always require medication.

Emphasis is placed on care in the community either in people's own homes or in supported housing. Community psychiatric nurses (CPNs) visit people at home to provide support through difficult times and to help with medication regimes. Social workers can assist with housing and financial issues as well as transport, meals and daily chores. Self-help groups and mental health charities like MIND and SANE provide free services for people with mental health problems.

1. Schizophrenia can run in families. ☐

2. In the NHS, most people with mental health problems attend an outpatient clinic. ☐

3. A psychiatrist is a qualified medical doctor who works with a team of healthcare professionals. ☐

4. Psychotherapy could be described as a 'talking treatment'. ☐

2. Time and temperature (300 words)

Food poisoning is still prevalent in the UK, with more than 90,000 reported cases in 2007, though unreported cases could be as much as 10 times higher, because most people with mild symptoms fail to report the incident. Millions of bacteria are needed to produce food poisoning. Under favourable conditions, rapid multiplication takes place by binary fission every 10 to 20 minutes. Pathogenic bacteria can grow at temperatures as low as 5 °C and as high as 63 °C; food kept in this 'danger zone' should never be reheated. Fridges and cold stores at 1 to 4 °C stop the multiplication of pathogenic bacteria but not of food spoilage bacteria. The latter can continue to grow at temperatures as low as minus 18 °C, below which they remain dormant. Bacteria are not destroyed by freezing and can multiply again after the food thaws out.

Campylobacter is responsible for most of the food poisoning in the UK, with about four times as many cases as occur with Salmonella. Campylobacter is also referred to as a 'food-borne' disease because it remains dormant at room temperature but multiplies rapidly at body temperature (37 °C); it is destroyed at temperatures above 48 °C. Most cases of Salmonella food poisoning are caused by storing prepared food at room temperature. Salmonella is quickly destroyed at temperatures above 74 °C. Other food-borne pathogens include Listeria, E. coli and Clostridium perfringens, which is spore forming and can survive cooking.

Both Campylobacter and Salmonella are associated with raw meat, poultry, eggs and unpasteurized milk. Examples of cross-contamination include kitchen staff failing to wash their hands when taking eggs out of the fridge, a drop of juice from a fresh chicken at the top of the fridge contaminating cooked foods below, and using the same chopping board to prepare meat and vegetables. Spread is not normally from person to person.

5. Pathogenic and food spoilage bacteria remain dormant below minus 18 °C. ☐

6. A single cell of Campylobacter can multiply to more than 1,000 bacteria in less than two hours on food at room temperature. ☐

7. The ingestion of a small number of Campylobacter cells could make you ill. ☐

8. Heating food to 75 °C will destroy most bacteria responsible for food poisoning in the UK. ☐

3. Fumes (275 words)

The word 'smog' was first used to describe the 'smoke fog' that arose from the burning of coal during the early 19th century. Today's smog is associated more with vehicle exhaust emissions and industrial pollutants that combine in the presence of sunlight to produce a 'photochemical smog'. This modern smog has implications for human health and global warming.

Car exhausts emit unburnt hydrocarbons, carbon monoxide, carbon dioxide and oxides of nitrogen (NOx). Hydrocarbons can cause liver damage, and carbon monoxide is harmful to people with ischaemic heart disease (IHD). Carbon dioxide is a major greenhouse gas, and nitrogen oxides contribute to acid rain. Power stations release sulphur dioxide, which is an irritant when inhaled and can cause breathing difficulties. Sulphur dioxide is oxidized to sulphur trioxide, which combines with water vapour in the atmosphere to form sulphuric acid, giving rise to acid rain. The acid is environmentally damaging and can become a risk to human health if it leaches carcinogenic metals into the food chain.

Volatile organic compounds (VOCs) constitute the volatile components in paints, aerosol sprays and solvents and they are released when fuel is not completely burnt. VOCs can be split into two groups – methane-containing and non-methane-containing. Methane is a significant greenhouse gas and contributes to global warming. Some non-methane VOCs react with nitrogen oxides in the presence of sunlight to form ozone, which can exacerbate chronic obstructive pulmonary disease (COPD) and asthma.

The formation of ozone and acid rain is not instantaneous, so concentrations of secondary pollutants are highest downwind of the precursor chemicals. Consequently, choosing to live in the countryside where there are fewer sources of pollutants no longer guarantees good air quality.

9. The passage states that carbon monoxide is a major greenhouse gas. ☐

10. Non-methane-containing VOCs do not contribute to global warming. ☐

11. Sulphur dioxide is the only pollutant that forms acid rain. ☐

12. The precursor chemicals referred to in the final paragraph include nitrogen oxides, sulphur dioxide and methane. ☐

4. Pennies make pounds (350 words)

In business, it's not just what you spend and earn that counts, it's how you account for it as well. The accounts of a simple business might just keep track of what has been paid out, what has been received and what is due in. Even so, it is easy to get in a mess. A business makes goods or provides a service. It then needs to record the sales invoices sent out in the sales day book and in the customers' sales ledger account (debtors' account). Upon payment of the invoice the payment is recorded in the cash book and in the customers' sales ledger account.

A business will also receive goods or use a service. It then needs to record the invoice received in the purchase day book and in the suppliers' purchase ledger account. On paying the invoice the payment is recorded in the cash book and in the suppliers' purchase ledger account. Bank reconciliation checks the accuracy of cash book entries against the bank statements. Differences between the bank columns of the cash book and the bank statement may reflect errors made by the business or by the bank; however, they can usually be explained by cheques the business has written out that have yet to be presented to the bank or equally by any uncleared deposits.

A petty cash book is used to maintain an office float, for example £50, to pay for miscellaneous office items like stamps, stationery and travelling expenses. The petty cash float cuts down on the need to write out cheques for small items and then have to make numerous bookkeeping entries. However, payments received in the form of notes and coins should be paid into the bank in the normal way and not into the petty cash box. Ideally receipts should be provided for petty cash claims and a petty cash voucher made out for monies paid out. In this way the sum of the receipts, vouchers and petty cash in the box should always equal the float (£50). When the float runs low the payments recorded in the petty cash book are totalled up and the equivalent sum is withdrawn from the bank to top up the float to its original level.

13. One sale will result in three bookkeeping entries in three ledgers. ☐

14. The purchase ledger account could be described as a creditors' account. ☐

15. No notes or coins are paid into the petty cash box. ☐

16. There will be no discrepancy between the bank statement and the cash book. ☐

5. Bee's knees (300 words)

Honey is making a comeback as a wound care product. The use of honey for medicinal purposes dates back to Egyptian times when it was used both topically and internally to treat a wide range of health problems ranging from skin infection to gaping wounds and stomach ulcers. However, modern civilizations have regarded honey more as foodstuff than as medicine. Today, medical-grade manuka honey from New Zealand is healing wounds where more conventional treatments have failed. It can be used on partial or full thickness wounds including pressure sores, leg ulcers, surgical wounds, burns and graft sites. The honey is applied directly to the wound bed followed by an occlusive dressing, or as top-up to a honey-impregnated wound dressing.

Honey is able to clean wounds because the high sugar content provides an osmotic potential that draws moisture into the skin. Moisture management is a key feature of wound healing; the benefits of maintaining a warm, moist environment are widely accepted. Infection control is fundamental to wound care, and the high acidity or low pH of honey makes it bactericidal. Consequently, honey may be able to control wound infection where antibiotics have failed. Honey has anti-inflammatory properties and it reduces wound exudate, which if not contained can macerate the surrounding skin to increase the risk of infection.

Honey treatments are generally well received by patients, who view them as a natural cure, although body temperature makes honey very runny, creating a sticky mess that may require more frequent dressing changes. The only contraindication to using honey is a known allergy to bee venom. Some patients may experience an increase in pain due to its osmotic action. Whilst eating honey is not an option for patients with diabetes, there are no reports of topical honey increasing blood glucose levels, though the manufacturers advise that these levels are closely monitored.

17. In ancient times honey was used more as a medicine than a foodstuff. ☐

18. The application of medical-grade manuka honey to a wound could render it sterile. ☐

19. Controlling moisture is the main aim of wound care. ☐

20. The possibility of a topical honey dressing increasing the blood sugar level in a patient with diabetes cannot be ruled out. ☐

6. Weighty problem (300 words)

The World Health Organization (WHO) reports that obesity has reached epidemic proportions worldwide, with three times as many overweight adults as there were 20 years ago. Almost one-quarter of the adult population of the UK are now classed as obese, and they are over-represented in their use of NHS services.

The most widely used tool to assess obesity is body mass index (BMI), which divides weight in kilograms by height in metres squared to give the units kg/m^2. A BMI of 25 or above is defined as overweight or pre-obese, and a BMI of 30 or more is defined as obese. People with a BMI of 40 or above are morbidly obese; they are at severe risk of developing co-morbidities like cardiovascular disease and type 2 diabetes, which reduce life expectancy and increase hospital stay. Patients weighing more than 20 stone are described as bariatric – the word originated from the Greek word *baros* meaning heavy and *iatrics* meaning medical treatment. The large size of bariatric patients often leads to poor mobility, with implications for manual handling, equipment, beds, chairs and space.

Most bariatric patients will have a BMI in excess of 40, though not all bariatric people will be morbidly obese nor will every person with a BMI over 30 be obese. For example, a six-foot-five rugby player weighing 21 stone (BMI = 35) with a muscular build and a good weight distribution might be athletic. In these larger people the waist-to-hip ratio can serve as a more reliable indicator of a weight problem. A ratio of 1.0 or more is consistent with an excess of fat around the waist and the need to lose weight. From a health perspective, maximum safe waist measurements are reported as 40 inches (102 cm) for men and 35 inches (89 cm) for women irrespective of fat distribution.

21. At least one-quarter of obese adults use NHS services. ☐

22. A patient with a BMI of between 25.0 and 29.9 is pre-obese. ☐

23. A patient with a waist-to-hip ratio of 1.1 is obese. ☐

24. A patient with a waist measurement over 40 inches is obese. ☐

7. Votes count (200 words)

The United Kingdom has had a full parliamentary democracy since 1928 when women were allowed to vote in general elections at age 21, the same as men. Women were first given the right to vote in 1918 after the First World War, but only if they were over the age of 30. In 1969 the voting age for men and women was reduced to 18. Today, no person can vote unless their name appears on the electoral register, and the earliest you can register is age 16.

Citizens of the Commonwealth and those of the Irish Republic are eligible to vote in all public elections (general and local) as long as they are resident in the UK. British nationals who move abroad retain the right to vote in British and EU elections for a further 15 years. Some people are disenfranchised, including convicted prisoners (but not those on remand), non-UK EU citizens, Church of England archbishops and bishops, members of the House of Lords and people lacking the mental capacity to vote on polling day. However, all of the above people (convicted prisoners and those lacking mental capacity excepted) can vote in local elections, and all EU citizens can also vote in European elections, though only in one country and not two.

25. A woman born in 1889 would not have been allowed to vote in the 1918 UK general election. ☐

26. A 55-year-old male born in Northern Ireland and domiciled in Spain five years ago is entitled to vote in a UK general election. ☐

27. Non-UK EU citizens over age 18 with mental capacity who are not prisoners are entitled to vote in a UK general election. ☐

28. A 19-year-old female born in the Irish Republic is entitled to vote in a UK general election. ☐

8. Park and fly (300 words)

For most people, parking the car is a mundane activity devoid of planning. However, Heathrow airport has so many car parks and parking options that if you park in the wrong place the charges could exceed the cost of the flight. Terminal 5's car park can hold 2,200 cars, and the long-stay car park can hold 3,800 cars and 150 motorcycles, so finding a space should never be a problem, but the turn-up prices can be much higher than those offered for pre-booking. The multi-storey car parks at Heathrow airport are mainly for short-stay parking where there is a general vehicle height restriction of 2 metres. Charges are designed to discourage a stay of more than six hours, and the daily rate is punitive. Vehicles up to 2.4 metres in height can park on the ground floor of car park 3 (serving Terminals 1, 2 and 3).

Customers using Terminal 4 can park vehicles up to 2.6 metres in height on the roof of car park 4 or alternatively they can use business parking, where they will be charged the short-stay tariff for stays of up to six hours, after which time long-stay tariffs apply. Terminal 5 customers can also use business parking combined with a short courtesy coach transfer. Vehicles up to 2.6 metres in height can use the Terminal 4 forecourt for the purposes of dropping off and picking up only. Vehicles taller than 2.6 metres need to park in the long-stay car parks (one-day minimum stay) or at business parking. The former charges a variable daily rate depending on the number of days stayed, whilst the latter charges a fixed amount per day for stays between 1 and 13 days and a fixed sum for stays between 14 and 28 days. Stays longer than 28 days incur the fixed sum plus the fixed amount per day charge for the additional days.

29. A vehicle that is 1.9 metres in height can be parked for two days in a multi-storey car park. ☐

30. Vehicles taller than 2.6 metres can park at business parking for the purposes of short- or long-term parking. ☐

31. Parking a vehicle at business parking costs twice as much for 26 days as it does for 13 days. ☐

32. A vehicle that is 2.3 metres in height can be parked on the roof of car park 3. ☐

9. Minted (280 words)

Coins have been struck in Britain for over 2,000 years, but it was not until the 13th century that a properly instituted mint was formed. Sited in the Tower of London between the inner and outer walls, it employed primitive methods of coining money with hand-held tools. In the 17th century, human-powered screw presses were introduced that could strike up to 30 coins per minute.

With the advent of the Industrial Revolution, steam-powered machinery was available and a private mint was opened in Birmingham by the entrepreneur Matthew Boulton. He secured contracts for pennies and twopences, producing much higher-quality coins than the Tower, which lacked the space for steam-powered presses. A decision was taken to transfer facilities from the Tower to Tower Hill, where the Royal Mint began production in 1810. The new presses were capable of striking up to 100 coins per minute. UK coins were circulated in various parts of the British Empire, and after the First World War the Royal Mint sought orders from countries all over the world.

In 1964 the government decided to adopt a decimal system of currency and a new Royal Mint was constructed in readiness for decimalization on 15 February 1971. The new Mint was constructed at Llantrisant in south Wales in 1967 and the first phase was opened by the queen on 17 December 1968. Later, an up-to-date foundry was installed, followed by engraving, tool-making and assay departments along with a special section for striking proof coins for the collectors' market. The original site on Tower Hill was run down once the Llantrisant facility had the full range of minting facilities. Tower Hill struck its last coin in November 1975.

33. The Royal Mint was not the first to utilize steam power. ☐

34. All of the minting facilities had been transferred from Tower Hill to Llantrisant by 1968. ☐

35. Only Llantrisant could strike special proof coins. ☐

36. The mint at Tower Hill continued to operate after decimalization. ☐

10. Talking rot (280 words)

Despite its name, dry rot is anything but dry; it needs water to grow. It is caused by the fungus *Serpula lacrymans*, which colonizes damp wood in the form of red-brown fruit bodies. Wood consists of cellulose and lignin, and the fungus metabolizes the cellulose to its sugar components and eventually to carbon dioxide and water, which the fungus soaks up. The affected timber takes on a dull brown appearance, dries up and rapidly loses mechanical strength. Dry rot can threaten the structure of a building because it can spread beyond its source to penetrate the walls and brickwork.

In the short term, timber affected with dry rot can be removed and the adjacent wood treated with a chemical fungicide. However, prevention is better than cure, and dry rot will not grow in an environment with less than 20 per cent moisture. Wet rot is more common in buildings than dry rot but is a far less serious problem because it cannot spread into the brickwork. Like dry rot, wet rot cannot grow in dry wood. Both dry and wet rot can usually be traced to a distinct source of rainwater ingress into a building, for example broken tiles, guttering or brickwork. Painting timbers with primer and top coat can stop water from penetrating wood, thereby preventing the germination of wood rot spores. However, an intact paint surface can mask fungal penetration that may have entered the wood at an exposed surface, for example where the timber is embedded in wet brickwork. The presence of dry rot can be confirmed by probing with a screwdriver, when the timber will easily give way, and also by tapping with a hammer, when it will sound hollow.

37. Both dry and wet rot are caused by the fungus *Serpula lacrymans*. ☐

38. Wood with an intact paint surface is free of wood rot. ☐

39. The normal water content of wood is less than 20 per cent. ☐

40. Dry rot can occur only in environments that have a high percentage of moisture. ☐

UKCAT-style verbal reasoning timed test 2

(10 sets of four questions in 20 minutes.)

1. ET (230 words)

From a space exploration point of view, a satellite is a human-made object placed into orbit around a planet, for example the Earth, Saturn or Jupiter. In astronomy, a satellite is any celestial body orbiting around a planet or star, so the moon is a natural or non-artificial satellite of the Earth; the other planets encircling the sun are natural satellites of the sun. Mercury and Venus are the only planets to have no moons. Mars has two small asteroid-like moons called Phobos and Deimos. Saturn has at least 30 orbiting moons. The largest of Saturn's moons, Titan, is 1.5 times larger than the Earth's moon, making it the second-largest moon in the solar system. Titan is larger than the planets Mercury and Pluto. The four largest of Jupiter's 60 moons are Ganymede, Io, Callisto and Europa. These four Galilean satellites were discovered in 1610 and are all planet-sized. Europa has an icy surface at minus 170 °C. However, heat linked to volcanic activity on Europa may be sufficient to maintain a layer of liquid water below the ice sheet, making it one of the few places in the solar system capable of sustaining life. This possibility featured in the 1984 science fiction film *2010*, based on an Arthur C Clarke novel. NASA now plans to send a probe to Europa to see if it harbours life.

1. The Earth's moon is the third-largest moon in the solar system. ☐

2. Jupiter has more moons than any other planet. ☐

3. The low number of craters on the surface of Europa results from volcanic activity and lava flows. ☐

4. The atmosphere on Europa is capable of sustaining life. ☐

2. Burning issues (230 words)

Fire extinguishers come in several different types depending on the nature of the material that can combust. There are six classifications of combustible material as described below:

Class A: flammable organic solids (eg wood, paper, coal, plastics, textiles)
Class B: flammable liquids (eg petrol, spirits) but not cooking oil
Class C: flammable gas (eg LPG, butane)
Class D: combustible metals (eg magnesium, titanium)
Class E: electrical equipment (eg computers, photocopiers)
Class F: cooking oil and fat

Pressurized water fire extinguishers can only be used to tackle Class A fires; carbon dioxide extinguishers are especially suitable for Class E fires, as they do not damage electrical equipment such as computers; they can find limited use with Class B fires, though there is a risk of reignition due to a lack of cooling; foam-filled fire extinguishers are suitable for Class B fires and can be used on Class A fires though not in confined spaces; they are not for electrical equipment fires or cooking oil; dry powder fire extinguishers can be used for Class A, B, C and E fires, with specialist powders for Class D fires; dry powder fire extinguishers smother the fire but do not cool it or penetrate very well, so there is a risk of reignition; wet chemical fire extinguishers are designed specifically to tackle cooking oil fires, especially with high temperature deep fat fryers.

5. Class F fires can be extinguished with wet chemical fire extinguishers. ☐

6. Class A fires can be tackled with three types of fire extinguisher. ☐

7. Foam-filled fire extinguishers should not be used on Class D fires. ☐

8. Flammable liquids are more likely to reignite than flammable solids. ☐

3. World's language (290 words)

The pre-eminence of the English language globally may be under threat. One billion people in the world speak Mandarin, the dominant language of China, more than three times the number who speak English. If economic trends continue then China is set to dominate world trade and quite possibly global communication with it. It is perhaps surprising then that learning English is growing fast in China, where there are more English-language teaching jobs than in any other country. The International English Language Testing System or IELTS is taken by more than one million people worldwide, and last year 270,000 tests were taken in China. This fact belies the notion that the number of speakers of a language determines its status. English is set to remain influential because it is seen as the language of academia, diplomacy and especially science, where 95 per cent of scientific publications worldwide are written in English.

The language of English is robust because it has a great literary heritage and prestige (though notably so did Latin, which subsequently declined), and it is the main language of the prosperous and stable nations of the West. The use of English became widespread following the expansion of the British Empire, and it remains the primary language of at least 45 countries and the official language of many international organizations. Above all else, it is the popularity of English as a second and third language that confirms its status as the world's language. Globally there are almost three times as many non-native speakers of English as native speakers. The number of people who can speak English in India now exceeds the number in the United States. In Nigeria, more people can speak English (pidgin) than in the UK.

9. There are fewer English-language teaching jobs in the UK than in China. ☐

10. The language of Latin was gradually displaced by English. ☐

11. More people speak English outside of the UK than in the UK. ☐

12. In terms of English speakers, four countries are ranked as follows: India, United States, Nigeria, UK (highest number first). ☐

4. Waterways (280 words)

At the height of the Industrial Revolution in the mid-19th century, huge quantities of coal had to be transported from the pithead for iron smelting, manufacturing and domestic use. Coastal shipping, navigable rivers and horse-drawn carts were either slow or restrictive in comparison to the new purpose-built canals. A horse could pull a narrowboat weighing 50 times as much as a cart. The UK soon developed a national network of canals and by the middle of the 19th century almost all major towns and cities had a canal. At the same time, there was controversy as to the rival merits of transporting coal by canal or by railway. Stephenson's locomotive could transport vast quantities of coal and other goods more quickly than by canal and also offered a new means of passenger transport. The canal network was doomed, and investment was redirected into railways, with local lines laid down in the coal districts developed into a national system for the whole of the country.

Road haulage in the 20th century brought more competition for canals, and only a few remained open until the Second World War. Further declines were inevitable, and the use of canals for industrial purposes was minimal in the 1960s. However, interest in canals for leisure purposes had begun to grow, and some were restored and reopened by volunteers in the 1970s. This trend has continued, with canals attracting government funding for restoration projects. Canals are now a major tourist industry, with more than 10 million visitors per year and 30,000 craft. Today there are more boats on the canals than at the height of the Industrial Revolution.

13. A network of canals was in place before a national system of railways. ☐

14. The 1960s saw more interest in canals for leisure than for industry. ☐

15. Stephenson's locomotive succeeded because it could transport vast quantities of coal. ☐

16. There are more narrowboats on the canals today than at the height of the Industrial Revolution. ☐

5. Internet chat (340 words)

The transmission control protocol/internet protocol (TCP/IP) is a spin-off from military communications. TCP/IP is an electronic handshake that connects networks using routers. It defines what happens when data packets are transmitted and received and includes data formatting, timing, and error checking. An in-house TCP/IP network is called an intranet and it allows members of an organization to access a private website. An internet service provider (ISP) is required to share public web pages on the internet. In a local area network or LAN, several computers or workstations and their associated peripherals (eg printers) are connected together in the same building. In a wide area network or WAN, multiple LANs are connected over a large area of several kilometres.

Topology is a term that refers to the physical layout of the network or the architecture of its cabling system. Problems with the cabling can lead to a network 'going down'. There are three basic types of LAN topology, which are the star, ring and bus, and each has its own advantages and disadvantages. With a star topology each workstation has its own cable connected to a central hub. Signals pass into the hub and then out to each of the workstations. Failure of a single system will not affect any of the other workstations, but the failure of the hub will disconnect every computer. A star topology makes adding more workstations easy, though only one computer can send and receive data from the hub at any one time. In a ring topology, or closed loop network, each workstation is joined to a common ring at a node. If one computer fails, it can bring the entire network down. In a bus topology, the workstations are 'daisy-chained' together, with all the computers connected to a backbone or bus cable; if two computers try to send a signal along the cable at the same time a collision occurs; every collision slows the network down. Network faults are difficult to troubleshoot with a bus topology, because the workstations share a cable, unlike the star and ring topologies.

17. In a star topology, a computer can be disconnected from the network without causing the system to go down. ☐

18. In a star topology, several computers can send and receive data from the hub at any one time. ☐

19. If too many computers are 'daisy-chained' together on a bus cable then the network system might grind to a halt. ☐

20. In a ring topology with six workstations, every node in the network is connected to two other nodes. ☐

6. Beneficence (300 words)

In the 18th century, there were great improvements in surgery, midwifery and hygiene. In London between 1720 and 1745, Guy's, Westminster, St George's, the London and Middlesex general hospitals were all founded. Other hospitals were established in Exeter (1741), Bristol (1733), Liverpool (1745) and York (1740). In the course of 125 years after 1700, at least 154 new hospitals and dispensaries were founded in towns across Britain. These were not municipal undertakings; they were benevolent efforts that relied on voluntary contributions and bequests. It worked well for 250 years prior to the creation of the NHS in 1948.

The first medical school in England was the London Hospital medical college founded in 1785. The teaching and practice of medicine and surgery were improving, but treatments remained limited, encouraging medical fakers with homemade remedies. There was minimal knowledge of the disease process, and diagnosis remained poor, so the same medication was given regardless of the ailment. The most popular treatment was laudanum, a mixture of an opiate-based drug and alcohol, prescribed for pain relief and common ailments such as headaches and diarrhoea. Unfortunately some people became dependent on it and died from overdoses.

Anaesthetics (chloroform and ether) were not used to relieve pain in surgery until 1847. Suturing of wounds was common practice, though needles and thread were not sterile, so infection was rife. Hygiene and infection control remained non-existent until the 1870s, when Louis Pasteur's germ theory of disease had become widely accepted. A Scottish surgeon named Joseph Lister atomized carbolic acid (phenol) for use as an antiseptic, leading to a major decline in blood poisoning following surgery, which had normally proved fatal. The hygiene and nursing practices of Florence Nightingale were adopted by hospitals and led to a reduction in cross-infection and an improvement in recovery rates.

21. On average at least one new hospital per year was founded in Britain between 1700 and 1825. ☐

22. A hospital in Exeter was established before a hospital in Liverpool but after hospitals in Bristol and York. ☐

23. In the 1870s the germs responsible for a disease could be identified. ☐

24. Operations prior to 1847 were carried out without any pain relief. ☐

7. Drive alive (280 words)

The monotony of driving along straight roads and motorways, especially with driver aids like cruise control, increases the chances of falling asleep at the wheel. Working night shifts and driving home afterwards can be particularly risky. Younger drivers are more likely to feel tired in the morning and older drivers can doze off in the afternoon. A period of increased drowsiness and fighting sleep pre-empts falling asleep. It is important to recognize these warning signs and to stop driving. Winding the window down for cold air and turning the radio up provide only temporary relief from drowsiness. Drivers should act responsibly and stop driving to prevent an accident. One solution is to take a short break (15 minutes) with a cup of coffee (caffeine stimulant). The same counter-measures can be employed every two hours during daytime driving.

Long journeys should be planned in advance to avoid hold-ups that increase the time spent behind the wheel. Other preventative measures include sharing the driving with others, turning the heat down or the air conditioning on, not driving after a large meal or heavy exercise, and avoiding even the smallest amount of alcohol. Some medications, such as cold and flu remedies, antihistamines and motion sickness tablets, can cause drowsiness as a side-effect. Ideally, it is better not to upset the body's natural circadian rhythm by driving at a time normally spent sleeping, for example in the early hours of the morning, and to limit the total number of hours spent behind the wheel to a maximum of eight per day. Self-awareness of one's vulnerability to falling asleep and of fighting sleep is also important. Feeling sleepy is perfectly natural but, narcolepsy excepted, nobody falls asleep without prior warning.

25. Ideally, a driver spending a maximum of eight hours per day behind the wheel should take three 15-minute coffee breaks at regular intervals. ☐

26. Driving home after a night shift with the window of the car open and the radio turned up will prevent you from falling asleep. ☐

27. Driving in the early hours of the morning upsets the circadian rhythm. ☐

28. Reaction times are slower in the early hours of the morning. ☐

8. Non-PC (305 words)

Political correctness has eroded our freedom of speech. In the UK, political correctness came to the fore in the 1980s when it sought to protect minority groups from offensive language, attitudes and discrimination as well as banish stereotypes. In recent times it has influenced language, ideas and behaviour to the extent that only one viewpoint can be tolerated, ie that of the politically correct majority, and as such has seriously undermined our freedom of expression. The government has pandered to the 'PC brigade', who more often than not fail to consult the minority groups they claim to support.

The NHS has not escaped the culture of political correctness. Equality and diversity are the latest NHS buzzwords. Anti-discrimination laws have been in place since the 1970s and they were updated in 2003, so much of the new material covers old ground. Furthermore, the PC brigade has failed to understand that the best way to prevent discrimination is to stop looking for it at every turn. For example, why should NHS employees and patients be asked to tick boxes that request information about sexuality or ethnic origin? Highlighting differences is a form of discrimination in itself.

The pervasiveness and absurdity of political correctness was highlighted recently when the NHS suspended a nurse for offering to pray for an elderly patient. In this case, the NHS discriminated against the nurse on the basis of her religious beliefs whilst at the same time claiming to respect equality and diversity. Clearly the PC brigade within the NHS believes that spiritual needs are at odds with its equality and diversity policy; hospital chaplains beware. The only PC the NHS should concern itself with is patient care. The NHS should not waste resources pandering to political correctness when all that is required is a little more common sense.

29. The author believes that equality and diversity within the NHS are largely within the scope of anti-discrimination laws. ☐

30. NHS patients must declare their sexuality by ticking a box. ☐

31. The nurse was suspended for breaching the NHS equality and diversity policy. ☐

32. The author believes that political correctness is contrary to freedom of thought. ☐

9. Pink ladies (290 words)

In 1973, the antipodean John Cripps cross-bred the Australian Lady Williams apple with the American Golden Delicious to combine the best features of both apples in the Cripps Pink. Today it is one of the best-known varieties of apples and is grown extensively in Australia and New Zealand, and in California and Washington in the United States. By switching from northern hemisphere fruit to southern hemisphere fruit the apple is available at its seasonal best all year round. The highest-quality apples are marketed worldwide under the trademark Pink Lady™ and, in order to preserve its premium appeal and price, about 65 per cent of the apples that do not meet the highest standard are sold under the name Cripps Pink™. These standards are based on colour intensity and flavour. Both the Pink Lady™ and the Cripps Pink™ have become increasing popular with UK consumers. The Pink Lady™ held approximately 10 per cent of the UK apple market in 2005.

The Cripps Red variety, also known as Cripps II, sells equally as well as the Pink Lady™, with which it shares the same parentage. The premium grade is marketed as the Sundowner™. This apple is harvested in late May to early June, three weeks after Cripps Pink and a few weeks before Lady Williams™. It can be cold-stored for longer than Cripps Pink and has an excellent shelf life. Cripps Red is sweeter than Lady Williams™ but not as sweet as Golden Delicious. Unlike the genuinely pink Pink Lady™, the Sundowner™ is a classic bi-coloured apple, about 45 per cent red from Lady Williams™ and 55 per cent green from Golden Delicious™. Apples that fall outside this colour ratio are rejected at the packing station and used for juice, whilst the smaller apples are retained for the home market.

33. Approximately two-thirds of the Cripps Pink variety fail to meet the highest standards required of the Pink Lady™ trademark. ☐

34. Pink Lady™ is more expensive than Sundowner™. ☐

35. The Pink Lady™ is equally as popular as the Sundowner™. ☐

36. Colour is an important factor in the selection of both of the premium grades of Cripps apples referred to. ☐

10. Blighty (270 words)

Are the British Isles, the UK, Great Britain and Britain one and the same thing? Well, no, actually. The British Isles is a non-political, geographical term that refers to an archipelago, or cluster of islands, that includes the two main islands that encompass England, Wales and Scotland and the whole of the island of Ireland, as well as all of the many small surrounding islands.

The UK is an abbreviated form of the United Kingdom of Great Britain and Northern Ireland, whereas Great Britain is England, Wales and Scotland (and their adjacent islands) but not Northern Ireland, making Great Britain a geographical term but not a political entity. The adjacent islands referred to include the Isle of Wight, the Isles of Scilly, the Isle of Anglesey (Ynys Mon in Welsh) and the islands of Scotland (Orkney and Shetland Islands and the Inner and Outer Hebrides). The term Britain is often used to mean Great Britain, though strictly speaking Britain covers England and Wales but not Scotland, because Britain stems from the Roman word Britannia, which did not include the area now called Scotland, which was never conquered. To add to the confusion, the term British Islands encompasses the United Kingdom, the Channel Islands (Jersey and Guernsey) and the Isle of Man; the small islands are not part of Great Britain, the UK or the European Union but are self-governing British Crown dependencies. Finally, the term Ireland defines both a political entity, ie the Republic of Ireland (or Eire), that is Southern Ireland, and the geographical entity that is both Northern and Southern Ireland, the single land mass.

37. The British Islands include Northern Ireland whilst the British Isles include all of Ireland. ☐

38. The Isle of Anglesey is not part of Great Britain. ☐

39. Northern Ireland is not part of Great Britain but it is part of the UK. ☐

40. Jersey is not part of Great Britain but it is part of the British Isles. ☐

3

Decision analysis

These tests are about making good judgements in less than ideal circumstances – as is often the case in real life. The information provided is deliberately incomplete, and the rules being followed are deliberately ambiguous. It is your task to decipher the code and then, despite the fact that the information is incomplete and that there is uncertainty, decide which of the suggested answers are best. You have to do this within a tight time frame.

This chapter contains a total of 128 questions. It starts with 20 that require you simply to identify synonyms, antonyms, or expanded or contracted terms and correctly identify terms that are similar (a key competency assumed in the decision analysis sub-test and one that speakers of English as a second language in particular may find it beneficial to practise). These are followed by 33 warm up questions to start you practising the key competencies and 75 realistic decision analysis practice questions.

Twenty questions on synonyms, antonyms, expanded or contracted terms and terms that are similar

One of the skills tested in the UKCAT decision analysis sub-test involves the identification of synonyms and antonyms and words that are related in some way. Use the following 20 questions to become confident in this important ability. Identify which of the suggested answers is correct and enter it in the answer box. These questions will prove particularly helpful to speakers of English as a second language. Feel free to skip this section if your English is fluent or native.

Q1. Turn around the word humble

A. Modest
B. Ordinary
C. Belittle
D. Self-important
E. Unpretentious

Answer ☐

Q2. Enlarge deepen

A. Lessen
B. Dig
C. Excavate
D. Hollow

Answer ☐

Q3. Decrease poisonous

A. Venomous
B. Corrupting
C. Fatal
D. Cleansing

Answer ☐

Q4. Find the equivalent to social

A. Friendly
B. Personal
C. Cool
D. Private

Answer ☐

Q5. Find the term least similar to block

A. Lump
B. Fool
C. Obstruction
D. Building

Answer ☐

Q6. Turn around request

A. Demand
B. Appeal
C. Offer
D. Seek

Answer ☐

Q7. Decrease unsurpassed

A. Best
B. Worst
C. Very good
D. Even better

Answer ☐

Q8. Past of copy

A. Scanned
B. Fake
C. Forgery
D. Reproduction

Answer ☐

Q9. Find the word that is not the equivalent to necessity

A. Requirement
B. Superfluous
C. Obligation
D. Essential

Answer ☐

Q10. Find the term least similar to display

A. Show
B. Reveal
C. Extend
D. Mask

Answer ☐

Q11. Find the term corresponding to enigma

A. Paradox
B. Axiom
C. Platitude
D. Message

Answer ☐

Q12. Find the contradictory of resemble

A. Like
B. Like chalk and cheese
C. Comparable
D. Kindred

Answer ☐

Q13. Extend carve

A. Cut
B. Etch
C. Chop
D. Engrave

Answer ☐

Q14. Find the term most akin to margin

A. Perimeter
B. Small
C. Middle
D. Major

Answer ☐

Q15. Shrink slap

A. Whack
B. Knock
C. Punch
D. Stroke

Answer ☐

Q16. Find the term analogous to assort

A. Mixed
B. Group
C. Miscellaneous
D. Sundry

Answer ☐

Q17. Make bigger peel

A. Thunder
B. Boom
C. Unwrap
D. Dissect

Answer

Q18. Diminish unwise

A. Sensible
B. Shrewd
C. Ill advised
D. Imprudent

Answer

Q19. Find the converse of might

A. May
B. Weakness
C. Strength
D. Force

Answer

Q20. Find the term most analogous to thing

A. Slender
B. Belongings
C. Article
D. Journal

Answer

Thirty-three warm up questions

You are provided with a short description of a situation – this is the context – and a list of codes and their corresponding meanings. The situation and codes are followed by questions, and each question involves a sequence of code and a series of suggested answers. In some instances more than one suggested answer is correct. It is your task to identify which of the suggested answers are the best interpretation of the code. Note that, in these warm up questions, and this is important, the sequence of codes can be used in a different order from that in which they are presented in the question. So, for example, the code xx (meaning rock) and yy (meaning paper) can be used to construct correctly the interpretation rock, paper or paper, rock. Also note that other words (not covered by the code and not contradicted by the context) can be added to the suggested answer and it can still be correct. For example, it would be correct to translate the code xx, yy as rock and paper, paper or rock and so on. Pay particular attention to the commas in the questions. If two codes are *not* separated by a comma then they relate to each other and only each other. If the codes are separated by commas then they may relate to any of the other codes in the given sequence.

Read each situation, interpret the question code and answer the questions that follow it, deciding which in your opinion is the best suggested answer or answers. Note that a question has only one best answer unless you are informed that you must select more than one best answer.

Situation 1

The official inflation rate is announced annually and determines monetary policy. Investors try to anticipate the rate and for this reason the government statisticians codify their internal communications. The rate is derived from monitoring the prices of a basket of goods and services sold. Each year items are deleted or new items added depending on consumer trends, and these changes are especially confidential because the inclusion of items that traditionally suffer inflation will inflate the official rate while the inclusion of deflationary items will deflate the official rate. A criminal investor has intercepted the following communications between statisticians working on the calculation of the official rate. Use your judgement to identify which of the suggested answers best explains the meaning of the coded messages.

Codes

Modifiers

321. Parallel
322. Append
323. Reverse
324. Lessen
325. Akin

Features and instructions

601. Elevated
602. Temperate
603. Tiny
604. Popular
605. Unfashionable
606. Add
607. Delete
608. Inflation
609. Deflation

Lexis

930. Service
931. Commodity
932. Wide-screen TV
933. Milk
934. Cigarettes
935. Banking
936. Landscape gardening
937. Pasta
938. Mobile phone contract
939. Refrigerator
940. Wooden flooring
941. Gasoline
942. Soft furnishings
943. The basket of goods and services

The first nine questions have only one correct answer.

Q1. 323 607, 940

A. Delete wooden flooring.
B. Add wooden flooring.
C. Should we add or delete wooden flooring?
D. Reverse the decision to delete wooden flooring.

Answer ☐

Q2. 606 937, 934 321 607

A. Delete cigarettes and add pasta.
B. Add cigarettes and delete pasta.
C. Add pasta and delete cigarettes.
D. Remove cigarettes and add pasta.

Answer ☐

Q3. 941, 325 606, 321 943

A. Gasoline is on the list.
B. Add gasoline to the inventory.
C. Put gasoline in the basket of goods and services.
D. Put gasoline in the basket.

Answer ☐

Q4. 322 604, 321 601, 937

A. Fashionable pasta is all the rage.
B. Promote pasta; it has become all the rage.
C. Pasta has become very popular.
D. Popular, eminent, pasta.

Answer ☐

Q5. 323 931, 938, 936

A. Landscape gardening and mobile phone contracts are services.
B. Remove from the basket of goods and services landscape gardening and mobile phone contracts.
C. Mobile phone contracts and landscape gardening are not commodities.
D. Mobile phone contracts and landscape gardening are not goods.

Answer ☐

Q6. 935, 322 930, 325 602, 608

A. Banking facilities are experiencing soaring inflation.
B. Pleasant inflation is occurring in banking provision.
C. Inflation is rising in the banking sector.
D. Banking services are experiencing moderate inflation.

Answer ☐

Q7. 933, 325 606, 608, 321 324

A. The inclusion of milk will cut inflation.
B. Remove milk and you will add to inflation.
C. Decrease inflation by cutting out milk.
D. Increase inflation by promoting milk.

Answer ☐

Q8. 605, 938, 937, 323

A. Reverse the decision not to include mobile phone contracts and pasta.
B. Pasta and mobile phone contracts are popular.
C. Mobile phone contracts and pasta are out of favour.
D. Pasta and mobile phone contracts are out of date.

Answer

Q9. 942, 324 607, 604, 321 601, 608

A. Soft furnishings are popular but they experience high inflation.
B. Soft furnishings are very popular but consider deleting them as they suffer very high inflation.
C. Think about deleting soft furnishings; while popular, they have high inflation.
D. Don't delete soft furnishings; though they experience inflation they remain very popular.

Answer

The next five questions have more than one correct answer. Enter your choice of correct answers in the answer box.

Q10. 321, 606, 941

A. Include gasoline.
B. Put petrol on the list.
C. Put gasoline on the list.
D. Add petrol.
E. Add gasoline.

Answer

Q11. 942, 607, 939

A. Delete soft furnishings and refrigerator.
B. Delete both soft furnishings and refrigerator.
C. Delete refrigerator or soft furnishings.
D. Delete soft furnishings not refrigerator.
E. Delete refrigerator not soft furnishings.

Answer

Q12. 321 607, 322 935

A. Remove banking and all other similar services.
B. Erase all financial services.
C. Cut out banking and financial services.
D. Eliminate banking and its related services.
E. Cancel everything involved with the entry banking.

Answer

Q13. 607, 941, 321 602, 604, 606, 934

A. Add gasoline as it has become moderately popular and delete cigarettes.
B. Delete cigarettes and add gasoline as it is quite popular.
C. Add gasoline because it is reasonably popular but delete cigarettes.
D. Delete moderate-strength cigarettes and add popular gasoline.
E. Delete gasoline even though mildly popular and add cigarettes.

Answer

Q14. 325 933, 943, 606, 323 603

A. Add butter to the basket of goods and services.
B. Sales of white paint are vast so add it to the basket of goods and services.
C. Sales of yogurt are minute but still add it to the basket of goods and services.
D. Trade in dairy products is immense so add them to the basket of goods and services.
E. Cows are big so why are they not in the basket of goods and services?

Answer

Situation 2

Gasoline and diesel generate large amounts of the pollutant carbon dioxide and the race is on to find green bio-fuel alternatives that do not require large-scale investment in new infrastructure. The returns on this research could be enormous because it would allow a whole-scale switch from polluting crude oil to green bio-fuels. Petro-corporations jealously guard the findings of this research, but some environmental activists hacked into one of the corporations' network and posted the following encrypted messages on the internet in the hope that someone would be able to decipher them. Some mathematicians from Bangalore have proposed the following matrix – use it to identify in your judgement the best interpretation of the messages.

Codes

Language

101. Vegetable
102. Oil
103. Octane
104. Alcohol
105. Ethanol
106. Gasoline
107. Diesel
108. Alternative
109. Investment
110. Bio
111. Fuel
112. Tell
113. Know

Transformers

311. Equivalent
312. Enlarge
313. Turn around
314. Decrease
315. Similar
316. Join

Features and values

521. New
522. High
523. Few
524. Green
525. Gain
526. More

Possibilities

731. Can
732. Could
733. May
734. Contradiction

Q15. 103, 104, 106, 521, 522

A. The new green fuel is high-octane alcohol.
B. Interest in high-octane alcohol has long surpassed gasoline and reached a new high.
C. High-octane alcohol is the new gasoline.
D. It's high time industry switched from gasoline to high-octane alcohol.

Answer ☐

Q16. 525, 313 734, 733

A. They may deny it but try to gain permission.
B. You may gain agreement.
C. This may mean we gain some opposition.
D. Gain their trust and you may just beat the challenge.

Answer ☐

Q17. 107, 524, 312 108, 315 521, 526

A. Today we have greener choices than just diesel.
B. This innovative alternative to diesel is more green.
C. There are innovative green alternatives to diesel.
D. Recent alternatives to diesel are more green.

Answer ☐

Q18. 109, 521, 110, 315 113, 111

A. No new investment in bio-fuel is needed.
B. He knows that new investment in bio-fuel is high risk.
C. I know someone who might invest in a new bio-fuel.
D. Investment in new bio-fuels is now risky.

Answer ☐

Q19. 112, 313 732

A. We couldn't tell the difference from the results.
B. This might possibly tell between the options.
C. The test ought to tell them apart.
D. Tell the project manager that we can do it.

Answer ☐

Q20. 524, 313 733, 105

A. Maybe ethanol is not all that green.
B. Might it be the case that ethanol is not all that green?
C. Ethanol may not be all that green.
D. Ethanol may well be the greenest of them all.

Answer

Q21. 312 108, 312 526, 109, 526

A. Additional alternatives require more investment.
B. Most alternatives need more investment.
C. More investment is required if alternatives are to be found.
D. Extra investment in alternatives is needed most.

Answer

Q22. 525, 315 522, 313 731, 112, 521, 102

A. The price will soar so gain as much new oil as you can.
B. Gain as high a price as possible for the new oil product.
C. You could sell the new oil product but better to wait for the forecast price gains.
D. We can't tell if oil will gain new highs.

Answer

The following questions have more than one correct answer. Enter the corresponding letter of each correct answer in the answer box.

Q23. 315 734, 315 109, 110, 111

A. The take-up of bio-fuel by the big consumer nations has been inconsistent.
B. Disagreement exists over how good a venture bio-fuel represents.
C. There is conflicting evidence as to how safe a speculation bio-fuel is.
D. The production of this bio-fuel is far less capital intensive.

Answer

Q24. 315 523, 105, 109, 108

A. The minority think ethanol a good alternative investment.
B. As an alternative investment hardly any think ethanol a good choice.
C. Only a small amount of investment is required in the alternative ethanol.
D. As the best investment in the alternative market ethanol is backed by many.

Answer

Q25. 313 525, 107, 111, 106, 313 521

A. Supplies of gasoline and diesel will dwindle as deliveries of substitute fuel increase.
B. Production of bio-fuel will increase as production of gasoline and diesel falls.
C. The decline in traditional gasoline and diesel markets will be sudden and novel.
D. Sales of all conventional fuel like diesel and gasoline will decrease.

Answer

Q26. 105, 106, 111, 103, 522

A. Ordinary fuel when blended with ethanol makes it high-octane.
B. An ethanol and gasoline mix is a high-octane fuel.
C. Cars can run on a high-octane ethanol gasoline mix.
D. Gasoline and ethanol are both classed as high-octane fuel.

Answer

Situation 3

The consequences that follow from the theft of valuable data cannot be overestimated. Most people perceive the threat to be an external one, and we are all aware of the threat posed by, for example, viruses, worms and spyware unintentionally downloaded from the internet. But the threat is just as likely to come from within an organization. A malicious employee is perfectly placed to know what information is the most valuable and to steal it. If that information includes details of bank accounts and personal information then criminal gangs are willing to pay large sums of money for it. You work in the security department of a large corporation and must decode the following messages, which all refer to an employee stealing the personal details of a large number of his colleagues, before a departmental meeting to review the progress in uncovering the identity of the thief. The risk is very serious, as all but the most secure of the organization's networks are known to be compromised. The letter S is used to signify the thief.

Codes

Modifiers

201. Past
202. Similar to
203. Same as
204. Reverse
205. Contract
206. Expand

Vocabulary

310. He or S
311. We
312. Know
313. Online
314. Try
315. Steal
316. Information
317. Staff
318. Believe
319. All
320. Ready
321. Prefers
322. High
323. Seems
324. Looks
325. Proves
326. No
327. Only
328. If
329. Works
330. Week

Select *one* of the following answers as in your judgement the best interpretation of the sequence of code.

Q27. 316, 206 314, 310, 313

A. S never tries to take information before 10 am.
B. The information he takes is always decrypted before it is copied.
C. We believe he simply e-mails the information to an outside contact.
D. Look, he is online now trying to access information.

Answer ☐

Q28. 329, 310, 323, 204 330

A. It seems S works at the weekend.
B. Some days he works later than others.
C. Weekly he seems to work from one particular terminal.
D. My hunch is that he works as a casual on an hourly contract.

Answer ☐

Q29. 311, 203 320, 313, 310

A. If news goes online that all this personal detail has been stolen we can expect a lot of negative publicity.
B. We are online and standing by.
C. We are all set for when he next goes online.
D. Until S is caught nothing online is safe and we have one major security headache.

Answer ☐

Q30. 317, 202 326, 316, 206 320, 310, 318, 311

A. We believe S already has information on over 1,000 staff.
B. He believes we do not have enough information or staff to catch him.
C. No, we don't believe he will stop until he has a lot more information.
D. The personal information of no member of staff is safe until we have caught this individual.

Answer ☐

The following questions have more than one correct answer.

Q31. 310, 325, 329

A. This proves he operates from the eastern seaboard.
B. S works from a US office and this proves it again.
C. That proves he works alone.
D. He works late many evenings but never when the New York Giants are playing.

Answer ☐

Q32. 311, 326, 202 310

A. They are sure we will get our man in the end.
B. She thinks we must wait until he makes a mistake.
C. He's so careful not to give away his identity.
D. We are nowhere near catching him.

Answer ☐

Q33. 205 311, 203 318, 325, 206 326

A. I expect it proves nothing.
B. I think it proves that none of the current theories are correct.
C. In my best judgement it proves we have our man.
D. I trust no one until they prove themselves.

Answer

UKCAT-style decision analysis timed tests

Hints and tips

In this section of the real test you have 30 minutes to answer 26 questions, or a little over one minute per question. After the warm up material, we now provide 75 questions in three blocks of 25 to provide ample practice. Each block comes with a table of codes that is applicable to all 25 questions in the test. The goal is to identify which of the five sentences is the correct match for the code. There is no need to decipher or break the code. You translate it literally and then compare your translation with the five answer choices to find the best fit.

There are two key steps, as follows:

Step 1: Translate the code words without interpretation. For example, B(7), G, 205, 101(A) translates as opposite large, male, seek, money increase (see the table 'Codes: test 1'). Do not attempt to interpret the code at this stage, deciding for example that opposite (large) means small, ie small, male, seek, money increase; this is a mistake.
Step 2: Look at the answer options to see which is the best fit. One answer will include all the concepts described by the code without leaving any out or introducing new ideas. Taking the example in step 1: B(7), G, 205, 101(A), the following sentences include all the concepts:
'Small man seeks more money.'
'The boy wants higher wages.'
'Little man aspires to wealth.'
The answer you choose must translate all the code words. If it fails to do so or includes additional concepts or incorrect concepts you can eliminate it from the answer options.

Example: E1, 20, 7(106), E14
Step 1: Translate literally: plural person, vision, large number, plural problem.
There are several correct possibilities, including:
'We see a large number of problems.'
'The group sees many difficulties.'
'The players look for numerous obstacles.'
'We see countless stumbling blocks.'

The following translations are wrong for the reasons given in brackets and would be eliminated from the answer choices:

'I see a large number of problems' (no concept of plural person).
'The group sees many difficulties ahead' (includes the concept of ahead, which is not coded for).
'The players meet with numerous obstacles' (no concept of vision).
'We see several stumbling blocks' (poor concept of large number).

The question would appear as follows:

E1, 20, 7(106), E14

A. I see a large number of problems.
B. The group sees many difficulties ahead.
C. The players look for numerous obstacles.
D. We see several stumbling blocks.
E. The players meet with numerous obstacles.

Step 1: Write down the code without interpretation: plural person, vision, large number, plural problem.
Step 2: Find the best fit; eliminate wrong answers (A, B, D, E).

In addition to translating codes, you can expect a few questions that ask you to identify which code, from the five given, best translates the message. There is neither time nor need to translate every code; look for the common elements between the answer choices, because these are the most likely choices, and anticipate what code you would expect to see. Some answers will be close matches for the code, whilst others will be contradictory.

In a third type of question, you may be asked to identify which two out of five words when added to the table of code words would be the most helpful in coding the sentence. To answer these questions you have to identify which two words in the sentence cannot be coded from any existing code in the table or, failing this, any word that cannot be coded accurately or without difficulty.

Practice questions, test 1

Codes: test 1

Operating	**Basic**	**Specialist**
A = Increase	1 = Person	101 = Money
B = Opposite	2 = Eat	102 = Rules
C = Similar	3 = Think	103 = Day
D = Positive	4 = Vehicle	104 = Danger
E = Plural	5 = Wrong	105 = Health
F = Always	6 = Time	106 = Number
G = Male	7 = Large	107 = Air
H = Personal	8 = Water	108 = Meal
J = Together	9 = Speak	109 = Heard
K = Specific	10 = Work	110 = Pain
L = Situation	11 = Fire	201 = Fix
M = Future	12 = House	202 = Light
	13 = Fall	203 = Expense
	14 = Problem	204 = Old
	15 = Short	205 = Seek
	16 = Few	206 = Notes
	17 = Space	207 = Object
	18 = Travel	● = Happy
	19 = Take	■ = Lonely
	20 = Vision	♦ = Friendly
	21 = Vessel	♥ = Anxious

Q1. HE, 2, B7(108), 15(6)

A. I eat lunch quickly.
B. We have finished our meal.
C. We eat breakfast quickly.
D. I eat breakfast in the morning.
E. We eat small meals in the morning.

Answer ☐

Q2. (106 10) 14, B16(E1)

A. Some people find numbers hard work.
B. Calculations are difficult for people.
C. Number work is complicated.
D. Equations are hard for many people.
E. I find equations hard to solve.

Answer ☐

Q3. HE, 10(BA), B10(A)

A. I should spend less time working.
B. People should work less not more.
C. People need to work and play.
D. We should work less and play more.
E. We need less work to do.

Answer ☐

Q4. 14(10), BF, A110, 1

A. Nobody likes hard work.
B. Hard work never hurt anyone.
C. Working hard makes money.
D. A little work is pain free.
E. There is no gain without pain.

Answer ☐

Q5. B(HE), B(C105)H

A. Others are not as fit as me.
B. Most people are healthier than me.
C. No people are less healthy than me.
D. Many people do not keep fit.
E. Few people keep fit and healthy.

Answer ☐

Q6. BD(7, 17), H(7G), 12

A. My boyfriend is not coming to stay.
B. My husband has left home.
C. There is no room in my father's house.
D. A small man takes up less space.
E. My father's home has plenty of space.

Answer ☐

Q7. H(BF), B201, C102

A. Sometimes I break the rules.
B. I never break the law.
C. I cannot change the rules.
D. We should never break the law.
E. It is not always unlawful.

Answer ☐

Q8. 105, 2(B7), 14, A6

A. It takes time to diet.
B. I eat a small amount of healthy food.
C. It is hard to remain on a healthy diet.
D. I find it hard to eat small, healthy meals.
E. Healthy people eat small meals.

Answer ☐

Q9. H, B10, B105

A. I don't like working when I'm ill.
B. I seldom take sickness absence.
C. I can play unless I am unwell.
D. I was off work due to illness.
E. I hate working when I'm ill.

Answer ☐

Q10. B16, C(E12), 16(7E, 17)

A. There are a few buildings and not many open spaces.
B. There are a few buildings and a few open spaces.
C. There are many buildings and a few open spaces.
D. There are many houses in open spaces.
E. There are few houses in several open spaces.

Answer ☐

Q11. H(10J), A(3C)

A. My friends and I are in agreement.
B. My colleagues and I hold the same view.
C. My workmates and I have similar thoughts.
D. We work together in the same place.
E. Working together increases my knowledge.

Answer ☐

Q12. EH, BF, 2, B(105), C2

A. We never eat healthy food.
B. We don't eat healthily.
C. We rarely eat unhealthy food.
D. We seldom eat fast food.
E. We never consume unhealthy food.

Answer ☐

Q13. EH, BA(BF), C(11 8)

A. We seldom drink alcohol.
B. We rarely drink hot drinks.
C. We never drink alcohol.
D. We don't like alcoholic drinks.
E. We seldom drink hot water.

Answer ☐

Q14. B10, A(B13, M)

A. Jobs are hard to find.
B. The jobless total is rising.
C. Unemployment is increasing.
D. Jobs are hard to find quickly.
E. Unemployment will rise.

Answer ☐

Q15. E1, 4K, 18(7, 8)

A. Boats sail on water.
B. People sail across oceans.
C. People take a ferry across the sea.
D. We go boating on the river.
E. Most people cross the channel by ferry.

Answer ☐

Q16. EH, 10(101), C(7, 12)

A. We all work for the same company.
B. We are all employed at the factory.
C. We all work from home.
D. They work on the shop floor.
E. We receive more pay working from home.

Answer ☐

Q17. Which ONE of the following words when added to the table of code words would be the most helpful in coding the sentence?

We sold our home in Scotland and moved away.

A. sell
B. Scotland
C. we
D. home
E. moved

Answer ☐

Q18. Which ONE of the following words when added to the table of code words would be the most helpful in coding the sentence?

Most people can lose weight with diet and exercise.

A. exercise
B. most
C. diet
D. lose
E. people

Answer ☐

Q19. Which TWO of the following words when added to the table of code words would be the most helpful in coding the sentence?

My old car passed its test.

A. my
B. old
C. car
D. failed
E. test

Answer ☐

Q20. Which TWO of the following words when added to the table of code words would be the most helpful in coding the sentence?

We sold our home in the city and moved to the countryside to live.

A. sell
B. city
C. moved
D. countryside
E. live

Answer ☐

Q21. Which TWO of the following words when added to the table of code words would be the most helpful in coding the sentence?

Neither of us found the restaurant meals appetizing.

A. food
B. appetizing
C. neither
D. both
E. restaurant

Answer ☐

Q22. Which of the following codes best translates the message?

Happy people are not depressed.

A. ●E1, BD (B●)
B. ●E1, B(B●)
C. ●1, BD(B●)
D. ●E1, BD(●)
E. ●E1, B(BD●)

Answer ☐

Q23. Which of the following codes best translates the message?

A thoughtful person avoids a dangerous situation.

A. 3E1, BD(205), 104L
B. 3(1), BD(205), 104L
C. 1(BM3) BD(205), 104L
D. 1(BM3), L(205), 104L
E. 1(BM3), 14(205), 104L

Answer ☐

Q24. Which of the following codes best translates the message?

Women earn less money than men.

A. BG, BA(101), G
B. B(G E1), BA(101), G E1
C. BG, 14(101), G
D. BG, 10, BA(101), G
E. B(G E1), 10, BA(101), G E1

Answer ☐

Q25. Which of the following codes best translates the message?

Children should be seen and not heard.

A. B7(E1), C20, B109
B. B204(E1), D(C20), BD109
C. B204(E1), BD109, C20
D. B7(E1), C20, BD109
E. 15(E1), BD109, D(C20)

Answer

Practice questions, test 2

Codes: test 2

Operating	**Basic**	**Specialist**
A = Increase	1 = Person	101 = Money
B = Opposite	2 = Eat	102 = Rules
C = Similar	3 = Think	103 = Day
D = Positive	4 = Vehicle	104 = Danger
E = Plural	5 = Wrong	105 = Health
F = Always	6 = Time	106 = Number
G = Male	7 = Large	107 = Air
H = Personal	8 = Water	108 = Meal
J = Together	9 = Speak	109 = Heard
K = Specific	10 = Work	110 = Pain
L = Situation	11 = Fire	201 = Fix
M = Future	12 = House	202 = Light
	13 = Fall	203 = Expense
	14 = Problem	204 = Old
	15 = Short	205 = Seek
	16 = Few	206 = Notes
	17 = Space	207 = Object
	18 = Travel	● = Happy
	19 = Take	■ = Lonely
	20 = Vision	♦ = Friendly
	21 = Vessel	♥ = Anxious

Q1. HG, A(C18), 12

A. He was evicted from the house.
B. They were asked to leave their home.
C. The man quickly left his house.
D. He was ordered to leave the home.
E. They were forced out of the premises.

Answer ☐

Q2. 101(BA), 102(BD), 18B, K4

A. You must pay for parking your car.
B. There are fines for illegally parking your car.
C. You can be fined for parking your car.
D. There are fines for illegally parking a vehicle.
E. You can receive a ticket for illegal parking.

Answer ☐

Q3. 8(B13), 8(14A)

A. The rising water caused great damage.
B. More floods caused water damage.
C. Flooding by water increased the damage.
D. The rising tide caused water damage.
E. Rising tides caused flooding.

Answer ☐

Q4. H■, BJ, B103, 6

A. I felt lonely after becoming separated.
B. I feel lonely on my own in the evening.
C. Night-time is a lonely time of day.
D. I feel all alone when we part.
E. People feel lonely at night-time.

Answer ☐

Q5. EH17(11 107), 104 105

A. Smoke inhalation is dangerous.
B. Smoking kills many people.
C. We do not smoke as it is unhealthy.
D. Smoking cigarettes is hazardous to health.
E. Passive smoking is harmful to health.

Answer ☐

Q6. H, J(E1), B♦(E1)

A. My neighbours are unfriendly towards me.
B. I am not friends with my neighbours.
C. I find neighbours unfriendly.
D. My neighbours are unfriendly people.
E. My neighbours are not my friends.

Answer ☐

Q7. B7(G), 19(5), H(G7), 7(101)

A. The small boy stole the large man's money.
B. The son inherited his father's money.
C. The boy stole his father's money.
D. The son inherited his father's estate.
E. The son stole his father's fortune.

Answer ☐

Q8. C(9), 18(MB), BA(12 2)

A. The letter will be posted shortly.
B. The e-mail was sent from an internet café.
C. The e-mail was sent from my computer.
D. The e-mail was opened at an internet café.
E. He sent the e-mail from an internet café.

Answer ☐

Q9. C(102,12), H(BD,5), (1,102)

A. The court found him not guilty of the crime.
B. He said he was not guilty of the crime.
C. The judge found him not guilty of the crime.
D. The court decided he was not guilty.
E. The court found him guilty as charged.

Answer ☐

Q10. B(16), E1, BD(105), 14(B●)

A. Many ill people are depressed.
B. Many sad people are ill.
C. Depression is an illness that makes many people sad.
D. Some people are unhappy with their health.
E. Depression makes all people feel sad.

Answer ☐

Q11. G(E1), 19(C12), A(C101), BG(E1)

A. Men earn more than women.
B. Men buy larger houses than women.
C. Men take home more pay than women.
D. Males take home similar money to females.
E. Males earn the same money as females.

Answer ☐

Q12. 7(12 101), (14 101), A16 (7, 6)

A. A mortgage is a loan paid back in instalments.
B. A large house takes years to buy.
C. An expensive house is hard to pay for.
D. A mortgage is a loan paid back over many years.
E. A mortgage is taken out to buy a home.

Answer ☐

Q13. 1E(B105), C19, C(105, 12), BD(B103)

A. Outpatients receive hospital care during the day.
B. Patients receive medical care but not at night.
C. Patients need less hospital care at night.
D. Outpatients attend hospital during the day.
E. Outpatients receive hospital care except at night.

Answer ☐

Q14. E1(B7), B(7, 101), (15, 6)

A. Pupils receive little money for school meals.
B. Young people are paid a minimum weekly wage.
C. Children receive weekly pocket money.
D. Children have little time to spend their money.
E. Children receive pocket money from their parents.

Answer ☐

Q15. E1, J, A(A●)

A. Couples like to be together.
B. Married people are happier.
C. People are happiest when together.
D. Married people are happy people.
E. Married people are the happiest.

Answer ☐

Q16. A16(E1), 18(10), B(E)1, 4

A. Some people drive to work by car.
B. A few people catch the bus to work.
C. Some people ride a motorcycle to work.
D. Most people drive to work.
E. Some people walk to work.

Answer ☐

Q17. 10J, BD(18), B10

A. The workforce went on strike.
B. The teammates did not travel together.
C. The workmen turned up late for work.
D. Team working saves time and effort.
E. The management stopped the strike.

Answer ☐

Q18. B(7, 1), H18, C(MB), 9

A. Some young people can see into the future.
B. Most children learn to walk and speak.
C. A child walks before it talks.
D. Children soon learn to walk and speak.
E. A child can walk and talk.

Answer ☐

Q19. Which TWO of the following words when added to the table of code words would be the most helpful in coding the sentence?

Successful business people are optimistic about the future.

A. optimistic
B. business
C. future
D. people
E. successful

Answer ☐

Q20. Which TWO of the following words when added to the table of code words would be the most helpful in coding the sentence?

Penalty points are on your licence for three years.

A. penalty
B. on
C. three
D. points
E. your

Answer ☐

Q21. Which TWO of the following words when added to the table of code words would be the most helpful in coding the sentence?

Time spent studying for the test is time spent well.

A. test
B. time
C. well
D. study
E. spend

Answer

Q22. Which TWO of the following words when added to the table of code words would be the most helpful in coding the sentence?

Parents can harm their child's development.

A. growth
B. child
C. hinder
D. their
E. parent

Answer

Q23. Which of the following codes best translates the message?

We paid a small deposit on the house.

A. E1, 12, B(19,7)101
B. E1, B7, 101, 12
C. E1, B19, 101, 12
D. E1, B19, 7(101)
E. E1, B(19)101, B7(101)

Answer

Q24. Which of the following codes best translates the message?

I eat one hot meal at night.

A. H, 2, 11(108), 103
B. H, 2, 11(108), B(103)
C. H, 2, BE, 11, 108, B(103)
D. E1, 2, 11(108), 103
E. 2, H, B(103)

Answer ☐

Q25. Which of the following codes best translates the message?

The meeting was held in cramped conditions.

A. E1, C19, B7(17)
B. E1(J), BM19, L(B7,17)
C. E1, 7(106), J, C(B7,17)
D. E1(BJ), 7(17)
E. E1, BM19, BA(17)

Answer ☐

Practice questions, test 3

Codes: test 3

Operating	**Basic**	**Specialist**
A = Increase	1 = Person	101 = Money
B = Opposite	2 = Eat	102 = Rules
C = Similar	3 = Think	103 = Day
D = Positive	4 = Vehicle	104 = Danger
E = Plural	5 = Wrong	105 = Health
F = Always	6 = Time	106 = Number
G = Male	7 = Large	107 = Air
H = Personal	8 = Water	108 = Meal
J = Together	9 = Speak	109 = Heard
K = Specific	10 = Work	110 = Pain
L = Situation	11 = Fire	201 = Fix
M = Future	12 = House	202 = Light
	13 = Fall	203 = Expense
	14 = Problem	204 = Old
	15 = Short	205 = Seek
	16 = Few	206 = Notes
	17 = Space	207 = Object
	18 = Travel	● = Happy
	19 = Take	■ = Lonely
	20 = Vision	♦ = Friendly
	21 = Vessel	♥ = Anxious

Q1. (107, 14), BD(H107)

A. Car exhaust fumes make breathing difficult.
B. I find it hard to breathe.
C. Exhaust fumes create pollution.
D. Pollution makes breathing difficult for many people.
E. Pollution is bad for my breathing.

Answer ☐

Q2. E1, B10, B15(4), 18

A. People rest on coach journeys.
B. People sleep on long train journeys.
C. Many people use public transport.
D. Trains stop for short periods.
E. We travel long distance.

Answer ☐

Q3. 2, 15(6), B204(108)

A. Food should not be eaten beyond its use-by date.
B. Old food is bad to eat.
C. Expiry dates are always shown on food.
D. Fresh food should be eaten soon.
E. Food should be eaten fresh.

Answer ☐

Q4. B16, B7(E1), 10(BD101)

A. Many young people do voluntary work.
B. Many young people are out of work.
C. Some children work for nothing.
D. Many young people receive little wages.
E. Most young people are paid less.

Answer ☐

Q5. BD(105A), E1(2,11,108)

A. It is unhealthy for me to eat hot dinners.
B. Eating undercooked food is a health hazard.
C. Food poisoning is dangerous for old people.
D. Eating barbecued food made them ill.
E. Food poisoning bacteria can kill.

Answer ☐

Q6. (108,K,105,14), B(202), E1, C(104)

A. Large people eat too much.
B. People with diabetes should watch their diet.
C. Eating too much makes people look overweight.
D. Obese people risk diabetes.
E. Diabetes is linked with obesity.

Answer ☐

Q7. C(BK), B105, M, H, B103, 17

A. After a night out I felt generally unwell.
B. Generally there was lack of space at night.
C. My diabetes required overnight treatment.
D. I stayed in hospital last night to recover.
E. I was admitted to the general hospital.

Answer ☐

Q8. BD(105), C(BD,14), E1

A. The solution was obvious to everyone.
B. The team diagnosed the problem.
C. We all understood the difficulty.
D. The health problem was obvious.
E. Doctors diagnose illness.

Answer ☐

Q9. E108, 202, BD(14), E(1,2)BA

A. Breakfast is the smallest meal of the day.
B. Diets are easy for poor eaters.
C. Light meals leave you feeling empty.
D. Small snacks are eaten between meals.
E. Lunch was an easy meal to prepare.

Answer ☐

Q10. 3, 14, 10, 106, 205, E1

A. Large numbers are difficult to manipulate.
B. Mental arithmetic is hard for some people.
C. Maths questions are the most problematic.
D. Numerical solutions are hard to find.
E. People find maths confusing.

Answer ☐

Q11. BD(10)E1, BD(203), 105, 206

A. Health advice is available for nothing.
B. A sick note is required if you take time off work.
C. Health records are freely available.
D. Illness causes unemployment and lack of money.
E. Prescriptions are free for unemployed people.

Answer ☐

Q12. (18,6) (207,110) C(B102)

A. Carrying a weapon is a crime.
B. Time travellers feel no pain.
C. An assault is a criminal offence.
D. Heavy cargo should not be transported.
E. Criminals carry weapons that inflict injuries.

Answer ☐

Q13. M, B7(8), 7(106), M(103)

A. Most of the country will be short of water.
B. There will be very little water for us.
C. Showers are forecast for tomorrow.
D. Tomorrow we will have plenty to drink.
E. It was raining earlier in the day.

Answer ☐

Q14 ♦ E1, ♦ BA, 12J

A. Friendly people make excellent housemates.
B. Our neighbours are unfriendly people.
C. Friendly people make satisfactory neighbours.
D. I am a good friend to my neighbour.
E. My friends live in the same house.

Answer ☐

Q15. BD(107A), H, BD(H107)

A. Air pressure decreases at high altitude.
B. Exercise increases my breathing rate.
C. Expiration follows inspiration.
D. I suffer from shortness of breath.
E. I can't breathe without oxygen.

Answer ☐

Q16. 17(18), 18E1, H18, BM(103)

A. Space travel will be available to everyone.
B. Long distances take several days on foot.
C. We travelled by car yesterday.
D. We crossed the bridge on foot yesterday.
E. There is no future in space travel.

Answer ☐

Q17. H(E14), 20M, 7, 106

A. I envisaged numerous problems.
B. We will experience many more problems.
C. I found the high number of questions problematic.
D. We anticipated more difficulties in the future.
E. There are many more problems to come.

Answer ☐

Q18. 104, BM(3), BD1

A. A negative person thinks about risk.
B. I find the hazards depressing.
C. Nobody had considered it risky.
D. We heard that it was dangerous.
E. It pays not to think about it.

Answer

Q19. Which TWO of the following words when added to the table of code words would be the most helpful in coding the sentence?

A reservoir provided the town with a source of fresh water.

A. source
B. reservoir
C. water
D. town
E. fresh

Answer

Q20. Which TWO of the following words when added to the table of code words would be the most helpful in coding the sentence?

We were unconcerned with the possibility of deterioration and complications.

A. possibility
B. complications
C. deterioration
D. concerned
E. we

Answer

Q21. Which TWO of the following words when added to the table of code words would be the most helpful in coding the sentence?

Clients' health records are filed away separately.

A. separate
B. client
C. health
D. store
E. records

Answer

Q22. Which TWO of the following words when added to the table of code words would be the most helpful in coding the sentence?

Nobody protested as the better player won.

A. player
B. protest
C. good
D. nobody
E. won

Answer

Q23. Which of the following codes best translates the message?

The women could see more with the light on.

A. BD(G1), 20D, 202A
B. B(G E1), 20A, 202D
C. B(G E1), 20A, 7(202)
D. B(G E1), 20A, 202L
E. BD(G1), 20A, 202A

Answer

Q24. Which of the following codes best translates the message?

A burn takes a long time to heal.

A. 11(110), 19, B15, 6, 201
B. 11(110), 19, B16(6), 105(201)
C. 11(110), 19, B(15,6), 201(105)
D. 11(110), 19, B15, 6, 105
E. 11(110,7), 19, B15, 6, 105

Answer ☐

Q25. Which of the following codes best translates the message?

The young woman solicited our help for her sick mother.

A. B204(B G1), 205(BM), L♦, B105, H(7,BG)
B. B204(B G1), 205, L♦, B105, H(7,BG)
C. B204(B GE1), 205(BM), L♦, B105, H(7,BG)
D. B204(B G1), 205(BM), L♦, B105, H(7,G)
E. B204(B G1), 205(BM), C♦, B105, B(7,G)

Answer ☐

4

Quantitative reasoning

Objectives

At the end of this chapter you will be able to answer questions of the type used in the UKCAT quantitative reasoning sub-test principally on the following subjects:

A. Addition, subtraction, multiplication and division
B. Proportion and ratios, including conversions
C. Powers and roots
D. Statistics, including mean, median, mode and range of both grouped and non-grouped data
E. Fractions, decimals and percentages
F. Formulae and equations

The intention of this chapter is to give you skills necessary to maximize your score by practising the type of questions you will meet in the quantitative reasoning sub-test.

The test

The test consists of 40 multiple-choice questions divided up into 10 blocks of 4 questions for which you will have 21 minutes, ie 2 minutes per block, or 30 seconds per question. As there are no penalties for incorrect answers, you have nothing to lose by guessing answers if you are short of time towards the end.

Format

Each block of questions starts with a brief description of the scenario and then some information, often in the form of a table. There are then four multiple-choice questions with five possible answers, A, B, C, D, E, of which only one is correct. This is the format used here for the examples.

The test is described by Pearson VUE as being more about testing your problem-solving ability than your numerical faculty. It is the intention of this chapter to develop not only your problem-solving ability, but also your numerical ability. Time is of the essence! The more familiar you are with number and mathematical concepts the quicker you will be in all numerical questions.

The questions in this chapter start easily and rapidly become more difficult at a level equivalent to an A level standard, not simply the 'good GCSE' as described by Pearson. You are aiming to get into a competitive field in a numerical subject; you need this ability with numbers.

There are a total of 192 questions, including some which are in the form of timed mini sub-tests. The chapter concludes with a timed test. Good luck.

Questions 1 to 4 concern the population of a certain town which can be divided into the following age groups:

Age group	Population
0–4	6,450
5–9	7,600
10–14	8,450
15–19	7,400
20–24	5,550
25–29	6,150
30–34	8,100
35–39	8,750
40–44	8,450
45–49	8,400
50–54	10,150
55–59	9,600
60–64	7,950
65–69	7,450
70–74	7,100
75–79	6,450
80–84	4,500
85–89	2,750

1. How many people are younger than 20?

   A. 5,550
   B. 7,400
   C. 29,000
   D. 29,900
   E. 30,000

Answer ☐

2. If the total population is 131,250, approximately what percentage are under 25?

   A. 10%
   B. 15%
   C. 20%
   D. 25%
   E. 30%

Answer ☐

3. If everyone retires at 65, what fraction of the population is within 10 years of retirement?

   A. 1/4
   B. 1/5
   C. 1/7
   D. 1/10
   E. 1/20

Answer ☐

4. What is the ratio of schoolchildren (5–19) to retired people (65+)?

   A. 4 : 5
   B. 4 : 3
   C. 1 : 1
   D. 2 : 1
   E. 1 : 2

Answer ☐

Questions 5 to 8 concern the television viewing of children in a town in the east of the country and a town in the west:

East		West	
Child	Minutes	Child	Minutes
A	95	K	145
B	78	L	70
C	91	M	102
D	87	N	121
E	65	O	109
F	71	P	89
G	92	Q	96
H	69	R	113
I	82	S	121
J	80	T	98

5. What is the average viewing time for a child in the east?

A. 82.3
B. 91.0
C. 79.9
D. 81.5
E. 81.0

Answer ☐

6. What is the median viewing time for a child in the east?

A. 80
B. 81
C. 82
D. 80.4
E. 81.7

Answer ☐

7. How does the range of the viewing times for the west compare with the east?

   A. The mode is greater.
   B. The median is greater.
   C. It is smaller.
   D. It is twice as big.
   E. It is two and a half times greater.

Answer ☐

8. What is the mode of the viewing times in the west?

   A. 75
   B. 106.4
   C. 121
   D. 105.5
   E. 145

Answer ☐

Questions 9 to 12 concern the cost of calling abroad. A student has two possible phone companies' cards she can use to call her home country:

	Green		Black	
	£10 card	£20 card	£10 card	£20 card
Connection cost (p)	10	10	8	6
Cost per minute (p)	0.4	0.35	0.5	0.4

9. If she intends to call home 10 minutes every day for a month (30 days), which card would be the cheapest?

   A. Green £10
   B. Green £20
   C. Black £10
   D. Black £20
   E. Black £20 or Green £20, the same price

Answer ☐

10. If she chooses the Black £10 card, but it is only valid for a month, what percentage of the cost will she have wasted, to the nearest 5%?

A. 40%
B. 60%
C. 45%
D. 55%
E. 50%

Answer ☐

11. She records her phone calls for a year in the table below. What is the average length of call in minutes?

Month	No. of calls	Total duration
January	20	226
February	25	320
March	40	330
April	32	450
May	33	290
June	29	237
July	23	211
August	5	37
September	26	233
October	26	256
November	30	338
December	36	315

A. 270.1
B. 10.0
C. 27.0
D. 10.1
E. 9.9

Answer ☐

12. If the Black company increases its prices per minute by 70%, which card would now be the cheapest for the calls described in question 9?

A. Green £10
B. Green £20
C. Black £10
D. Black £20
E. Black £20 or Green £20, the same price

Answer

Questions 13 to 16 concern the type of employment in a particular region in thousands of people:

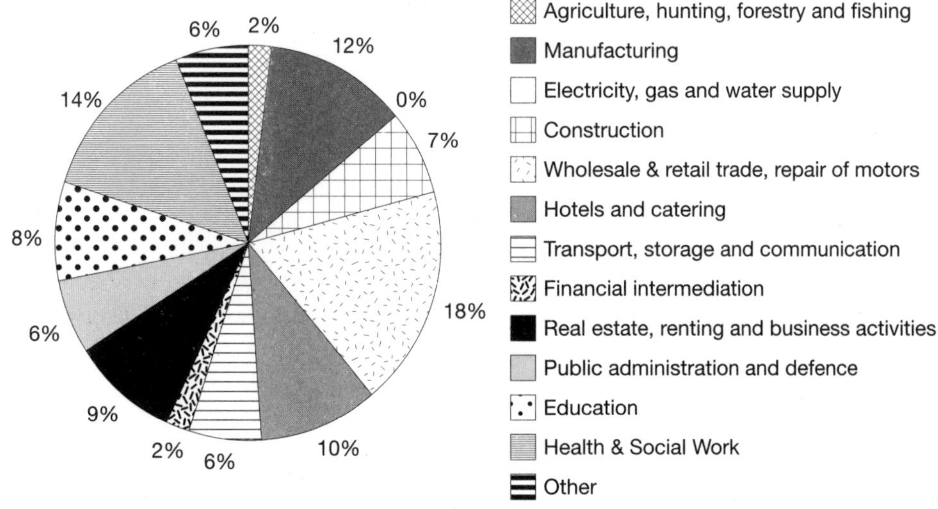

13. If the total population is 200,000, how many sectors employ more than 19,000 people?

A. 3
B. 4
C. 5
D. 6
E. 7

Answer

14. If those working in manufacturing generate a third more revenue per person than those in agriculture, fishing etc, how much more total revenue do they generate?

A. 8 times
B. 7 times
C. 6 times
D. 7.2 times
E. 6.75 times

Answer ☐

15. Half of the agricultural produce is sold to continental Europe. If the total revenue for the sector is £100m, calculate the revenue generated from these European sales in euros (1 pound = 1.25 euros).

A. 12.5m
B. 75m
C. 125m
D. 60m
E. 62.5m

Answer ☐

16. The average number of people employed per employer in hotels and catering is 20. How many employers are there?

A. 1,000
B. 4,000
C. 10,000
D. 400
E. 2,000

Answer ☐

Questions 17 to 20 concern the salt content in grams of some supermarket pre-prepared foods per 100 g:

Budget's Best Chicken Tikka with Pilau Rice	2.0
Charlie's Champion Chilli	1.2
Red Dragon Lo-salt Vegetable Chow Mein	0.3
Luigi Lambretta's Pasta Carbonara	1.8
Thai Me Up Prawn Curry	1.1
Barry's Bargain Range Paella	1.9
Cheap As Chips Shepherd's Pie	1.6
Luigi Lambretta's Spaghetti Bolognese	1.5
Sadek's Fish Curry	1.2
Mo's Cushy Couscous	1.7
John Bull's British Classics Toad In The Hole	1.8

17. Expressed as a decimal, what fraction of the above products are high in salt, ie greater than or equal to 1.5%?

A. 0.55
B. 0.54
C. 0.45
D. 0.44
E. 0.32

Answer ☐

18. If the maximum recommended daily intake of salt is 6 g, what percentage does a 350 g portion of Chicken Tikka with Pilau Rice represent?

A. 35%
B. 117%
C. 86%
D. 111%
E. 33%

Answer ☐

19. The Fish Curry is twice as expensive as the Paella, which itself is 10% more expensive than the Shepherd's Pie. If the pie costs £1.50, how much does the curry cost?

A. £3.00
B. £1.65
C. £3.60
D. £3.30
E. Cannot tell

Answer

20. The Toad in the Hole is also sold in continental Europe. The price in Britain is £2.65 and the exchange rate used to print the prices is £1 = €1.50. If the actual exchange rate is £1 = €1.25, how much more is the rest of Europe paying for it than it should?

A. 25 cents
B. 44.50 cents
C. 66.25 cents
D. 58.75 cents
E. 31.45 cents

Answer

Questions 21 to 24 concern the number of people in different groups. One hundred and six (106) people were stopped in the street and the following information obtained: 62 were born in this country, 50 were taller than 1.6 m and 14 were left-handed.

21. What percentage were 1.6 m or under?

A. 36%
B. 64%
C. 60%
D. 53%
E. 34%

Answer

22. If three people were taller than 1.6 m, born in this country and left-handed, how many people were only one of these things?

    A. 62
    B. 76
    C. 103
    D. 89
    E. Cannot tell

Answer ☐

23. What percentage of those born in this country were left-handed?

    A. 13%
    B. 60%
    C. 20%
    D. 25%
    E. Cannot tell

Answer ☐

24. There are three people who are left-handed, born in England and taller than 1.6 m, two people who are left-handed and taller than 1.6 m. There are twice as many people who are just left-handed as are left-handed and born in England. How many are just left-handed?

    A. 6
    B. 14
    C. 9
    D. 5
    E. Cannot tell

Answer ☐

Questions 25 to 28 concern the prices of different foods:

25. If an order of three cod and two portions of chips costs a total of £12.85 and two cod with three chips costs £10.40, what would be the formulae for determining the different prices?

    A. 2C + 3F = 12.85, 3C + 2Y = 10.40
    B. C + F = 7.85, F = 1.3
    C. X + Y = £5.00, 2X + 2Y = £10
    D. F = £3.50, C = £1.05
    E. 3X + 2Y = 1285, 2X + 3Y = 1040

Answer ☐

26. If the price of cod increases by 20% and the price of chips by 10%, what would be the new cost of a portion of cod and chips to the nearest penny?

A. £4.57
B. £5.47
C. £4.65
D. £4.10
E. £5.37

Answer ☐

27. What is the ratio of the old price to the new price?

A. 1 : 1.17
B. 1.55 : 1
C. 1.17 : 1
D. 1 : 1.18
E. 1.2 : 1

Answer ☐

28. If the shop accepts euros at an exchange rate of 1.20 euros = 1 pound, how much would a tourist pay at the original prices for three cod and three chips?

A. €13.95
B. €16.74
C. €20.91
D. €15.24
E. €11.26

Answer ☐

Questions 29 to 32 concern the results of an exam for schoolchildren:

29. A particular exam board requires schools to mark the work internally and send a sample of the work. The number of scripts required is given by the square root of the number of children sitting the exam rounded up to the nearest one. If 26 children sit the exam, how many scripts should be sent?

A. 21
B. 5
C. 6
D. 10
E. 13

Answer ☐

30. The student scores are shown below. If all those below the average mark fail, how many will do so?

Student no.	Score
1.	26
2.	91
3.	35
4.	55
5.	57
6.	59
7.	46
8.	63
9.	28
10.	34
11.	88
12.	62
13.	67
14.	29
15.	32
16.	51
17.	54
18.	56
19.	79
20.	75
21.	66
22.	63
23.	36
24.	51
25.	62
26.	60

A. 11
B. 13
C. 9
D. 10
E. 15

Answer ☐

31. If the system is set up so that 85–90% pass, what should the pass mark be?

A. 36
B. 35
C. 30
D. 33
E. 31

Answer ☐

32. If the pass mark is set at the lowest score plus 10% of the range, how many will fail?

A. 6
B. 5
C. 2
D. 3
E. 4

Answer ☐

Questions 33 to 36 concern fuel prices in Europe:

Country	Fuel price (p)
Austria	75
Belgium	95
Czech Rep	71.5
Denmark	92.2
Eire	74.5
Finland	89.4
France	85.2
Germany	90
Greece	65.7
Netherlands	100.3
Hungary	83.5
Italy	87.5
Luxembourg	76.5
Norway	94.8
Poland	79.5
Portugal	85.8
Spain	66.4
Sweden	82.1
Switzerland	72.1
United Kingdom (Av)	96.5

33. What would be the cost of driving a car that does 30 miles per gallon a distance of 95 miles in Italy if one gallon is 4.75 litres?

A. (95 / 30) × (87.5 / 4.75)
B. (95 × 30) / (87.5 × 4.75)
C. (95 × 30 × 4.75) / 87.5
D. (87.5 × 4.75) / (95 / 30)
E. (95 × 87.5 × 4.75) / 30

Answer ☐

34. The bar chart below shows the increase in price in one month. Which countries have seen the greatest increases?

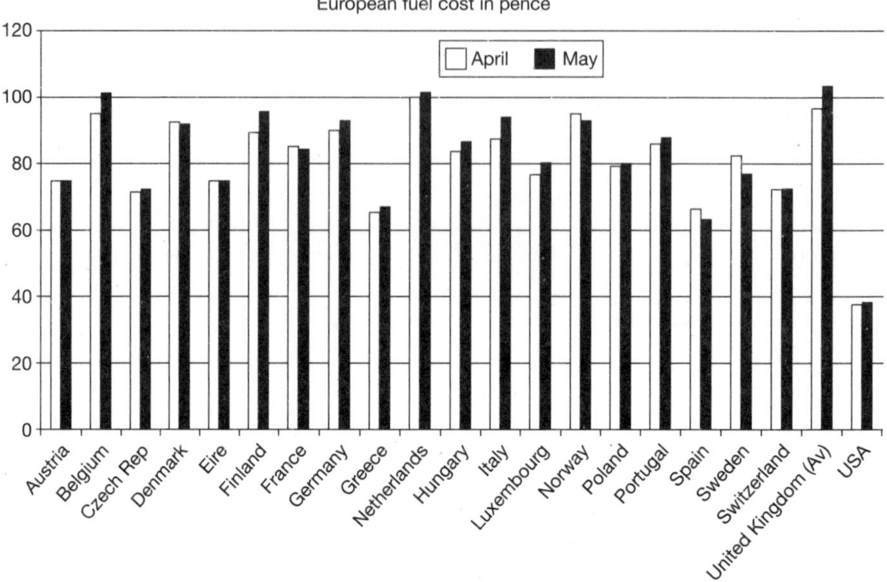

A. Hungary, Luxembourg, Germany
B. Sweden, Spain
C. Belgium, Finland, United Kingdom, Italy
D. Luxembourg, Germany, United Kingdom, Italy
E. Belgium, Finland, Germany

Answer ☐

35. If the price of fuel continues to rise at 7% per month in the UK, what would be the percentage increase to drive 100 miles with the car in question 33 after three months?

A. 14.0%
B. 21.0%
C. 21.7%
D. 22.5%
E. 28.0%

Answer ☐

36. If the driver is planning to drive 210 miles in the Netherlands starting at the German border, how much cheaper would it be to buy the fuel in Germany using the car and prices in question 33?

A. 297p
B. 342.5p
C. 333.275p
D. 10.3p
E. Cannot tell

Answer ☐

Questions 37 to 40 concern aircraft flight:

37. The power required to keep an aeroplane in flight is given by $P = Av^3$, where A is a constant and v the velocity. If the velocity increases by 25%, how much more power is required?

A. Nearly twice as much
B. Around 50% more
C. 25% more
D. About a third more
E. About the same

Answer ☐

38. If the pilot increases the thrust by 50%, how much faster will the plane fly?

A. 10%
B. 15%
C. 20%
D. 25%
E. 30%

Answer ☐

39. If a full fuel tank represents 60% of the total weight of the plane and the speed is proportional to the square root of the weight, how much slower can the plane fly when nearly empty of fuel?

A. $\sqrt{0.4}$
B. $\sqrt{0.6}$
C. 0.4^2
D. 0.6^2
E. Cannot tell

Answer ☐

40. How much more power is required on take-off (full) than on landing (empty)?

A. 0.6^3
B. $(0.6 / 0.4)^3$
C. 2.5
D. $2.5^{1.5}$
E. Cannot tell

Answer ☐

Questions 41 to 44 concern two tests to detect the presence of a certain substance:

SUBSTANCE PRESENT	Yes	Allcheck = 95% Truespot = 92%	Allcheck = 10% Truespot = 2%
	No	Allcheck = 5% Truespot = 8%	Allcheck = 90% Truespot = 98%
TRIAL RESULTS		Positive result	Negative result
		RESULTS OF TRIAL	

41. A trial was carried out on 780 samples using Allcheck. How many would be identified as having the substance present?

A. 702
B. 741
C. 78
D. 62
E. Cannot tell

Answer ☐

42. If 500 of the 780 have the substance present, how many samples would be expected to be incorrect?

A. About 43
B. 40
C. About 46
D. 10
E. Cannot tell

Answer ☐

43. If half the 780 samples had the substance present, what would be the difference in the number of wrong results for Allcheck compared to Truespot?

A. About 10 more
B. About 5 less
C. About 8 less
D. About 20 more
E. Cannot tell

Answer ☐

44. In another trial of 800 samples, Allcheck identifies 475 with the substance. How many are likely to have the substance present?

A. About 488
B. About 465
C. About 475
D. About 325
E. Cannot tell

Answer ☐

Questions 45 to 48 concern the video game-playing habits of students:

Time playing video games per week	
Hours	Number of students
10–14	2
15–19	12
20–24	23
25–29	60
30–34	77
35–39	38
40–44	8

45. What is the approximate average time spent playing games per week?

    A. 30
    B. 27
    C. 26
    D. 25
    E. 24

Answer ☐

46. How many play less than 20 hours a week?

    A. 35
    B. 37
    C. 14
    D. 206
    E. 24

Answer ☐

47. What fraction plays more than the average?

    A. 3/7
    B. 5/7
    C. 3/4
    D. 1/2
    E. 5/9

Answer ☐

48. If, during exam term, the three heaviest users reduce their playing by 10%, the three least-heavy user groups by 20% and the middle group remains unchanged, what would be the approximate average number of hours spent playing?

A. 24
B. 25
C. 26
D. 27
E. 28

Answer ☐

Questions 49 to 52 concern the measure of appropriate weight, the Body Mass Index (BMI):

49. BMI is defined as being the mass of a person (in kg) divided by the square of the height (in metres). Which of the following has the greatest BMI?

Person	Height (m)	Weight (kg)
A	1.45	45
B	1.50	50
C	1.55	55
D	1.70	60
E	1.80	70

A. A
B. B
C. C
D. D
E. E

Answer ☐

50. If an adolescent's height increases by 10% and their mass by 10%, by how much will their BMI change?

A. Plus 11%
B. Plus 10%
C. Minus 9%
D. Minus 10%
E. Unchanged

Answer ☐

51. Person A has a BMI index of 28, but would like to be in the 'normal' range, 18.5–24.9. If person A weighs 80 kg, how much do they need to lose?

A. 9 kg
B. 8 kg
C. 7 kg
D. 6 kg
E. 5 kg

Answer

52. A 1.8 m person has a BMI of 24.9, at the top end of the 'normal' range. By what fraction will their weight have to increase to be in the 'obese' range?

A. 1/3
B. 1/4
C. 1/5
D. 1/6
E. 1/7

Answer

Questions 53 to 56 concern house prices in two different regions:

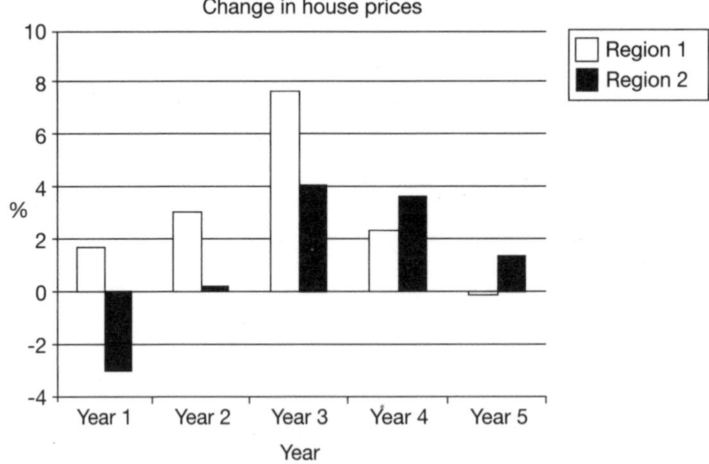

53. Where and when did prices fall most?

A. Region 1, year 3
B. Region 2, year 3
C. Region 2, year 2
D. Region 1, year 5
E. Region 2, year 1

Answer

54. Which year had the greatest difference in price changes between the two regions?

A. Year 1
B. Year 2
C. Year 3
D. Year 4
E. Year 5

Answer

55. If a region 1 house and a region 2 house are both worth £200,000 at the start of year 3, what will be the difference in value at the end?

A. £15,000
B. £7,000
C. £8,000
D. £7,500
E. Cannot tell

Answer

56. What is the total price change over the five years for region 1?

A. $1.5 + 3 + 7.5 + 2.3 - 0.1$
B. $1.05 \times 1.03 \times 1.075 \times 1.023 \times -1.01$
C. $1.05 \times 1.03 \times 1.075 \times 1.023 \times 0.99$
D. $1.05 + 1.03 + 1.075 + 1.023 + -1.01$
E. Cannot tell

Answer

Questions 57 to 60 concern the habits of a group of people surveyed in the street:

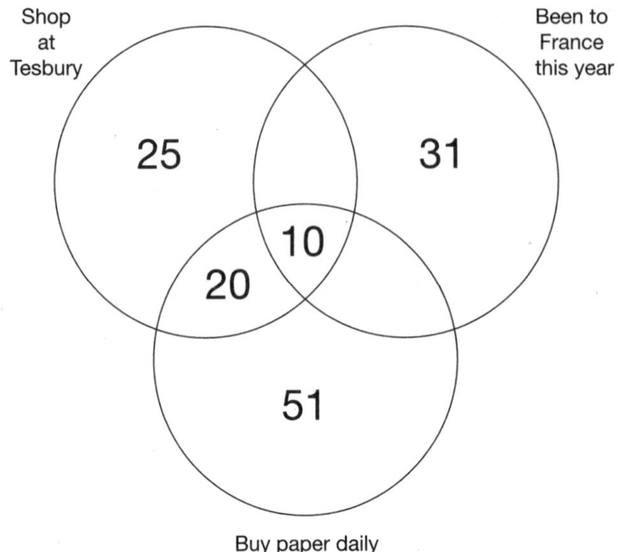

57. How many people were surveyed?

A. 51
B. 108
C. 98
D. 118
E. Cannot tell

Answer ☐

58. What is the largest number that could be in the group having 'been to France this year' and 'buy paper daily'?

A. 21
B. 41
C. 51
D. 32
E. 25

Answer ☐

59. How many 'buy paper daily' and 'shop at Tesbury'?

A. 20
B. 30
C. 51
D. 25
E. Cannot tell

Answer

60. If the two blank spaces both contain the number 20, how many people answer yes to two questions?

A. 20
B. 30
C. 50
D. 60
E. Cannot tell

Answer

Questions 61 to 64 concern the results of two political parties, the Direct Union for Democracy and the People's Union for Power, in monthly polls showing voting intentions. People expressed a preference for one or other party or the intention not to vote:

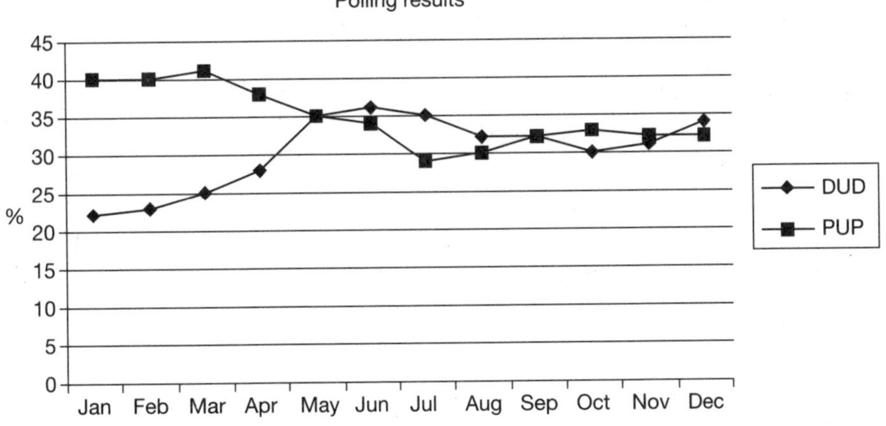

61. What fraction of those intending to vote would have chosen the Direct Union for Democracy party in September?

A. 1/3
B. 1/4
C. 1/5
D. 1/2
E. 2/3

Answer

62. Which month would have seen the greatest number of abstentions?

A. August
B. September
C. October
D. November
E. December

Answer

63. If 10% of the people abstaining now decide to vote following the pattern of the other voters, what would be the expected results for the parties in January? From 40% and 22% to:

A. 44.0% and 24.2% respectively
B. 42.5% and 23.5% respectively
C. 44.0% and 22.0% respectively
D. 36.0% and 19.8% respectively
E. 41.5% and 20.5% respectively

Answer

64. Which month saw the biggest relative gain for any party?

A. September to October
B. June to July
C. July to August
D. March to April
E. April to May

Answer

Questions 65 to 68 concern the exchange rates at different bureaux de change:

Financial institution	Exchange rate (£1 buys…)
Happy Holidays	€1.20 + £1.20 fee and 3% commission
Better Bank	€1.18 + no fee and no commission
X-change	€1.22 + £2.50 fee and 2% commission
Four Eyes Currency	€1.22 + no fee and 3% commission
Concurrency	€1.20 + £2.00 fee and no commission

65. Which of the following equations gives the number of euros for £200 with Happy Holidays?

A. (200 × 1.20) – (0.03 × 200)
B. 0.03 × 200 × 1.20 – 1.20
C. 0.97 × 200 × 1.20 + 1.20
D. (200 – 1.20) × 0.97 × 1.20
E. (200 – 0.03) × 1.20 – 1.20

Answer ☐

66. Which would be the most worthwhile for converting a large sum?

A. Happy Holidays
B. Better Bank
C. X-change
D. Four Eyes Currency
E. Concurrency

Answer ☐

The table below shows the number of euros for different sterling transactions:

£	Bureau de change				
	HH	BB	XC	FEC	CON
10	10.24	11.80	8.97	11.64	9.60
20	21.88	23.60	20.92	23.28	21.60
30	33.52	35.40	32.88	34.92	33.60
40	45.16	47.20	44.84	46.56	45.60
50	56.80	59.00	56.79	58.20	57.60
60	68.44	70.80	68.75	69.84	69.60
70	80.08	82.60	80.70	81.48	81.60
80	91.72	94.40	92.66	93.12	93.60
90	103.36	106.20	104.62	104.76	105.60
100	115.00	118.00	116.57	116.40	117.60
110	126.64	129.80	128.53	128.04	129.60
120	138.28	141.60	140.48	139.68	141.60
130	149.92	153.40	152.44	151.32	153.60
140	161.56	165.20	164.40	162.96	165.60
150	173.20	177.00	176.35	174.60	177.60
160	184.84	188.80	188.31	186.24	189.60
170	196.48	200.60	200.26	197.88	201.60
180	208.12	212.40	212.22	209.52	213.60
190	219.76	224.20	224.18	221.16	225.60
200	231.40	236.00	236.13	232.80	237.60
210	243.04	247.80	248.09	244.44	249.60
220	254.68	259.60	260.04	256.08	261.60
230	266.32	271.40	272.00	267.72	273.60
240	277.96	283.20	283.96	279.36	285.60
250	289.60	295.00	295.91	291.00	297.60

67. What is the biggest difference between the different bureaux for changing £150?

A. 3%
B. 4.4%
C. 2.5%
D. 3.5%
E. 2%

Answer

68. If the exchange rate is €1.22 to the pound, what fraction is lost changing £10 with Concurrency?

A. 1/10
B. 1/5
C. 1/4
D. 1/7
E. 1/3

Answer

Questions 69 to 72 concern the market share of different soft drinks:

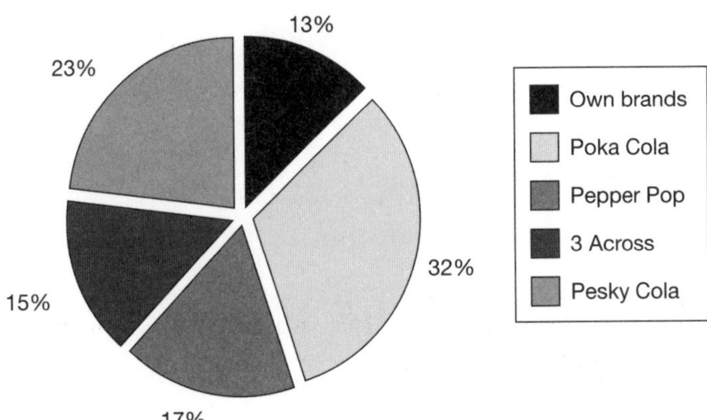

69. Approximately what fraction of the market do the colas represent?

A. 1/3
B. 1/2
C. 3/4
D. 1/5
E. 5/9

Answer ☐

70. If Pepper Pop increases its market share by 3% at the expense of 3 Across, what would be the new ratio of Pepper Pop to 3 Across?

A. 4 : 3
B. 1.67 : 1
C. 3 : 5
D. 20 : 15
E. 17 : 15

Answer ☐

71. A new brand is launched which succeeds in capturing 5% of the market within a year. If the ratio of Pesky Cola to Pepper Pop to 3 Across to Poker Cola remains the same, what is the maximum market share of the own brands?

A. 8%
B. 15%
C. 20%
D. 25%
E. 95%

Answer ☐

72. If Pepper Pop increases its sales by 15%, what would be its new market share, if the sales of the others remain static?

A. 15%
B. 16%
C. 17%
D. 20%
E. 30%

Answer ☐

Questions 73 to 76 concern the dosage of a particular treatment:

Dosage in millilitres, $D = 0.5 \times H^{0.5} \times W^{0.75}$, where W is the weight in kilograms and H the height in metres. (1 in = 2.54 cm, 1 kg = 2.2 lbs and 1 stone = 14 lbs)

73. If a patient's weight increases by 10% during the treatment, by what factor will the dose increase?

A. 1.1
B. $1.1^{0.75}$
C. $10^{0.75}$
D. 1.01
E. Cannot tell

Answer ☐

74. A 1.80 m patient has a brother who is 5 cm taller and 3 kg heavier. How much larger will the brother's dose be?

A. $\sqrt{(1.85/1.80)} \times (1.03)^{0.75}$
B. $(1.85/1.80)^{0.5} \times ((1.03)^{0.25})^3$
C. $(1.85/1.80)^{0.5} \times ((1.03)^3)^{0.25}$
D. $(1.85/1.80)^{0.5} \times (1.03)^{0.75}$
E. Cannot tell

Answer ☐

75. If the average height of a particular population is 5' 10" and the average weight 10 stone, what would be the average dose?

A. 110 ml
B. 120 ml
C. 130 ml
D. 140 ml
E. 150 ml

Answer ☐

76. If the weight of a particular population is 20% higher than here and the cost of the drug 15% more, how much more will it cost to treat people?

A. 20%
B. 32%
C. 38%
D. 30%
E. 35%

Answer

Questions 77 to 80 concern the time taken from receiving a call to the ambulance arriving at the destination:

Time in minutes	0–4.9	5–9.9	10–14.9	15–19.9	20–24.9	25–29.9
Number	15	157	154	92	51	4

77. In which group is the median time?

A. 0–4.9
B. 5–9.9
C. 10–14.9
D. 15–19.9
E. 20–24.9

Answer

78. Estimate the average response time.

A. 12.5 mins
B. 10 mins
C. 15 mins
D. 11.5 mins
E. 15.5 mins

Answer

79. What percentage were above 12.5 minutes?

A. 50%
B. 35%
C. 40%
D. 45%
E. Cannot tell

Answer ☐

80. If the ambulance consumes 0.1 litres per minute, roughly how much fuel was consumed getting to these destinations?

A. 900 litres
B. 9,000 litres
C. 6,000 litres
D. 600 litres
E. 90 litres

Answer ☐

Questions 81 to 84 concern the distance travelled by a falling object, where velocity is the rate of change of distance with time and acceleration is the rate of change of velocity with time:

Time (s)	Distance (m)
1	5
2	20
3	45
4	80
5	125
6	180
7	245
8	320
9	405

81. Estimate the speed at 6 seconds in metres per second.

A. 30
B. 60
C. 40
D. 20
E. 180

Answer ☐

82. Estimate the acceleration.

A. 10
B. 30
C. 20
D. 40
E. 50

Answer ☐

83. A second object is dropped which produces the following set of results. If the first object is dropped 3 seconds after the second object, how long will it take to overtake the second?

Time (s)	Distance (m)
1	8.0
2	11.8
3	16.1
4	20.7
5	25.4
6	30.2
7	35.2
8	40.1
9	45.1

A. Between 0 and 1 second
B. Between 1 and 2 seconds
C. Between 2 and 3 seconds
D. Between 3 and 4 seconds
E. Cannot tell

Answer ☐

84. What is the time at which this second object has greatest acceleration?

A. 1 second
B. 2 seconds
C. 3 seconds
D. 4 seconds
E. None of the above

Answer

Questions 85 to 88 concern the prices of petrol observed at various garages in a certain city:

Price in pence
96.5
99.9
97.5
98.3
99.6
99.6
100.3
100.1
100.5
99.9
99.9
98.7

85. How much bigger is the mode than the average, 99.2?

A. 0.55
B. 0.70
C. 0.75
D. 0.65
E. 0.45

Answer

86. The program used to calculate the average was only designed to accept prices up to 99.9p. If it reads 101.3 as 01.3, what will be the difference between the actual numerical mean and that calculated by the program?

A. 12
B. 4
C. 12.5
D. 25
E. 9.5

Answer ☐

87. If the prices all increase by 2%, what fraction will be above 100p?

A. 1/4
B. 9/12
C. 5/6
D. 2/3
E. All of them

Answer ☐

88. If, as a result of price increases, all the prices are between 100 and 200 and the same program is used to determine the average, which of the following could be used to give the correct answer?

A. Answer + 100
B. Answer × (number of samples) × 100 / (number of samples)
C. Answer + ((number of samples) × 100)
D. Answer + 200
E. Answer + number of samples

Answer ☐

Questions 89 to 92 concern the reliability of various brands based on the number of warranty claims of various brands of car:

Brand	Claims per 100	Average claim cost (£)
Bonza	9.9	325
Havanaisday	16.2	135
Frort	36.4	223
Perja	30.8	228
MT	37.7	433

89. Which brand has the lowest cost per 100?

A. Bonza
B. Havanaisday
C. Frort
D. Perja
E. MT

Answer ☐

90. If the cost of the claims has not been factored in, how much will MT have to add to the price of a car to take this into account?

A. £143
B. £149
C. £155
D. £160
E. £163

Answer ☐

91. Through improved quality and better working practices, Frort is able to reduce the number of claims per hundred to 25 and the cost per claim to £200. What is the fractional saving?

A. 2/5
B. 1/4
C. 3/10
D. 1/3
E. 4/9

Answer ☐

92. Perja decides to offer an additional insurance policy beyond the warranty period. If the probability of a breakdown with an average repair cost of £250 is 1 in 12 per year, what price should the premium be to make a 20% return?

A. £25
B. £20.74
C. £30.92
D. £20.10
E. £27

Answer ☐

Questions 93 to 96 concern exchange rates:

Dollally	Kroni	Pounze	Robbers	Yangs	Barts
1	5.91	1.97	23.69	104.93	33.15

93. What is the exchange rate from Robbers to Yangs?

A. 0.226
B. 4.429
C. 0.262
D. 23.69
E. 4.492

Answer ☐

94. If the exchange rate from Dollally to Pounze drops by 20% and the rate from Dollally to Yangs increases by 25%, by how much will the Pounze–Yangs rate change?

A. 56%
B. 45%
C. 5%
D. 20%
E. 25%

Answer ☐

95. A virtual currency is defined as the value of Dollally times Robbers divided by Pounze times Kroni. If the value of the Pounze drops 20% against the Dollally, by how much will this virtual currency change?

A. Up 1/4
B. Up 1/5
C. Down 1/5
D. Down 1/4
E. Down 1/3

Answer ☐

96. A tourist changes 100 Dollally to Barts. If the tourist then returns home and changes the remaining 100 Barts back to Dollally, how much would they have lost in total if the commission is 3% in both directions?

A. 6.00 Dollally
B. 3.00 Dollally
C. 3.09 Dollally
D. 6.33 Dollally
E. 4.27 Dollally

Answer ☐

Mini-tests

Mini-test 1

You have four minutes to answer eight questions in the two sections below.

Questions 97 to 100 concern the sales of ice cream:

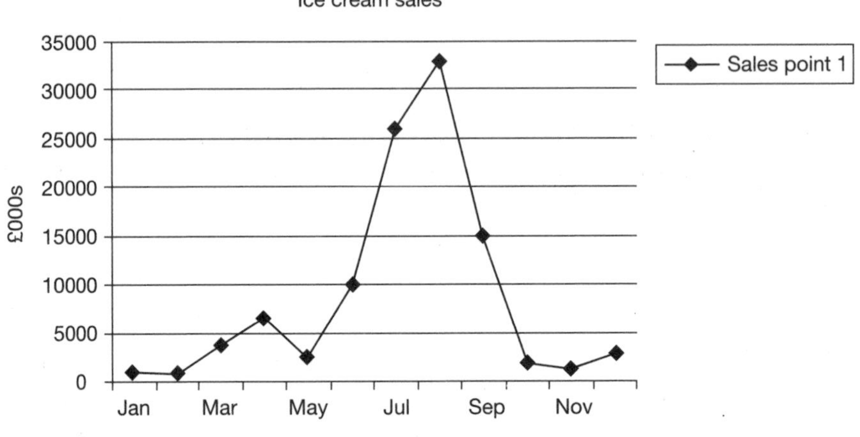

97. What fraction were the minimum sales of the maximum?

A. 1/10
B. 1/20
C. 1/30
D. 1/40
E. 1/25

Answer ☐

98. By how much do sales increase from January to April?

A. 500%
B. 600%
C. 60%
D. 450%
E. 550%

Answer ☐

99. If the company needs £5m sales per month to break even, how much profit does it make in the year?

A. £0.5m
B. £400m
C. £500,000
D. £5m
E. £45m

Answer

100. If inflation rises at 0.1% per month, what is the increase in cost at the end of the year?

A. 1.001^{12}
B. 12×0.1
C. 1.1^{12}
D. 0.1^{12}
E. $(1 + (12 \times 0.001))$

Answer

Questions 101 to 104 concern the recovery rates of trials of different drugs, based on number of days for substance X in blood to drop to certain level:

Number of days				
Drug A	Drug B	Drug C	Drug D	Drug E
20	11	5	11	25
21	20	6	16	26
27	16	30	12	24
19	15	25	13	23
28	19	9	15	25
25	15	24	17	25
23	14	11	14	26
21	13	15	16	23
20	12	27	13	21
21	12	9	15	29
22	12	8	15	27
21	11	25	15	25
19	15	13	11	26
26	16	25	12	26
23	18	8	13	24
21	20	24	11	23
20	16	15	13	21
17	17	21	16	20

101. Which drug has the best average?

A. Drug A
B. Drug B
C. Drug C
D. Drug D
E. Drug E

Answer ☐

102. Which drug has the lowest median value?

A. Drug A
B. Drug B
C. Drug C
D. Drug D
E. Drug E

Answer ☐

103. If each of the values in the drug C trials were 10% nearer the average, how would this affect the average?

A. 10% larger
B. 10% smaller
C. 20% larger
D. Cannot tell
E. Unchanged

Answer ☐

104. If the range of values in the drug C trials changed by 10%, how would this affect the average?

A. 10% larger
B. 10% smaller
C. 20% larger
D. Cannot tell
E. Unchanged

Answer ☐

End of test

Mini-test 2

You have four minutes to answer eight questions in the two sections below.

Questions 105 to 108 compares the time taken for various journeys:

Journey	Distance (miles)	Time (hours and mins)
A	115	1h 55m
B	97	2h 6m
C	65	1h 11m
D	88	1h 45m
E	95	1h 35m

105. Which journey has the fastest average speed?

A. A
B. A and E
C. E and C
D. C
E. E

Answer ☐

106. Which formula gives the average speed for journey C in miles per hour?

A. s = 65 / 1.11
B. s = 65 / 1 + (11/60)
C. s = 65 / (1 + (11/60))
D. s = 65 × 1 .11
E. s = 65 / (1 × (11/60))

Answer ☐

107. The time taken for journey C can vary by as much as plus or minus 20%. By how much will the corresponding average speed change?

A. + 20%, –20%
B. +25%, –25%
C. +25%, –17%
D. +17%, –20%
E. Cannot tell

Answer ☐

108. If there are 1.609 km to a mile, what is the average speed for journey E in metres per second?

A. 26.82 m/s
B. 1609 m/s
C. 96552 m/s
D. 25.66 m/s
E. 95562 m/s

Answer

Questions 109 to 112 concern traffic on the internet through a particular server during the day (1 TeraByte = 1,000 GigaBytes):

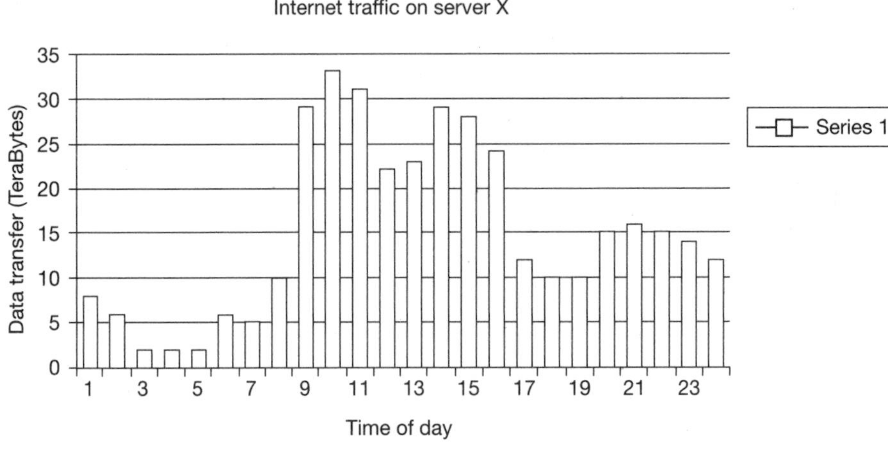

109. What is the approximate total traffic in the day?

A. 36 TeraBytes
B. 360 TeraBytes
C. 24 TeraBytes
D. 240 TeraBytes
E. 2,400 TeraBytes

Answer

110. What fraction of the day exceeded 15 TeraBytes?

A. 5/6
B. 1/2
C. 1/ 4
D. 11 /24
E. 9/24

Answer

111. Between which times did the traffic increase the most?

A. 8 and 9
B. 5 and 6 or 8 and 9
C. 5 and 6
D. 16 and 17
E. 30%

Answer ☐

112. In order to cope with demand a second server is activated when the data transfer rate exceeds 3 GigaBytes per second. Approximately how many hours a day will this occur?

A. 14
B. 10
C. 3
D. 2
E. 0

Answer ☐

End of test

Mini-test 3

You have four minutes to answer eight questions in the two sections below.

Questions 113 to 116 concern Boyle's law relating pressures and volumes of a gas, PV = constant:

113. If the pressure changes by a factor of 3/4, by how much does the volume change?

A. 3/4
B. 4/3
C. 1.5
D. 2
E. 1.25

Answer ☐

114. If the volume changes to 5/6 the original volume, by how much must the pressure change?

A. −1/ 6
B. +1/6
C. +1/ 5
D. +5/6
E. −5/6

Answer ☐

115. The following results were taken during an experiment. It appears that the experimenter has made a mistake. Where?

Pressure (kPa)	Volume (m^3)
100	0.020
95	0.021
90	0.022
65	0.031
150	0.133

A. The volume 0.020 should read 0.200.
B. The pressure 100 should read 10.
C. The volume 0.022 should read 0.220.
D. The volume 0.133 should read 0.013.
E. Cannot tell.

Answer ☐

116. The pressure in the above experiment is increased to 900 KPa. If the experimenter only reads to three decimal places, what percentage error will this introduce?

A. 10%
B. 15%
C. 5%
D. 2%
E. 3%

Answer

Questions 117 to 120 concern the results of a comparison test between two populations and two types of orange juice. The percentages give the number who preferred the particular juice:

	Population X	Population Y
Juice A	85%	55%
Juice B	10%	30%

117. What fraction of population Y was undecided?

A. 85/100
B. 25/100
C. 1/5
D. 3/20
E. 15/50

Answer

118. If the population Y were twice as big as population X, what would be the average preference percentage for Juice A for the entire population of X and Y together?

A. 83%
B. 79%
C. 65%
D. 70%
E. 67%

Answer

119. The polling company then carried out a later test where juice A was identified as being 10% more expensive than juice B and the question asked as to which juice people would buy. Which section has shown the greatest points change?

	Population X	Population Y
Juice A	65%	62%
Juice B	29%	32%

A. Population X for juice A
B. Population X for juice B
C. Population Y for juice B
D. Population Y for juice A
E. Cannot tell

Answer

120. Given that the same quantity of juice is sold and the populations remained as in question 118, by how much would it benefit the makers of juice A to sell it at the higher price?

A. Around 10% more
B. Around 10% less
C. Around 7% more
D. Around 5% more
E. Cannot tell

Answer

End of test

Mini-test 4

You have four minutes to answer eight questions in the two sections below.

Questions 121 to 124 concern the results of a particular competition:

Team	Won	Drawn	Lost	Points
A	2	2	0	26
B	1	3	1	18
C	0	3	3	18
D	1	2	1	19
E	2	1	0	21

121. How many points for a draw?

A. 1
B. 2
C. 3
D. 4
E. 5

Answer ☐

122. How many matches are left to play if each team plays the others twice?

A. 9
B. 8
C. 7
D. 6
E. 5

Answer ☐

123. What is the maximum total number of points?

A. 175
B. 192
C. 183
D. 157
E. 162

Answer ☐

124. If all the remaining matches are drawn, what fraction of the teams will have less than 30 points?

A. 1/5
B. 2/5
C. 3/5
D. 4/5
E. Cannot tell

Answer

Questions 125 to 128 concern mathematical functions:

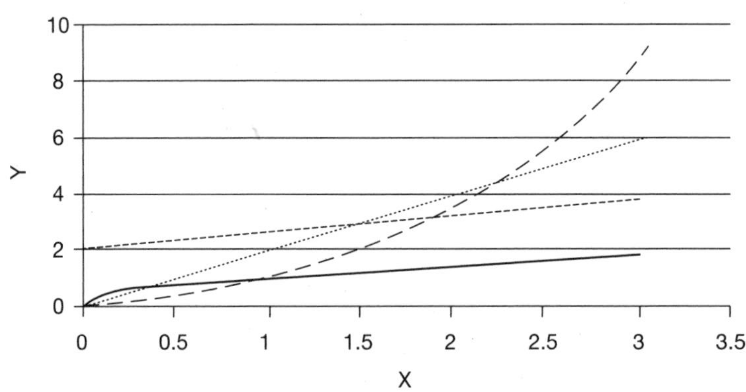

125. Which function does the line A represent?

A. $y = \sqrt{x}$
B. $y = 5x + 2$
C. $y = 0.58x$
D. 81.5
E. 81.0

Answer

126. Which has the highest average value between 0 and 3?

A. A
B. B and C
C. D
D. C
E. Cannot tell

Answer

127. What is the value of y when line D has an x value of 10?

A. 12
B. 10
C. 5
D. 6
E. 7

Answer

128. If all the y values of line C were reduced by a factor of 3, at what value of x would it cross line C?

A. 3
B. 4
C. 5
D. 6
E. 7

Answer

End of test

Mini-test 5

You have four minutes to answer eight questions in the two sections below.

Questions 129 to 132 concern a set of exam results:

Student	Result (%)
A	44
B	46
C	55
D	91
E	88
F	66
G	57
H	80
I	72
J	55
K	36
L	38
M	48
N	57
O	87
P	83
Q	55
R	61
S	59
T	54

129. If the exam board intends that only 10% of students should receive the maximum grade, what mark should be the minimum to achieve this grade?

A. 80
B. 87.5
C. 88
D. 87
E. 82.5

Answer ☐

130. If 10% also fail, what is the largest range between the mark separating the top group and the mark separating the bottom group?

A. 49
B. 45
C. 47.5
D. 48.5
E. 50

Answer

131. A second set of results was obtained as follows. By how much has the mode improved?

Result (%)
37
39
45
47
49
55
56
56
56
58
58
60
62
67
73
82
85
89
90
93

A. 1
B. 2
C. 3
D. 4
E. 5

Answer

132. If all the scores in the first set improved by 3%, how many would now achieve the top grade if the dividing mark remained unchanged?

A. 2
B. 3
C. 4
D. 5
E. Cannot tell

Answer

Questions 133 to 136 concern the speeds of different types of transport:

Transport	Speed
Running	10 m/s
Horse	23 m/s
Bicycle	16 m/s
Electric car	32 m/s
Car	50 m/s

133. If the electric car starts ahead of the car, what is the car's closing speed?

A. 18 m/s
B. 32 m/s
C. 50 m/s
D. 82 m/s
E. 9 m/s

Answer

134. If all the forms of transport pass the start together at their given speeds, how much further will the car have gone compared to the horse after one minute?

A. 3,000 m
B. 1,380 m
C. 1,620 m
D. 960 m
E. 1,220 m

Answer

135. How many metres' head start should the horse give the bicycle if they are to finish the 100 m together?

A. 7 m
B. 70 m
C. 39 m
D. 25.25 m
E. 30.43 m

Answer [ ]

136. If the runner has a 100 m head start over the horse, what will the distance, s, between them be at time, t?

A. $s = 100 + 23t - 10t$
B. $s = 100 - 13t$
C. $s = (100 + 10)\, t - 23$
D. $s = (10 - 23)t - 100$
E. $s = 33t - 100$

Answer [ ]

End of test

Mini-test 6

You have four minutes to answer eight questions in the two sections below.

Questions 137 to 140 concern rates of interest:

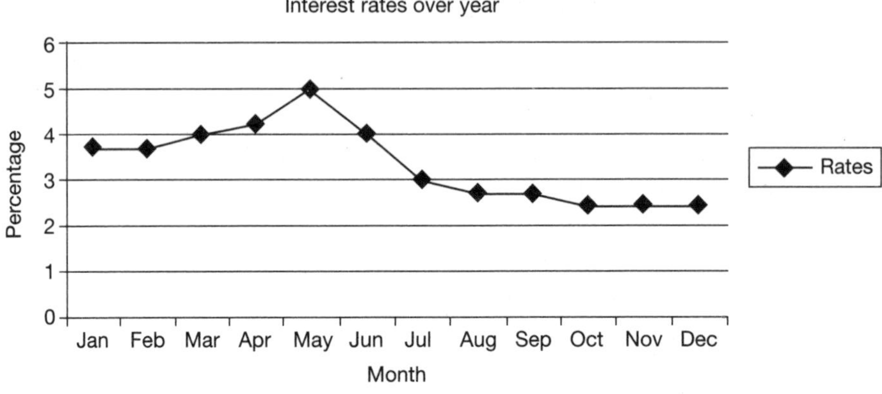

137. Which four months had the highest rates of interest?

A. January, February, March, April
B. February, March, April, May
C. March, April, May, June
D. April, May, June, July
E. September, October, November, December

Answer

138. What fraction of the May interest rate is the September rate?

A. 11/20
B. 1/2
C. 3/5
D. 2.5/5
E. 6/10

Answer

139. If the average interest rate over the year can be used to determine the interest paid on borrowings, how much will be paid on a £250,000 loan?

A. £102,000
B. £10,200
C. £840
D. £8,500
E. £9,600

Answer

140. If £50,000 is borrowed for the month of May, how much will it cost?

A. $C = 50{,}000 \times 5^{(1/12)}$
B. $C = 50{,}000 \times 1.05^{(1/12)}$
C. $C = 50{,}000 \times 5 / 12$
D. $C = 50{,}000 \times 1.05 / 12$
E. Cannot tell

Answer

Questions 141 to 144 concern the activity of a typical student during a college day:

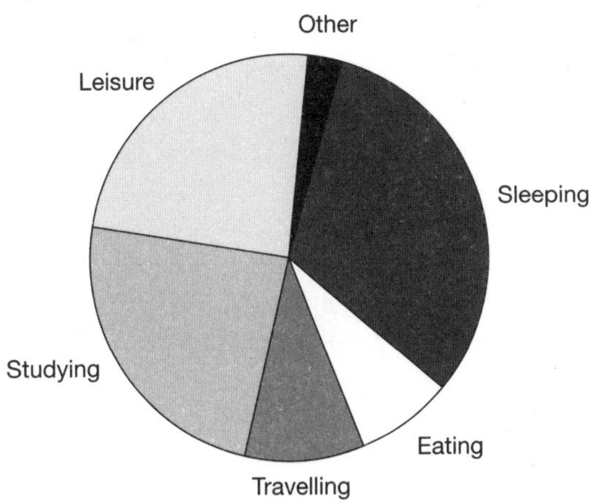

141. How much more time is spent on leisure than on travelling?

A. 300%
B. 400%
C. 40%
D. 200%
E. 25%

Answer

142. If the travelling time is double at the expense of leisure time, what is now the ratio of leisure to travel?

A. 4 : 1
B. 3 : 2
C. 2 : 1
D. 2 : 3
E. 1 : 4

Answer ☐

143. During the holidays the study time is replaced by working at £6.50 per hour. If the travel costs are £1.20 to get to work, how long does the student have to work to pay the travel costs?

A. 10.5 minutes
B. 20 minutes
C. 18.5 minutes
D. 11 minutes
E. 15.5 minutes

Answer ☐

144. If the student can work six hours a day and they find a job which is more lucrative, but further away, travel costs are now £3.00. How much more will they have to earn to make the new job worthwhile?

A. 10p/hour
B. 15p/hour
C. 20p/hour
D. 25p/hour
E. 30p/hour

Answer ☐

End of test

Mini-test 7

You have four minutes to answer eight questions in the two sections below.

Questions 145 to 148 concern the equations associated with the increase of a certain value, V, with time in seconds, t:

Equation 1: $V_1 = 3t + 5$
Equation 2: $V_2 = t^2$
Equation 3: $V_3 = 4t + 1$
Equation 4: $V_4 = 10(1 - e^{-0.2t})$
Equation 5: $V_5 = 5\sqrt{t}$

145. If t is very large, which equation would give the highest =t value of V?

A. Equation 1
B. Equation 2
C. Equation 3
D. Equation 4
E. Equation 5

Answer ☐

146. How much larger is the V_2 than V_1 at 5 seconds?

A. 10%
B. 15%
C. 20%
D. 25%
E. 30%

Answer ☐

147. If V_2 and V_5 are started together, when will they have the same value?

A. $t^3 = 25$
B. $t = 1$
C. $t = \sqrt{25}$
D. $25t = t^2$
E. 30%

Answer ☐

148. Which equation has the highest average value between 0 and 1?

A. Equation 1
B. Equation 2
C. Equation 3
D. Equation 4
E. Equation 5

Answer ☐

Questions 149 to 152 concern the student satisfaction levels in various faculties of a university:

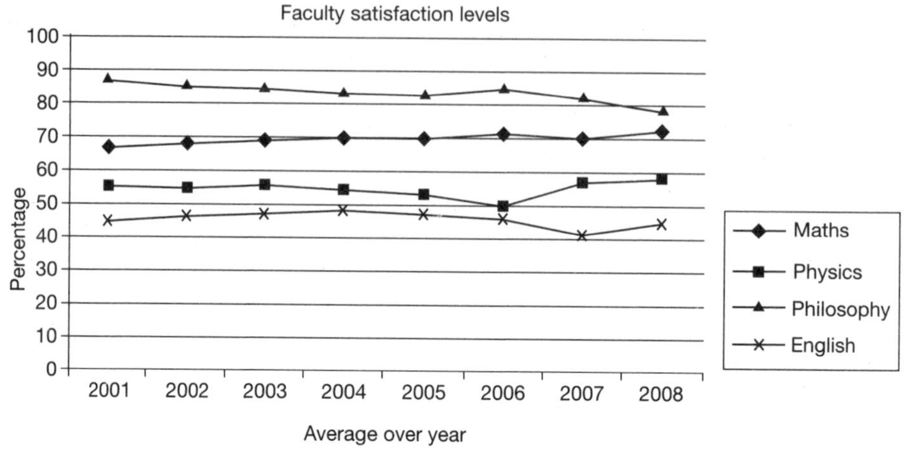

149. Which year had the greatest difference in points between the best performing and the worst?

A. 2001
B. 2003
C. 2005
D. 2007
E. 2004

Answer

150. The graph shows that...

A. Teaching is consistently better in the Philosophy faculty than in Maths.
B. Teaching is consistently better in the Maths faculty than in English, but not as good as in Philosophy.
C. Teaching is consistently better in the Physics faculty than in English, but not as good as in Philosophy.
D. All the above.
E. None of the above.

Answer

151. The respondents had three choices for most questions, A 'not good', B 'good' and C 'very good'. If the number of people polled was n, the score, S, was calculated as S = 100 × (B + 2C) / 2n. What would the score be if everyone replied 'good'?

A. 100
B. 75
C. 50
D. 25
E. 60

Answer ☐

152. If the English results continue to improve and the Philosophy results continue to decline as in the year 2007–2008, how long will it take for the English faculty to overtake the Philosophy faculty?

A. 2
B. 3
C. 4
D. 5
E. 6

Answer ☐

End of test

UKCAT-style timed tests

There are 40 questions (10 sets of four) in 21 minutes.

1. *Three Rs*

A school has recorded the performance of its pupils in reading, writing and arithmetic, and presented the information in the table shown below.

Class 4a: Attainment level

Name	Reading	Writing	Arithmetic
Alan	6	5	5
Barry	5	4	5
Charlie	5	6	6
Ethan	4	6	4
Harry	5	5	6
Joshua	5	4	5
Leanne	6	6	6
Nicola	5	6	7
Phoebe	7	7	7
Soraya	5	5	4
Yasmin	4	4	5
Zara	6	6	5
Percentage at level 5 or above		75.0	83.3
Percentage at level 6 or above	25.0	50.0	41.7

Questions

1. What proportion of the pupils achieved level 5 or above in reading?

   A. 58.3%
   B. 66.7%
   C. 83.3%
   D. 75.0%
   E. 90.0%

Answer ☐

2. What percentage of the pupils who achieved level 5 or above in reading also achieved level 5 or above in arithmetic?

A. 58.3%
B. 66.7%
C. 83.3%
D. 75.0%
E. 90.0%

Answer ☐

3. What percentage of the pupils achieved level 5 or above in all three subjects?

A. 58.3%
B. 66.7%
C. 83.3%
D. 75.0%
E. 90.0%

Answer ☐

4. What percentage of the pupils who achieved level 5 or above in all three subjects achieved level 6 or above in arithmetic?

A. 41.6%
B. 50.0%
C. 66.7%
D. 71.4%
E. 83.3%

Answer ☐

2. Pie in the sky

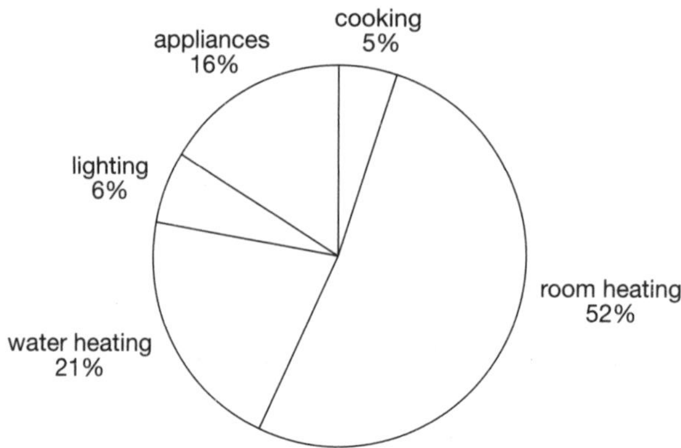

Pie chart showing carbon footprint activities of Household X

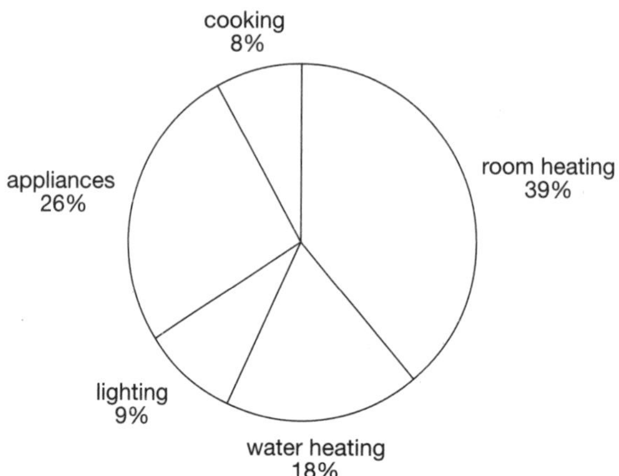

Pie chart showing carbon footprint activities of Household Y

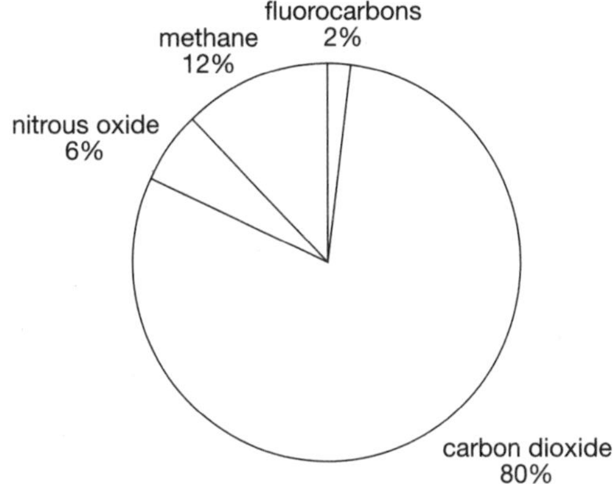

Pie chart showing Household Y's emissions of greenhouse gases during the year

Carbon dioxide, nitrous oxide, methane and fluorocarbons are the main gases that contribute to global warming. The combined emission of these gases constitutes the household carbon dioxide emission. Each of the four gases has a different impact on global warming depending upon how much heat it traps. Fluorocarbon emissions are particularly damaging to the environment because they trap 1,000 times as much heat as carbon dioxide. The ability to trap heat relative to carbon dioxide is as follows:

carbon dioxide × 1
methane × 22
nitrous oxide × 300
fluorocarbons × 1,000

The carbon footprint is found by multiplying the household carbon dioxide emissions by 12/44 or 0.273 (the ratio of the atomic weights of carbon and carbon dioxide). Household X generated 5,241 kilograms of carbon dioxide from room heating during the year.

Questions

5. What was the carbon footprint of Household X in kilograms of carbon during the year?

   A. 2,751
   B. 3,160
   C. 5,241
   D. 8,793
   E. 10,079

Answer ☐

6. What was the carbon footprint of Household Y if Household Y generated 20 per cent less carbon dioxide through room heating than Household X?

A. 2,747
B. 2,935
C. 3,264
D. 5,793
E. 10,751

Answer

7. The compressor pump failed in Household Y's fridge and it lost 0.5 kilogram of fluorocarbon refrigerant. By how much did this increase the carbon footprint of Household Y?

A. 65 kilograms
B. 137 kilograms
C. 326 kilograms
D. 500 kilograms
E. 1,000 kilograms

Answer

8. What percentage of household carbon dioxide emissions are attributable to fluorocarbons?

A. 2%
B. 6%
C. 12%
D. 36%
E. 48%

Answer

3. Onwards and upwards

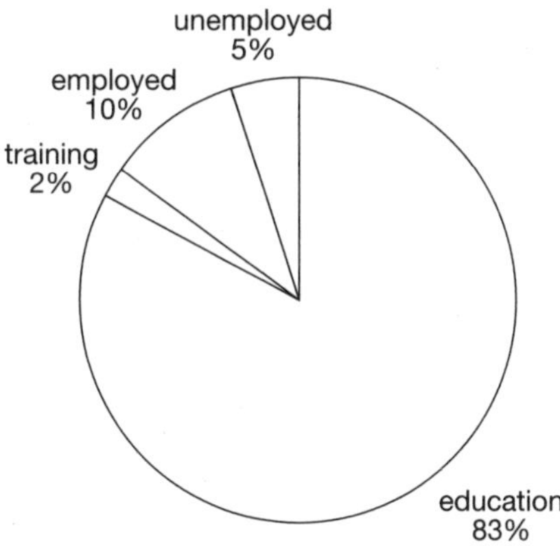

Pie chart showing destination of Year 11 pupils

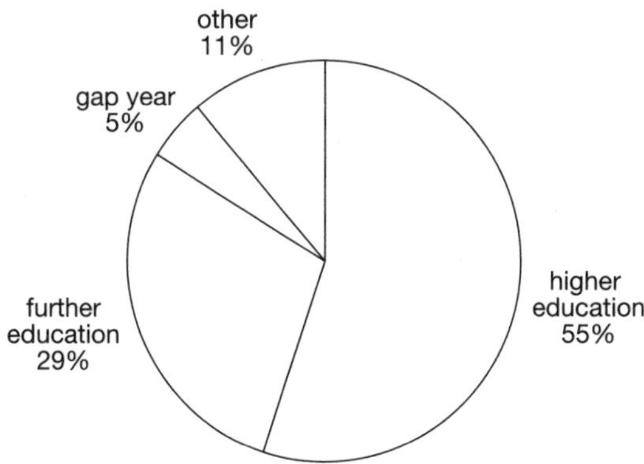

Pie chart showing destination of Year 13 pupils

After completing their education at Robert Nubegin School, pupils in Year 11 have several options available to them, including staying on in full-time education, training for a job or finding employment. Of the pupils who chose to continue their education, three out of seven did so at Robert Nubegin School.

Questions

9. In Year 11, the number of pupils who did not stay on in full-time education was 1,701. How many pupils were there in Year 11?

   A. 7,074
   B. 8,506
   C. 9,748
   D. 10,006
   E. 11,080

Answer ☐

10. How many pupils in Year 11 left the school to find employment or training?

   A. 1,101
   B. 1,201
   C. 1,301
   D. 1,401
   E. 1,501

Answer ☐

11. What percentage of the pupils in Year 11 at Robert Nubegin School decided to stay on at the school beyond Year 11?

   A. 27.7%
   B. 29.4%
   C. 35.6%
   D. 38.8%
   E. 42.9%

Answer ☐

12. Assuming that all the pupils who stay on at Robert Nubegin School after Year 11 remain until the end of Year 13, how many students are likely to end up in higher education, including those who take a gap year?

   A. 2,136
   B. 2,095
   C. 2,042
   D. 2,004
   E. 1,986

Answer ☐

4. Young man's game

Company ABC Ltd has carried out an audit of its sales staff, measuring average weekly sales in relation to sex and age. All the sales people under age 35 are men, and all the sales people over 44 are women. Two-thirds of the sales staff aged 35 to 44 are men.

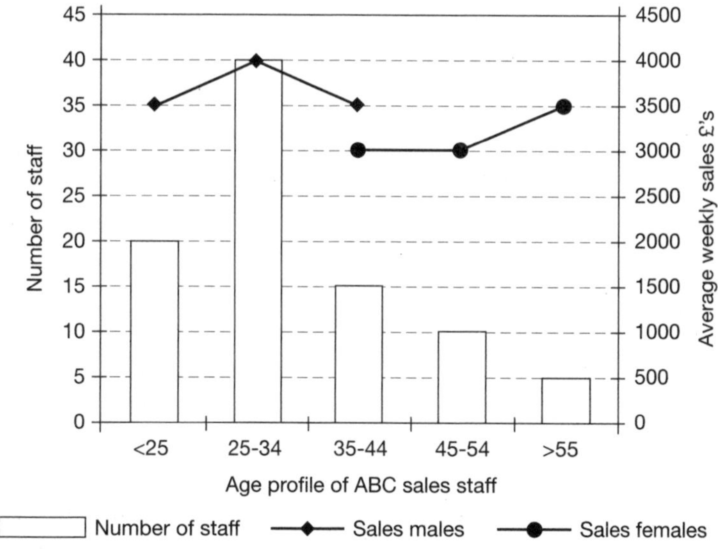

Age distribution of ABC sales staff versus sales

Questions

13. What was the total average weekly sales revenue of all the sales staff under age 35?

A. £160,000
B. £170,000
C. £200,000
D. £230,000
E. £260,500

Answer ☐

14. What was the total average weekly sales revenue of the female staff?

A. £42,500
B. £62,500
C. £92,500
D. £102,500
E. £112,500

Answer ☐

15. What percentage of the company's average weekly sales is generated by the male workforce?

A. 61%
B. 71%
C. 75%
D. 81%
E. 86%

Answer ☐

16. In the following year, sales by the men remained unchanged whilst sales by the women rose 10 per cent. What was the annual sales total?

A. £14.63 million
B. £15.99 million
C. £17.36 million
D. £18.95 million
E. £20.15 million

Answer ☐

5. Sip it

Ensure Twocal™ and Calogen™ are two high-energy nutritional supplements. Taken together they can provide the recommended daily calorific intake of 1,940 kilocalories (kcal) for women and 2,550 kilocalories (kcal) for men. Ensure Twocal™ is supplied in 200-millilitre bottles. The recommended dose of Calogen™ is 3 × 30 ml per day. Nutritional data are as follows:

Nutrition per 100 ml	Carbs	Protein	Fat
Ensure Twocal™	21 g	8.4 g	8.9 g
Calogen™	0 g	0 g	50 g

Fat provides more calories per gram than carbohydrate and protein, as shown below:

Nutrient	Carbs	Protein	Fat
kcal per g	4	4	9

Questions

17. How many kcal are provided by the recommended daily dose of Calogen™?

    A. 400
    B. 405
    C. 410
    D. 425
    E. 450

Answer ☐

18. A male patient, who cannot eat solid food, consumes the recommended daily dose of Calogen™ and six bottles of Ensure Twocal™. What percentage of the recommended daily calorific intake will he achieve?

    A. 69%
    B. 79%
    C. 89%
    D. 99%
    E. 109%

Answer ☐

19. What proportion of the calorific content of Ensure Twocal™ is supplied by its fat content?

A. 41%
B. 46%
C. 51%
D. 56%
E. 61%

Answer ☐

20. How many millilitres of Ensure Twocal™ will a female patient need to consume to achieve 100 per cent of her recommended daily calories if she takes 30 ml of Calogen™ per day?

A. 684 ml
B. 779 ml
C. 824 ml
D. 913 ml
E. 980 ml

Answer ☐

6. Duplicated

The table shows the annual amount of photocopying done by office workers in five different companies. The cost per copy is based on single-sided copies, and it is equal to the cost of the photocopying paper at £5 per ream of 500 sheets plus the cost of toner, which varies from company to company.

Company	Cost per copy in pence	Copies per employee	Number of employees
Valu	2 p	8,000	2,000
Wilats	3.5 p	6,000	3,000
Xsels	1.5 p	10,000	1,000
Yamit	2.5 p	4,000	5,000
Zonika	3 p	5,000	6,000

Questions

21. Which company spent the most money on photocopying?

    A. Valu
    B. Wilats
    C. Xsels
    D. Yamit
    E. Zonika

Answer ☐

22. What proportion of Wilats' photocopying costs went on toner?

    A. 71%
    B. 73%
    C. 75%
    D. 77%
    E. 79%

Answer ☐

23. To reduce its copying costs Xsels asks its staff to make duplex copies (double-sided) to cut its paper costs in half. How much money will Xsels save annually?

    A. £25,000
    B. £50,000
    C. £60,000
    D. £75,000
    E. £90,000

Answer ☐

24. To reduce copying costs, Yamit asks its office staff to reduce all its documents to A5 size to get two copies on to one A4 sheet. This cuts paper costs in half and reduces the consumption of toner by 50 per cent. How much money will Yamit spend on toner annually?

    A. £25,000
    B. £50,000
    C. £75,000
    D. £100,000
    E. £125,000

Answer ☐

7. Skin you're in

The Mosteller equation can be used for estimating body surface area (BSA) in metres squared, when the height and weight of a patient are known. It is given by the square root of the height in centimetres (cm) multiplied by the weight in kilograms (kg), divided by 3,600. Alan is 1.8 metres tall and weighs 80 kg.

$$\text{BSA (m}^2) = \sqrt{\frac{\text{cm} \times \text{kg}}{3{,}600}} \text{ or } \text{BSA}^2 \times 3{,}600 = \text{cm} \times \text{kg}$$

$$= 1/60 \times \sqrt{\text{cm} \times \text{kg}}$$

Patient	Height in metres	Weight in kg
Alan	1.8	80
Jack	1.7	–
Paula	1.6	60

Questions

25. What is Alan's BSA in metres squared?

A. 1.8
B. 2.0
C. $\sqrt{3}$
D. $\sqrt{8}$
E. $2\sqrt{2}$

Answer ☐

26. How heavy is Jack if he has the same body surface area (BSA) as Alan?

A. 79.5 kg
B. 80.2 kg
C. 83.0 kg
D. 84.7 kg
E. 85.0 kg

Answer ☐

27. What is Paula's BSA in metres squared?

A. 2.25
B. $2/3\sqrt{3}$
C. $\sqrt{5}/2$
D. $\sqrt{7}/2$
E. $4/\sqrt{6}$

Answer ☐

28. How much weight must Paula put on to reach a BSA of 1.732?

A. 1.0 kg
B. 2.5 kg
C. 5.0 kg
D. 7.5 kg
E. 10.0 kg

Answer ☐

8. Making hay

A straw merchant has to transport hay bales on a trailer 11 metres long and 2.4 metres wide. The bales are stacked one bale high and must not overhang the sides of the trailer. Bales come in five sizes, as shown in the table.

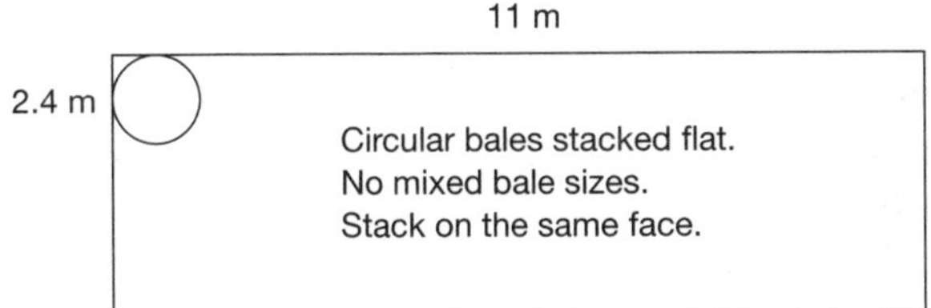

Bale type	Dimensions (cm)	£ per bale
Small	80 × 80 × 80	10
Medium	120 × 80 × 60	12
Conventional	200 × 80 × 60	20
Large cube	100 × 100 × 100	22
Circular	120 diameter	30

Questions

29. How many small bales will fit on the trailer?

 A. 39
 B. 42
 C. 45
 D. 47
 E. 50

Answer

30. How much will the merchant sell his straw for if he stacks the trailer with circular bales?

 A. £420
 B. £460
 C. £500
 D. £540
 E. £580

Answer

31. Which size bale should the merchant transport if he wants to sell hay with the highest value?

 A. small
 B. medium
 C. conventional
 D. large cube
 E. circular

Answer

32. The straw merchant can stack the conventional bales in one of three ways. Proportionally, how much less money will he receive from the sale of one trailer-load if he stacks them in the least inefficient of the three ways?

 A. 32%
 B. 48%
 C. 50%
 D. 63%
 E. 76%

Answer

9. Mine's a double

Daily limits for sensible drinking are 3 to 4 units for men and 2 to 3 units for women. One unit is 10 ml or 8 g of pure alcohol. The table shows the alcohol content by volume (ABV) of selected liquors. A standard single measure is 25 ml, a large single measure is 35 ml and a double measure is 50 ml.

Liquor	Percentage alcohol (ABV)
Bailey's Irish Cream	17%
Cointreau	40%
Malibu	21%
Pimm's No 1	25%
Southern Comfort	37%
Tia Maria	26.5%

Questions

33. How many grams of alcohol are there in a large single measure of Cointreau?

A. 8.0 g
B. 11.2 g
C. 14.9 g
D. 32.0 g
E. 1.12 g

Answer ☐

34. How many large single measures of Bailey's Irish Cream are equivalent to the maximum sensible drinking limit for women?

A. 2
B. 3
C. 4
D. 5
E. 6

Answer ☐

35. The ingredients of a Mudslide cocktail are one-and-a-half measures of vodka (40% ABV), one-half measure of Tia Maria and one-half measure of Bailey's Irish Cream. What is the alcohol content (ABV) of a Mudslide cocktail?

A. 27.5%
B. 29.6%
C. 32.7 %
D. 35.5%
E. 36.7%

Answer ☐

36. John completes his meal with a 150-ml cup of Bailey's coffee (one-third Bailey's Irish Cream and two-thirds black coffee) followed by a double measure of Cointreau. What fraction of the maximum sensible drinking limit has he drunk?

A. 71%
B. 73%
C. 75%
D. 77%
E. 79%

Answer ☐

10. Student travel

Five students travel from a hall of residence to the faculty of medicine, a distance of two miles, for the 0915 hours lecture. Their chosen mode of transport is shown below, along with each person's departure time and average speed in miles per hour.

	Mode	Speed (mph)	Departure
Barbara	walks	3	8.15
Phillip	walks	3.25	8.15
Aran	cycles	10	8.40
Luke	bus	20	8.40
Katie	car	30	8.55

Questions

37. Who is the last person to arrive at the faculty of medicine?

A. Barbara
B. Phillip
C. Aran
D. Luke
E. Katie

Answer ☐

38. On Tuesday, Aran leaves five minutes later but cycles 10 per cent faster. What time does Aran arrive?

A. 8.56
B. 8.57
C. 8.58
D. 8.59
E. 9.00

Answer ☐

39. On Monday morning it starts to rain so Barbara decides to stop en route and catch the bus. She has walked a distance of one mile before catching the bus. What is her average speed for the two-mile journey?

A. 5.3 mph
B. $6.\dot{3}$ mph
C. 8.6 mph
D. 9.3 mph
E. 11.5 mph

Answer ☐

40. On Tuesday morning Katie leaves 10 minutes earlier than usual and stops enroute to give Barbara a lift. How far has Barbara walked when she is given a lift?

A. 1.0 miles
B. 1.25 miles
C. 1.33 miles
D. 1.5 miles
E. 1.67 miles

Answer ☐

5

Abstract reasoning

The abstract reasoning sub-test is described as being intended to assess an ability to identify patterns amongst abstract shapes. The way the UKCAT sub-test does this is by asking the candidate to identify to which group a particular shape, or set of shapes, belongs as illustrated below:

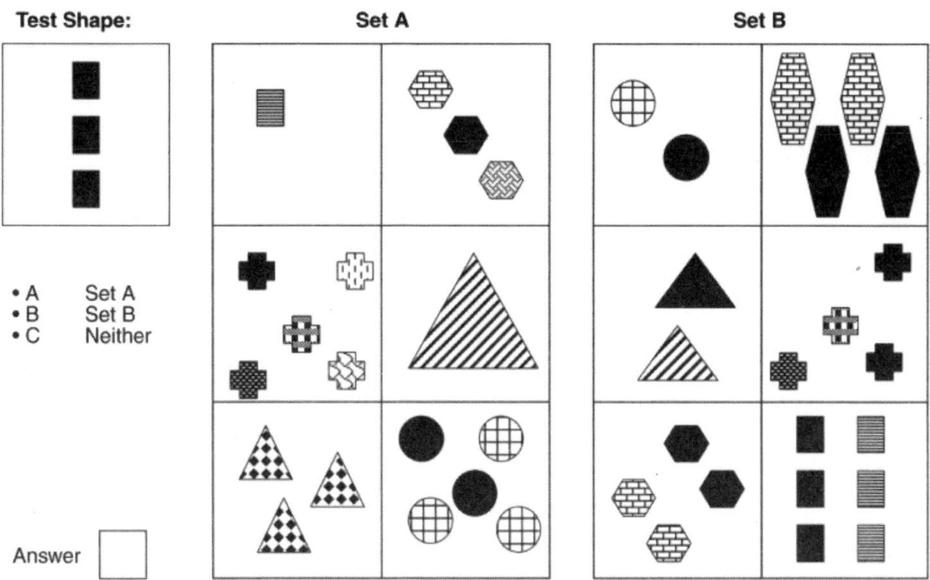

For each SET A and SET B there will be five items (screens) and you will have to click on one of the buttons, A, B or C, to indicate whether you think the test shape belongs to the set A, set B or to neither.

What you have to do, therefore, is to try to identify a particular rule, or set of rules, that governs the contents of the cells in each set. For example, set A may have an odd number of shapes and set B an even number. It is unlikely to be quite as simple, however, as this particular example would preclude the possibility of belonging to neither set. What is more likely is that there will be more than one rule, ie there is an odd number of shapes, triangles are shaded and other shapes may or may not have shading, and possibly even certain conditions – when there is a triangle present the rectangles are shaded, for example. Some of these rules will be readily apparent, but others, equally crucial for determining whether or not a particular test shape belongs, will be more obscure and will require careful scrutiny of *all* the cells in the set.

The kinds of things you should be looking for include:

- number;
- size;
- shape;
- number of sides;
- enclosed or not;
- type of shading or colour;
- patterns;
- position in the cell;
- direction (up or down, left or right, etc);
- rotation;
- reflection;
- intersection.

This particular sub-test will allow you one minute to read the instructions and 15 minutes to determine the appurtenance, or otherwise, of 65 test shapes divided into 13 groups. As before, the test screen will show the time remaining at the top right and the item number, out of 65, at the bottom right.

Simply dividing the time available by the number of test shapes to consider would give about 13 seconds for each shape. What you should do, however, is to spend a little time trying to establish the rules for each set and then more quickly determine the appropriate response (Set A, Set B or Neither) for each of the related five shapes. You should, therefore, aim to spend about one minute on each of the 13 groups of five test shapes.

This chapter provides 150 practice questions with answers, divided up into 70 warm up questions, 30 master class questions and 50 questions in the form of five mini-tests lasting two minutes, each containing 10 questions in two groups of five test shapes. Neither these examples nor the real test is intended to be easy. Good luck.

Warm up questions

Q1.

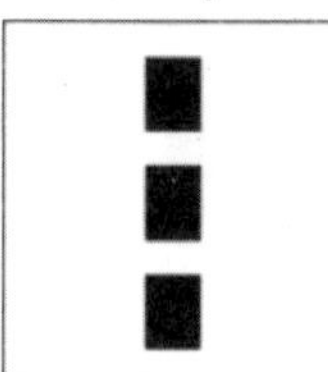

Set A

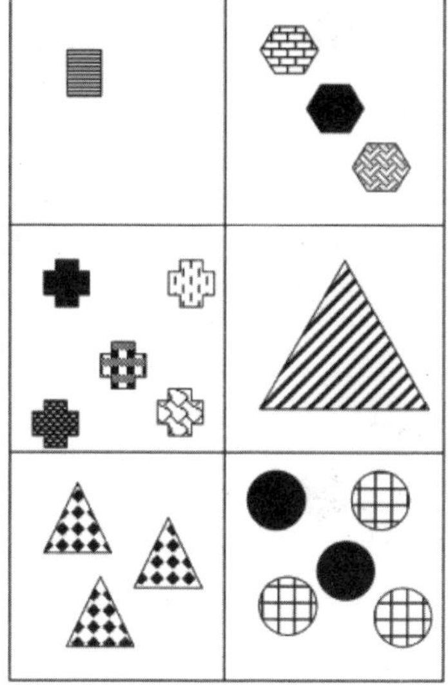

Set B

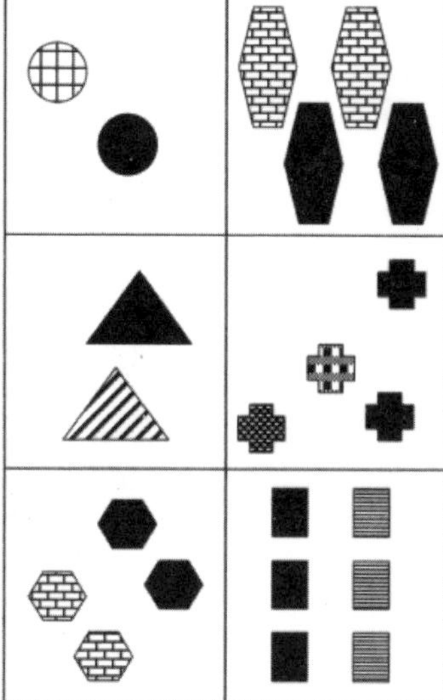

- A Set A
- B Set B
- C Neither

Answer ☐

Q2.

Test Shape:

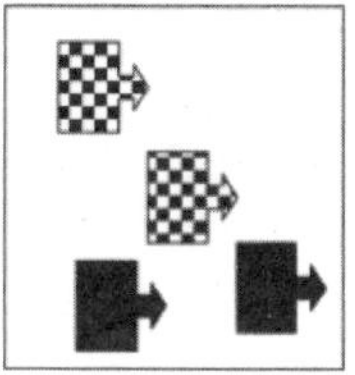

Set A

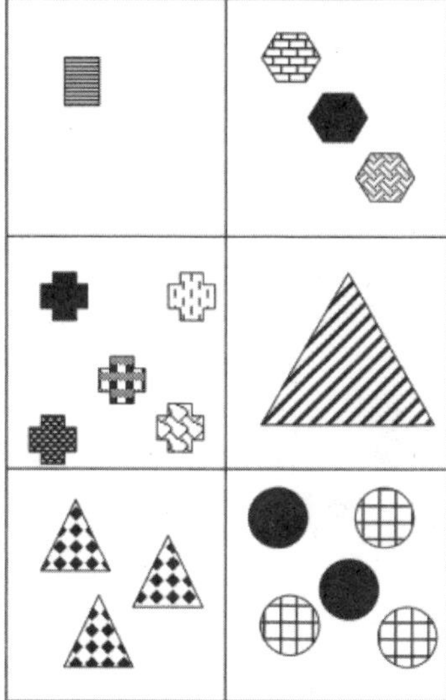

Set B

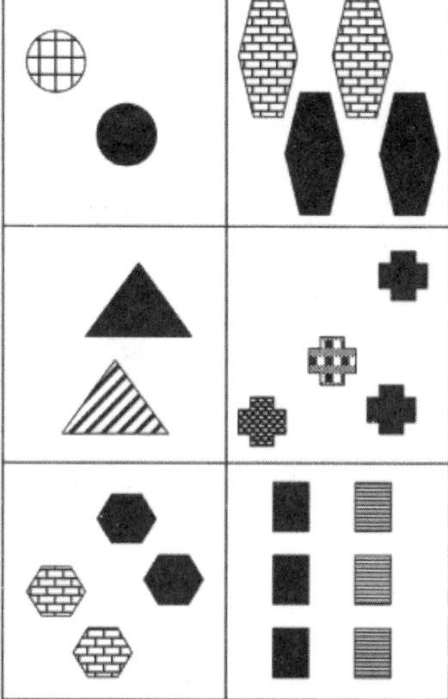

- A Set A
- B Set B
- C Neither

Answer ☐

Q3.

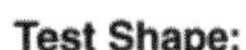

Test Shape:

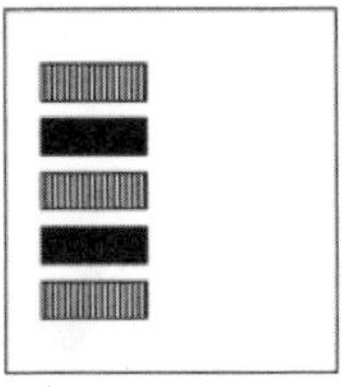

Set A

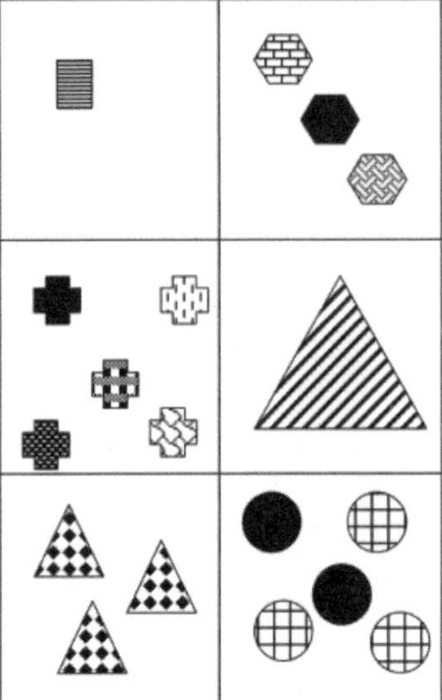

Set B

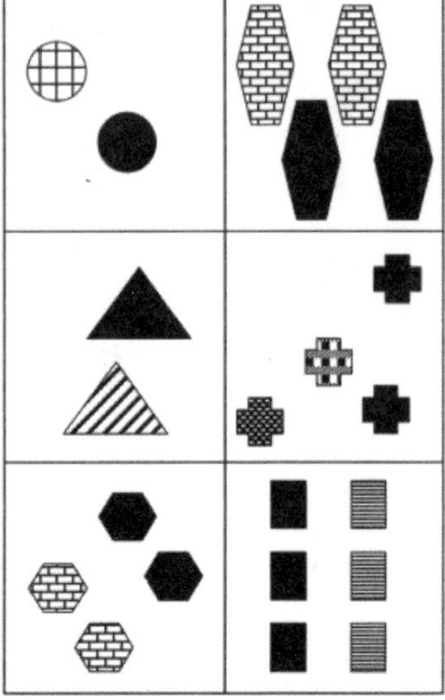

- A Set A
- B Set B
- C Neither

Answer ☐

Q4.

Test Shape:

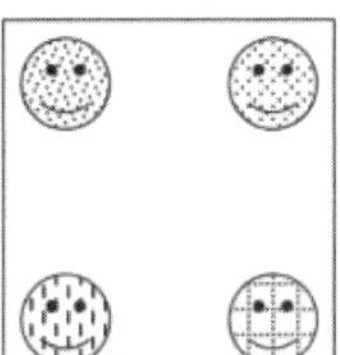

Set A

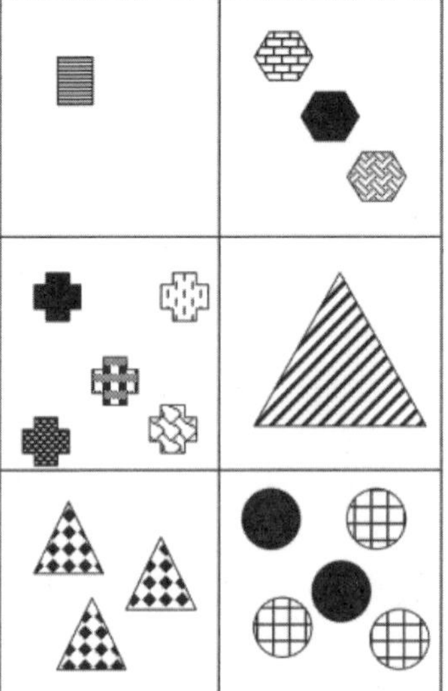

Set B

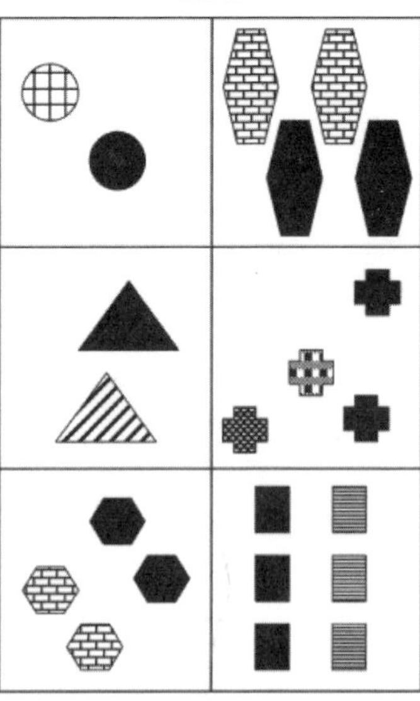

- A Set A
- B Set B
- C Neither

Answer ☐

Q5.

Test Shape:

Set A

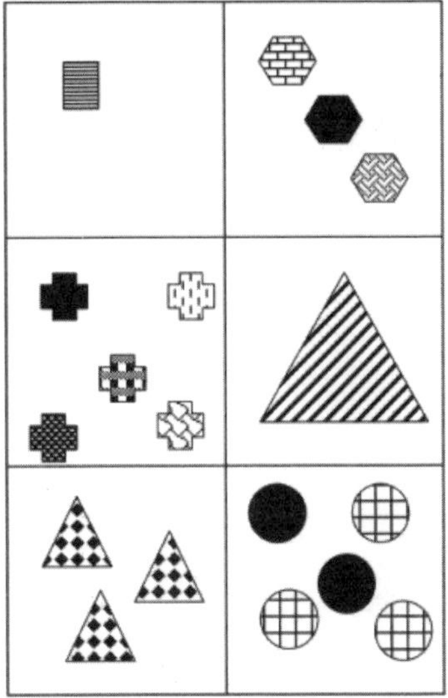

Set B

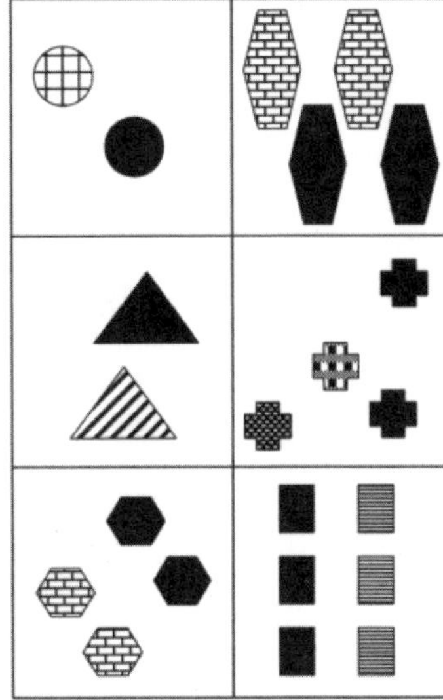

- A Set A
- B Set B
- C Neither

Answer

Q6.

Test Shape:

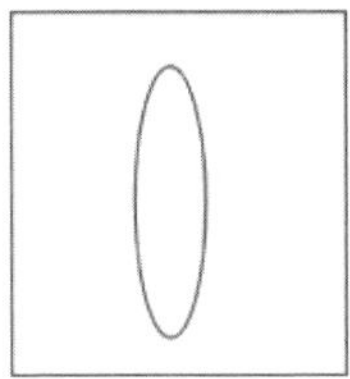

Set A

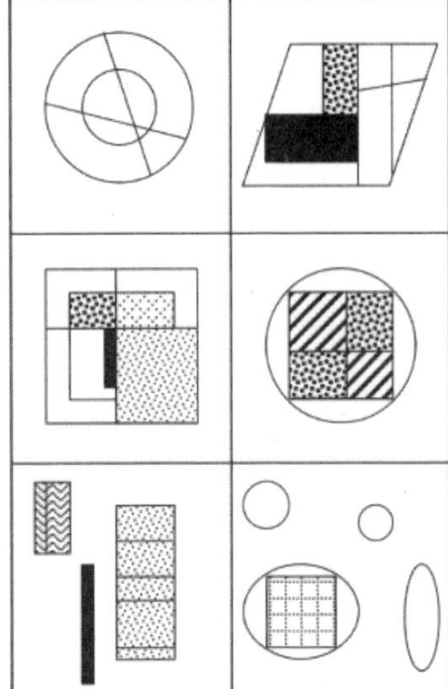

Set B

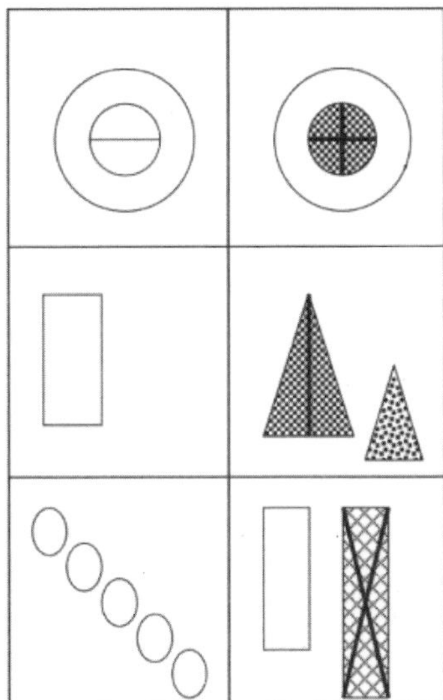

- A Set A
- B Set B
- C Neither

Answer

Q7.

Test Shape:

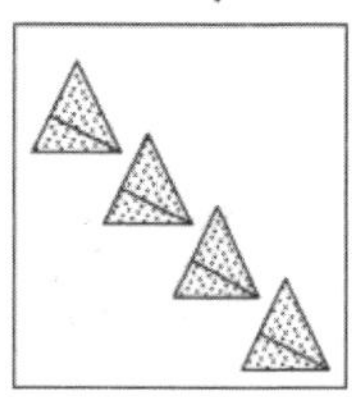

Set A

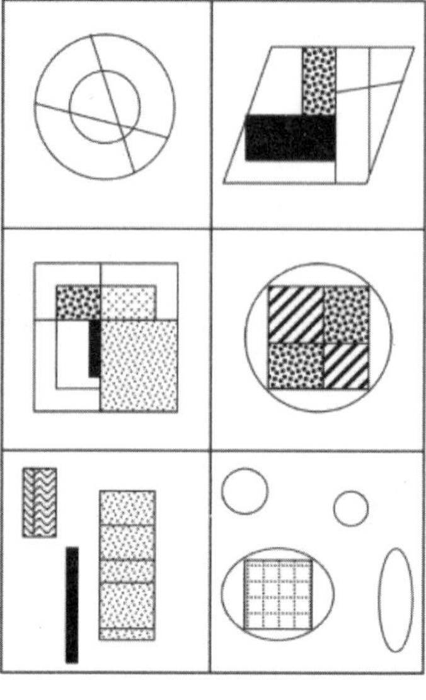

Set B

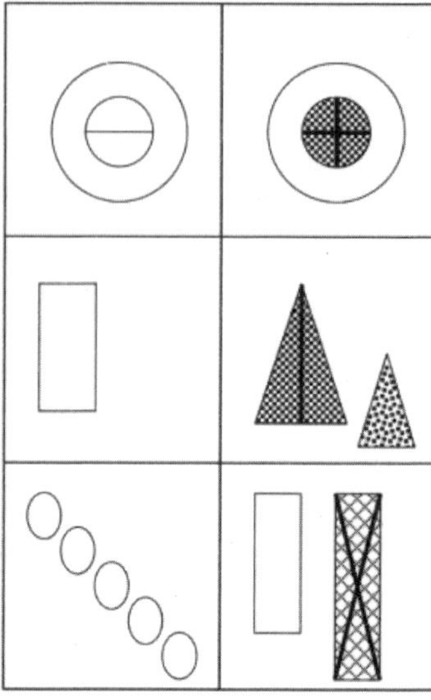

- A Set A
- B Set B
- C Neither

Answer

Q8.

Test Shape:

Set A

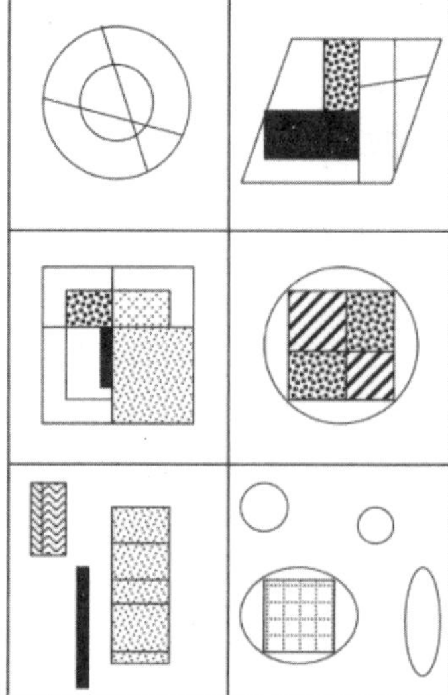

Set B

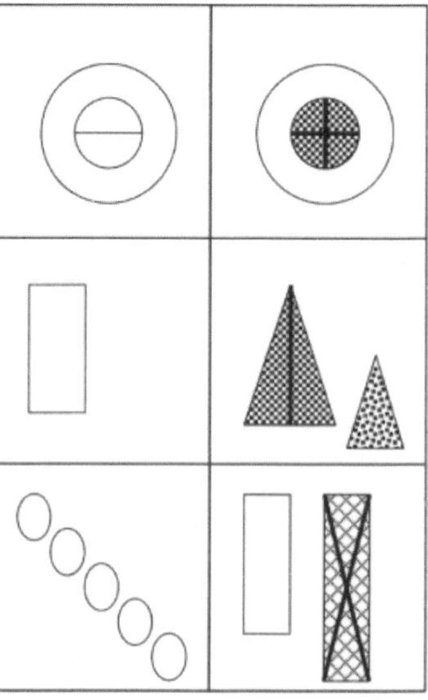

- A Set A
- B Set B
- C Neither

Answer

Q9.

Test Shape:

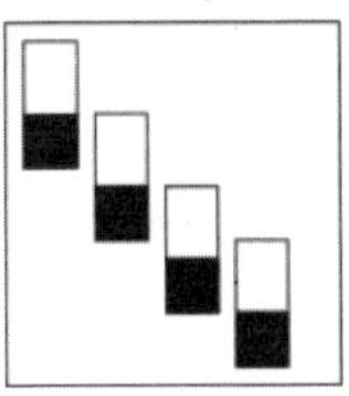

Set A

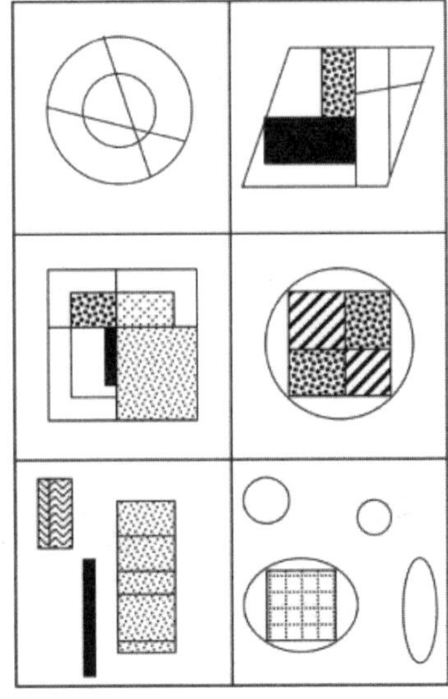

Set B

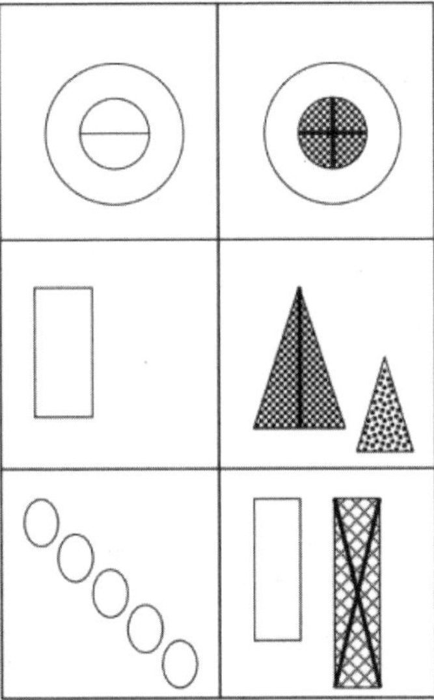

- A Set A
- B Set B
- C Neither

Answer

Q10.

Test Shape:

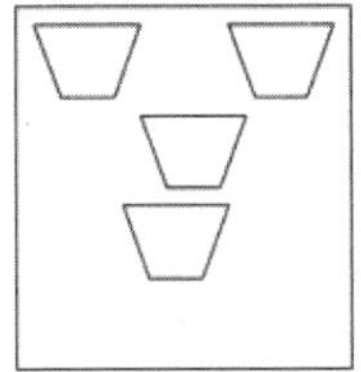

Set A

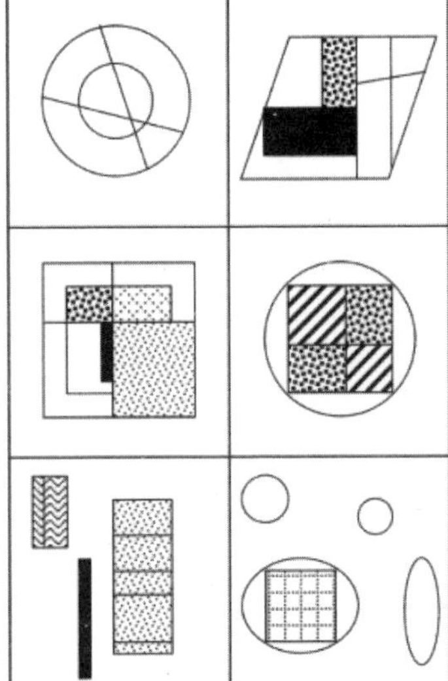

Set B

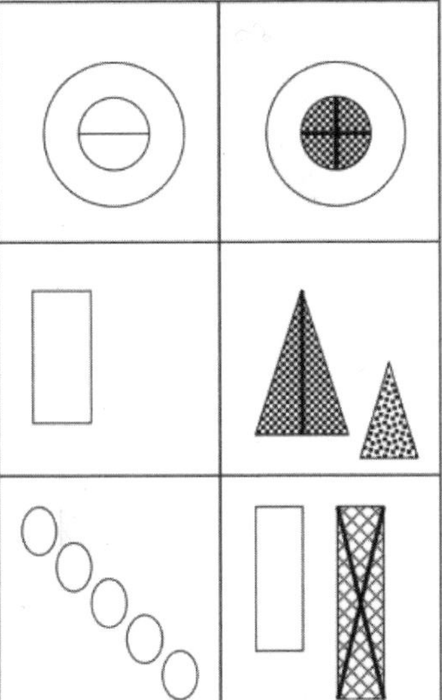

- A Set A
- B Set B
- C Neither

Answer

Q11.

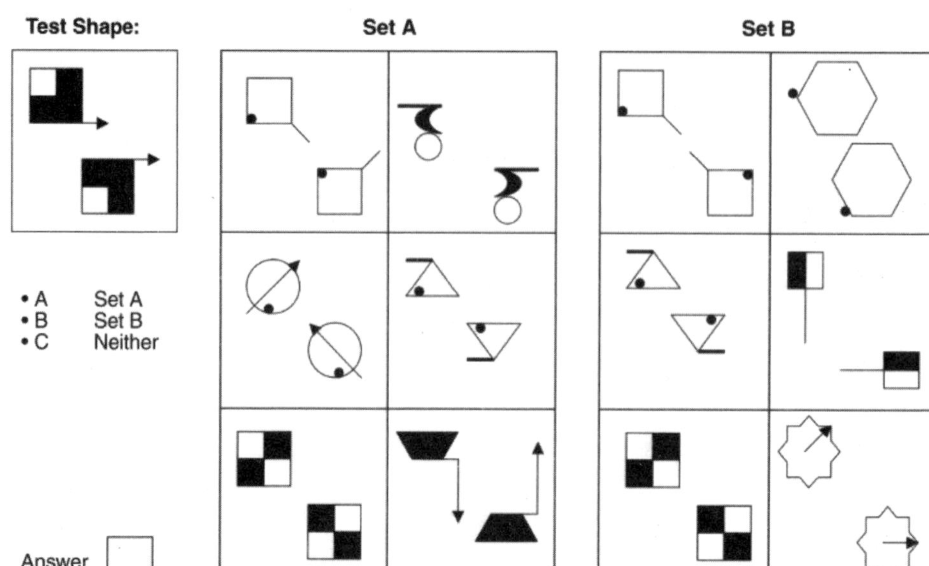
Test Shape:
Set A
Set B
• A Set A
• B Set B
• C Neither
Answer

Q12.

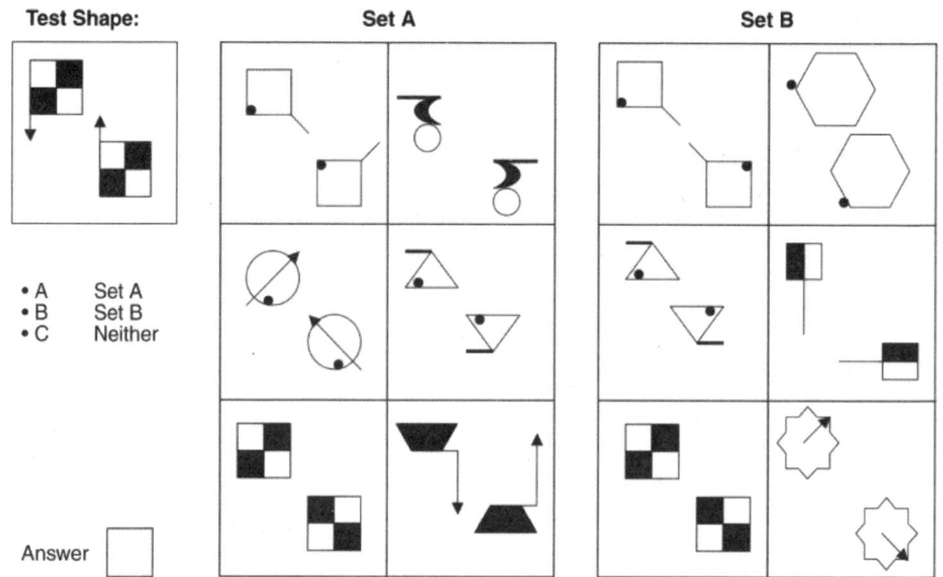
Test Shape:
Set A
Set B
• A Set A
• B Set B
• C Neither
Answer

Q13.

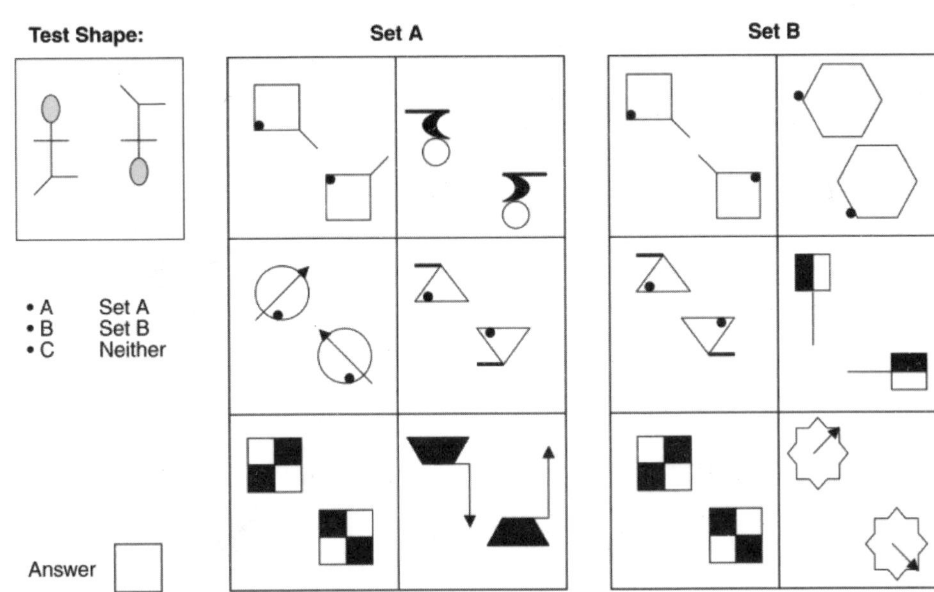
Test Shape:
Set A
Set B
• A Set A
• B Set B
• C Neither
Answer

Q14.

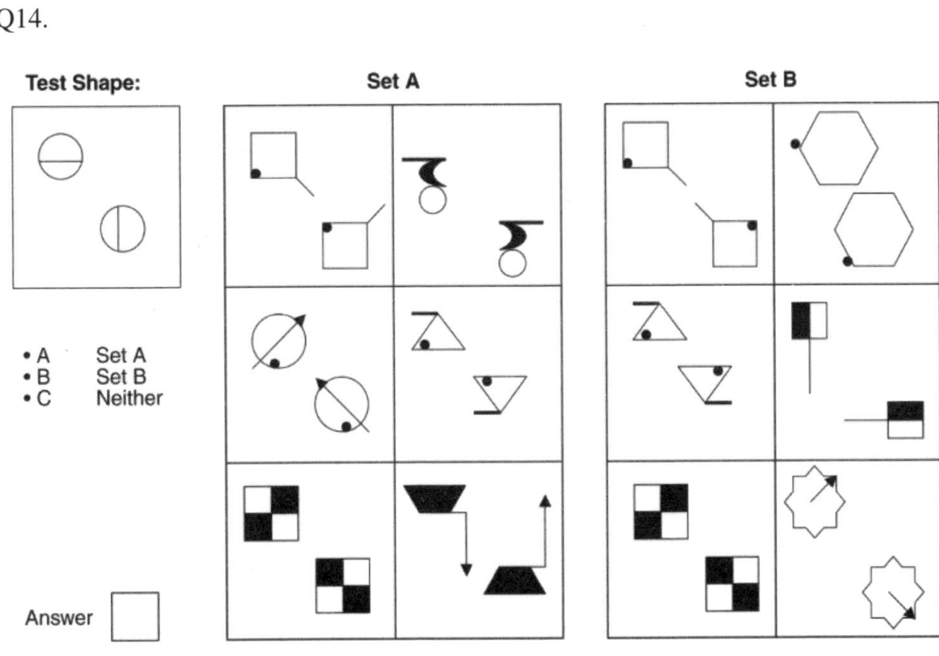
Test Shape:
Set A
Set B
• A Set A
• B Set B
• C Neither
Answer

Q15.

Test Shape:

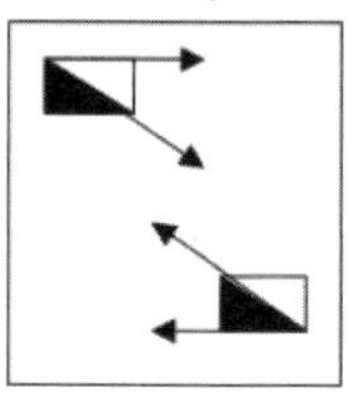

Set A

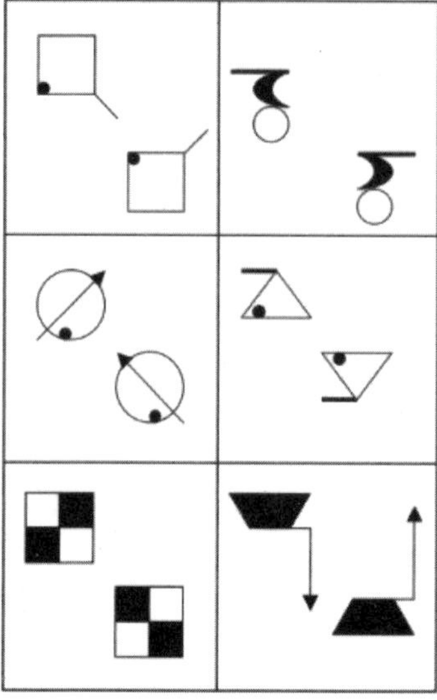

Set B

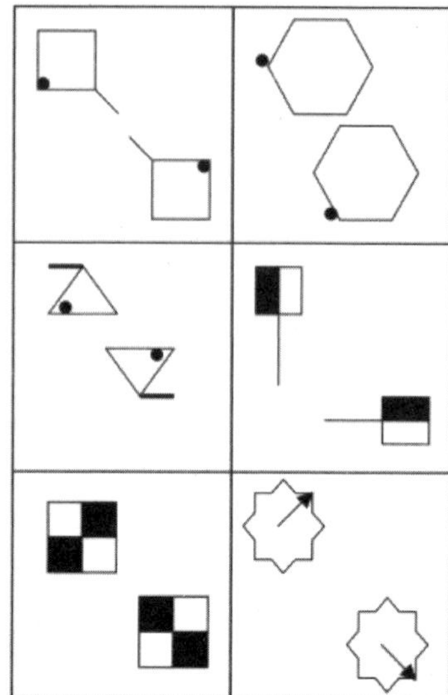

- A Set A
- B Set B
- C Neither

Answer ☐

Q16.

Test Shape:

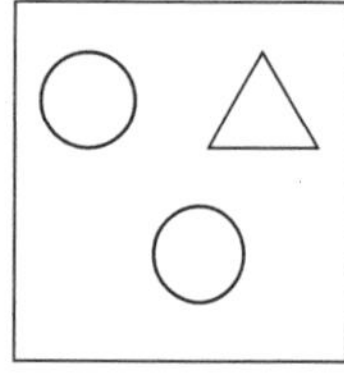

Set A

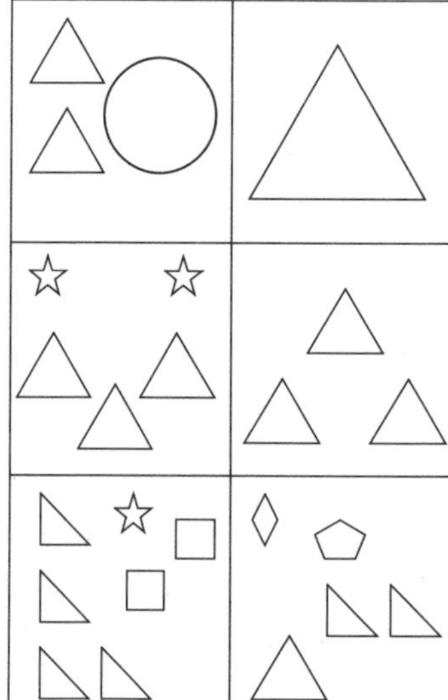

Set B

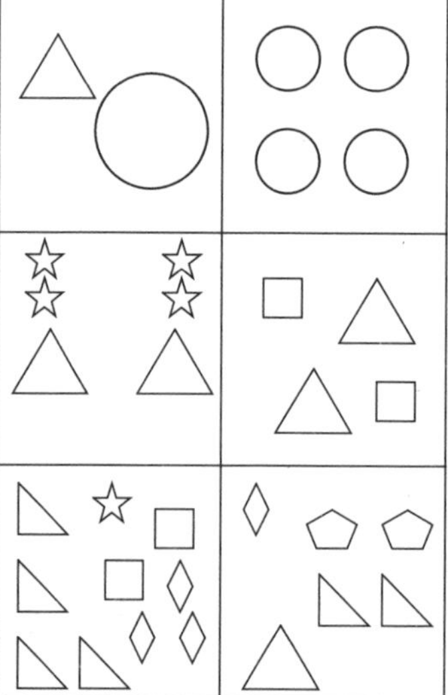

- A Set A
- B Set B
- C Neither

Answer ☐

Q17.

Test Shape:

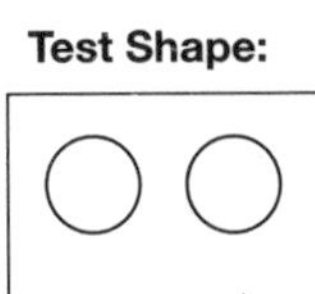

Set A

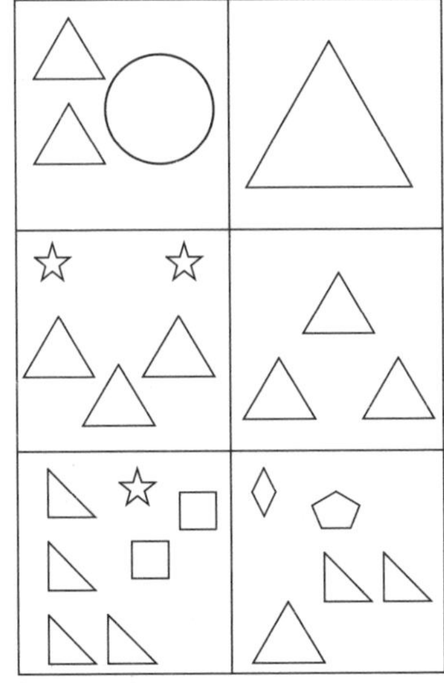

Set B

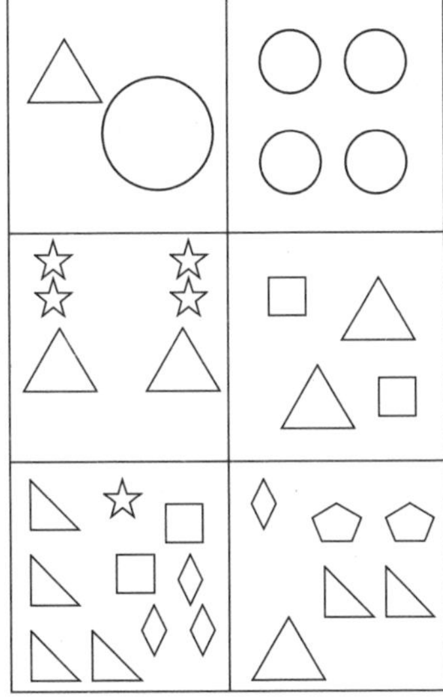

- A Set A
- B Set B
- C Neither

Answer

Q18.

Test Shape:

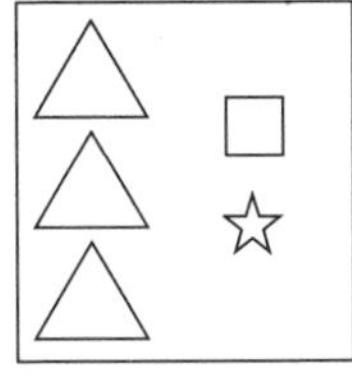

Set A

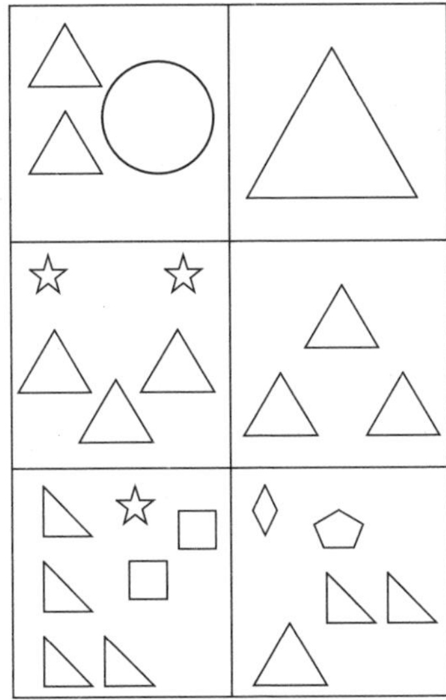

Set B

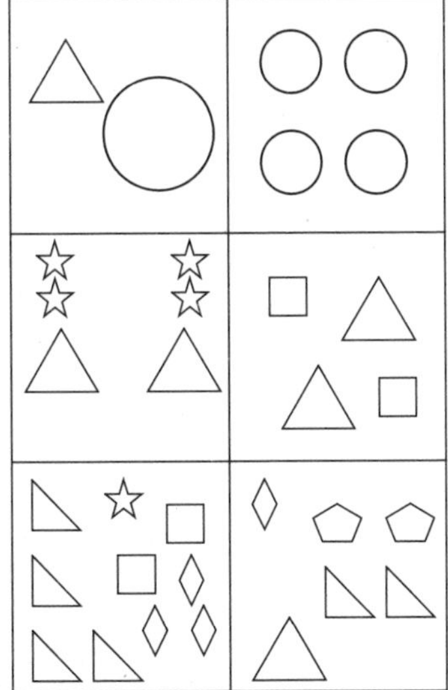

- A Set A
- B Set B
- C Neither

Answer

Q19.

Test Shape:

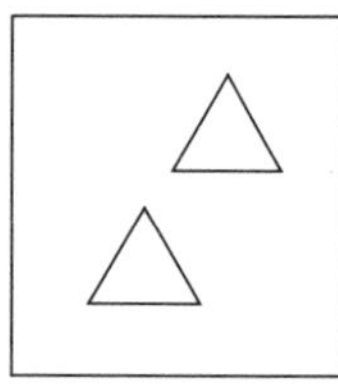

Set A

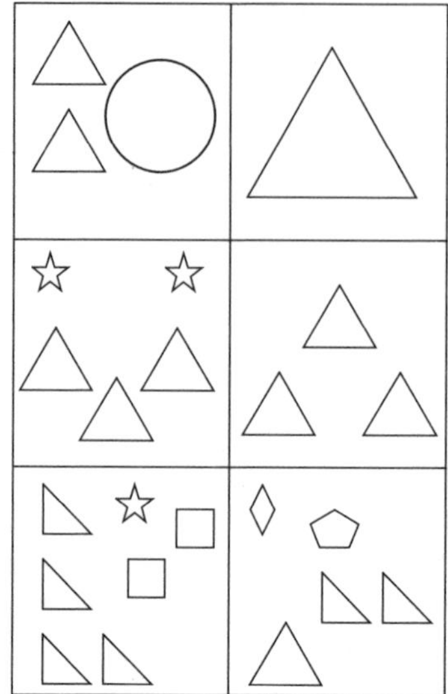

Set B

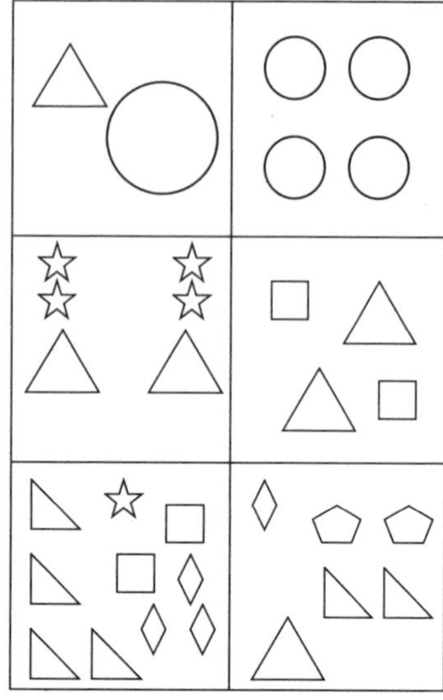

- A Set A
- B Set B
- C Neither

Answer

Q20.

Test Shape:

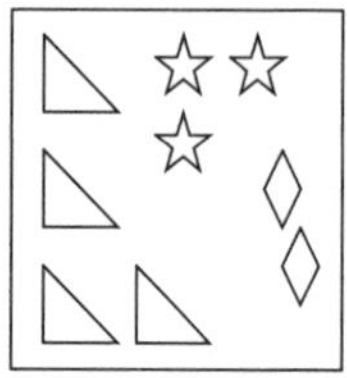

Set A

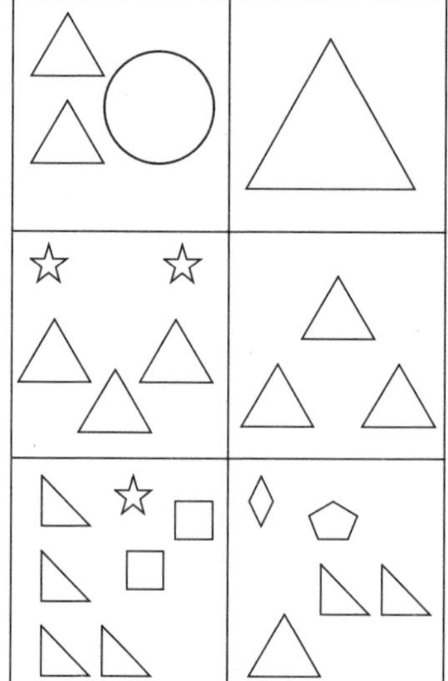

Set B

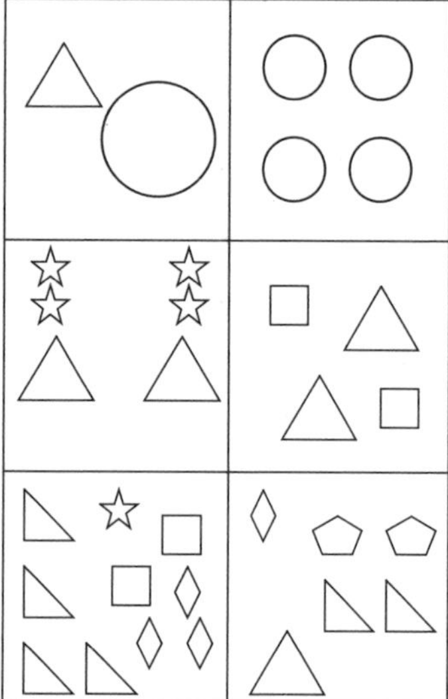

- A Set A
- B Set B
- C Neither

Answer

Q21.

Test Shape:

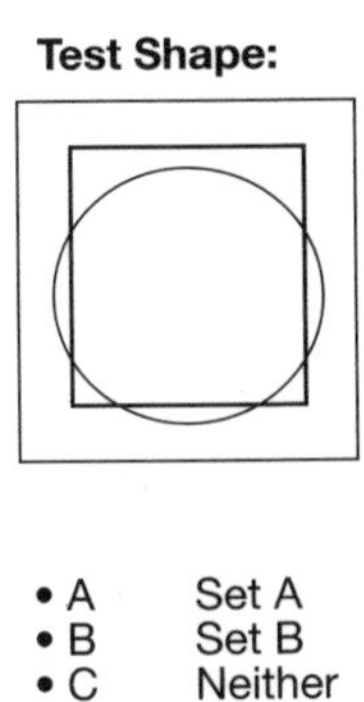

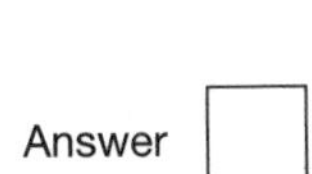

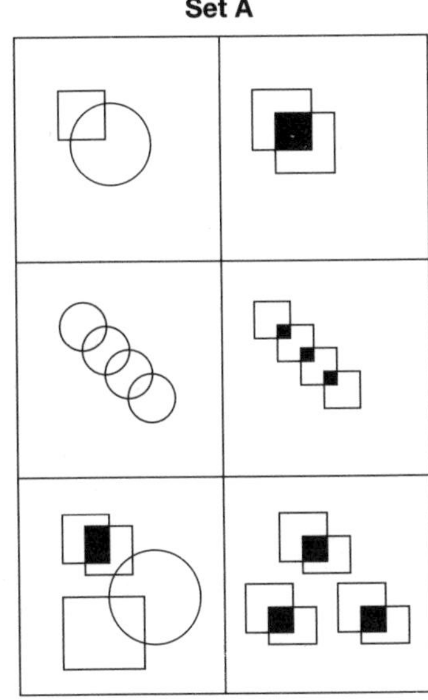

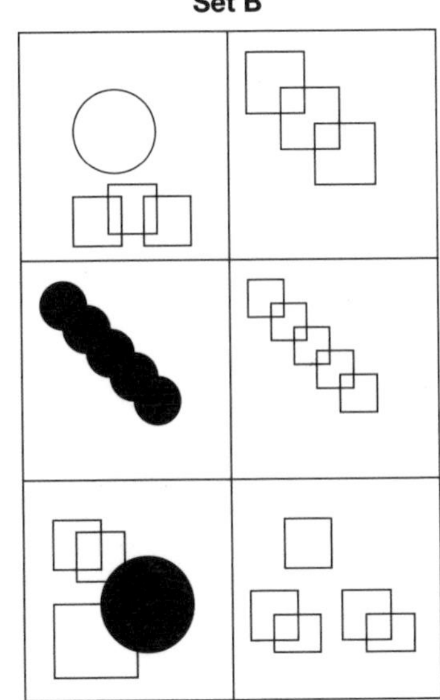

Answer

Q22.

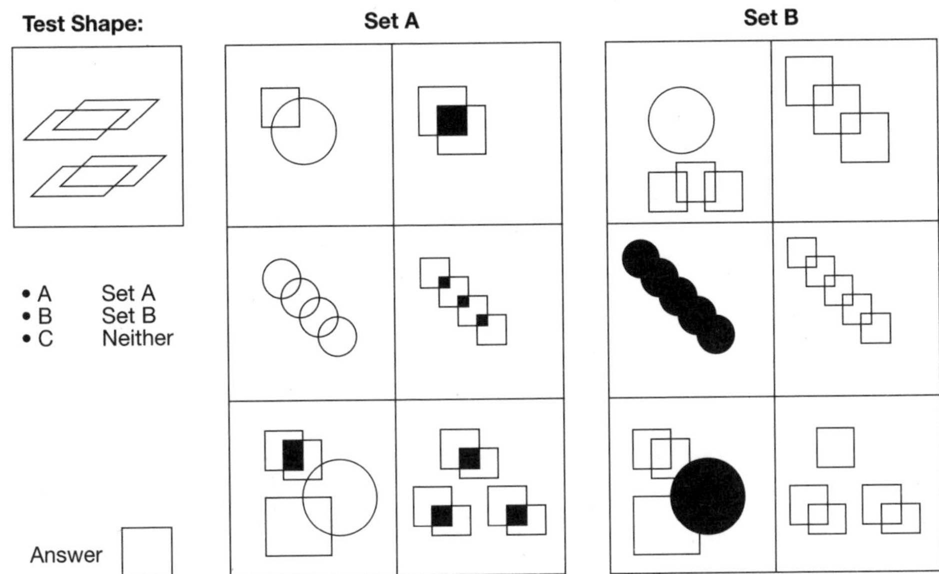

Q23.

Test Shape:

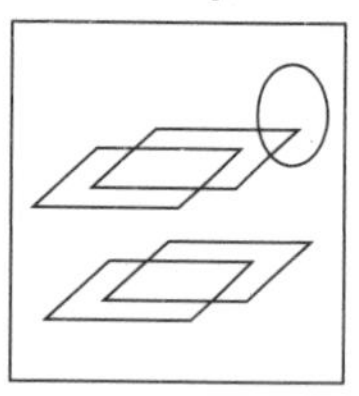

- A Set A
- B Set B
- C Neither

Answer

Set A

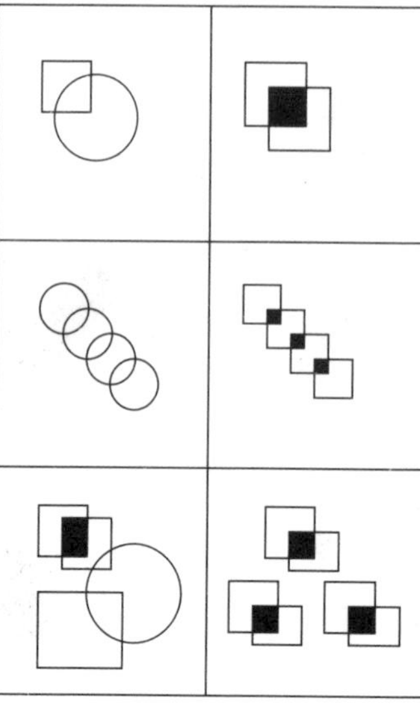

Set B

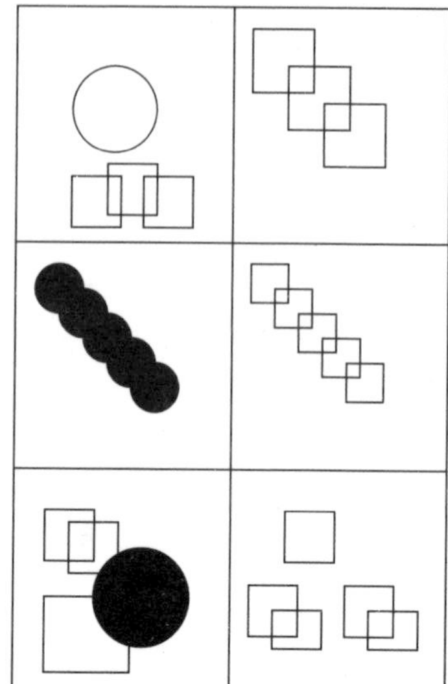

Q24.

Test Shape:

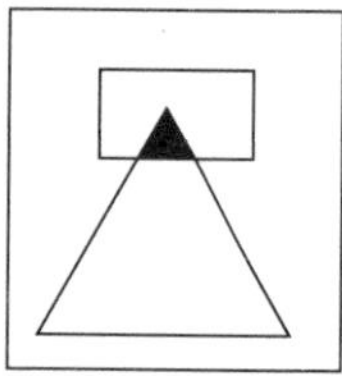

- A Set A
- B Set B
- C Neither

Answer

Set A

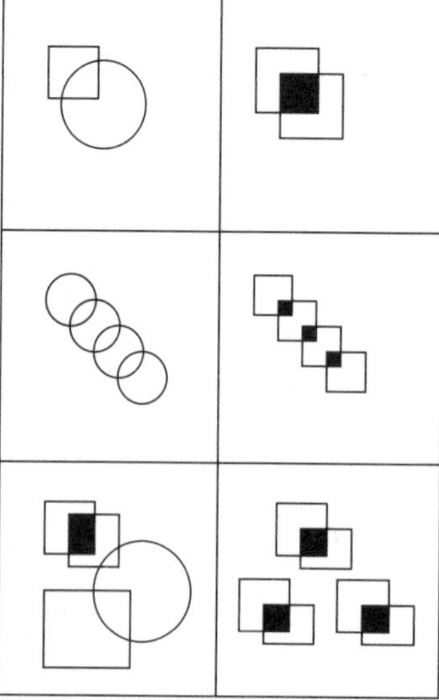

Set B

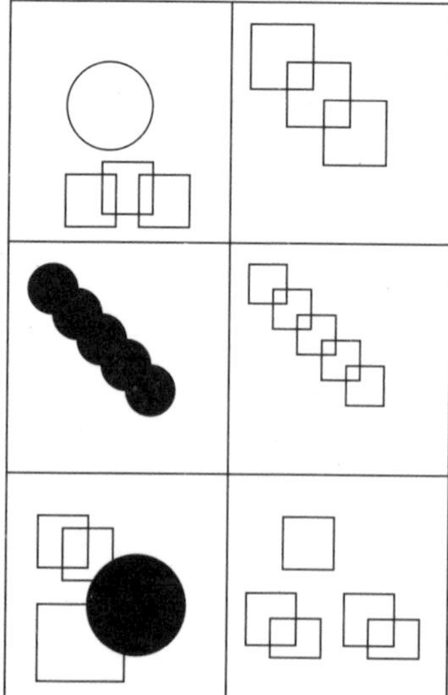

Q25.

Test Shape:

Set A

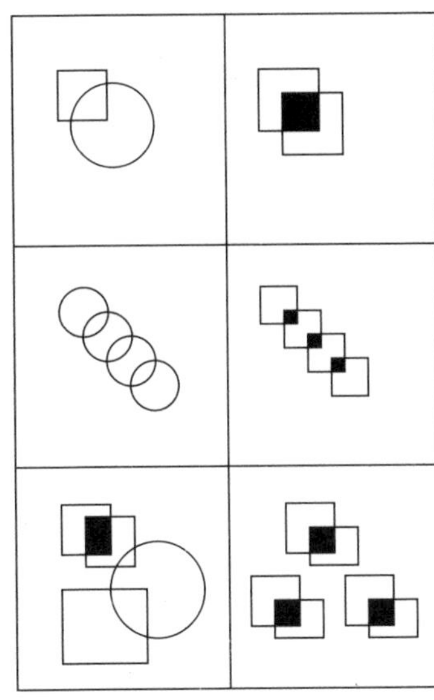

Set B

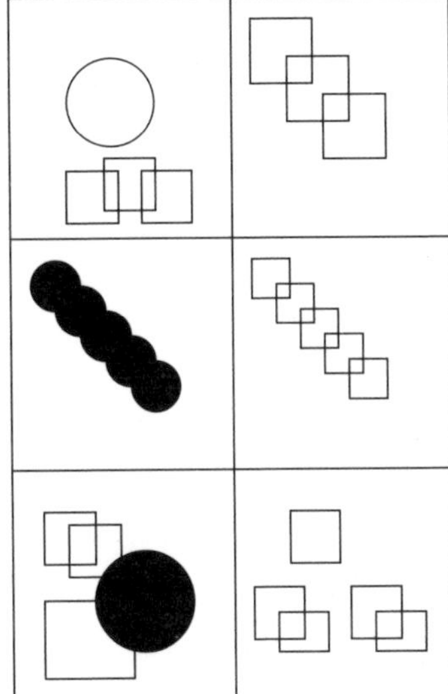

- A Set A
- B Set B
- C Neither

Answer

Q26.

Test Shape:

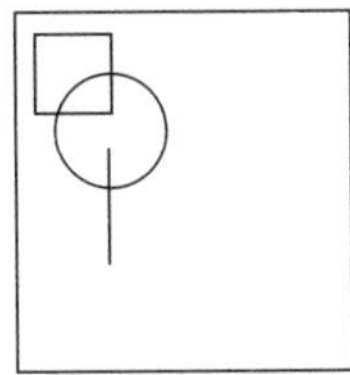

Set A

Set B

- A Set A
- B Set B
- C Neither

Answer 

Q27.

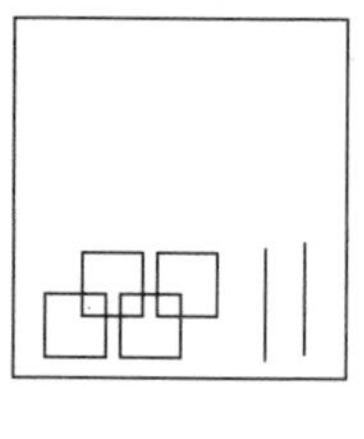

Set A

Set B

- A Set A
- B Set B
- C Neither

Answer

Q28.

Test Shape:

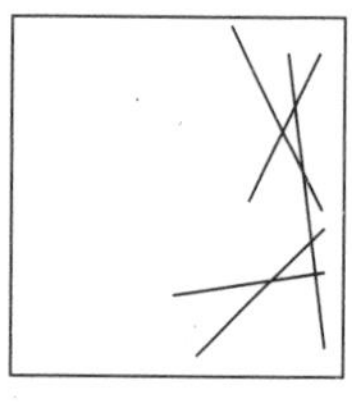

Set A

Set B

- A Set A
- B Set B
- C Neither

Answer

Q29.

Test Shape:

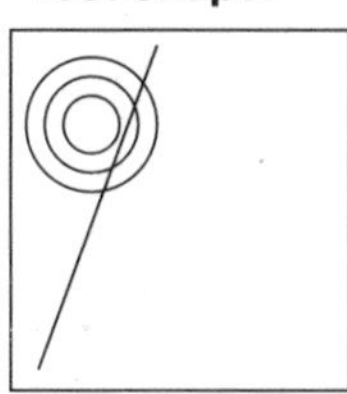

Set A

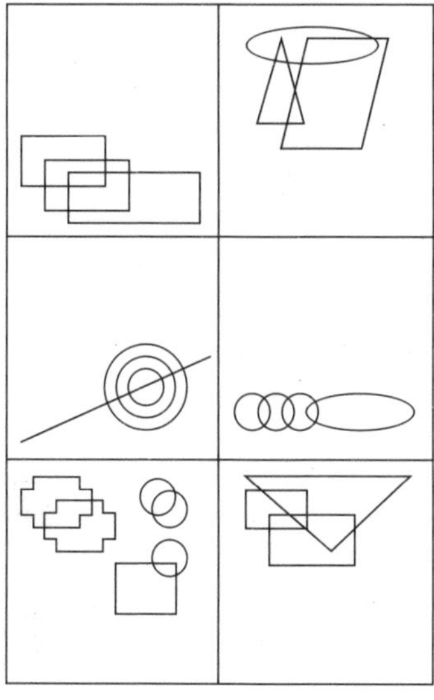

Set B

- A Set A
- B Set B
- C Neither

Answer

Q30.

Test Shape:

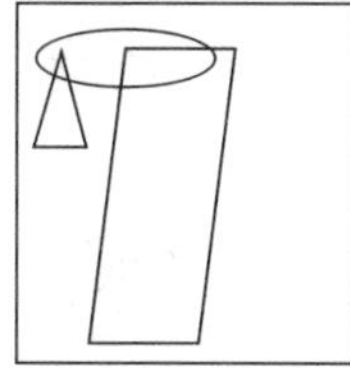

Set A

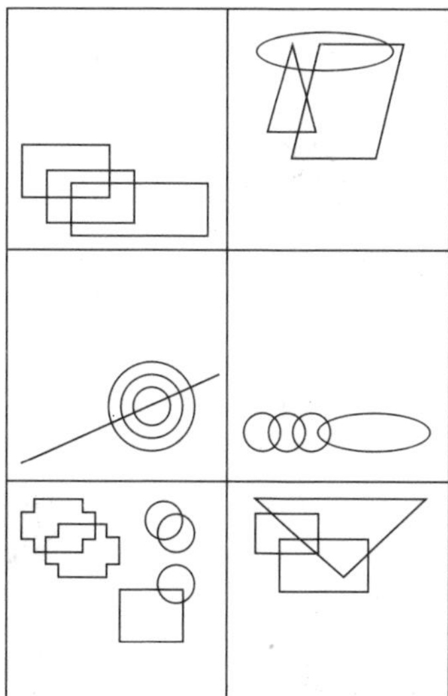

Set B

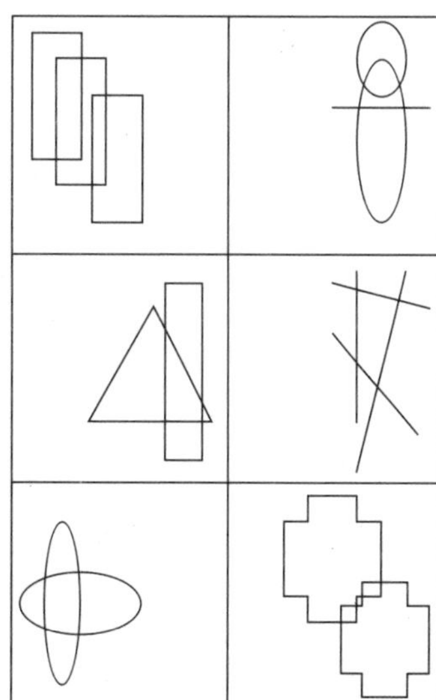

- A Set A
- B Set B
- C Neither

Answer

Q31.

Test Shape:

- A Set A
- B Set B
- C Neither

Answer

Set A

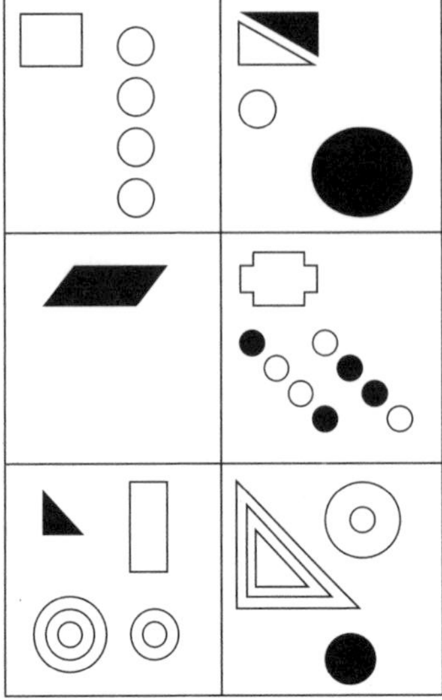

Set B

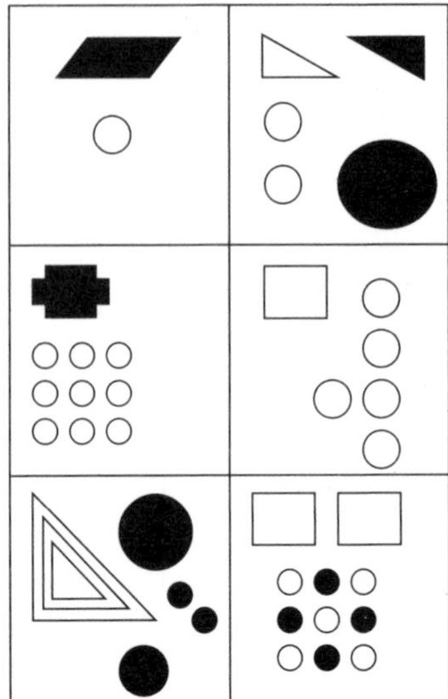

Q32.

Test Shape:

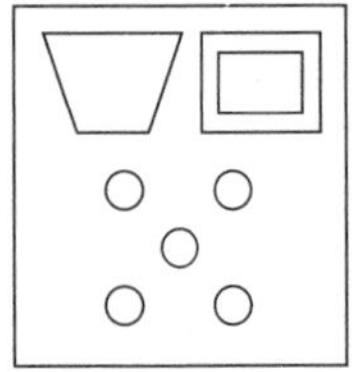

- A Set A
- B Set B
- C Neither

Answer

Set A

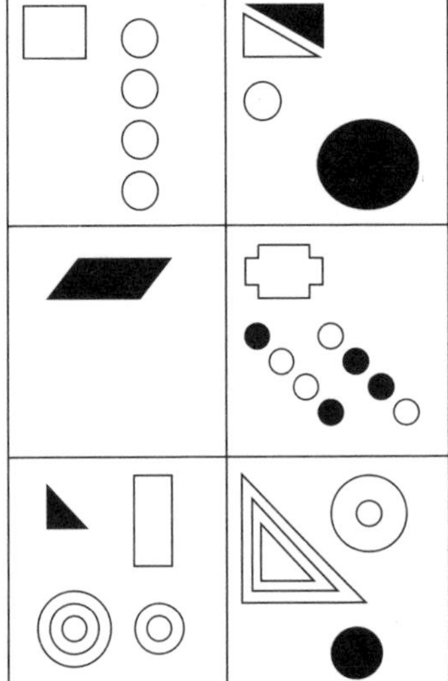

Set B

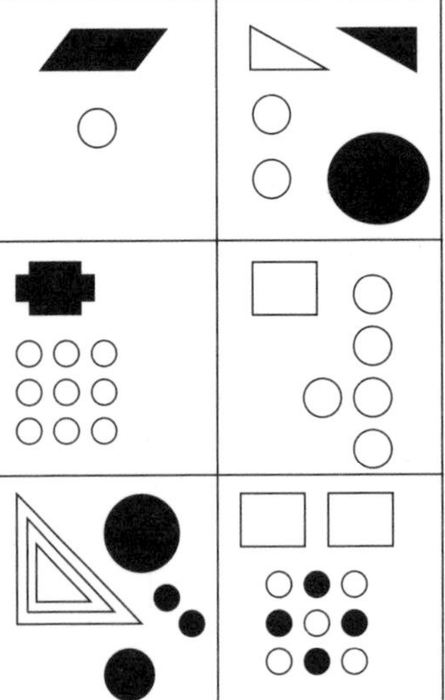

Q33.

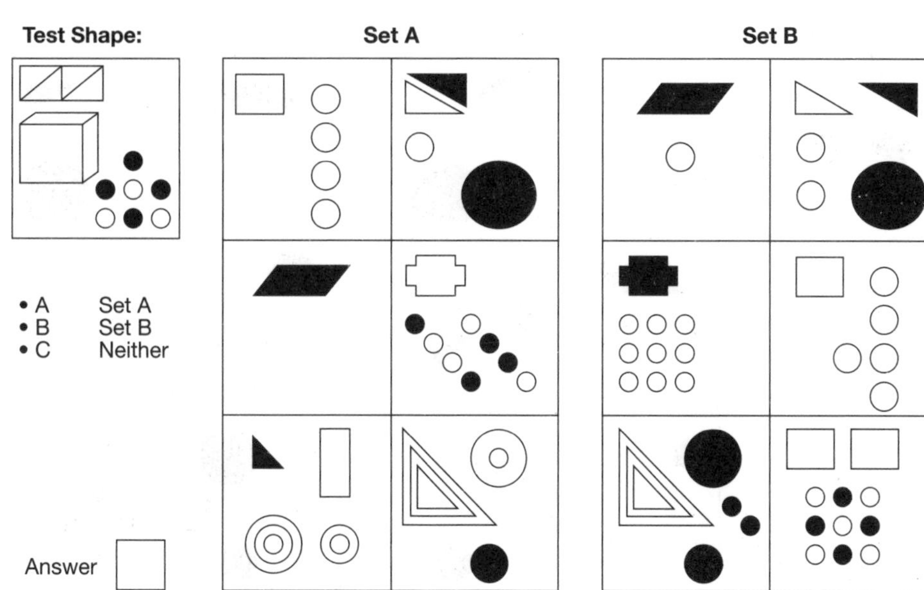
Test Shape:
Set A
Set B
• A Set A
• B Set B
• C Neither
Answer

Q34.

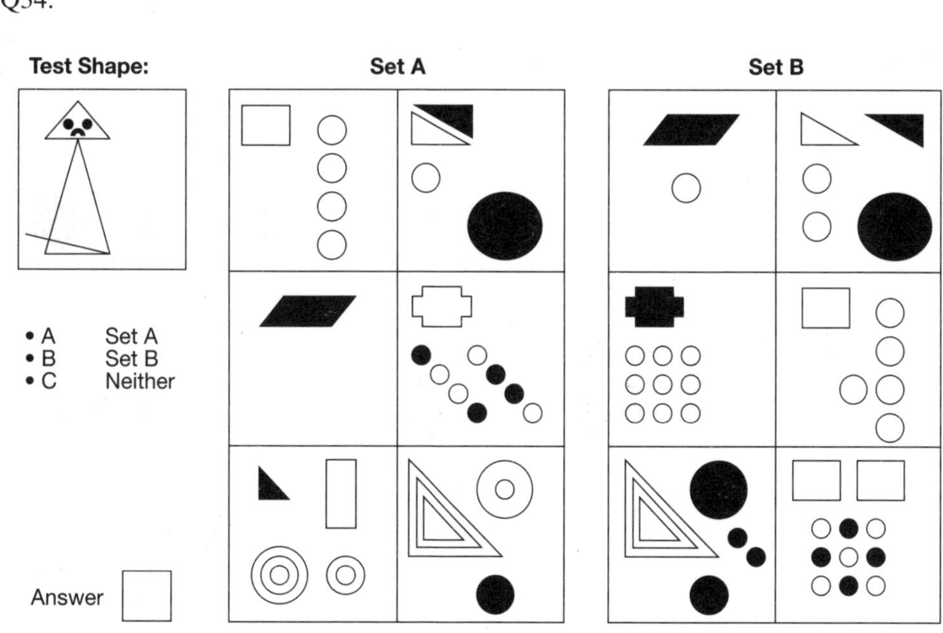
Test Shape:
Set A
Set B
• A Set A
• B Set B
• C Neither
Answer

Q35.

Test Shape:

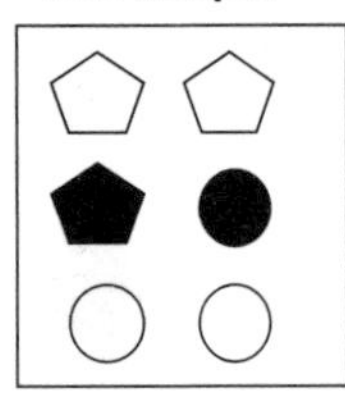

Set A

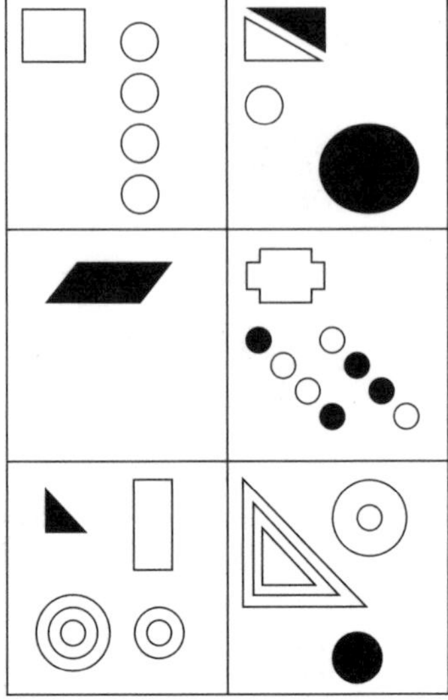

Set B

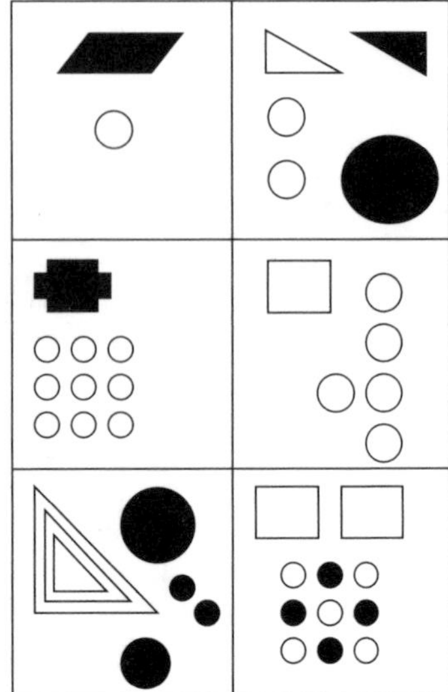

- A Set A
- B Set B
- C Neither

Answer

Q36.

Test Shape:

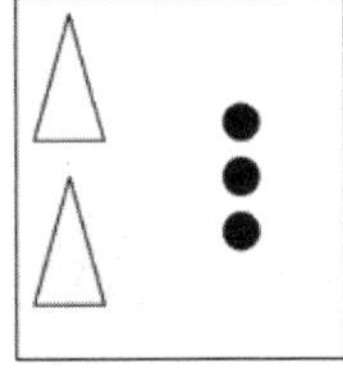

Set A

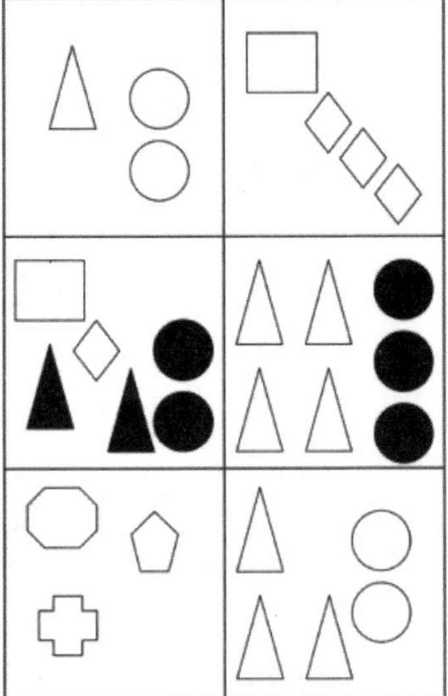

Set B

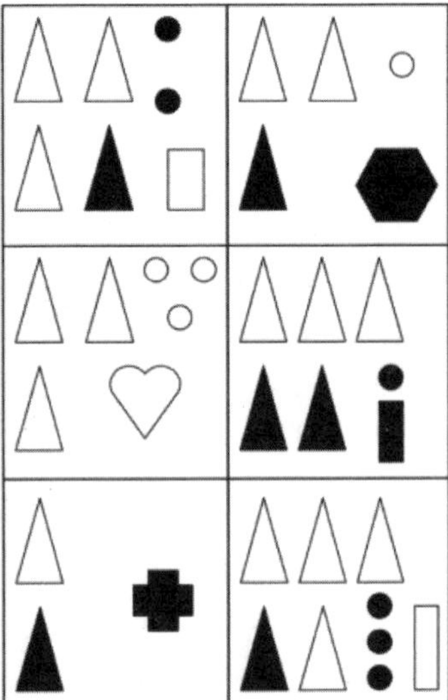

- A Set A
- B Set B
- C Neither

Answer

Q37.

Set A

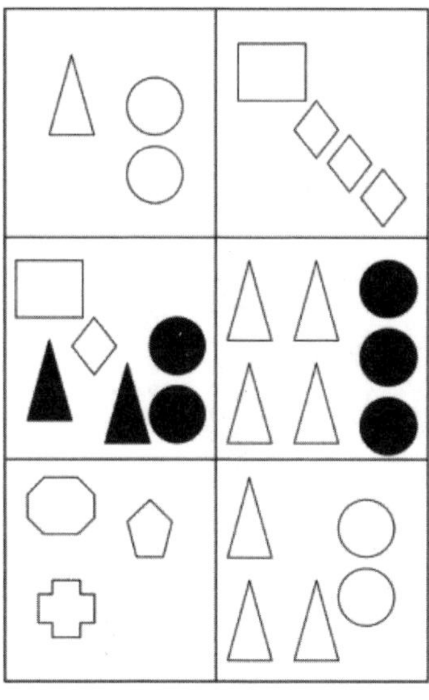

Set B

- A Set A
- B Set B
- C Neither

Answer ☐

Q38.

Test Shape:

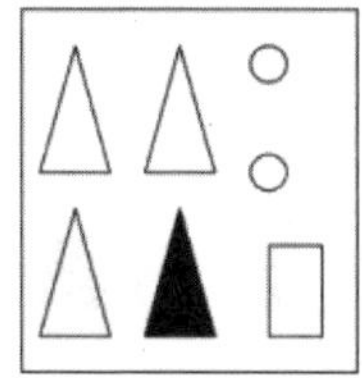

Set A

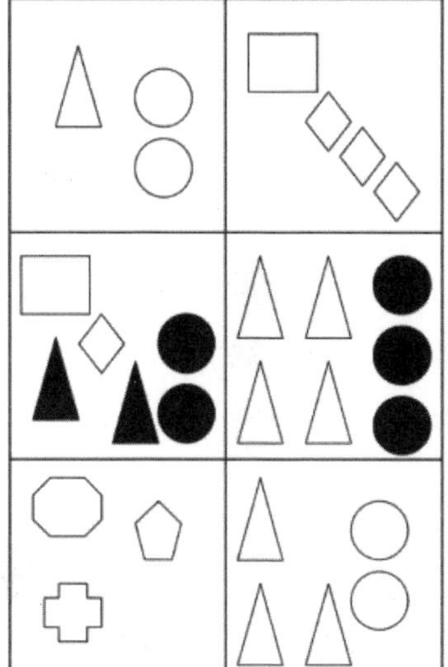

Set B

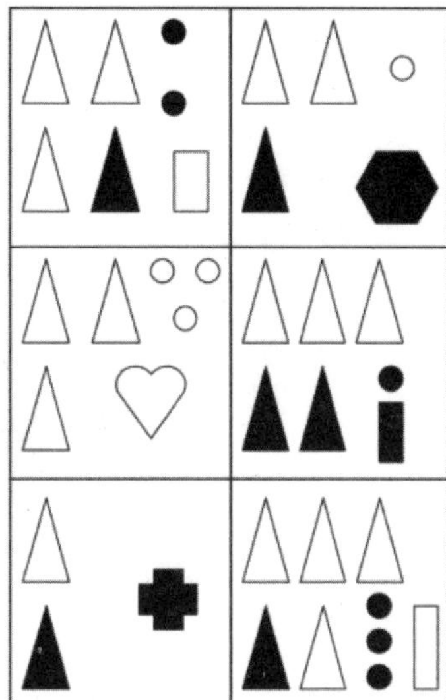

- A Set A
- B Set B
- C Neither

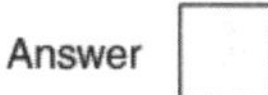

Q39.

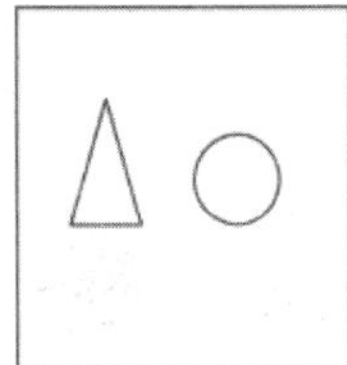

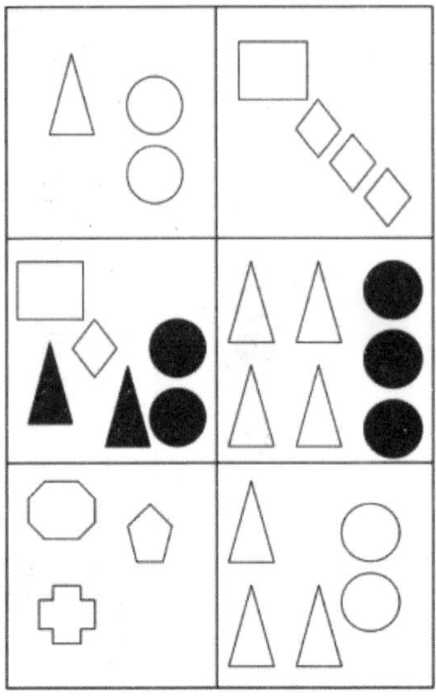

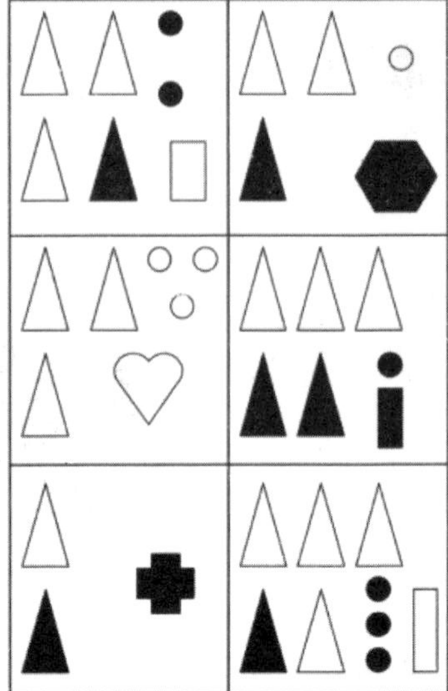

- A Set A
- B Set B
- C Neither

Answer ☐

Q40.

Test Shape:

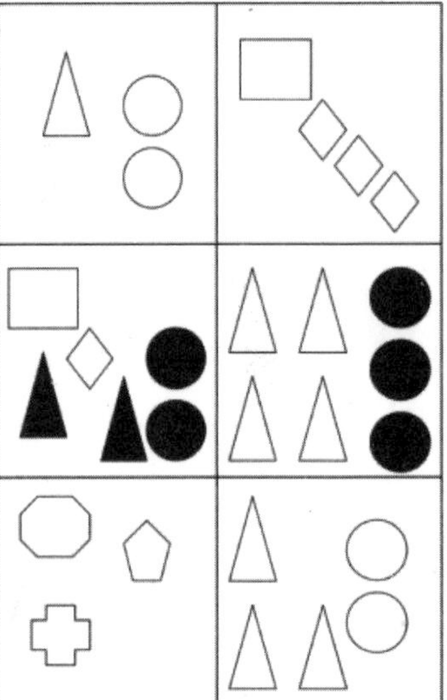

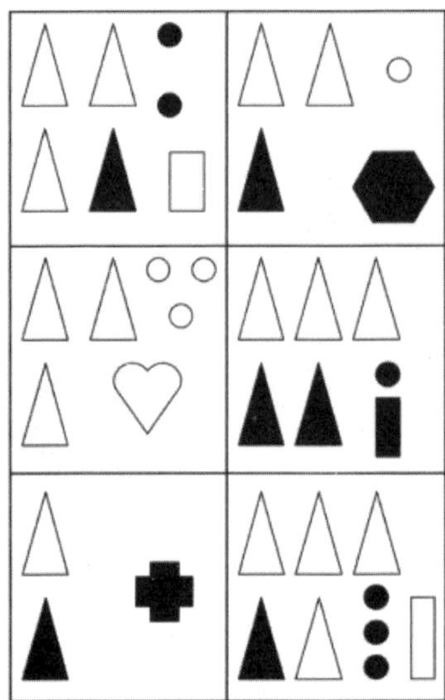

- A Set A
- B Set B
- C Neither

Answer ☐

Q41.

Test Shape:

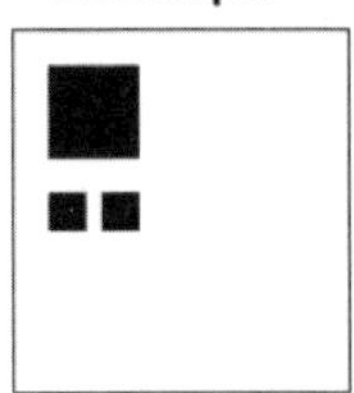

Set A

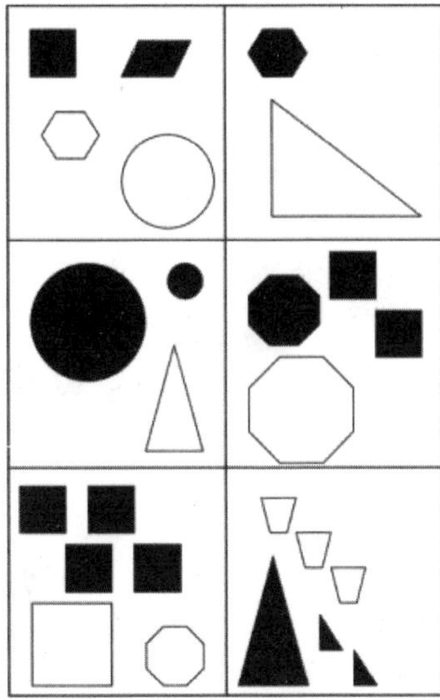

Set B

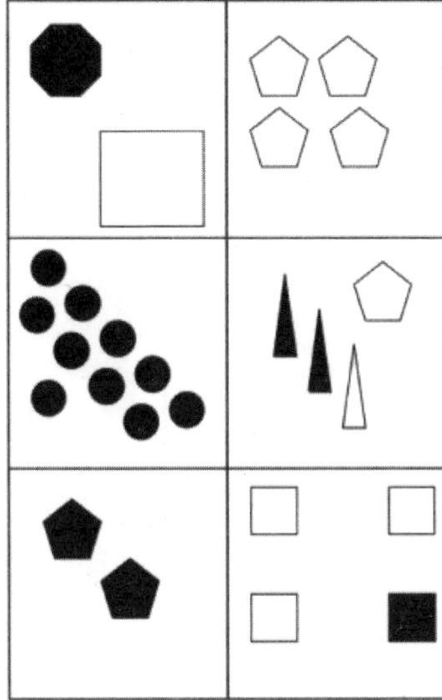

- A Set A
- B Set B
- C Neither

Answer

Q42.

Test Shape:

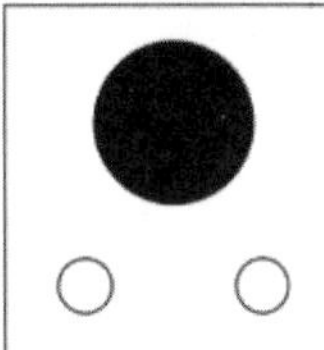

Set A

Set B

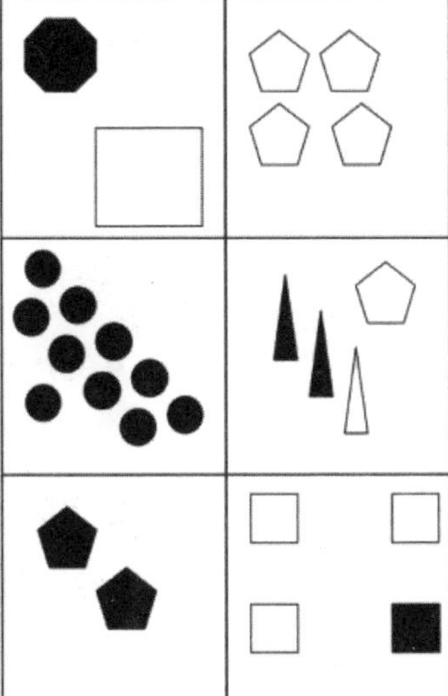

- A Set A
- B Set B
- C Neither

Answer

Q43.

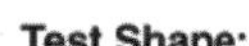

Set A **Set B**

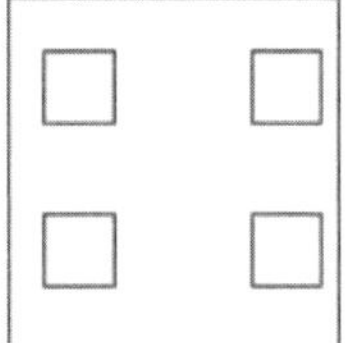

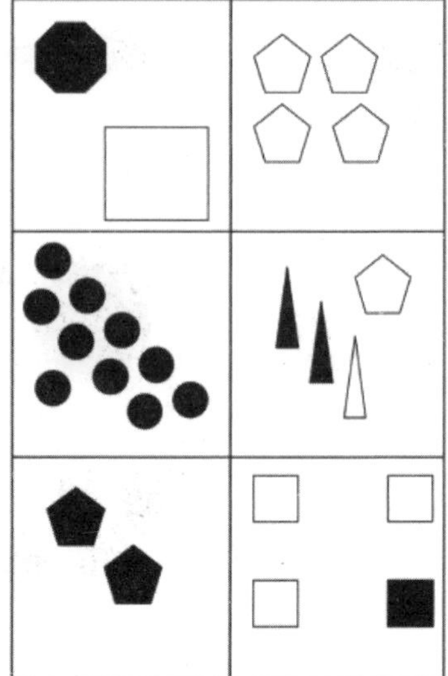

- A Set A
- B Set B
- C Neither

Answer

Q44.

Test Shape:

Set A **Set B**

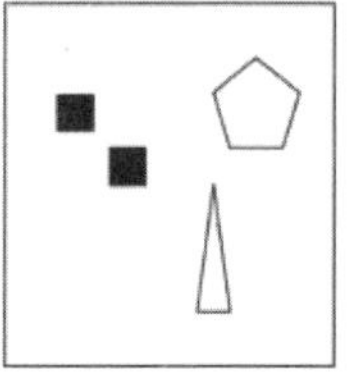

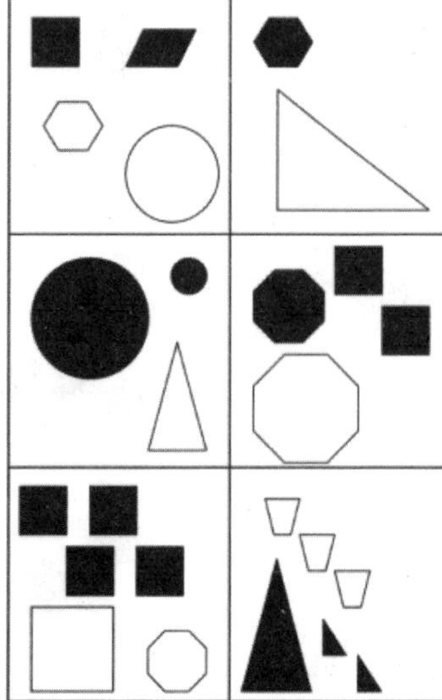

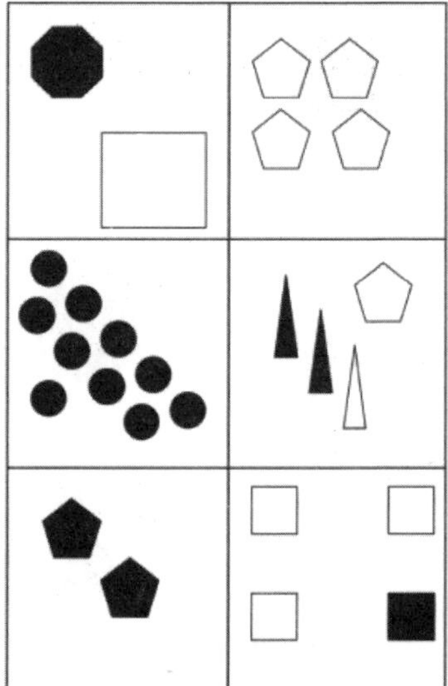

- A Set A
- B Set B
- C Neither

Answer

Q45.

Test Shape:

Set A

Set B

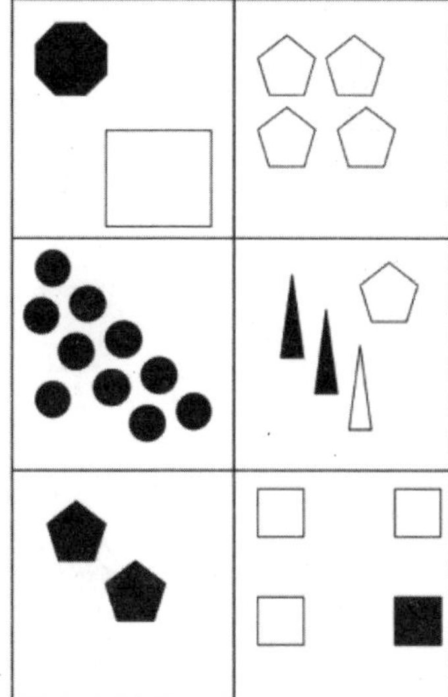

- A Set A
- B Set B
- C Neither

Answer

Q46.

Test Shape:

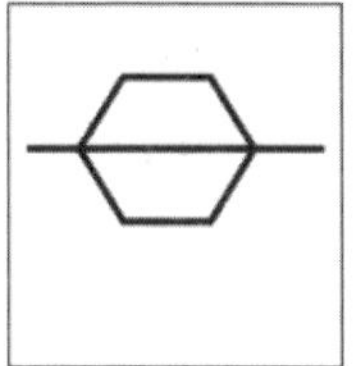

Set A

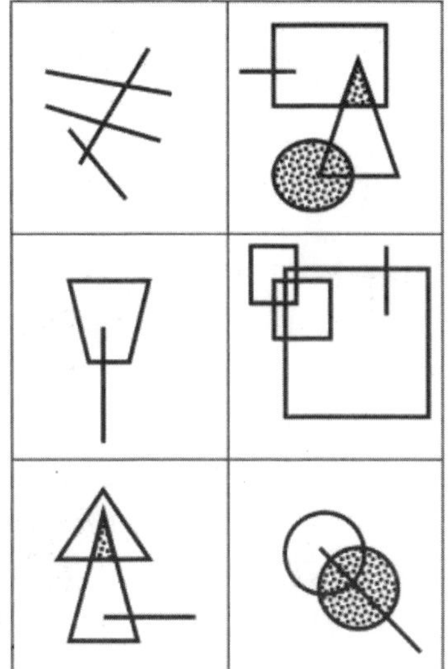

Set B

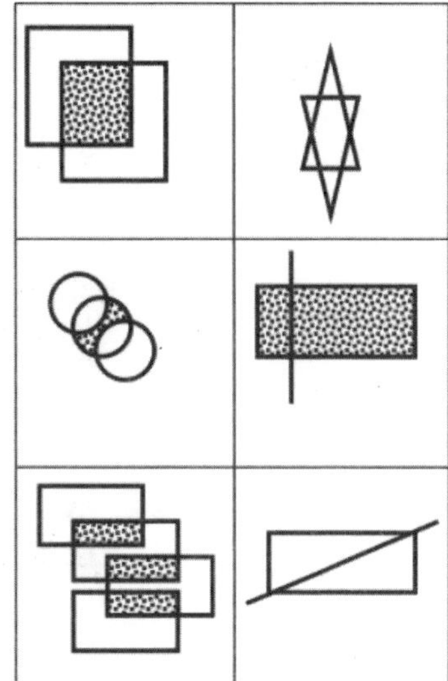

- A Set A
- B Set B
- C Neither

Answer

Q47.

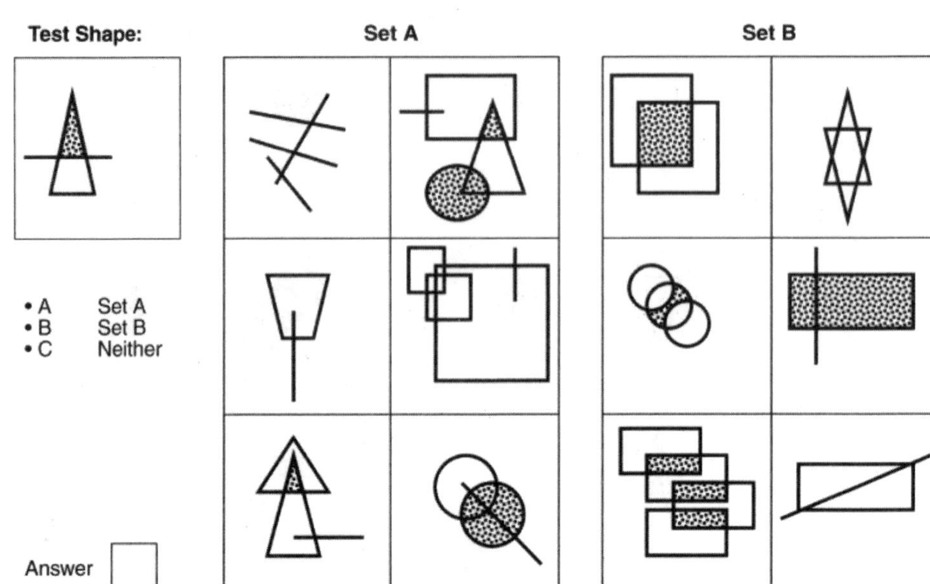
Test Shape:
Set A
Set B
• A Set A
• B Set B
• C Neither
Answer

Q48.

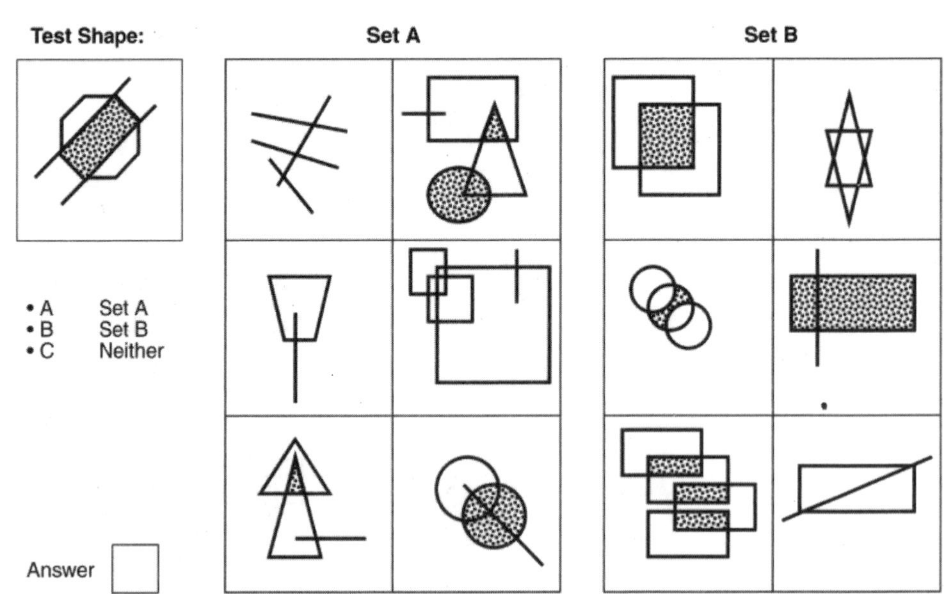
Test Shape:
Set A
Set B
• A Set A
• B Set B
• C Neither
Answer

Q49.

Test Shape:

Set A

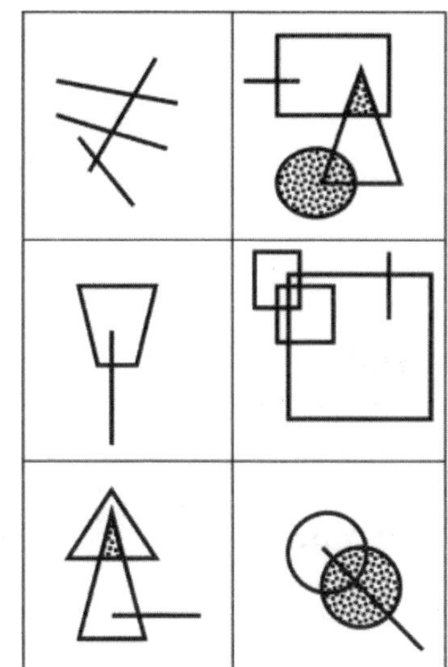

Set B

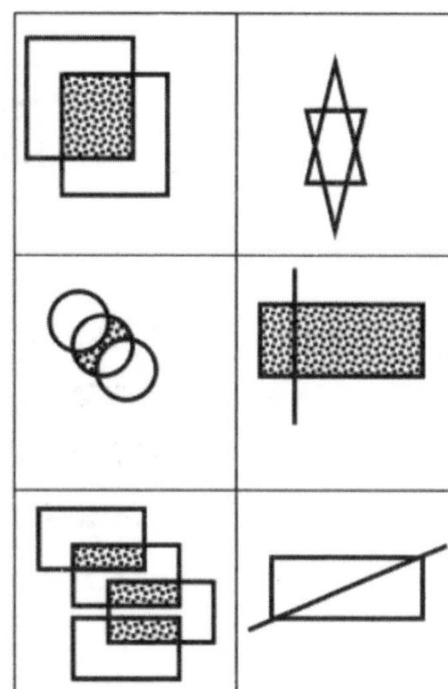

- A Set A
- B Set B
- C Neither

Answer

Q50.

Test Shape:

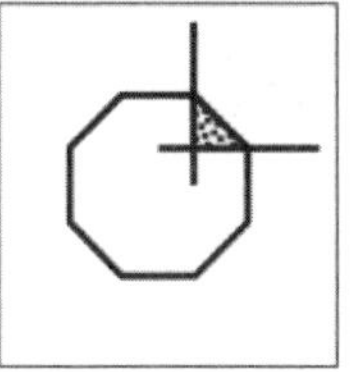

Set A

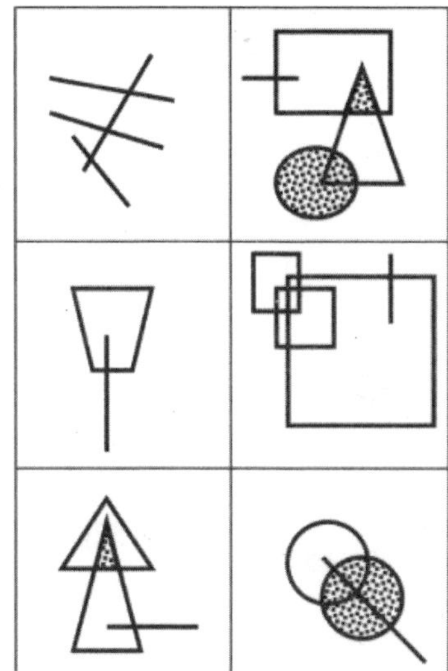

Set B

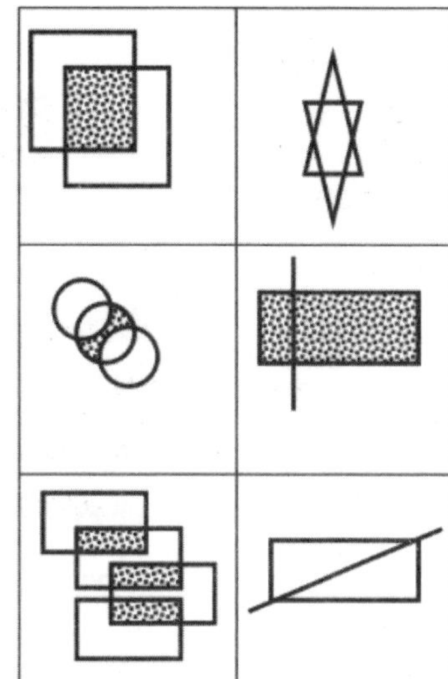

- A Set A
- B Set B
- C Neither

Answer

Q51.

Test Shape:

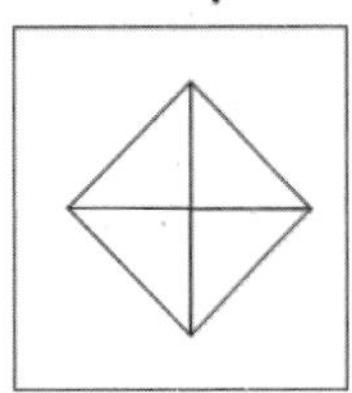

Set A

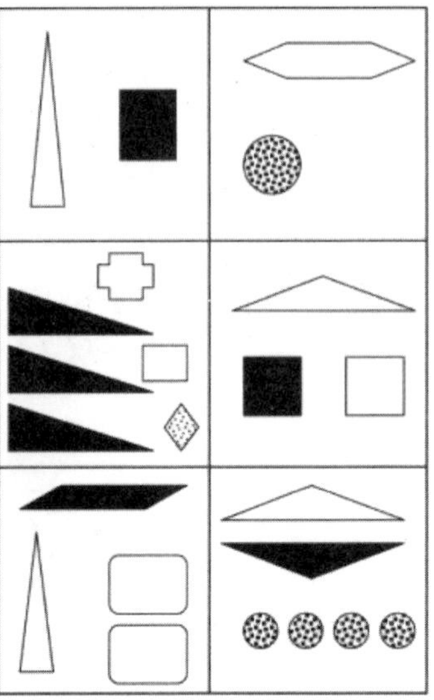

Set B

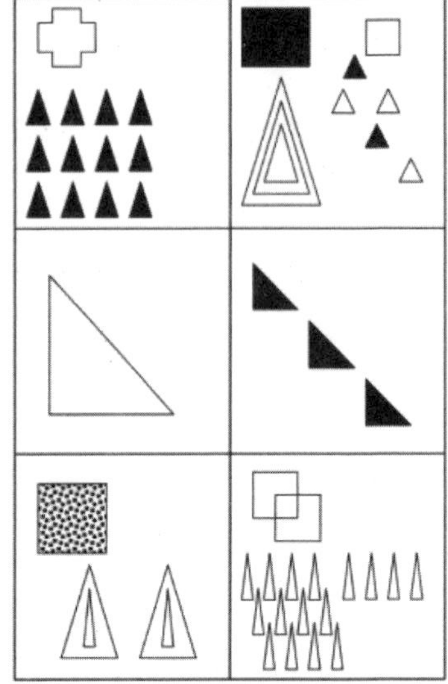

- A Set A
- B Set B
- C Neither

Answer

Q52.

Test Shape:

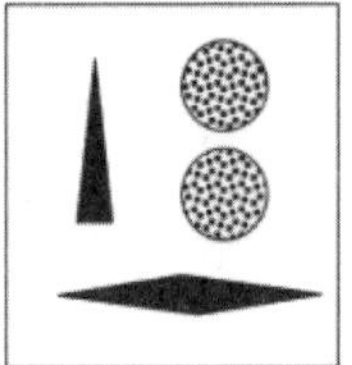

Set A

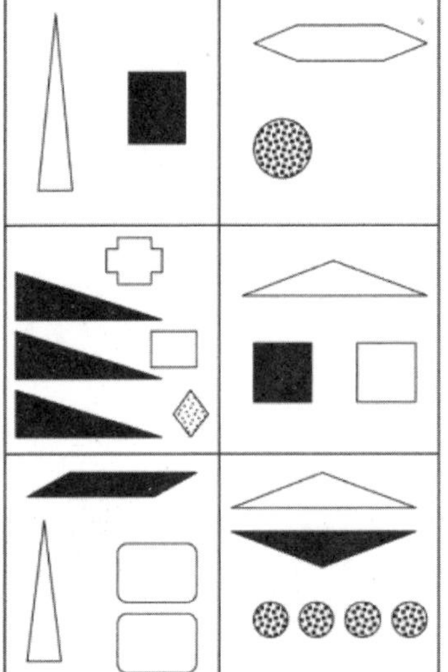

Set B

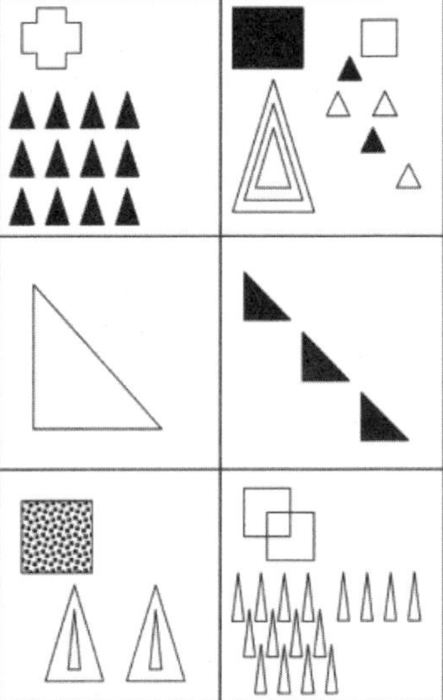

- A Set A
- B Set B
- C Neither

Answer

Q53.

Test Shape:

Set A

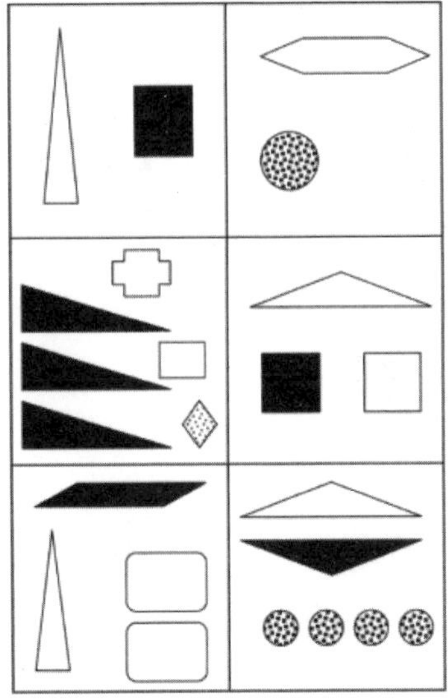

Set B

- A Set A
- B Set B
- C Neither

Answer ☐

Q54.

Test Shape:

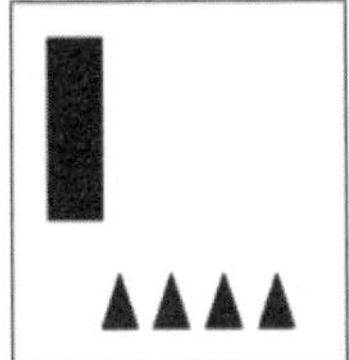

Set A

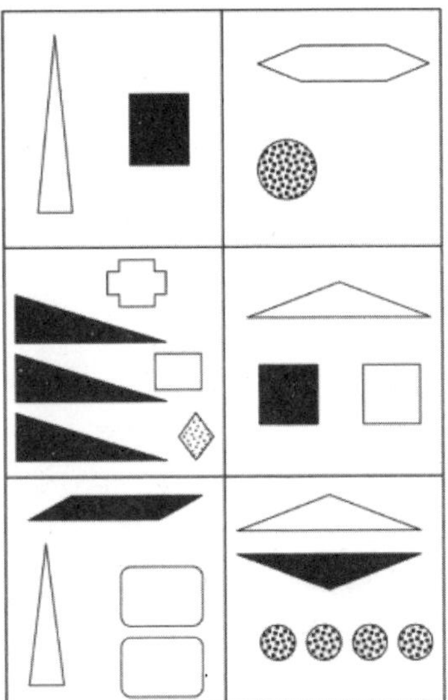

Set B

- A Set A
- B Set B
- C Neither

Answer ☐

Q55.

Set A

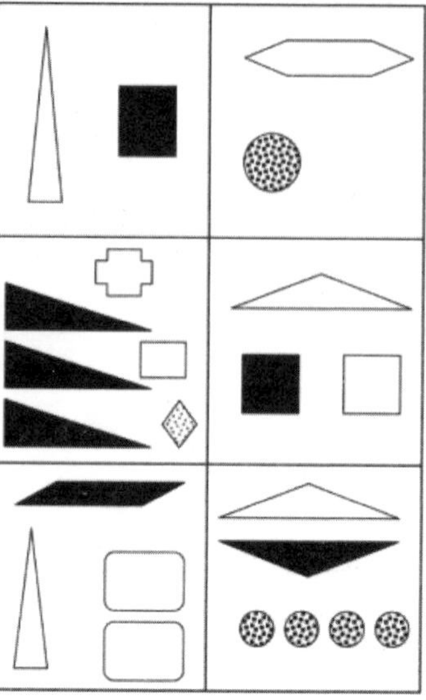

Set B

- A Set A
- B Set B
- C Neither

Answer ☐

Q56.

Test Shape:

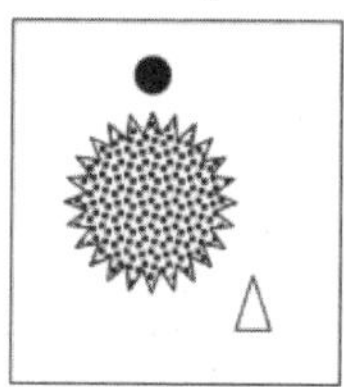

Set A

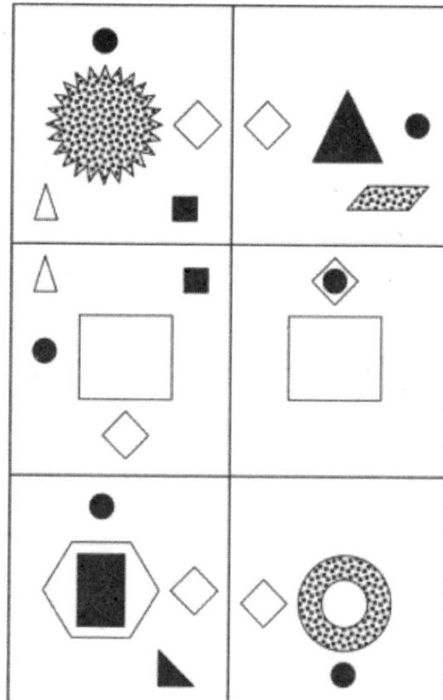

Set B

- A Set A
- B Set B
- C Neither

Answer ☐

Q57.

Test Shape:

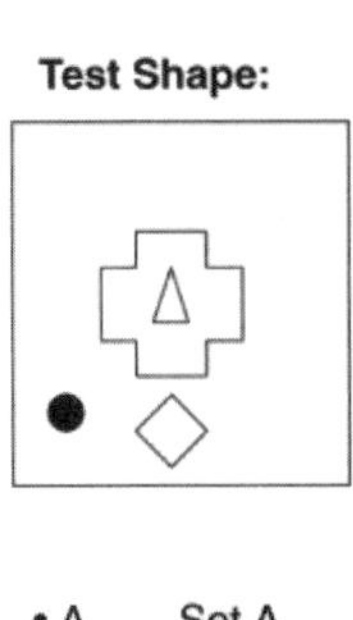

Set A

Set B

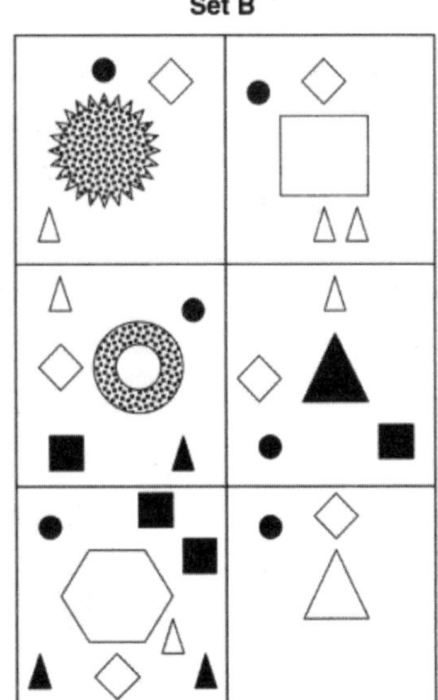

- A Set A
- B Set B
- C Neither

Answer

Q58.

Test Shape:

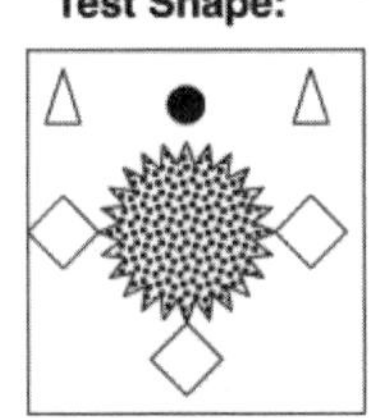

Set A

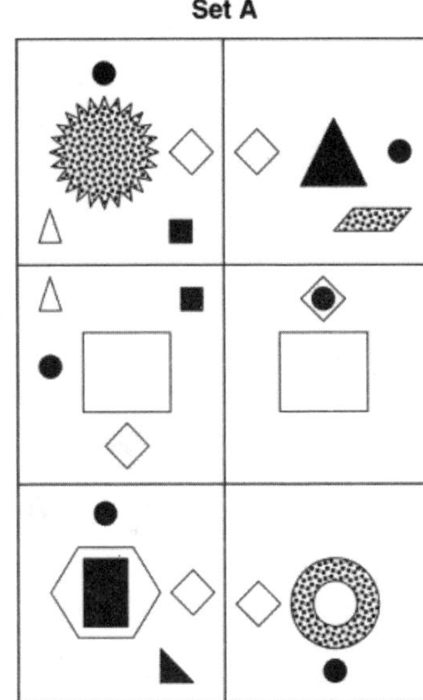

Set B

- A Set A
- B Set B
- C Neither

Answer

Q59.

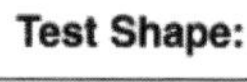

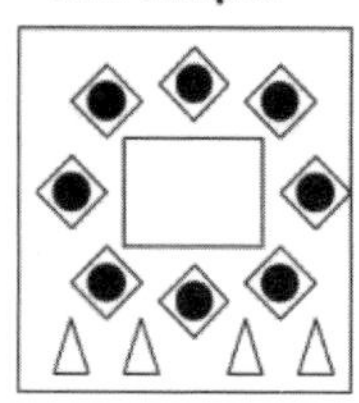

Set A

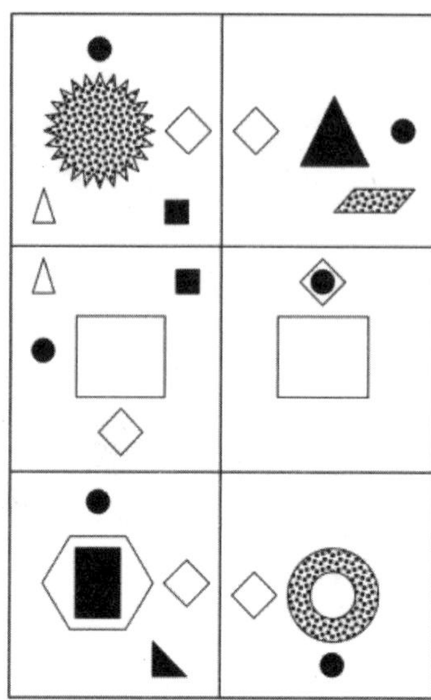

Set B

- A Set A
- B Set B
- C Neither

Answer

Q60.

Test Shape:

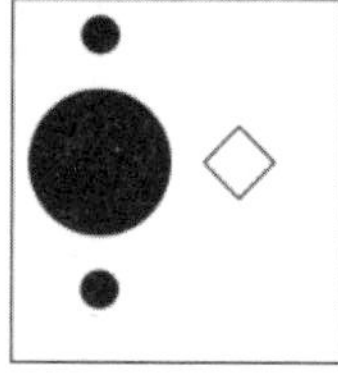

Set A

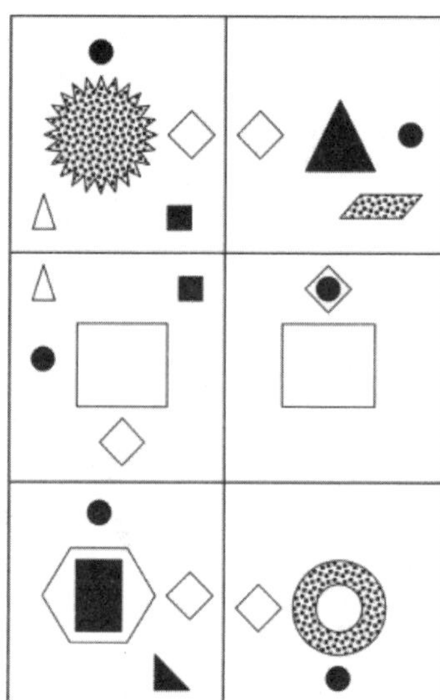

Set B

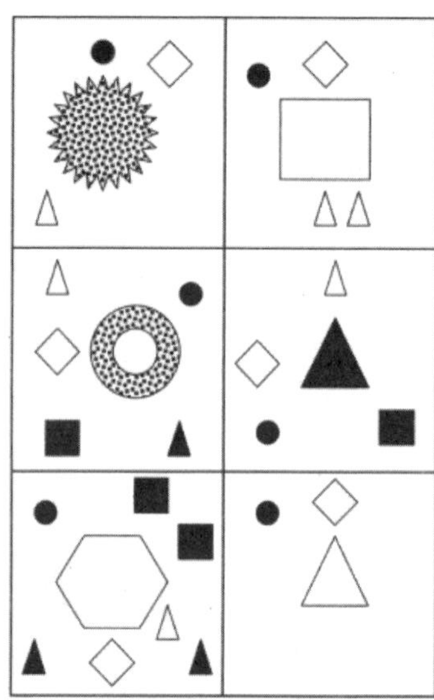

- A Set A
- B Set B
- C Neither

Answer

Q61.

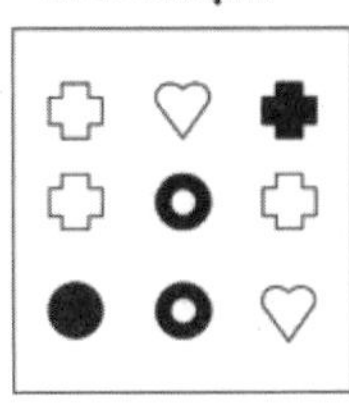

Set A

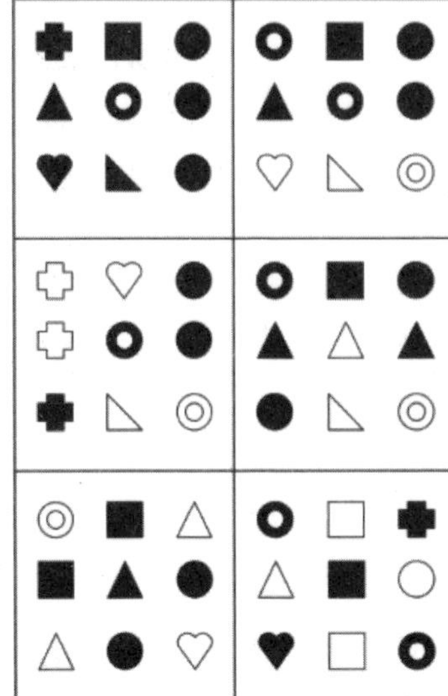

Set B

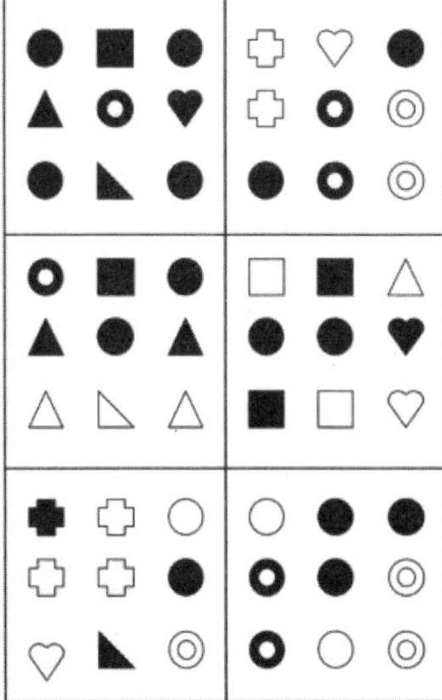

- A Set A
- B Set B
- C Neither

Answer

Q62.

Test Shape:

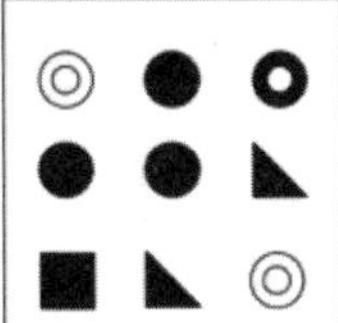

Set A

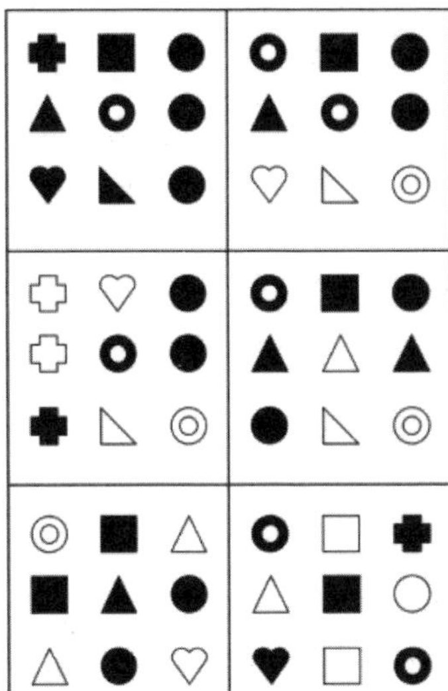

Set B

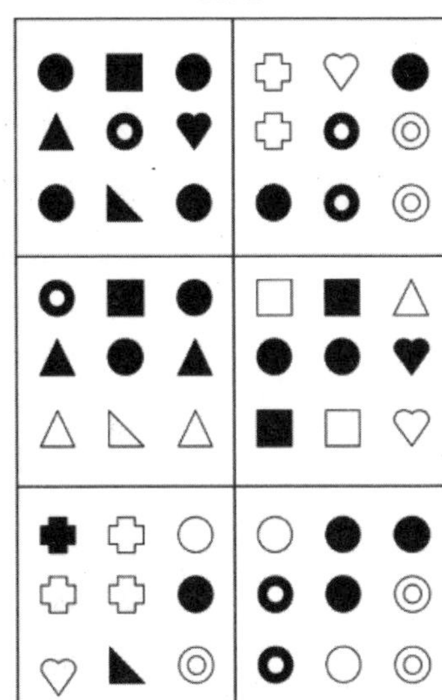

- A Set A
- B Set B
- C Neither

Answer

Q63.

Test Shape:

Set A

Set B

- A Set A
- B Set B
- C Neither

Answer

Q64.

Test Shape:

Set A

Set B

- A Set A
- B Set B
- C Neither

Answer

Q65.

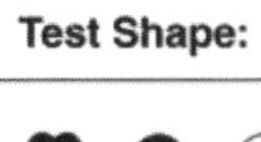

Test Shape:

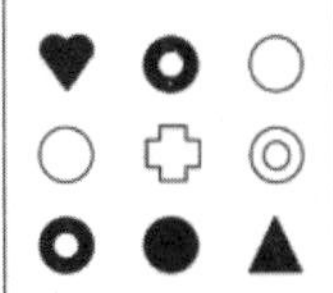

Set A

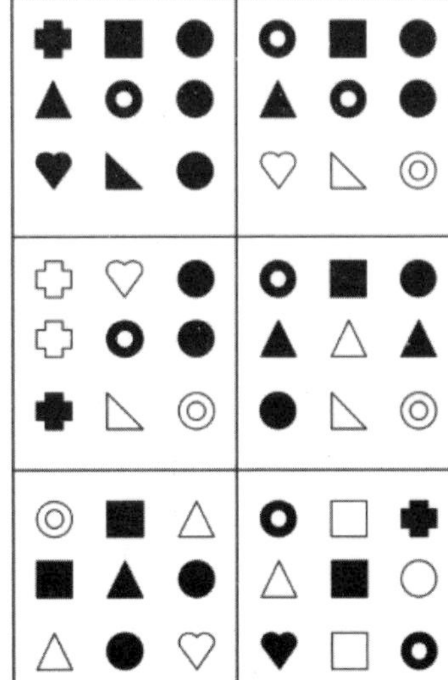

Set B

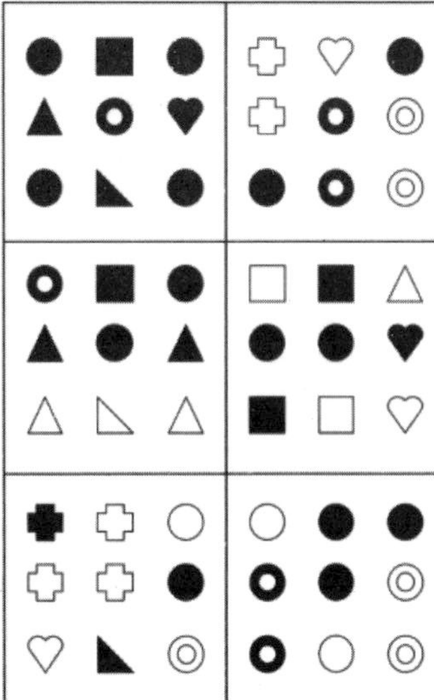

- A Set A
- B Set B
- C Neither

Answer ☐

Q66.

Test Shape:

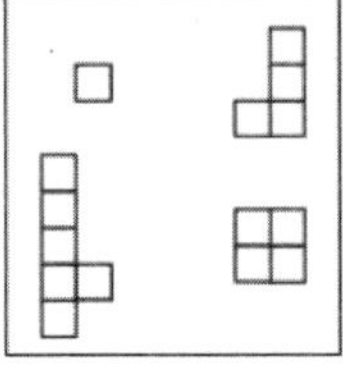

Set A

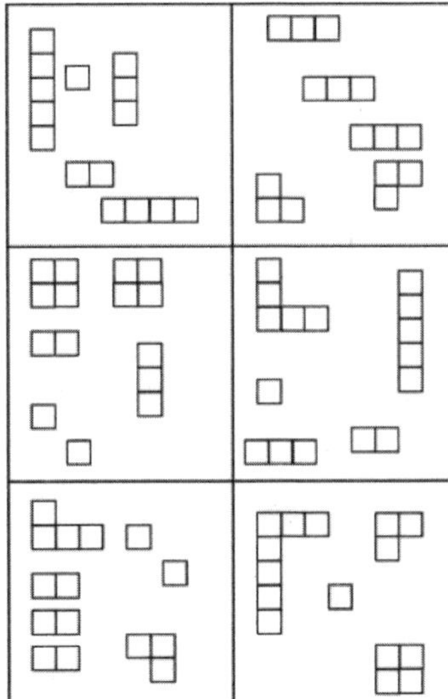

Set B

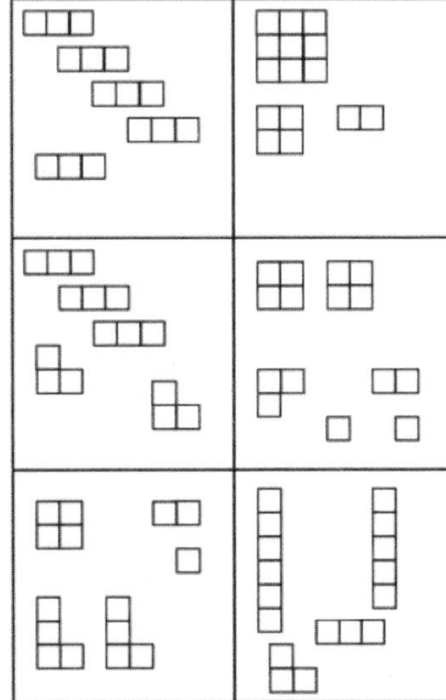

- A Set A
- B Set B
- C Neither

Answer ☐

Q67.

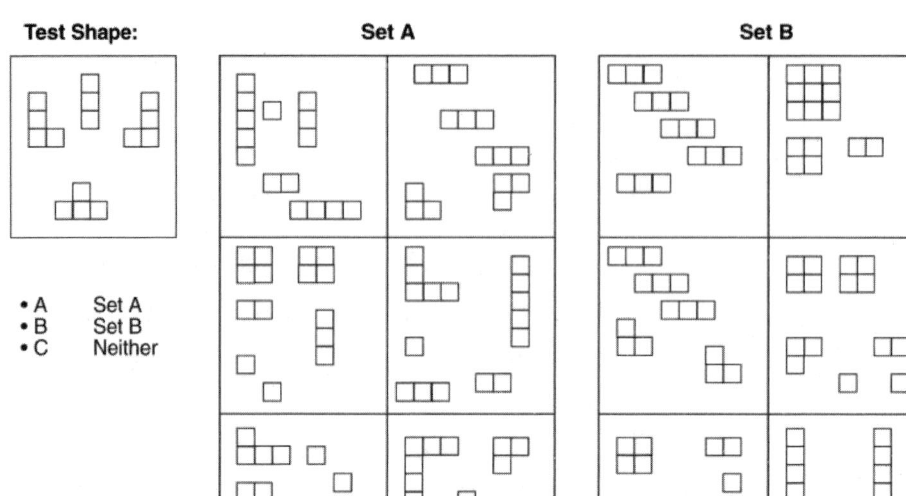
Test Shape:
Set A
Set B
• A Set A
• B Set B
• C Neither
Answer

Q68.

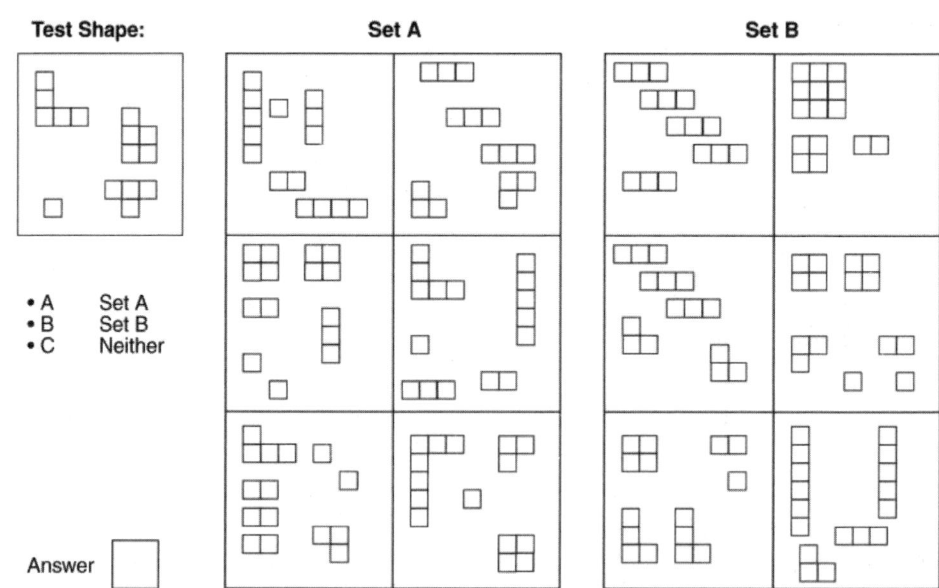
Test Shape:
Set A
Set B
• A Set A
• B Set B
• C Neither
Answer

Q69.

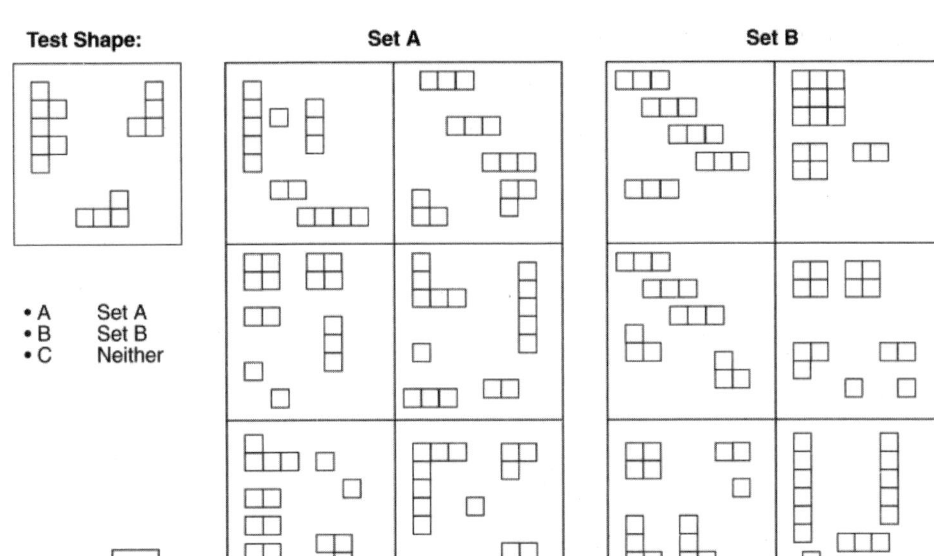
Test Shape:
Set A
Set B
• A Set A
• B Set B
• C Neither
Answer

Q70.

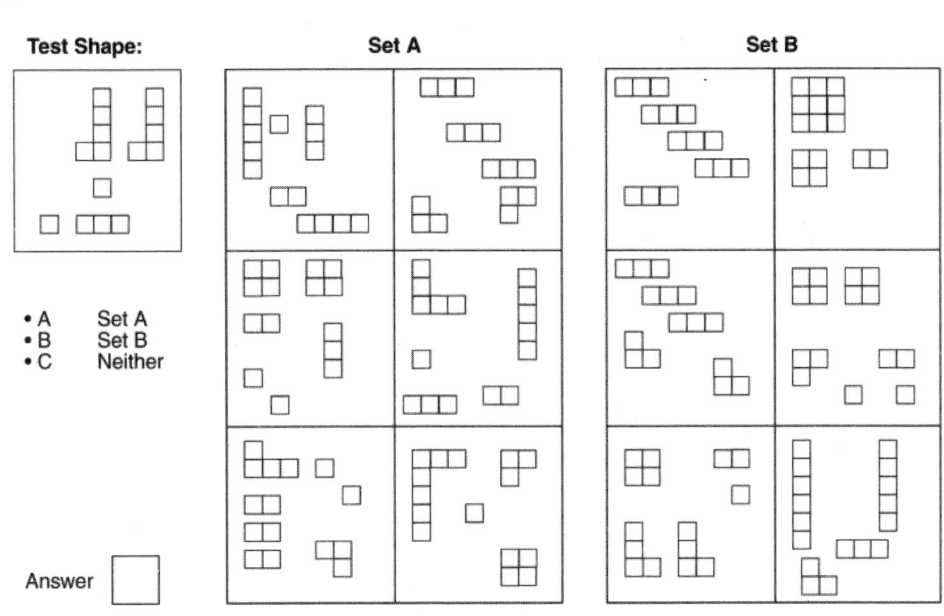
Test Shape:
Set A
Set B
• A Set A
• B Set B
• C Neither
Answer

Master class questions

The questions in the master class sections are harder than you'll find in the real test, but these are not supposed to make you anxious. We are providing them because it is proven that practising on more difficult material will give you the edge in the real test. If you can battle your way through these advanced questions under relaxed conditions, you are likely to do well in the real test answering easier questions when feeling anxious and under pressure.

Q71.

Test Shape:

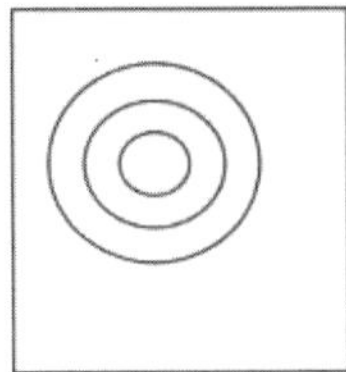

- A Set A
- B Set B
- C Neither

Answer

Set A

Set B

Q72.

Test Shape:

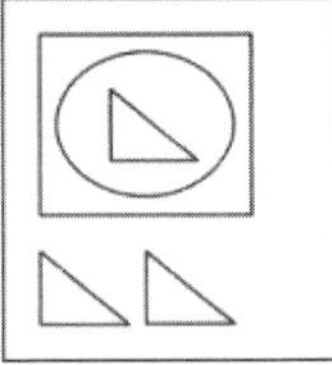

- A Set A
- B Set B
- C Neither

Answer

Set A

Set B

Q73.

Test Shape:

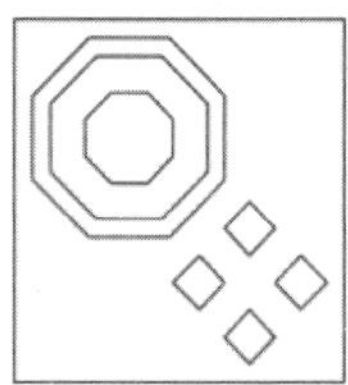

Set A

Set B

- A Set A
- B Set B
- C Neither

Answer

Q74.

Test Shape:

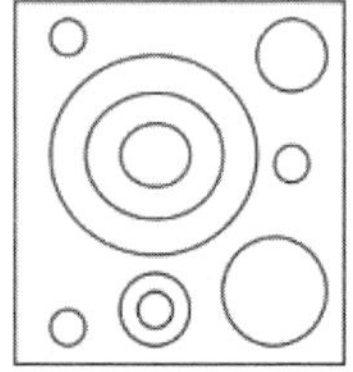

Set A

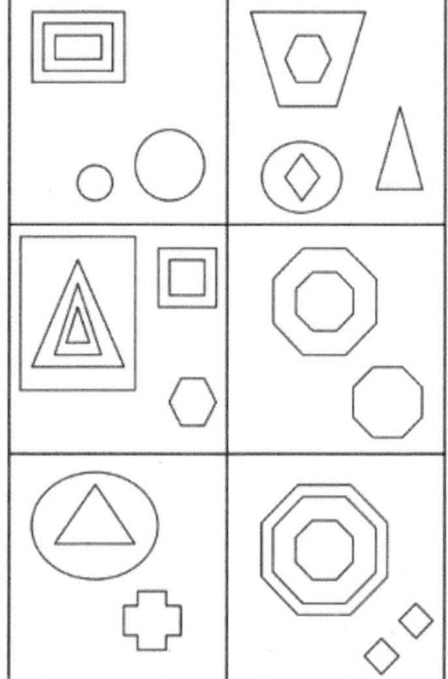

Set B

- A Set A
- B Set B
- C Neither

Answer

Q75.

Test Shape:

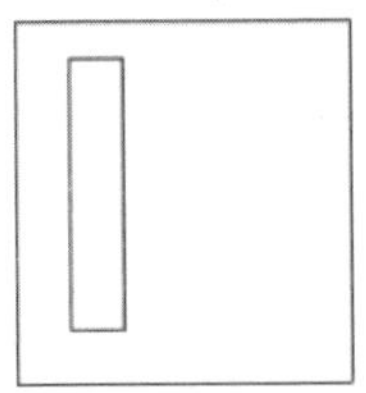

Set A

Set B

- A Set A
- B Set B
- C Neither

Answer

Q76.

Test Shape:

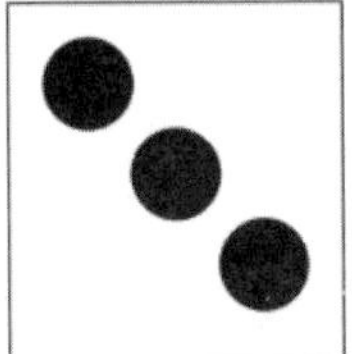

Set A

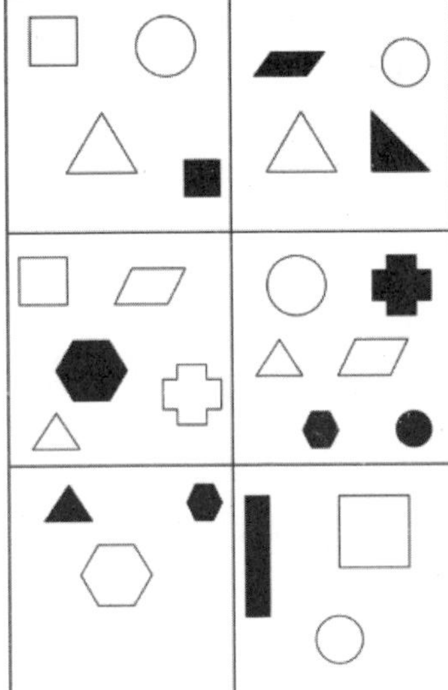

Set B

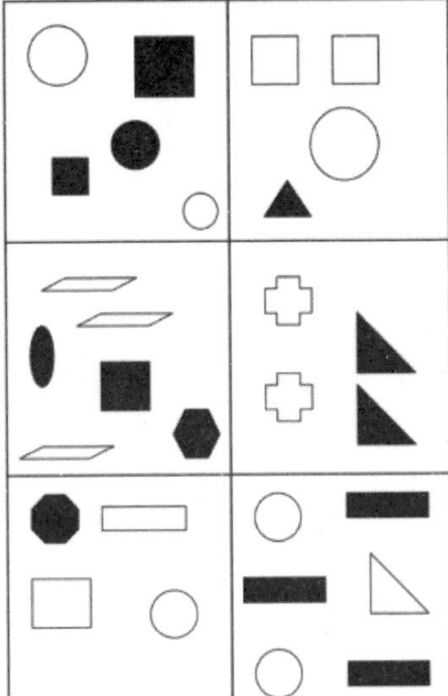

- A Set A
- B Set B
- C Neither

Answer

Q77.

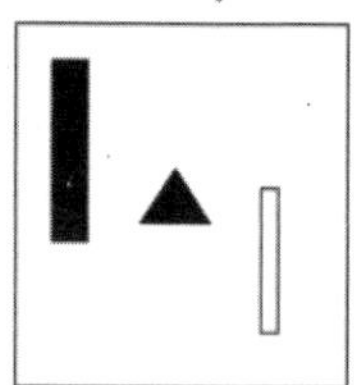

Set A

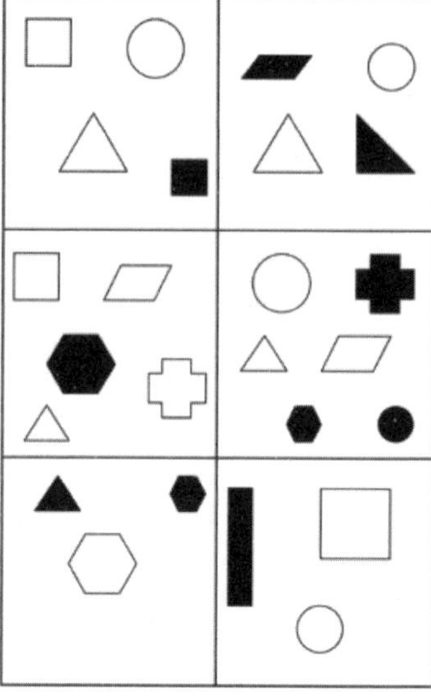

Set B

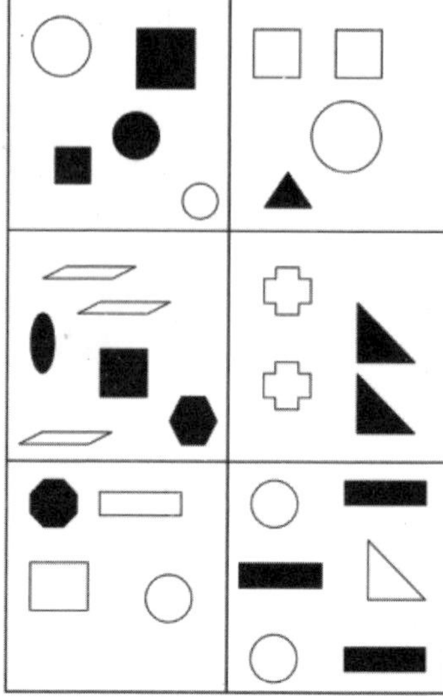

- A Set A
- B Set B
- C Neither

Answer

Q78.

Test Shape:

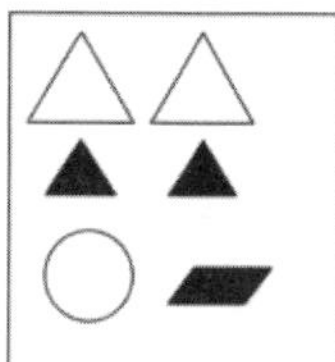

Set A

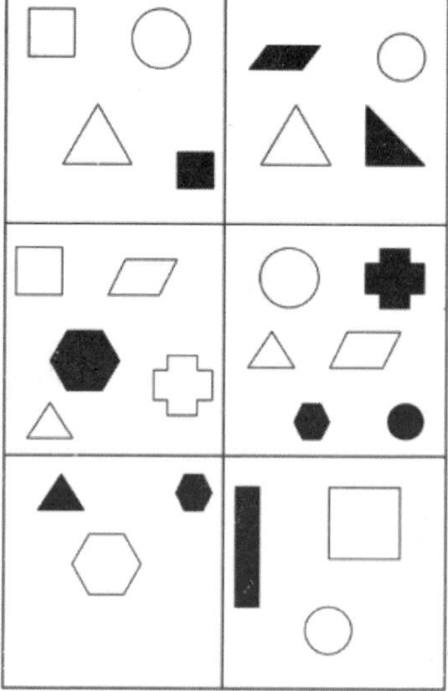

Set B

- A Set A
- B Set B
- C Neither

Answer

Q79.

Test Shape:

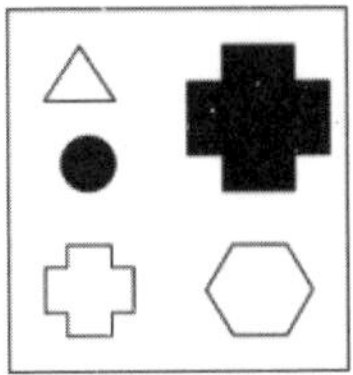

Set A

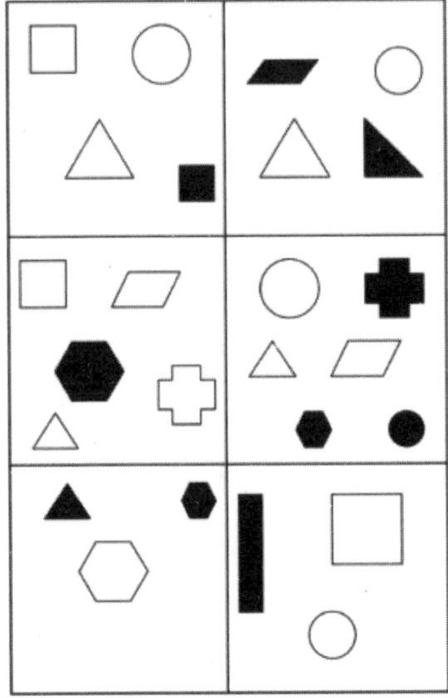

Set B

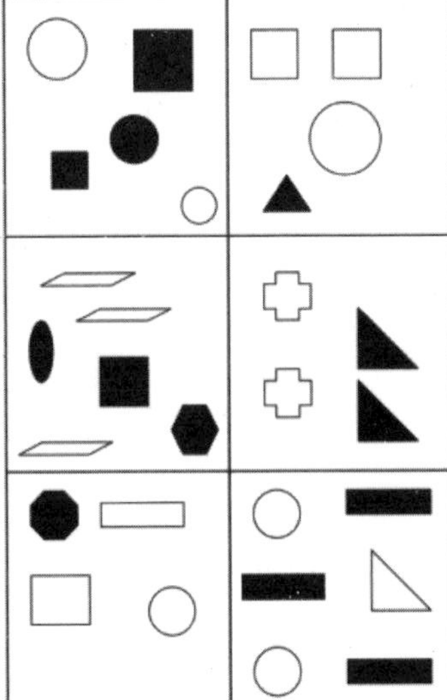

- A Set A
- B Set B
- C Neither

Answer

Q80.

Test Shape:

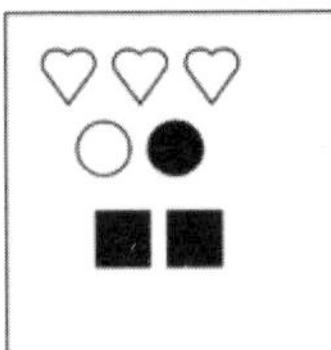

Set A

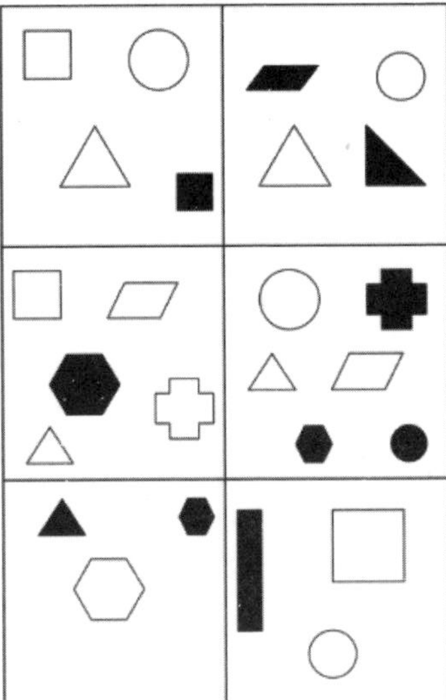

Set B

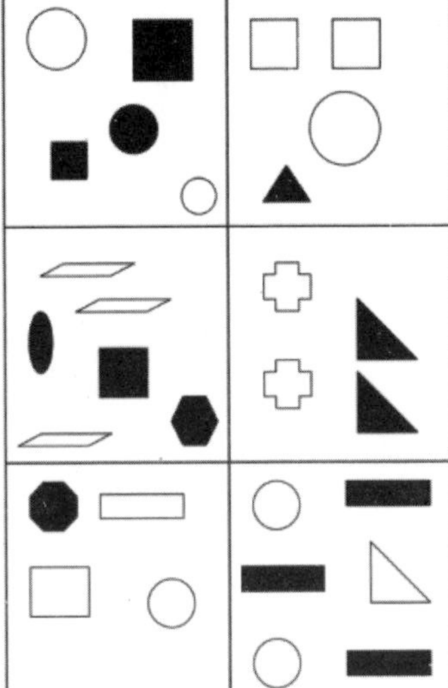

- A Set A
- B Set B
- C Neither

Answer

Q81.

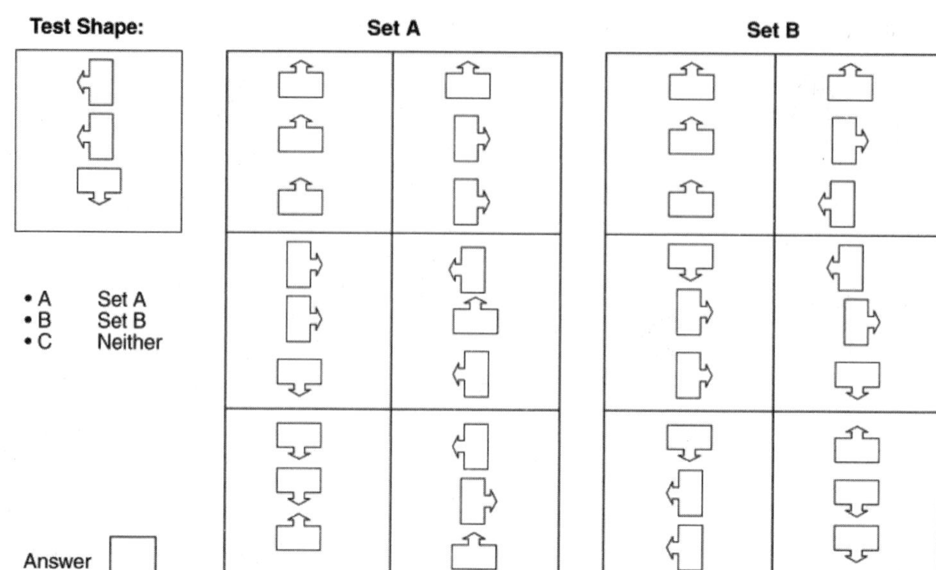
Test Shape:
Set A
Set B
• A Set A
• B Set B
• C Neither
Answer

Q82.

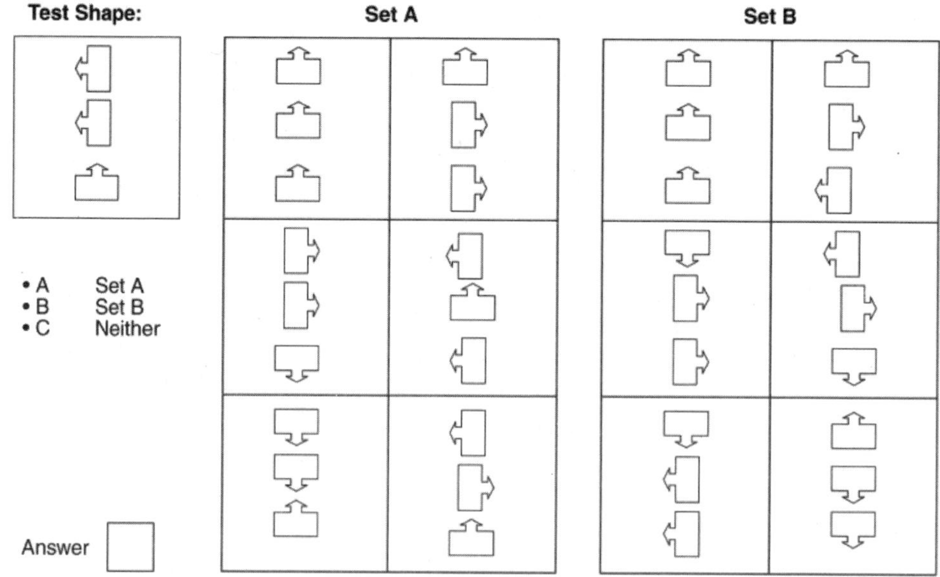
Test Shape:
Set A
Set B
• A Set A
• B Set B
• C Neither
Answer

Q83.

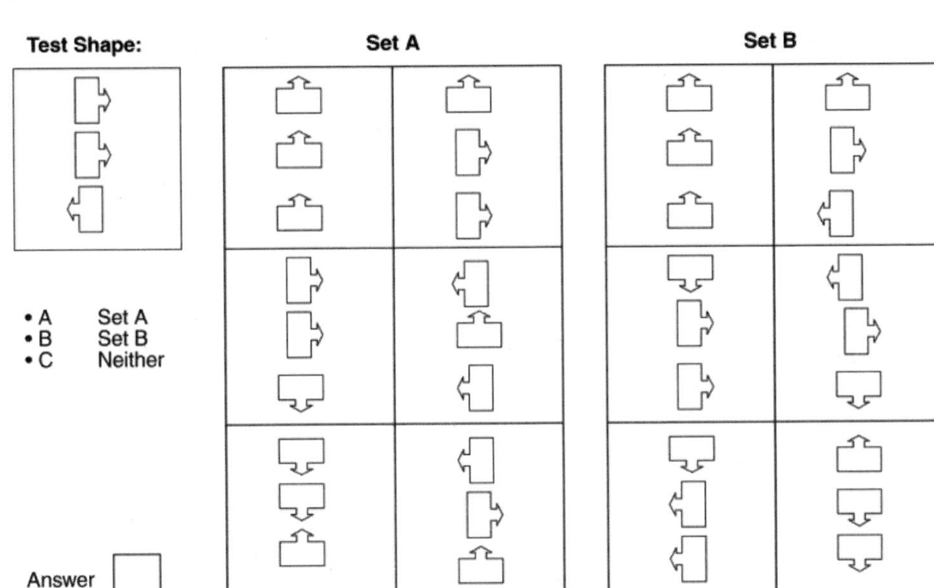
Test Shape:
Set A
Set B
• A Set A
• B Set B
• C Neither
Answer

Q84.

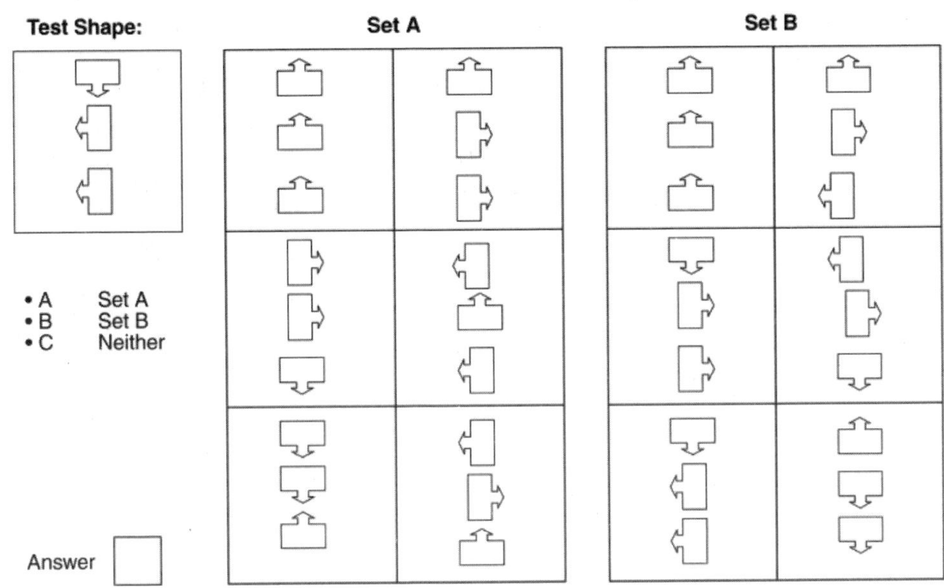
Test Shape:
Set A
Set B
• A Set A
• B Set B
• C Neither
Answer

Q85.

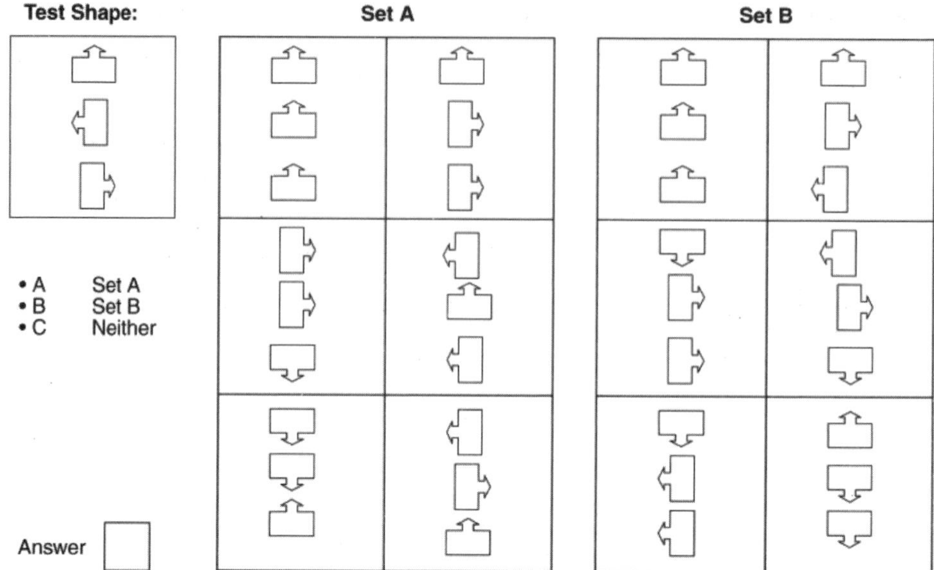
Test Shape:
Set A
Set B
• A Set A
• B Set B
• C Neither
Answer

Q86.

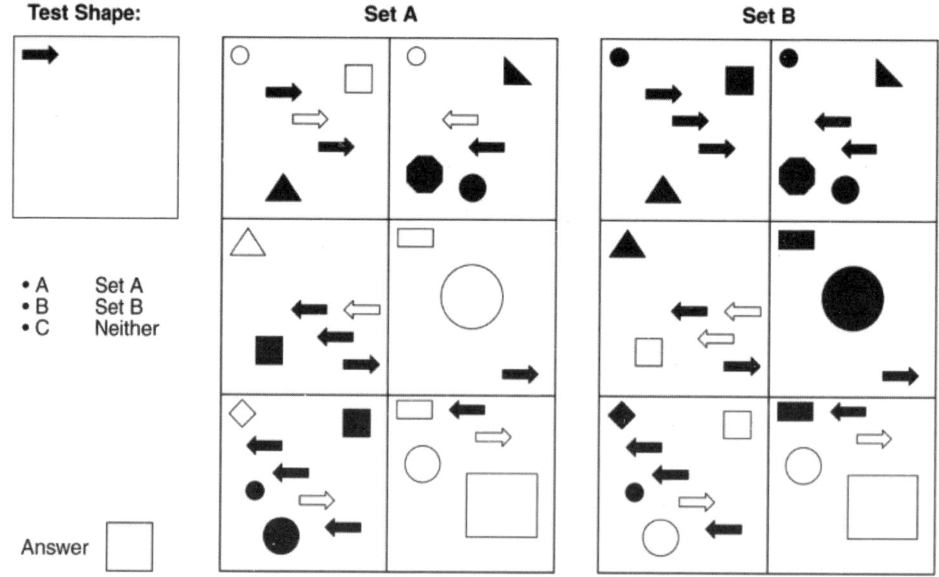
Test Shape:
Set A
Set B
• A Set A
• B Set B
• C Neither
Answer

Q87.

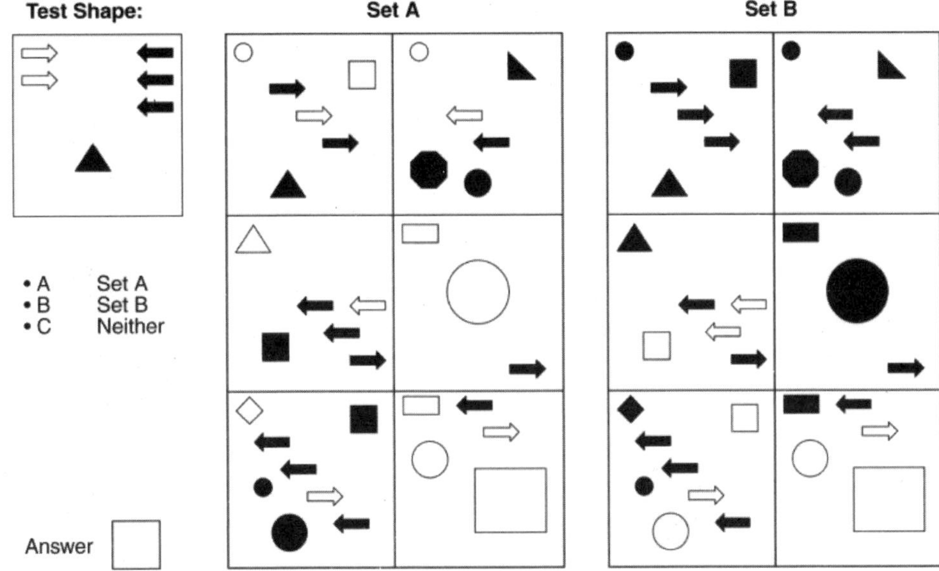
Test Shape:
Set A
Set B
• A Set A
• B Set B
• C Neither
Answer

Q88.

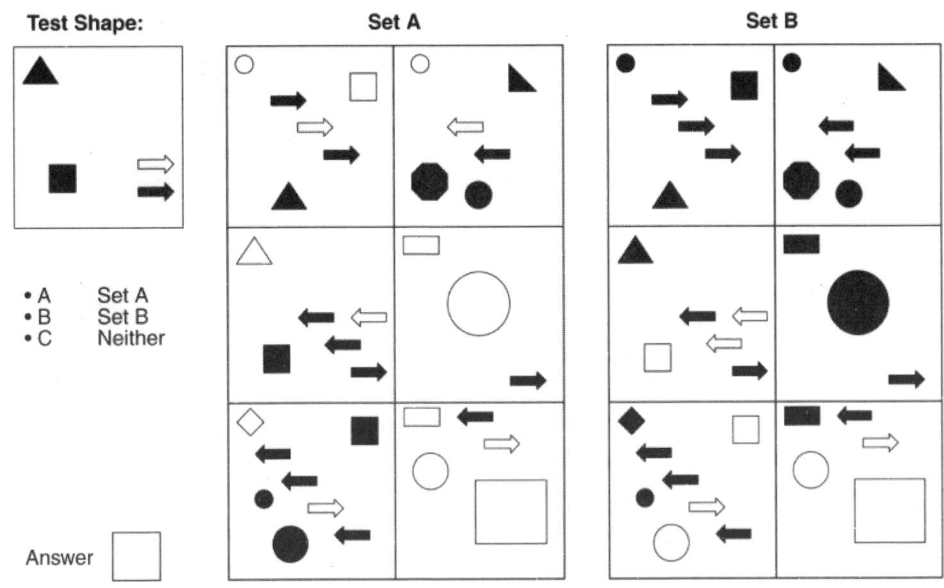
Test Shape:
Set A
Set B
• A Set A
• B Set B
• C Neither
Answer

Q89.

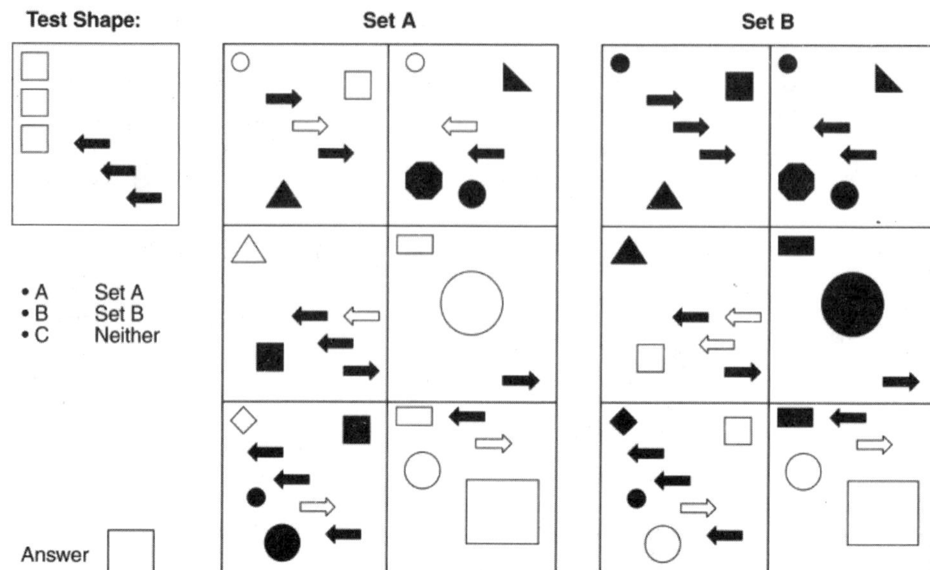
Test Shape:
Set A
Set B
• A Set A
• B Set B
• C Neither
Answer

Q90.

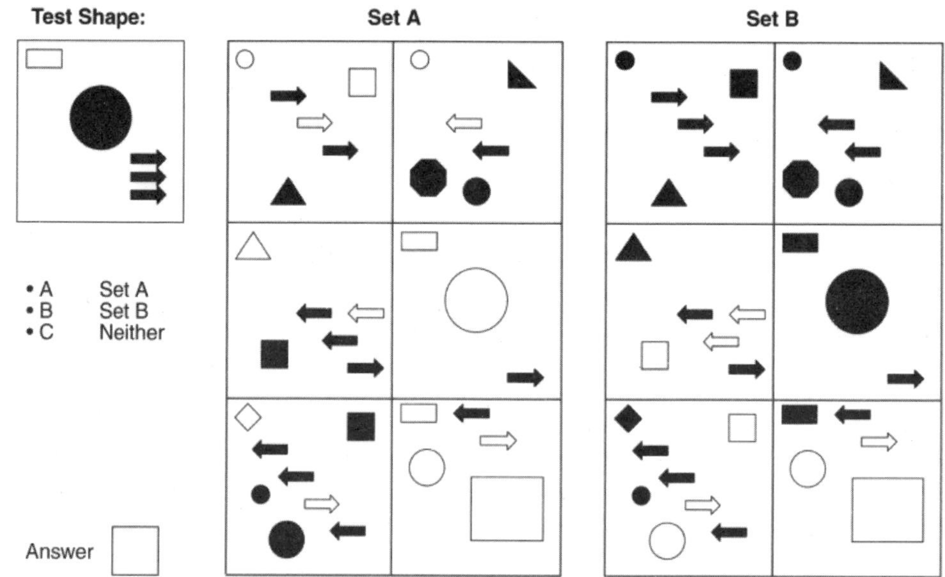
Test Shape:
Set A
Set B
• A Set A
• B Set B
• C Neither
Answer

Q91.

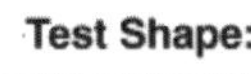

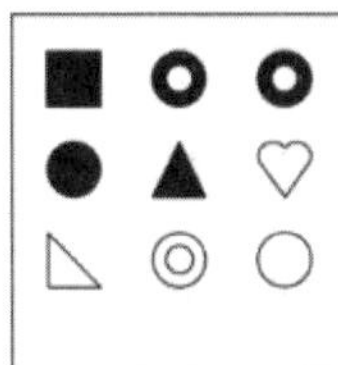

Test Shape:
Set A
Set B
• A Set A
• B Set B
• C Neither
Answer

Q92.

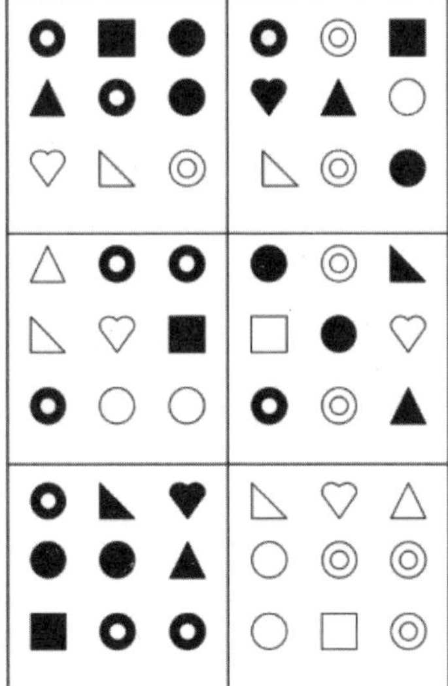

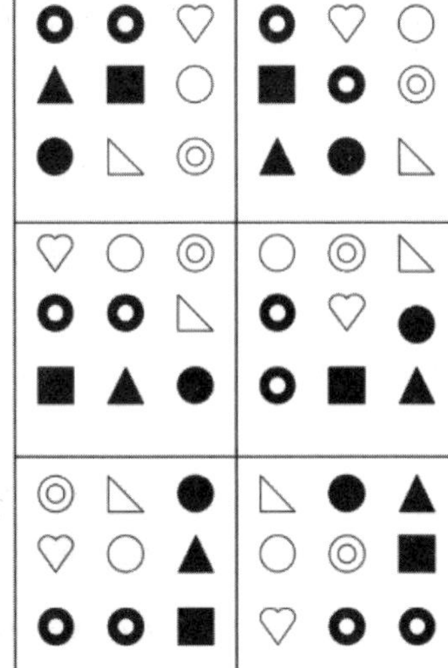

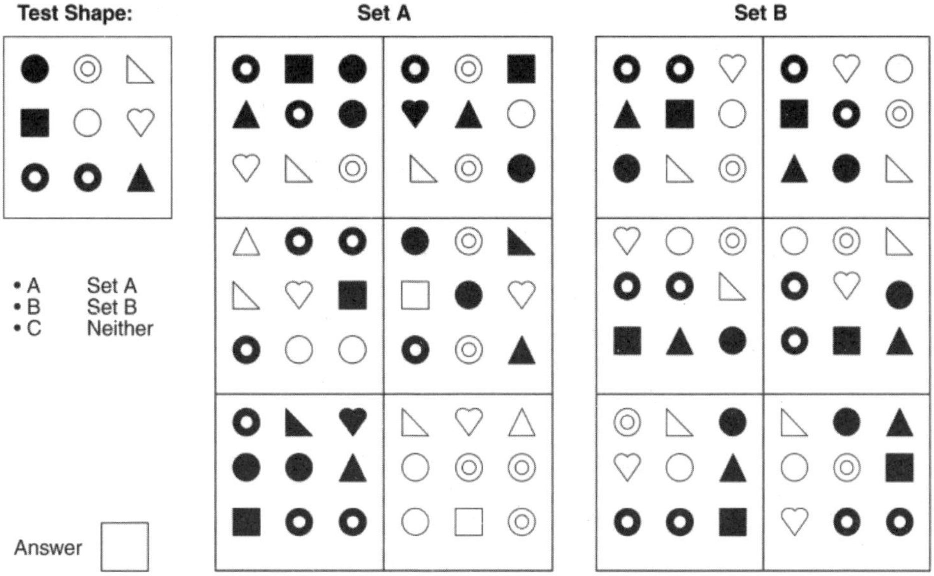

Test Shape:
Set A
Set B
• A Set A
• B Set B
• C Neither
Answer

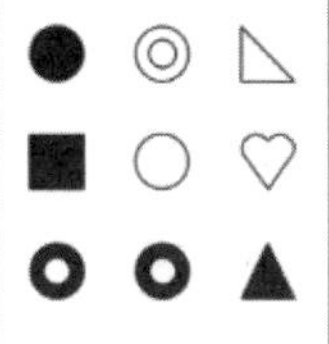

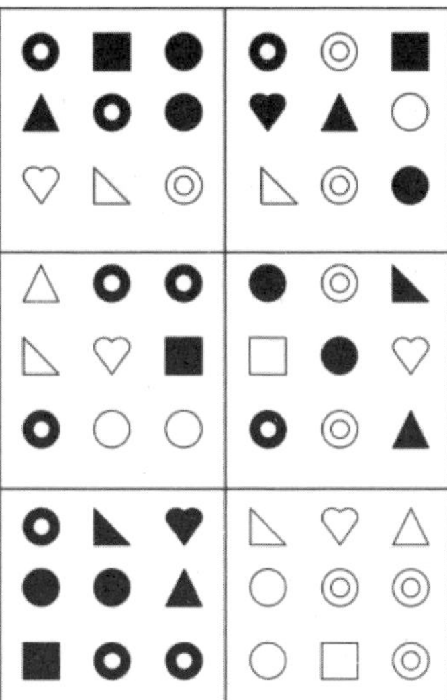

Q93.

Test Shape: **Set A** **Set B**

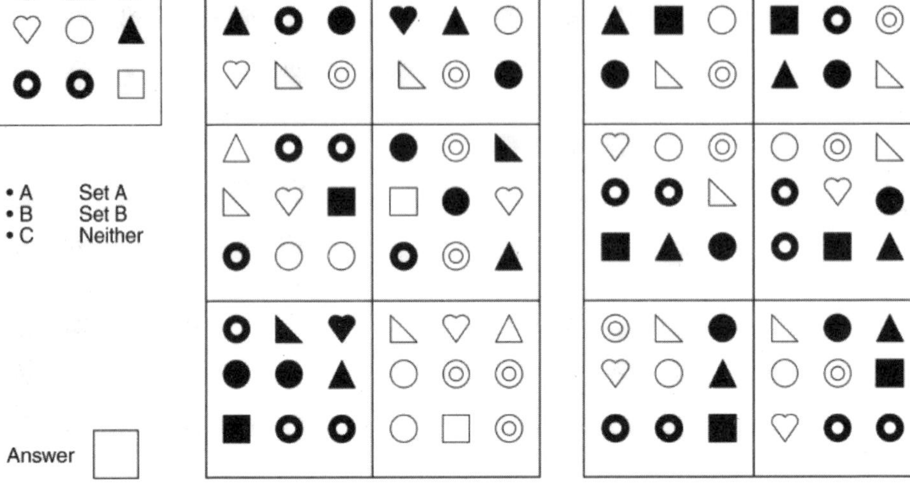

- A Set A
- B Set B
- C Neither

Answer

Q94.

Test Shape: **Set A** **Set B**

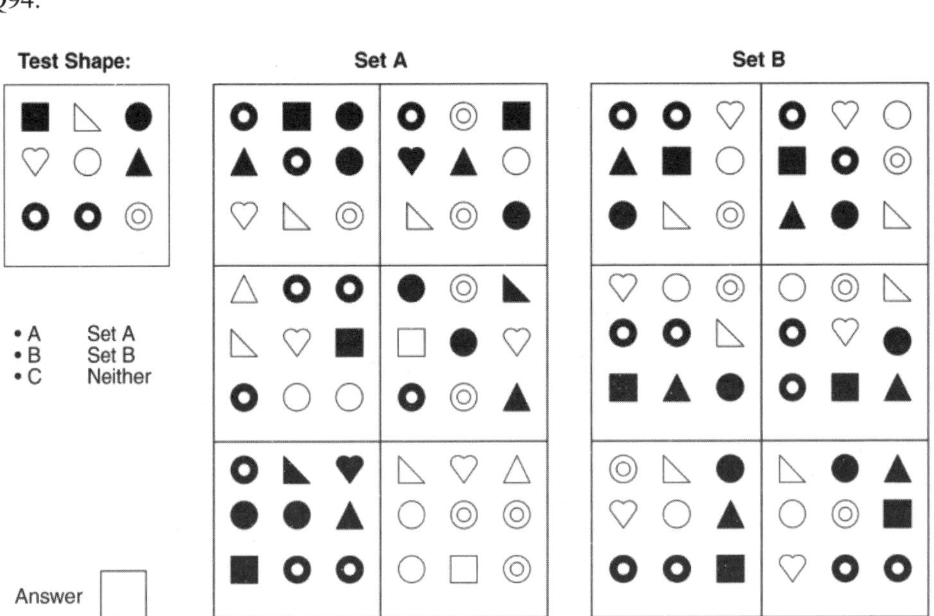

- A Set A
- B Set B
- C Neither

Answer

Q95.

Test Shape:

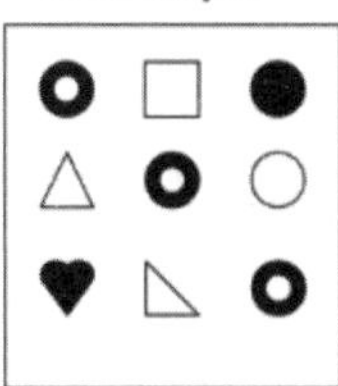

Set A

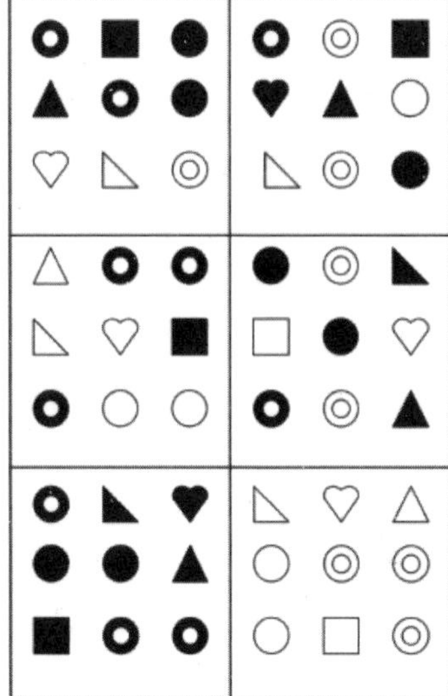

Set B

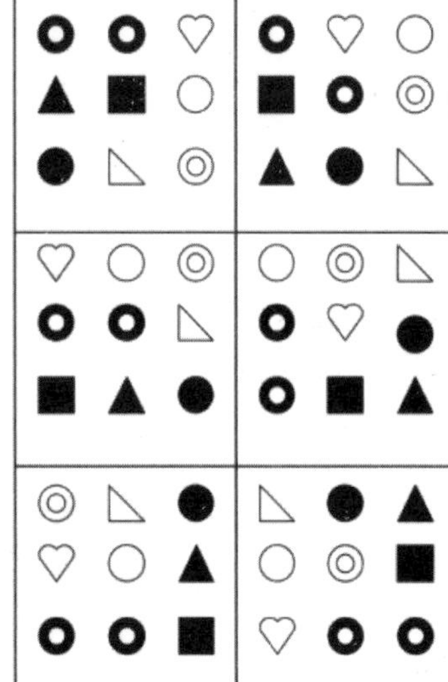

- A Set A
- B Set B
- C Neither

Answer

Q96.

Test Shape:

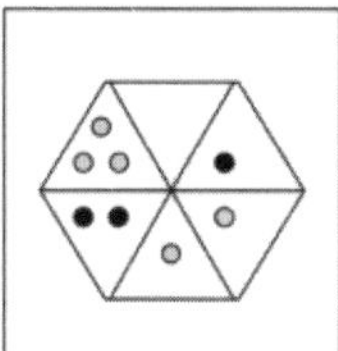

Set A

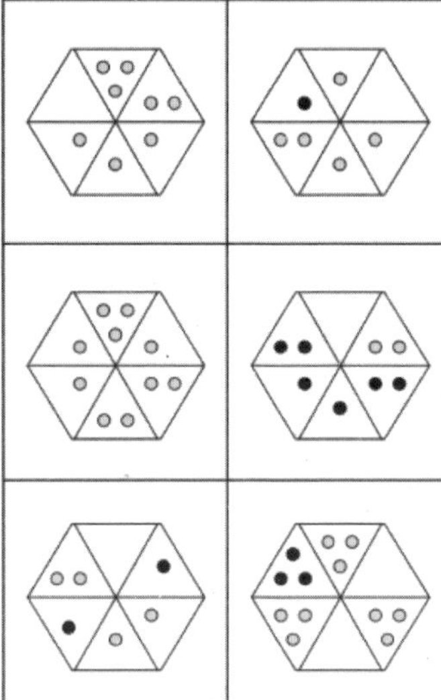

Set B

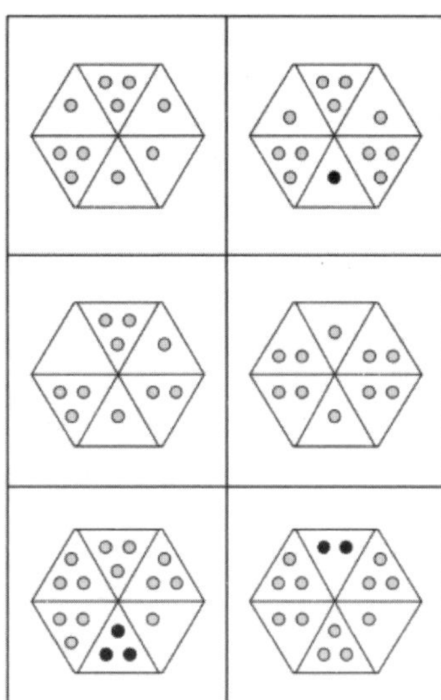

- A Set A
- B Set B
- C Neither

Answer

Q97.

Test Shape:

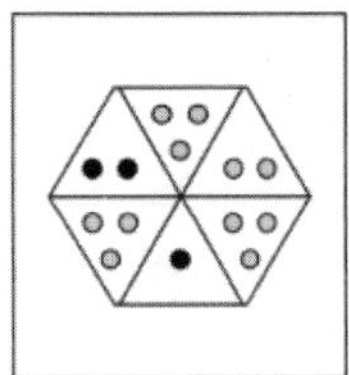

Set A

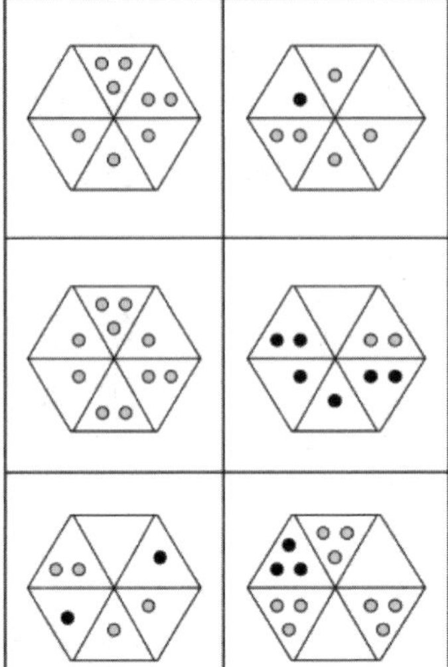

Set B

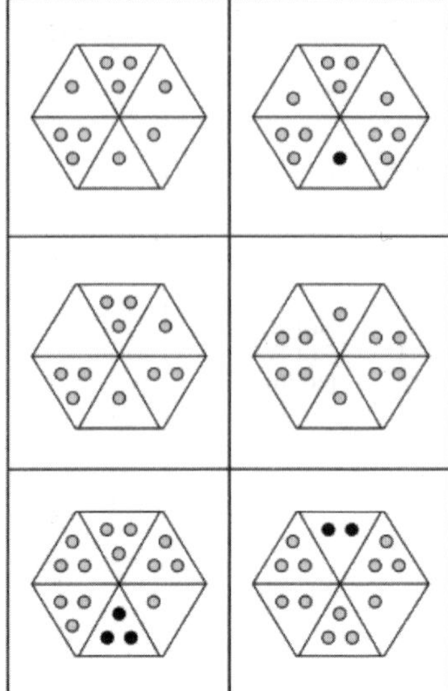

- A Set A
- B Set B
- C Neither

Answer

Q98.

Test Shape:

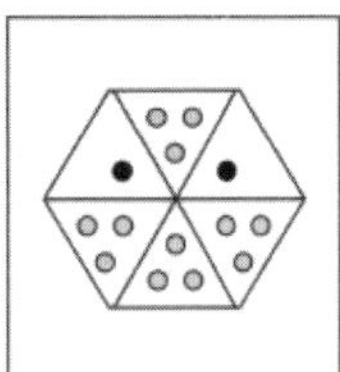

Set A

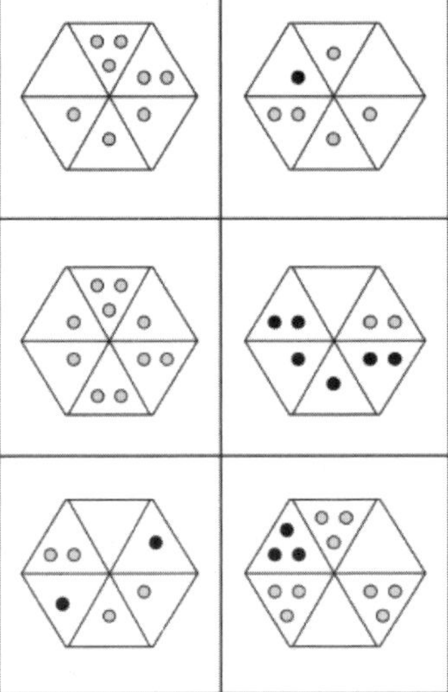

Set B

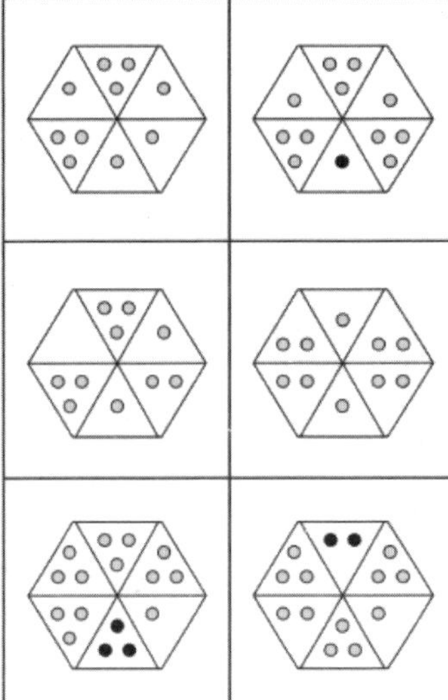

- A Set A
- B Set B
- C Neither

Answer

Q99.

Test Shape:

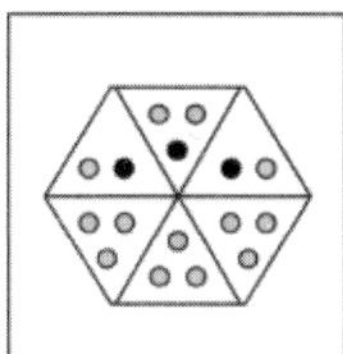

Set A

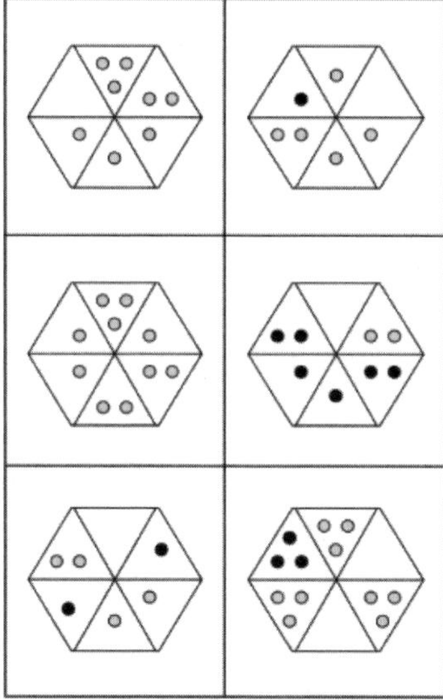

Set B

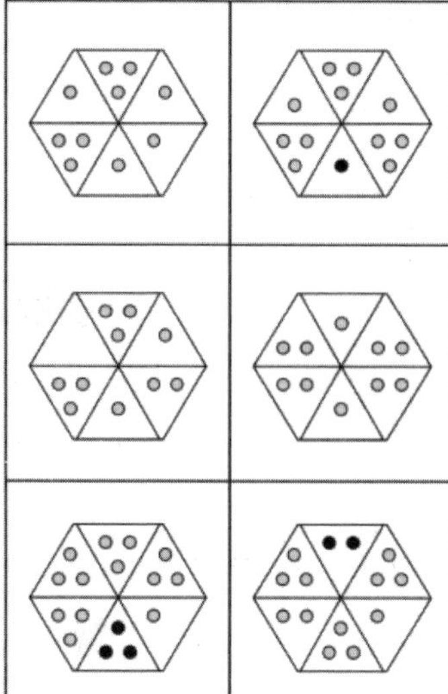

- A Set A
- B Set B
- C Neither

Answer

Q100.

Test Shape:

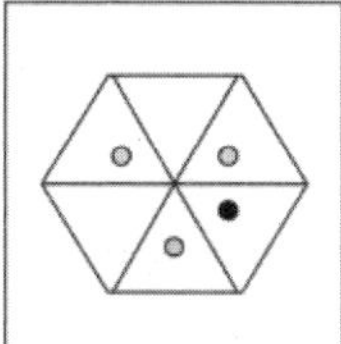

Set A

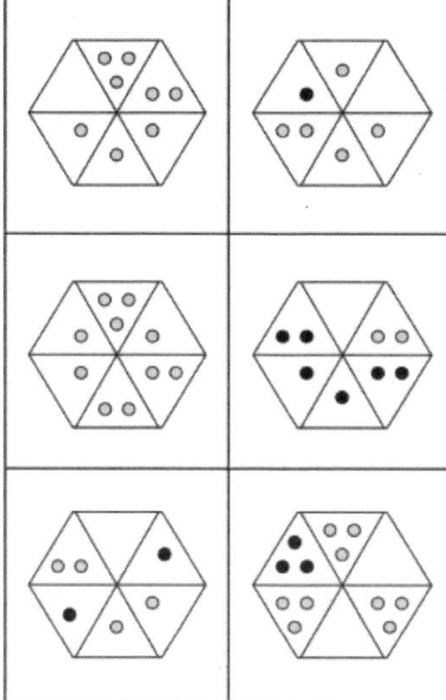

Set B

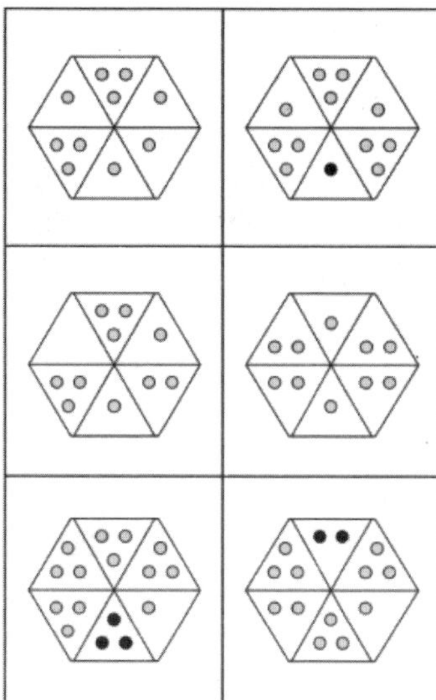

- A Set A
- B Set B
- C Neither

Answer

Mini-tests

Mini-test 1

Q101.

Test Shape: **Set A** 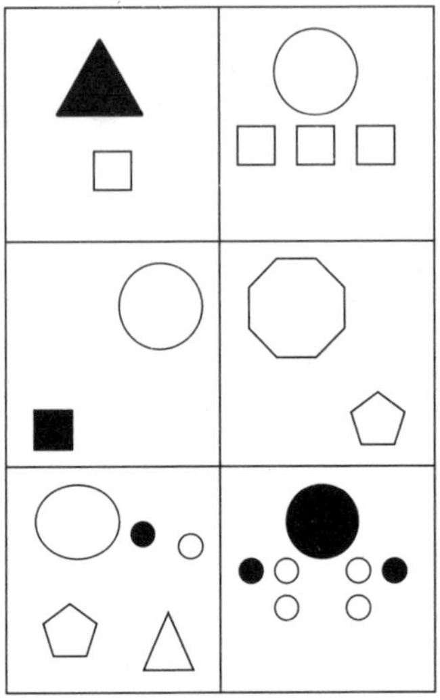 **Set B**

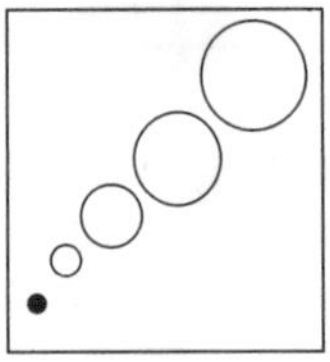

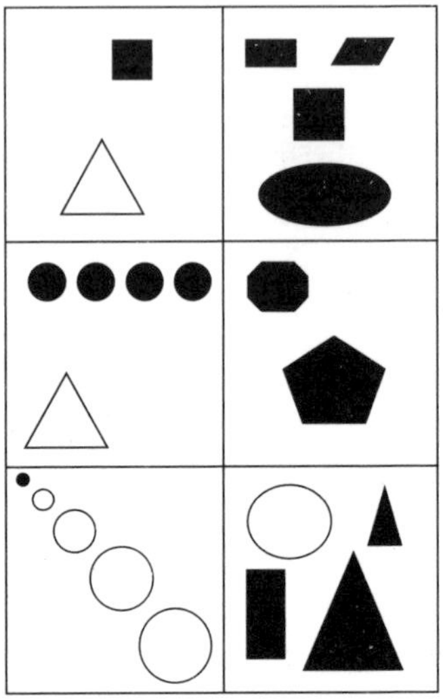

- A Set A
- B Set B
- C Neither

Answer

Q102.

Test Shape: **Set A** 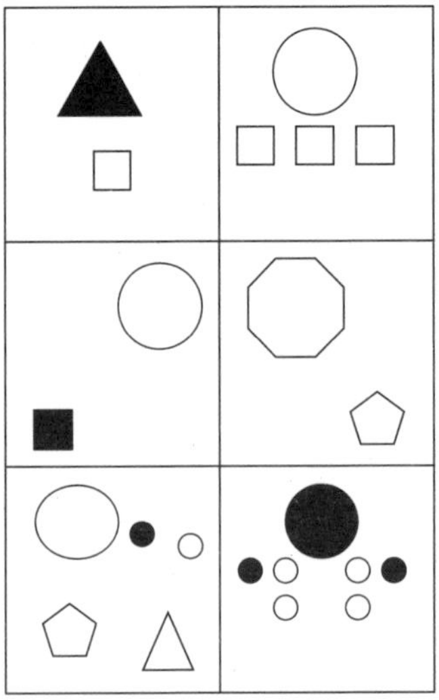 **Set B**

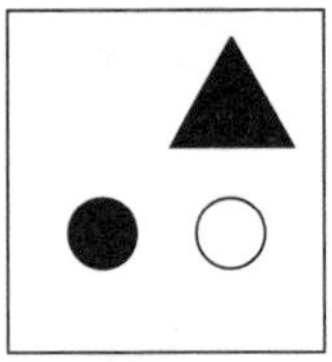

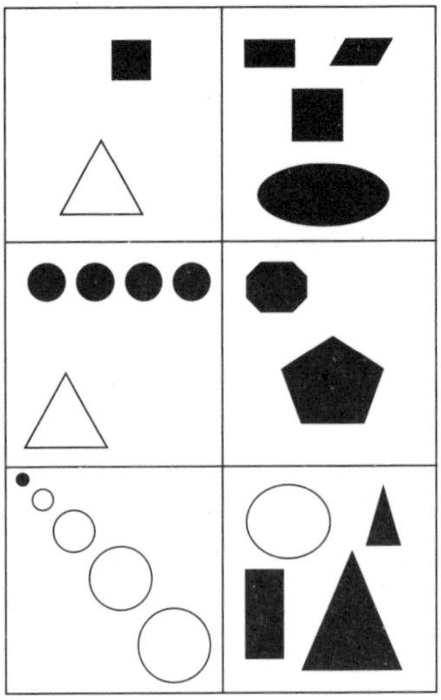

- A Set A
- B Set B
- C Neither

Answer

Q103.

Test Shape:

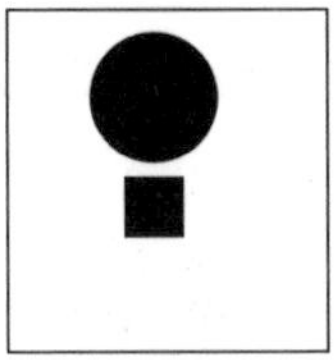

Set A

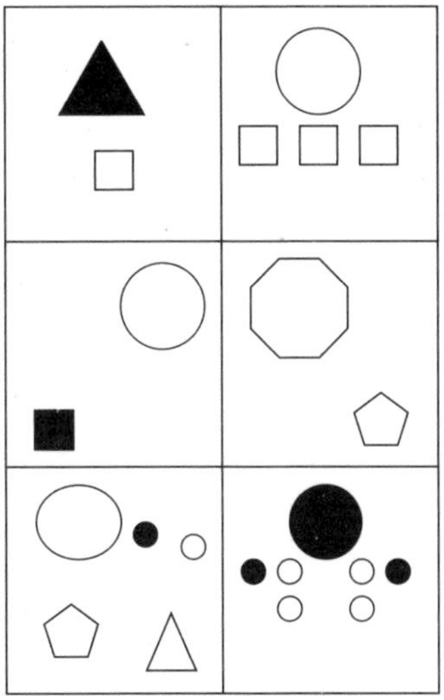

Set B

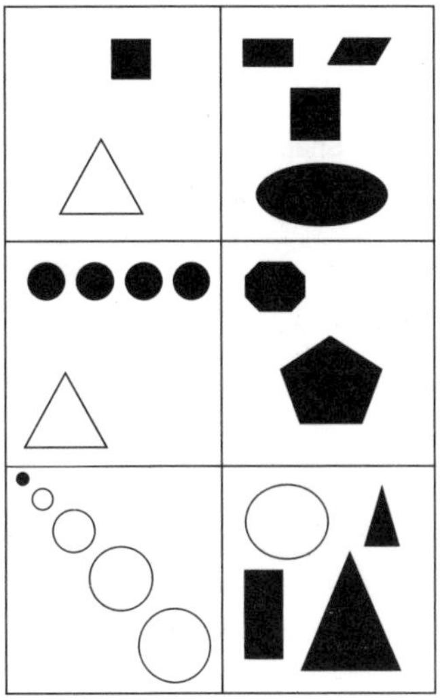

- A Set A
- B Set B
- C Neither

Answer

Q104.

Test Shape:

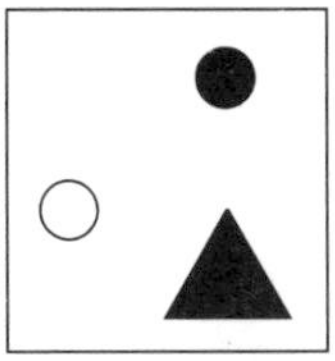

Set A

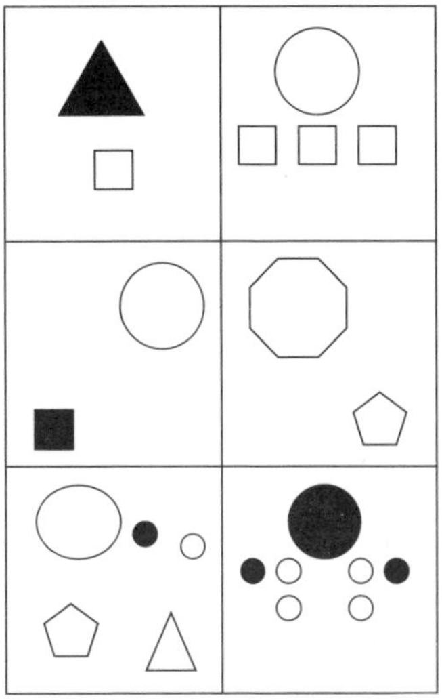

Set B

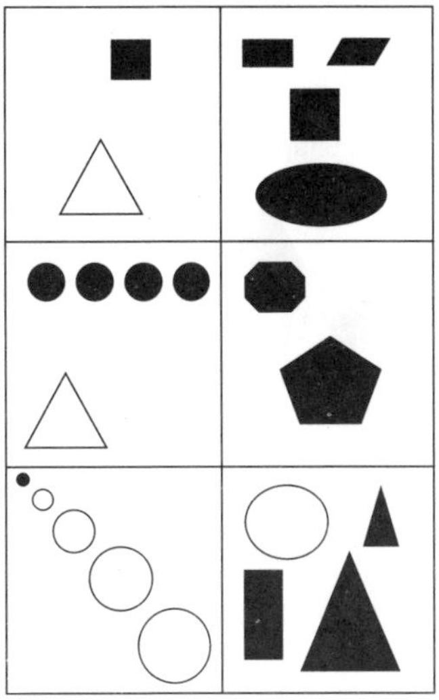

- A Set A
- B Set B
- C Neither

Answer

Q105.

Test Shape:

Set A

Set B

- A Set A
- B Set B
- C Neither

Answer

Q106.

Test Shape:

Set A

Set B

- A Set A
- B Set B
- C Neither

Answer

Q107.

Test Shape:

Set A

Set B

- A Set A
- B Set B
- C Neither

Answer

Q108.

Test Shape:

Set A

Set B

- A Set A
- B Set B
- C Neither

Answer

Q109.

Test Shape:

Set A

Set B

- A Set A
- B Set B
- C Neither

Answer

Q110.

Test Shape:

Set A

Set B

- A Set A
- B Set B
- C Neither

Answer

End of test

Mini-test 2

Q111.

Test Shape:

Set A

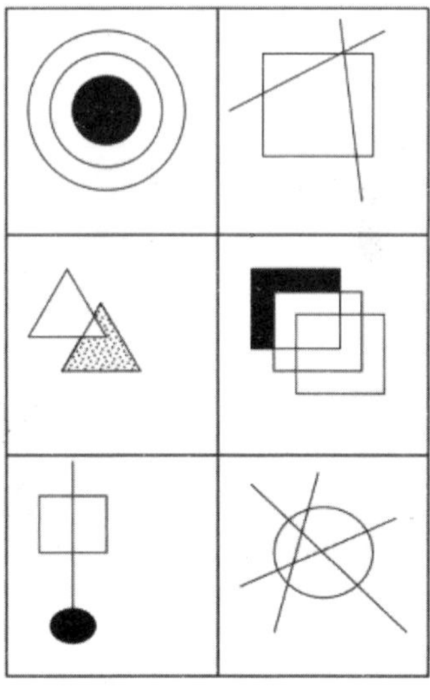

Set B

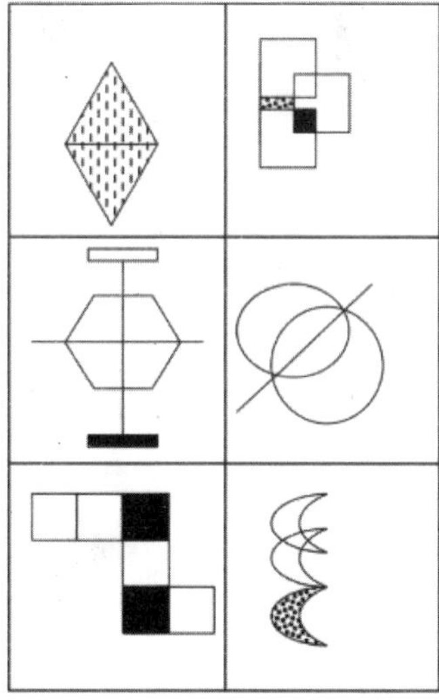

- A Set A
- B Set B
- C Neither

Answer

Q112.

Test Shape:

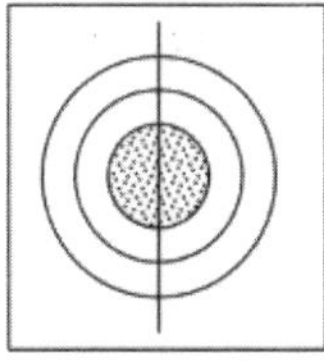

Set A

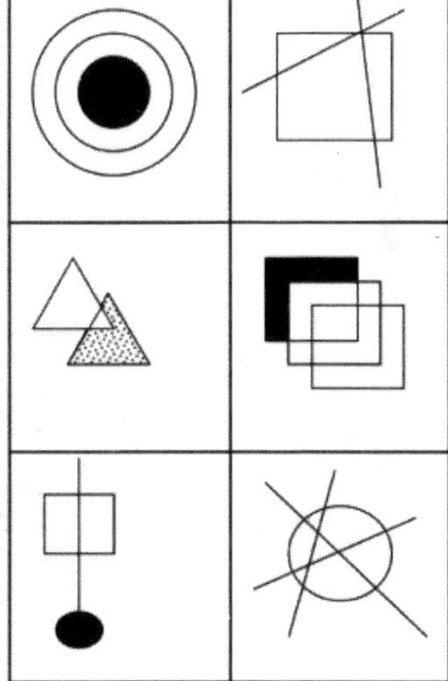

Set B

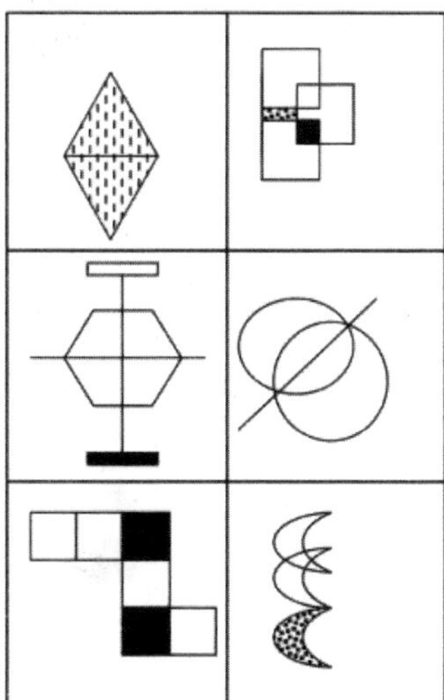

- A Set A
- B Set B
- C Neither

Answer

Q113.

Test Shape: **Set A** 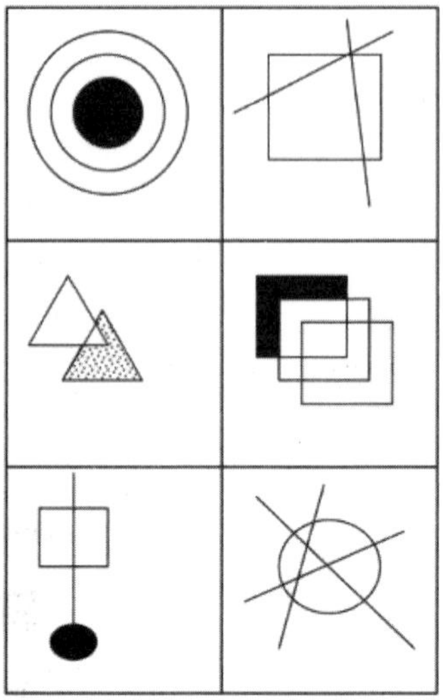 **Set B**

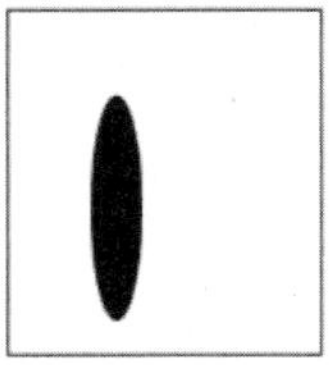

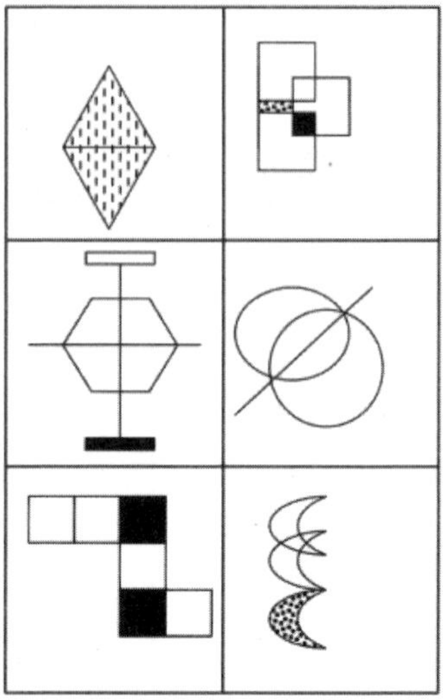

- A Set A
- B Set B
- C Neither

Answer

Q114.

Test Shape: **Set A** 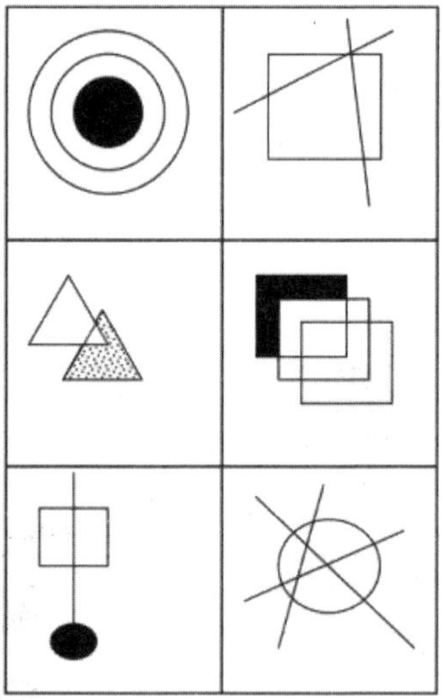 **Set B**

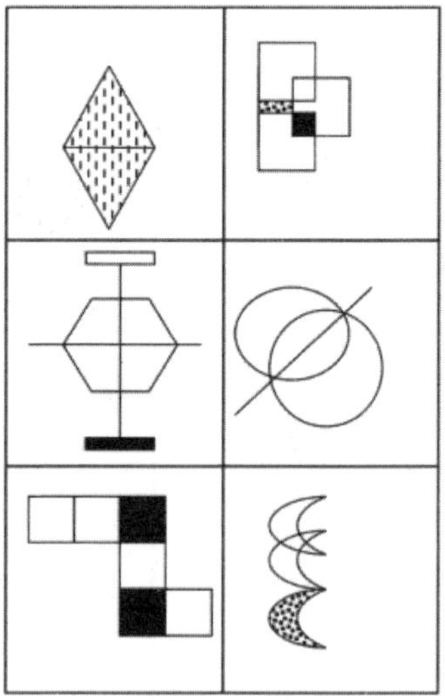

- A Set A
- B Set B
- C Neither

Answer

Q115.

Test Shape: **Set A** **Set B**

- A Set A
- B Set B
- C Neither

Answer

Q116.

Test Shape: **Set A** **Set B**

- A Set A
- B Set B
- C Neither

Answer

Q117.

Test Shape:

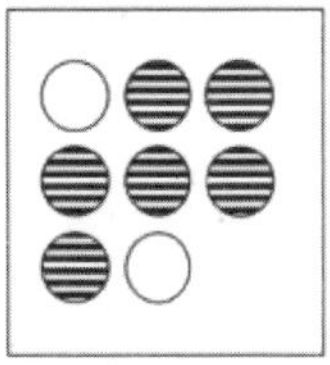

Set A

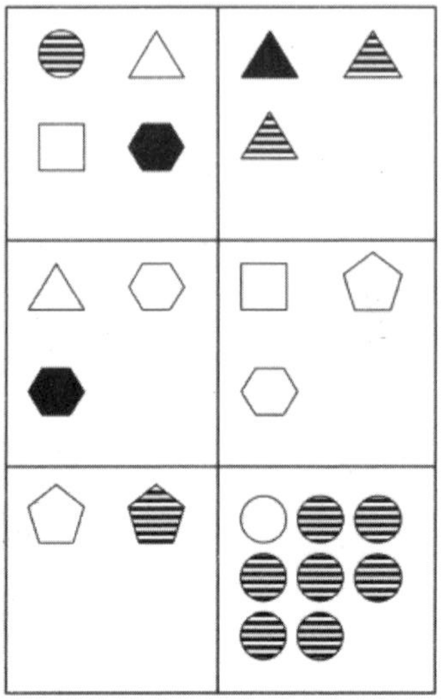

Set B

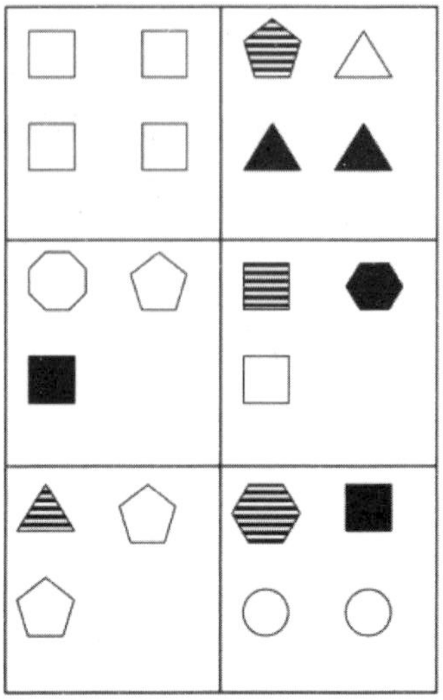

- A Set A
- B Set B
- C Neither

Answer

Q118.

Test Shape:

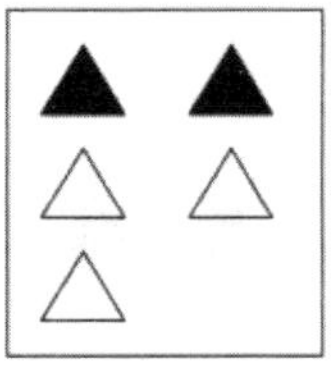

Set A

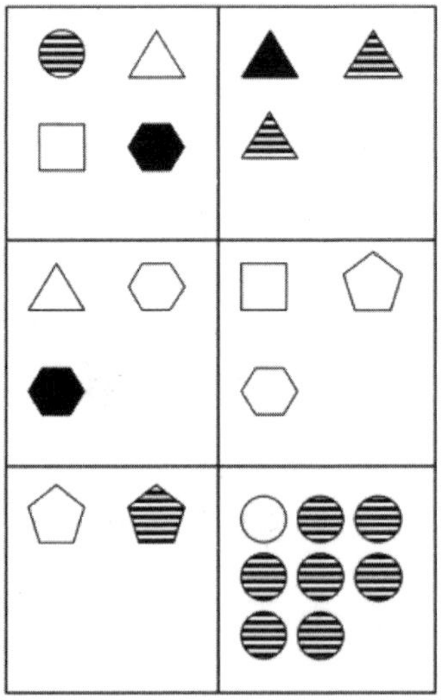

Set B

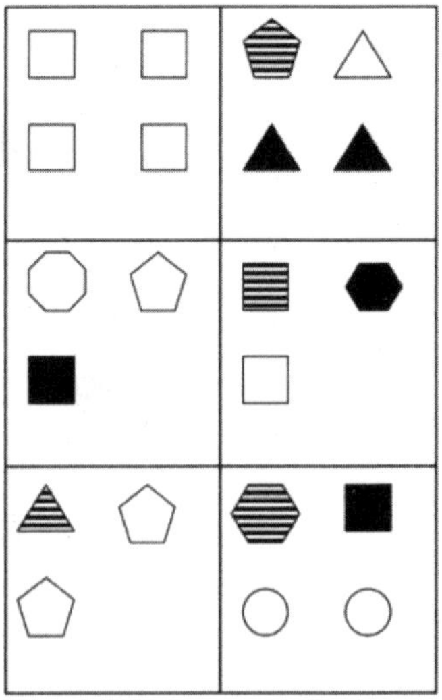

- A Set A
- B Set B
- C Neither

Answer

Q119.

Test Shape:

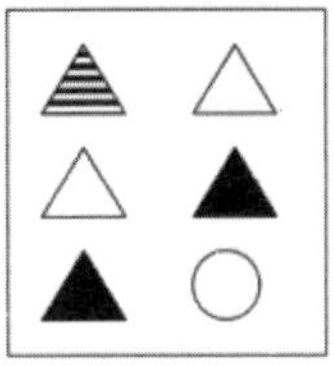

Set A

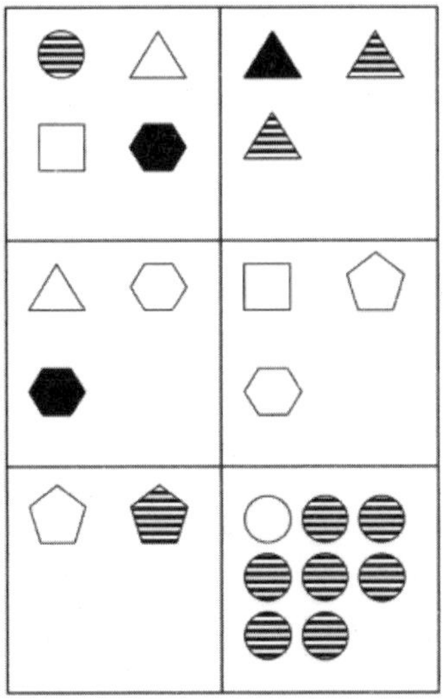

Set B

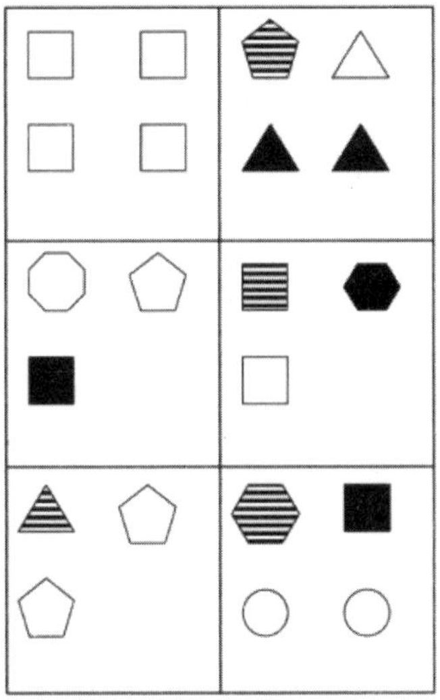

- A Set A
- B Set B
- C Neither

Answer

Q120.

Test Shape:

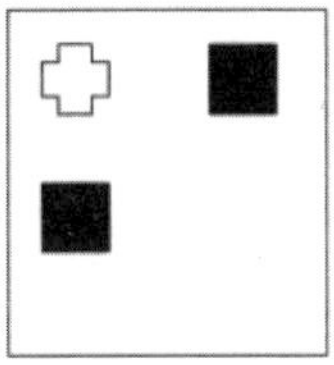

Set A

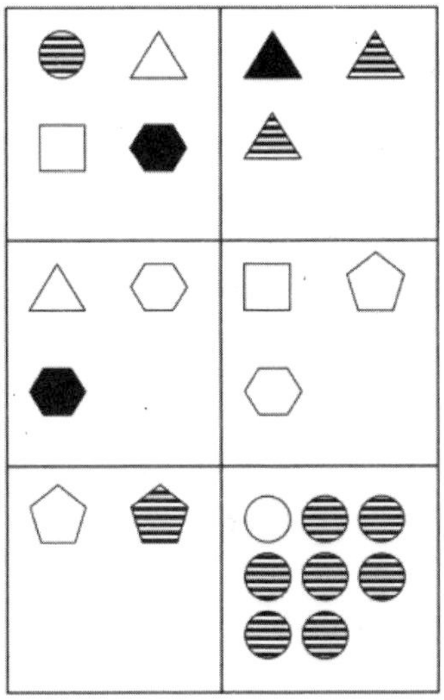

Set B

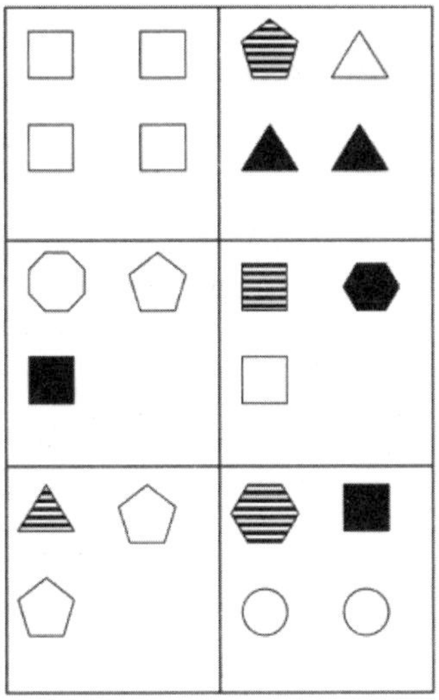

- A Set A
- B Set B
- C Neither

Answer

End of test

Mini-test 3

Q121.

Test Shape: **Set A** **Set B**

- A Set A
- B Set B
- C Neither

Answer

Q122.

Test Shape: **Set A** **Set B**

- A Set A
- B Set B
- C Neither

Answer

Q123.

Test Shape:

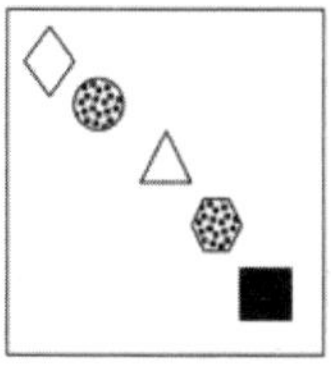

Set A

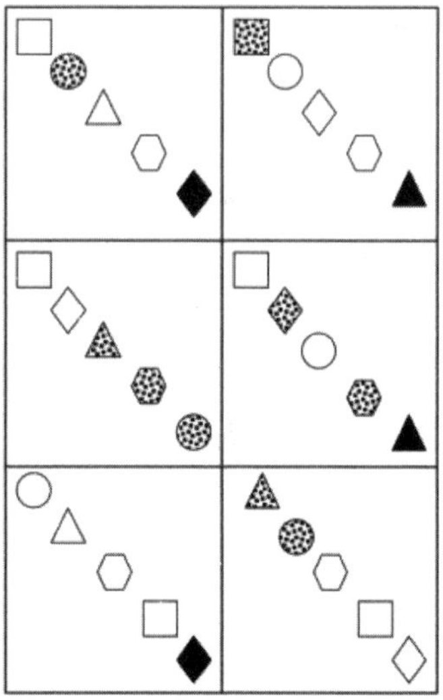

Set B

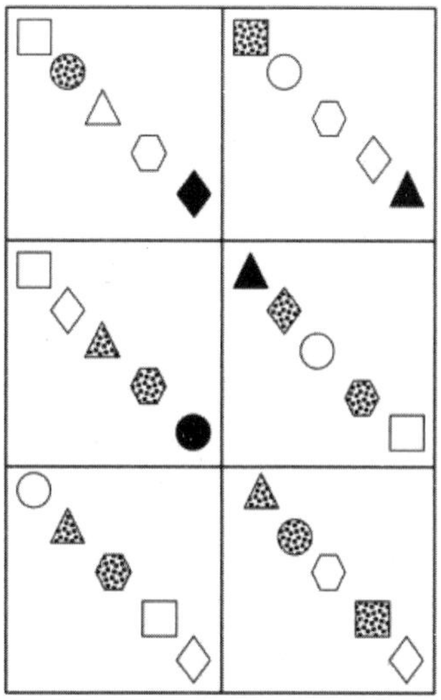

- A Set A
- B Set B
- C Neither

Answer

Q124.

Test Shape:

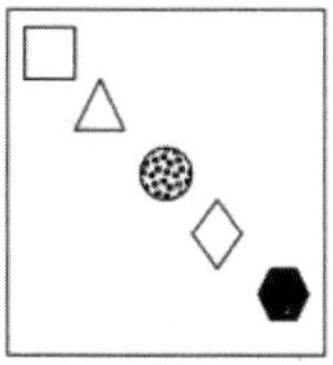

Set A

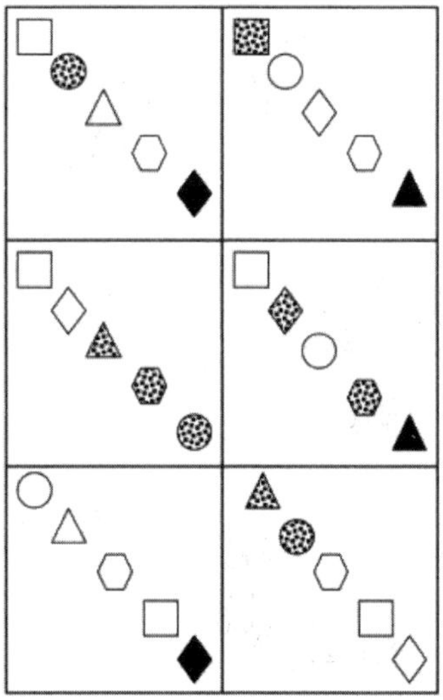

Set B

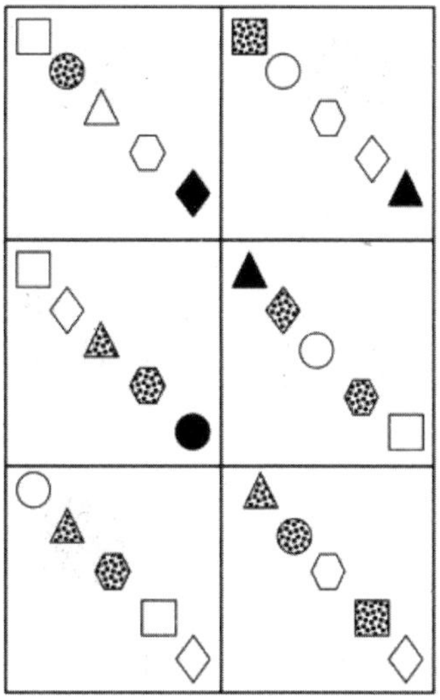

- A Set A
- B Set B
- C Neither

Answer

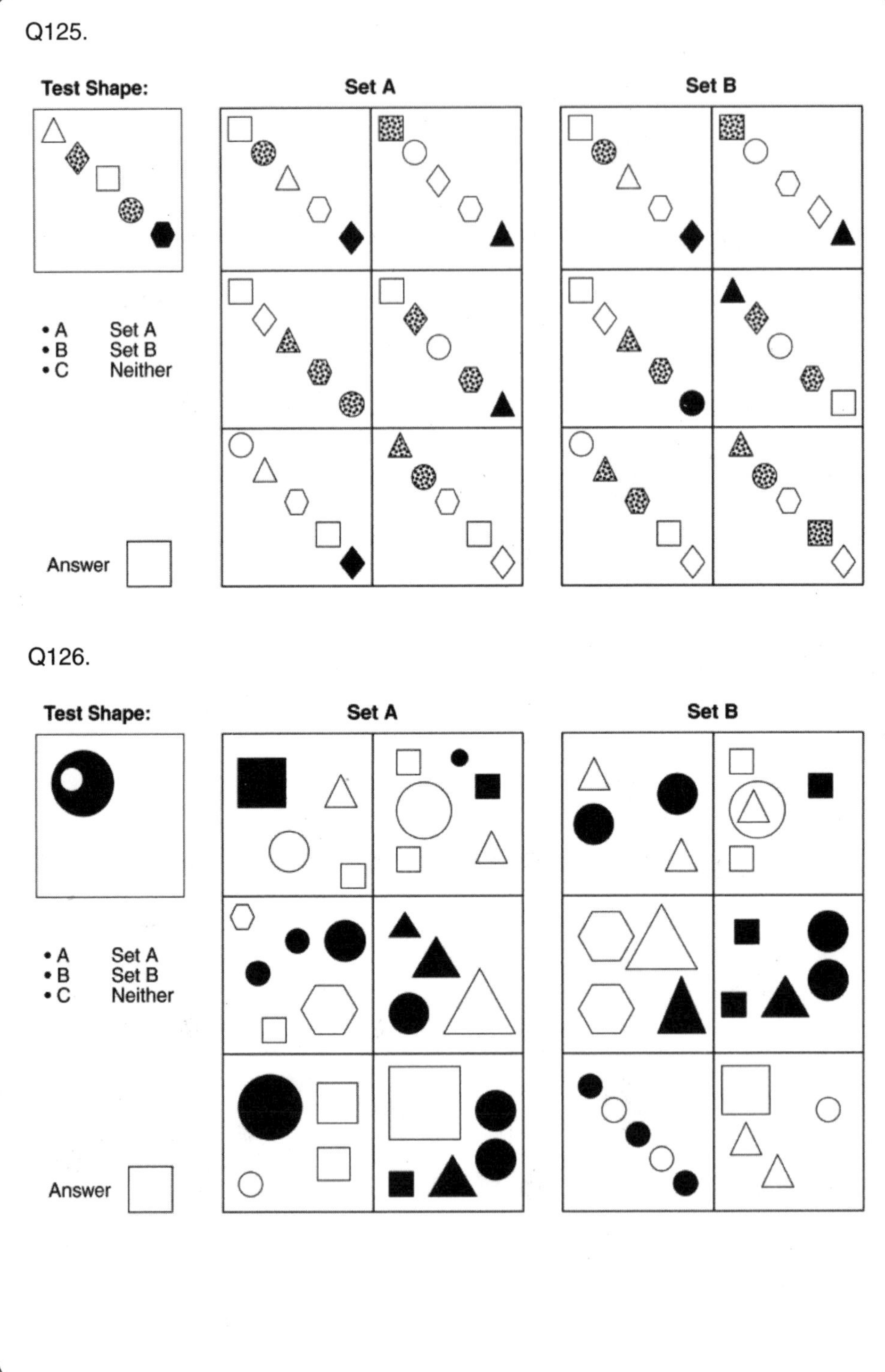
Q125.
Test Shape:
Set A
Set B
• A Set A
• B Set B
• C Neither
Answer
Q126.
Test Shape:
Set A
Set B
• A Set A
• B Set B
• C Neither
Answer

Q127.

Test Shape: **Set A** 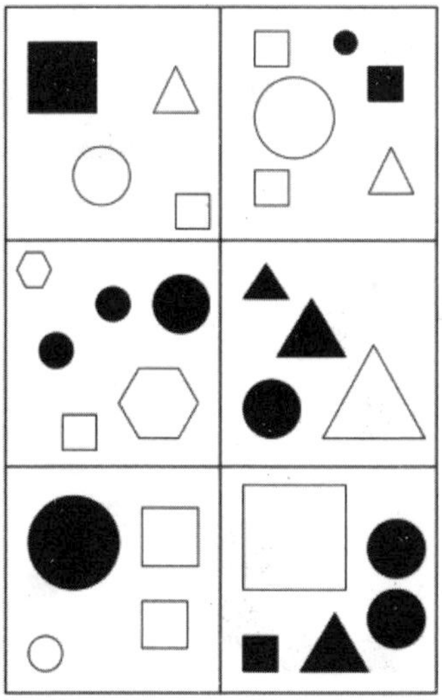 **Set B**

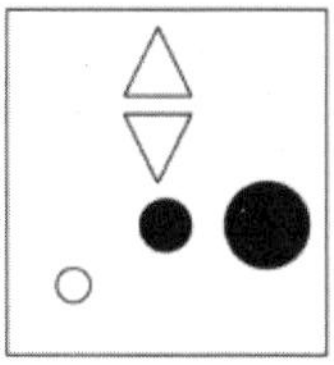

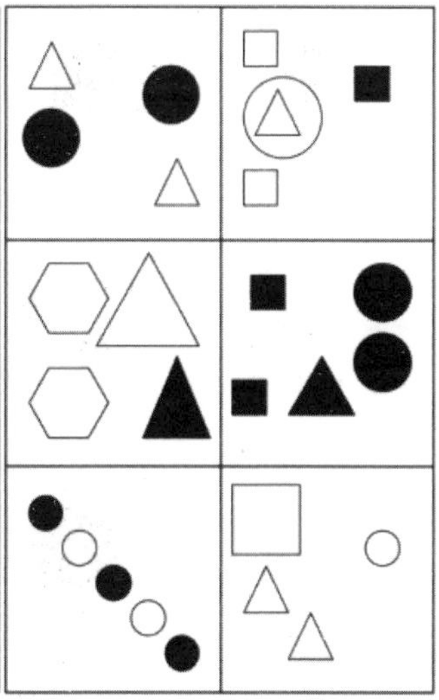

- A Set A
- B Set B
- C Neither

Answer

Q128.

Test Shape: **Set A** 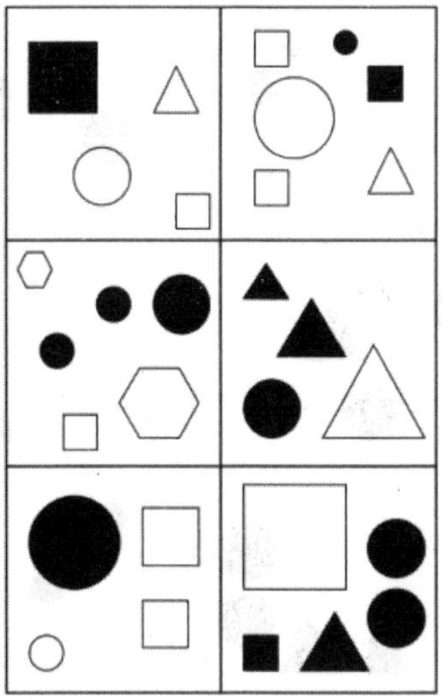 **Set B**

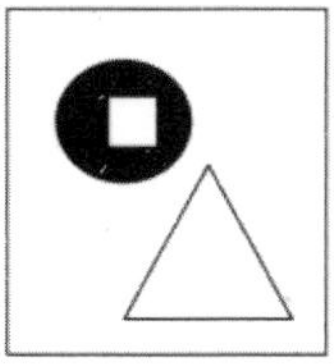

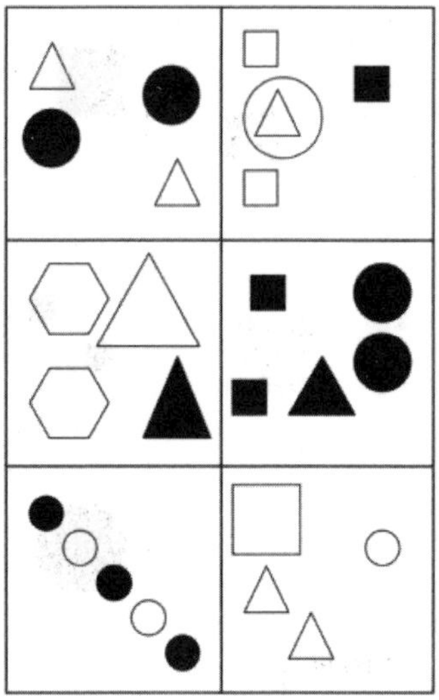

- A Set A
- B Set B
- C Neither

Answer

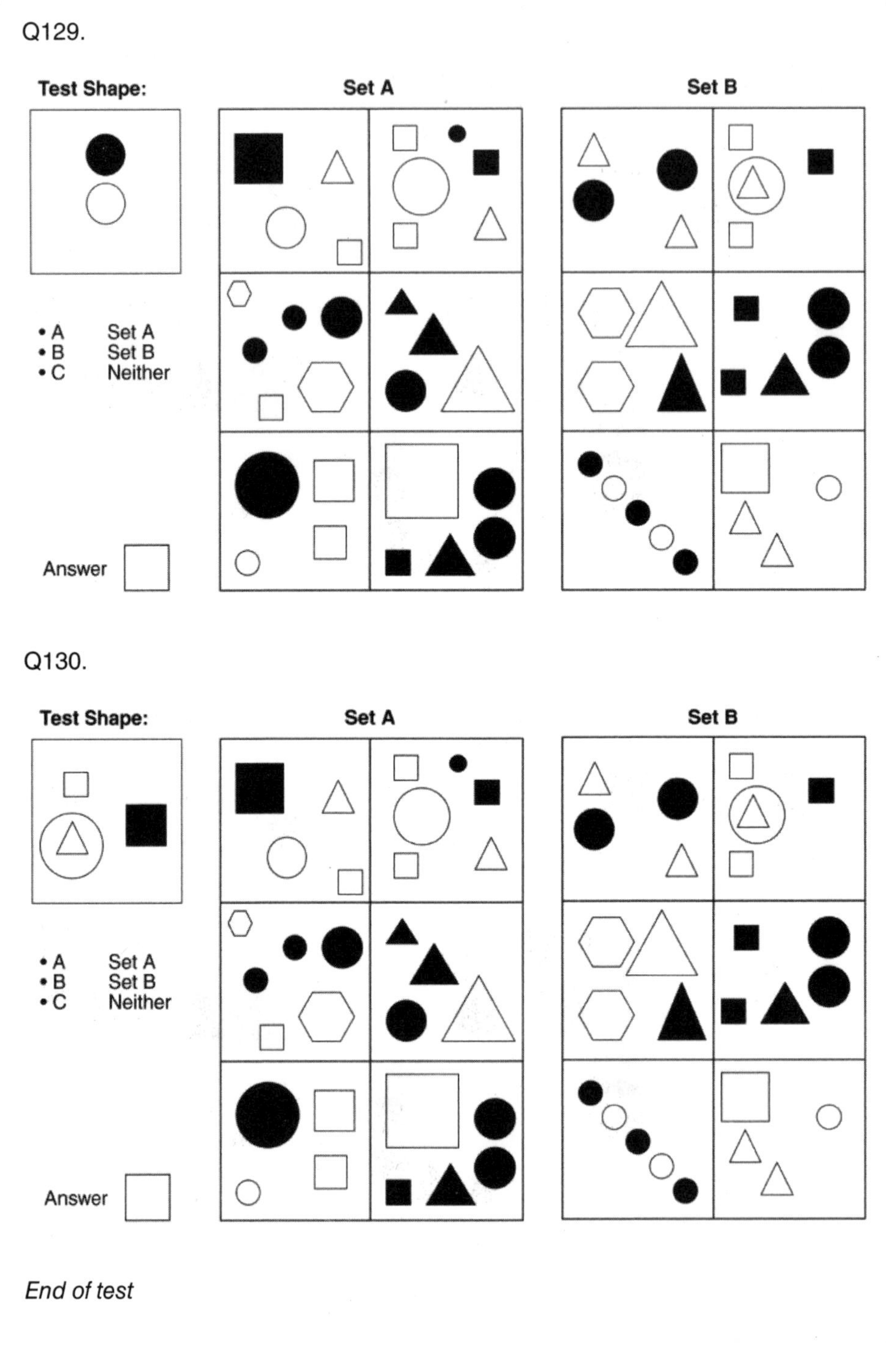
Q129.
Test Shape:
Set A
Set B
• A Set A
• B Set B
• C Neither
Answer
Q130.
Test Shape:
Set A
Set B
• A Set A
• B Set B
• C Neither
Answer
End of test

Mini-test 4

Q131.

Test Shape: **Set A** 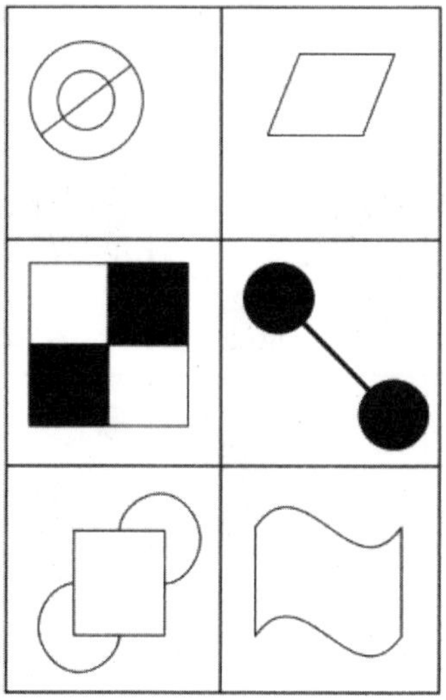 **Set B**

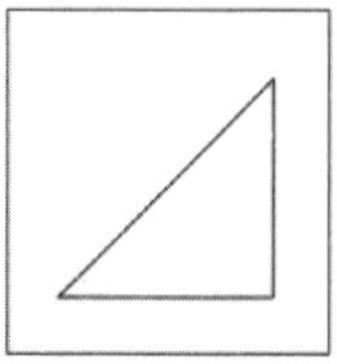

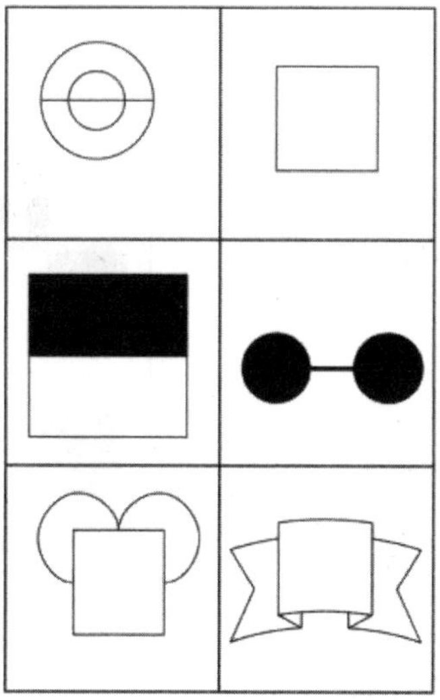

- A Set A
- B Set B
- C Neither

Answer

Q132.

Test Shape: **Set A** 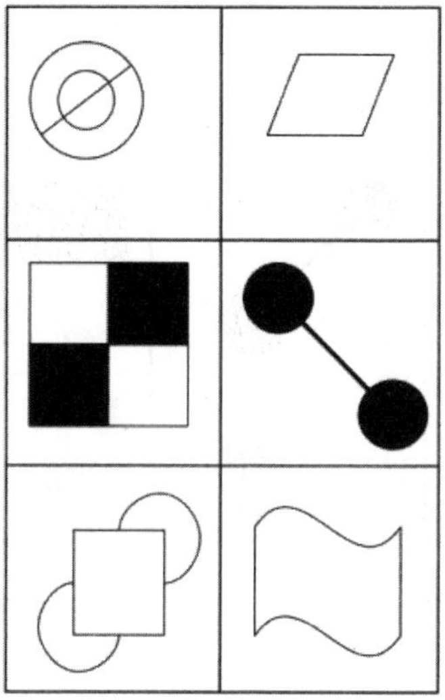 **Set B**

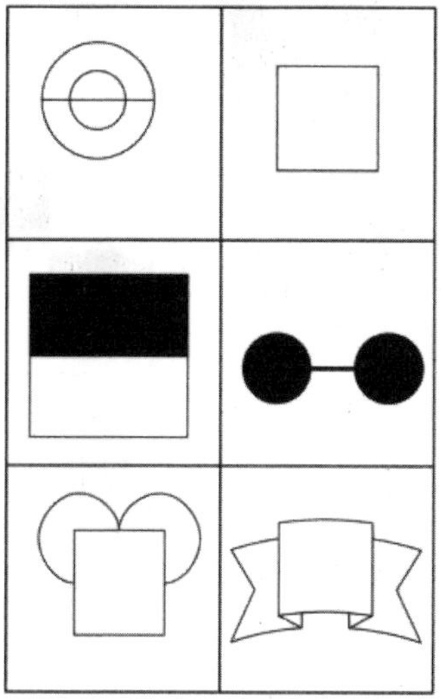

- A Set A
- B Set B
- C Neither

Answer

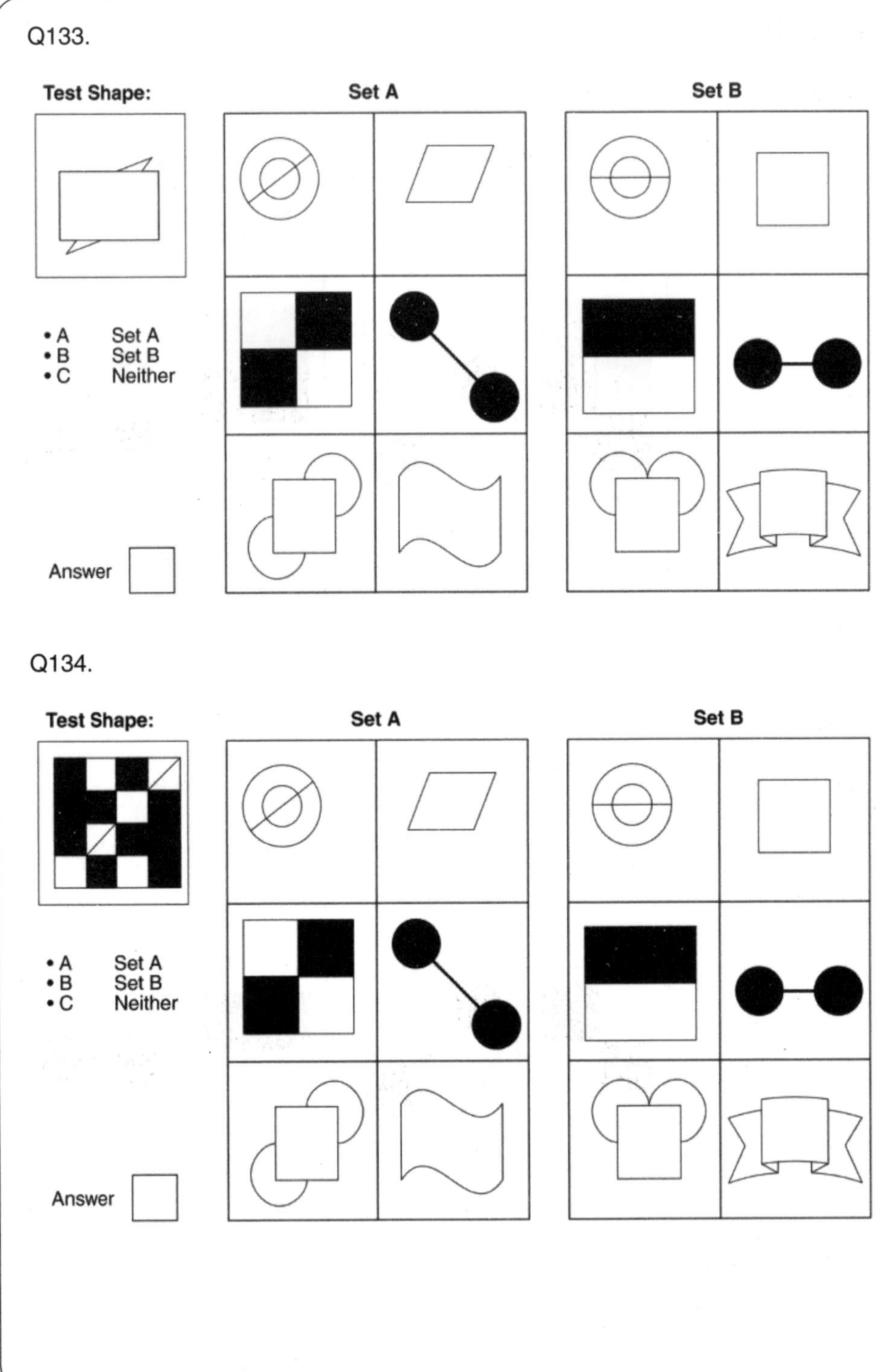
Q133.
Test Shape:
Set A
Set B
• A Set A
• B Set B
• C Neither
Answer
Q134.
Test Shape:
Set A
Set B
• A Set A
• B Set B
• C Neither
Answer

Q135.

Test Shape: **Set A** 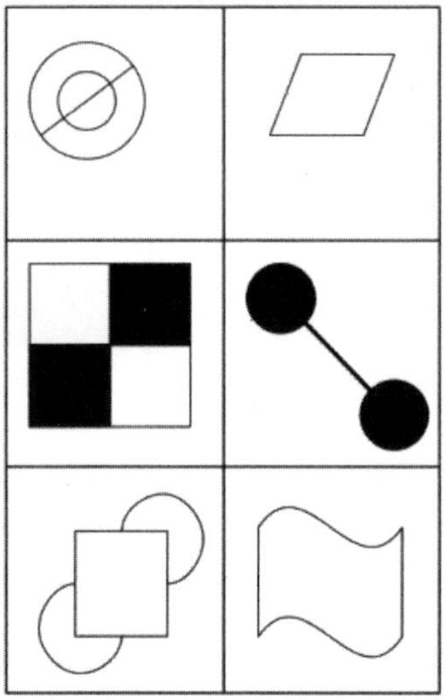 **Set B**

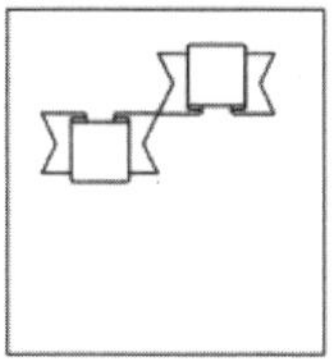

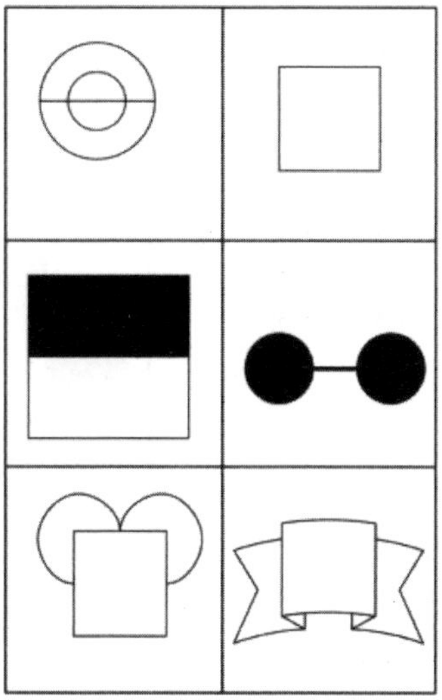

- A Set A
- B Set B
- C Neither

Answer

Q136.

Test Shape: **Set A**  **Set B**

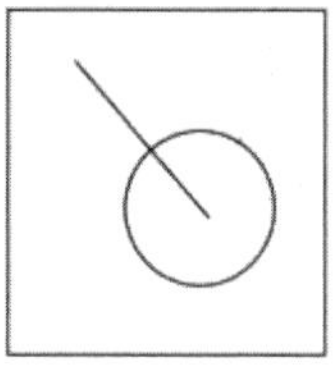

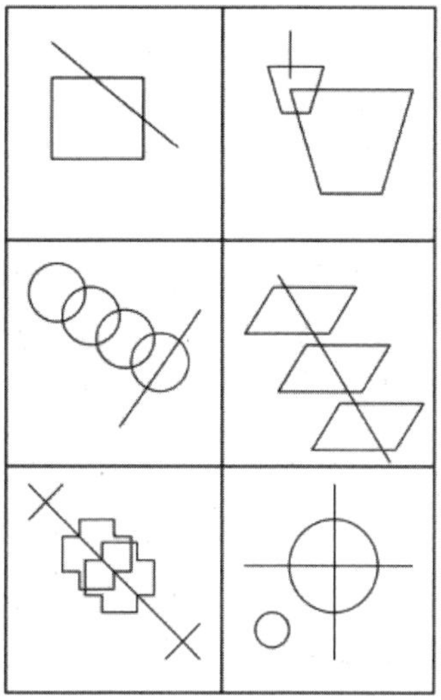

- A Set A
- B Set B
- C Neither

Answer

Q137.

Test Shape:

Set A

Set B

- A Set A
- B Set B
- C Neither

Answer

Q138.

Test Shape:

Set A

Set B

- A Set A
- B Set B
- C Neither

Answer

Q139.

Test Shape:

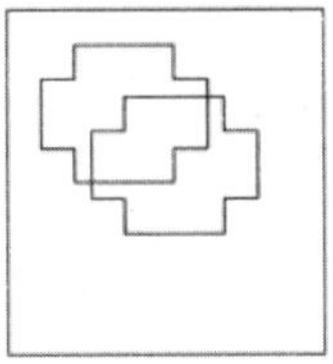

Set A

Set B

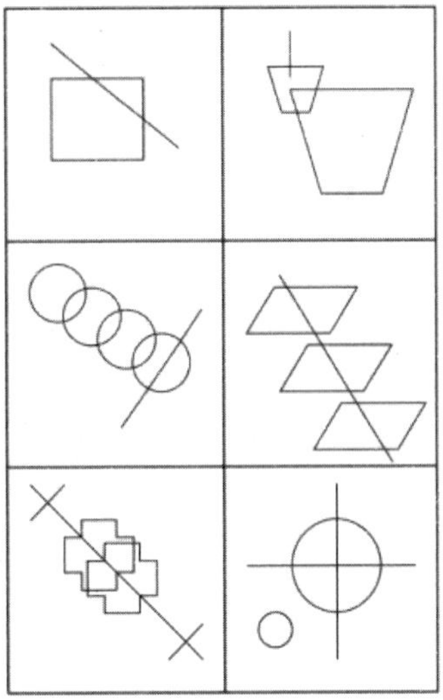

- A Set A
- B Set B
- C Neither

Answer

Q140.

Test Shape:

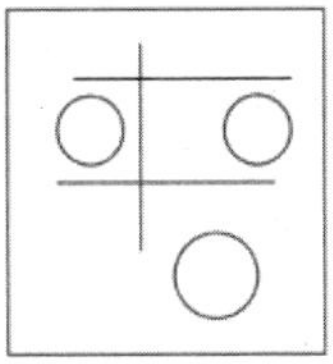

Set A

Set B

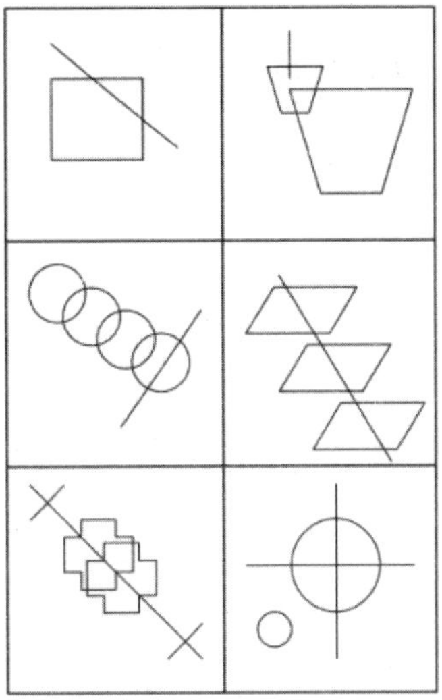

- A Set A
- B Set B
- C Neither

Answer

End of test

Mini-test 5

Q141.

Test Shape:

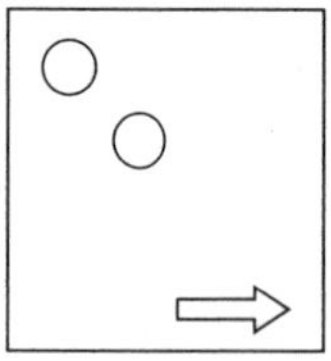

Set A

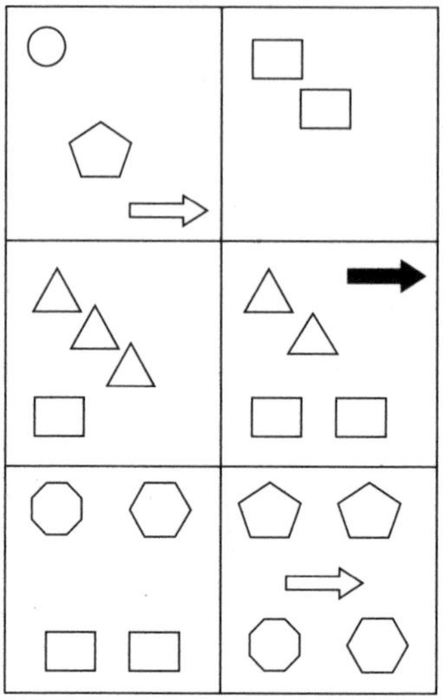

Set B

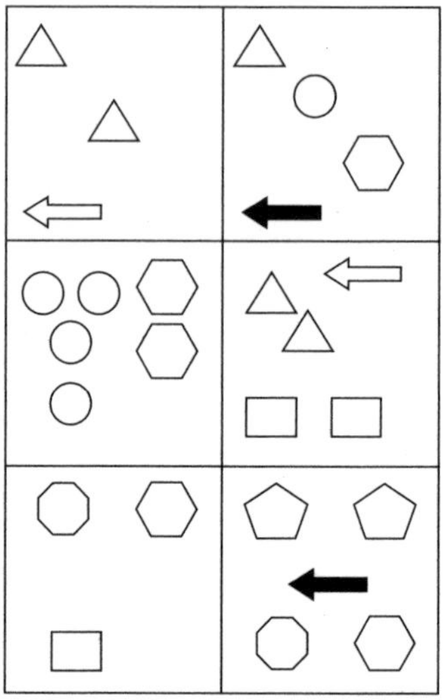

- A Set A
- B Set B
- C Neither

Answer

Q142.

Test Shape:

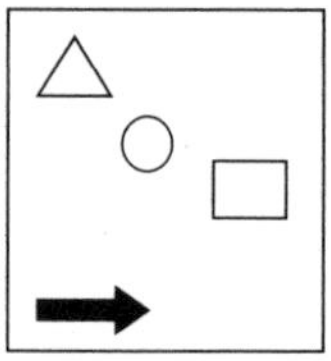

Set A

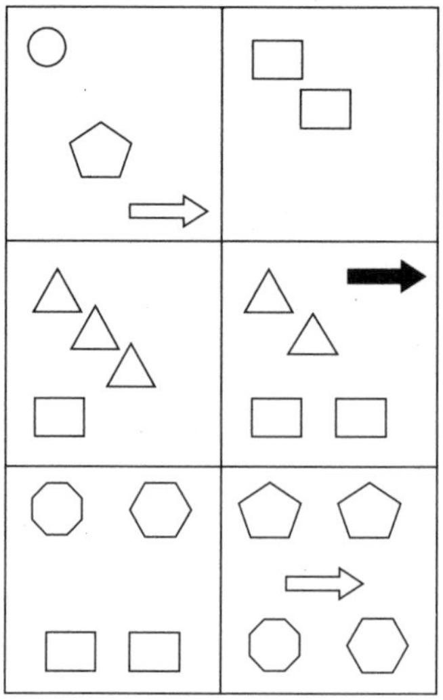

Set B

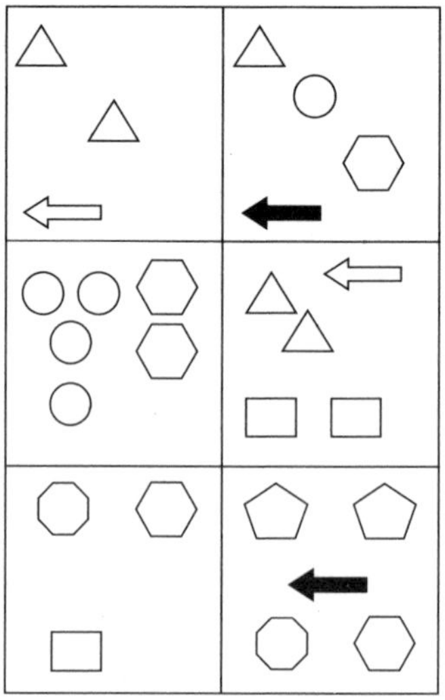

- A Set A
- B Set B
- C Neither

Answer

Q143.

Test Shape:

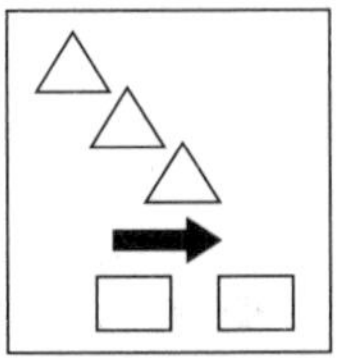

Set A

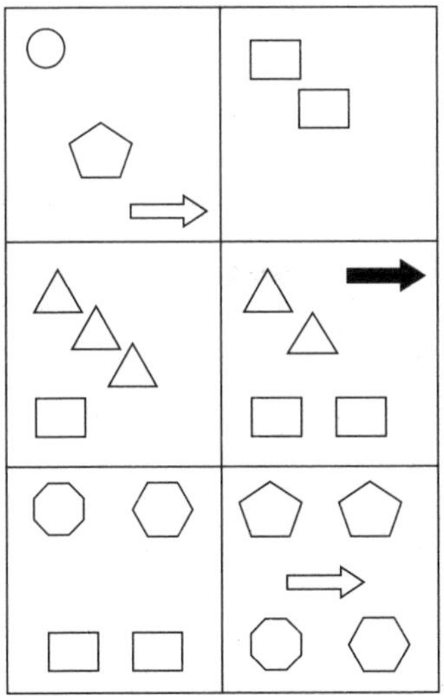

Set B

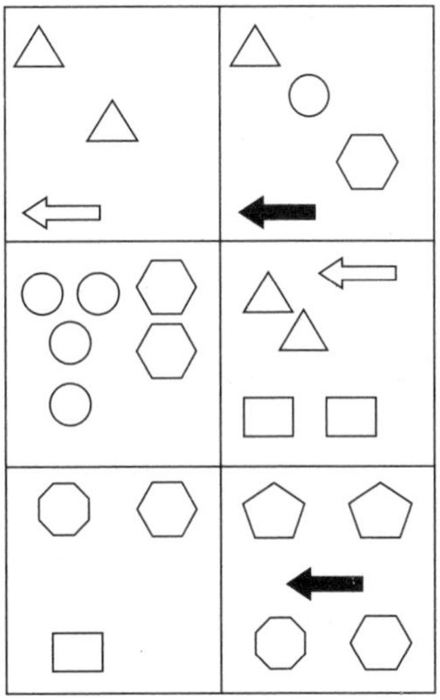

- A Set A
- B Set B
- C Neither

Answer

Q144.

Test Shape:

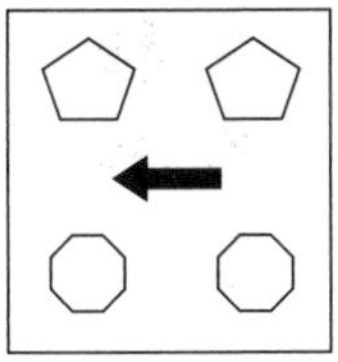

Set A

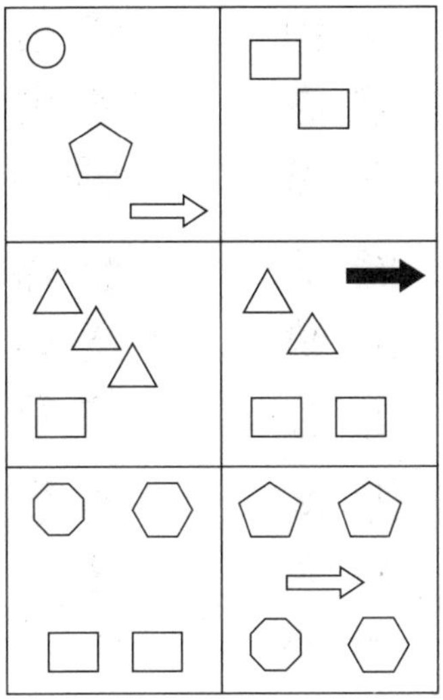

Set B

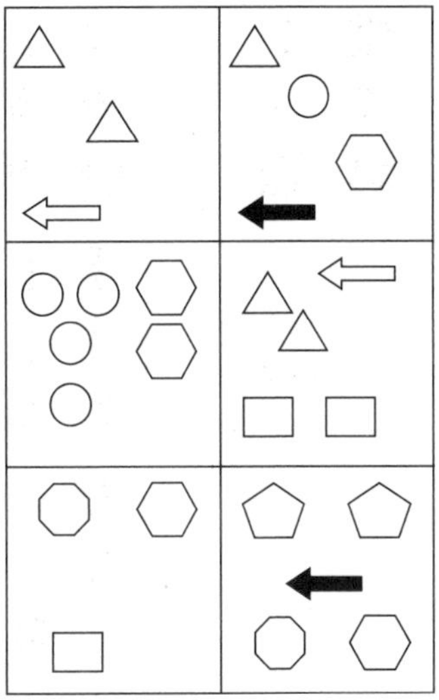

- A Set A
- B Set B
- C Neither

Answer

Q145.

Test Shape:

Set A

Set B

- A Set A
- B Set B
- C Neither

Answer

Q146.

Test Shape:

Set A

Set B

- A Set A
- B Set B
- C Neither

Answer

Q147.

Test Shape:

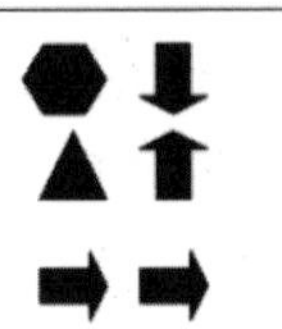

Set A

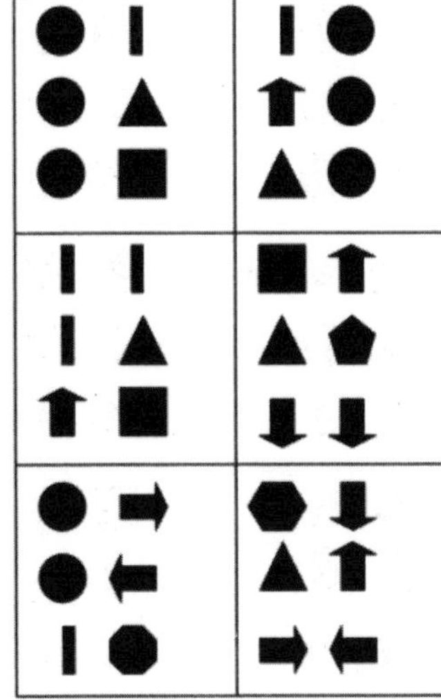

Set B

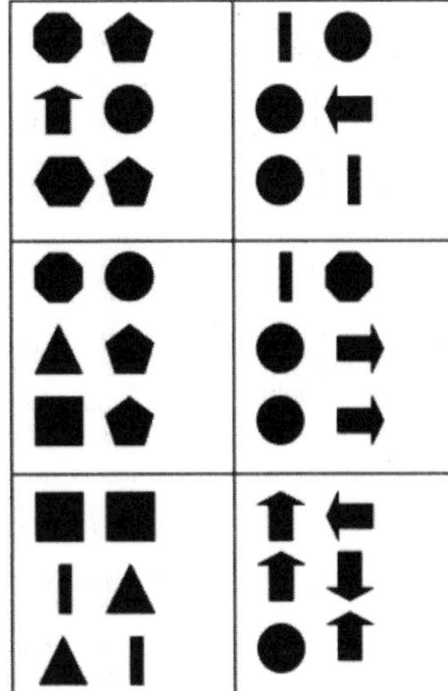

- A Set A
- B Set B
- C Neither

Answer

Q148.

Test Shape:

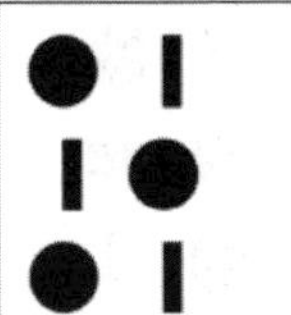

Set A

Set B

- A Set A
- B Set B
- C Neither

Answer

Q149.

Test Shape: **Set A** 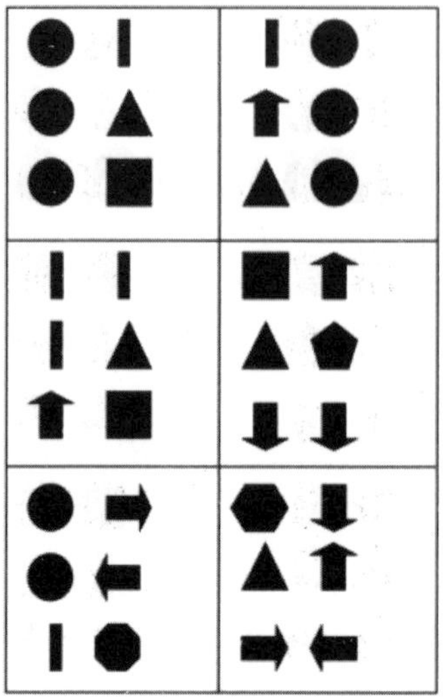 **Set B**

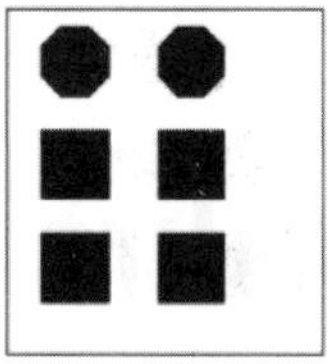

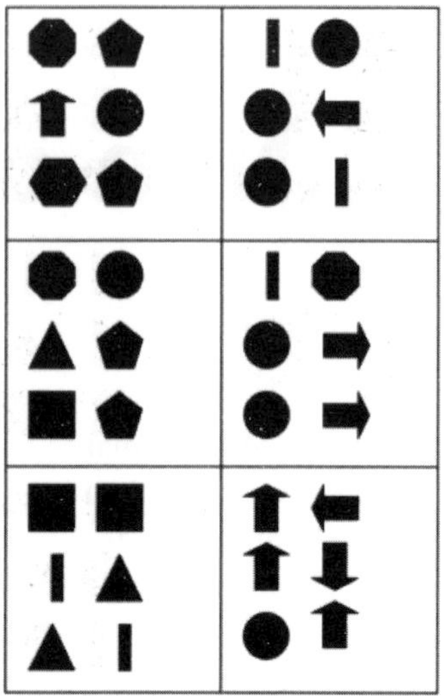

- A Set A
- B Set B
- C Neither

Answer

Q150.

Test Shape: **Set A** 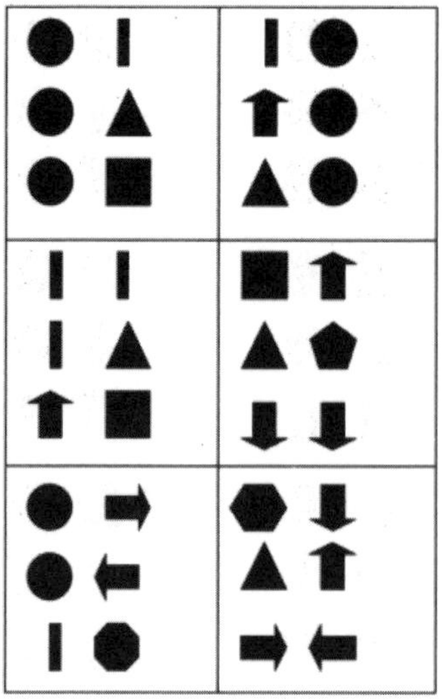 **Set B**

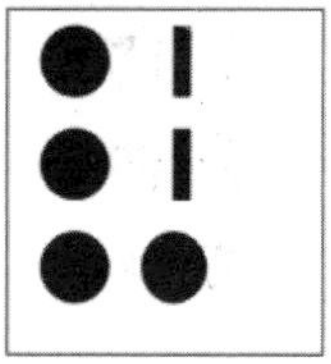

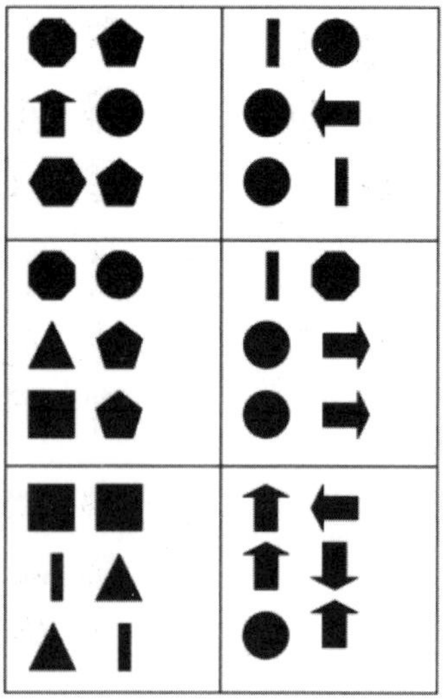

- A Set A
- B Set B
- C Neither

Answer

End of test

6

Non-cognitive analysis

The fifth sub-test that makes up the UKCAT is very different in nature from the other four and so we have saved it till last. In fact it is not a test in the true sense of the word (more a questionnaire) and is scored very differently from the other sub-tests. Its stated aim is to expand the range of information available on candidates by providing a report on attributes and characteristics regarding the candidate's personal style. Take this to mean that they will use your responses to build a psychometric profile of your attitude and personality. While people may be reluctant to call them tests and they say no answer is right or wrong, your responses may mean that you are offered counselling or advice on your working style. In the future your answers may be used to decide if your application should be accepted or rejected so take the questions seriously. You have 30 minutes in which to complete this section of the UKCAT and you are required to consider a list of statements and indicate your personal response to each of them. Be sure to download and work through the sample questions available as a PDF on the UKCAT website.

Some people mistakenly believe that you cannot improve your performance in this style of test. They are wrong, because many people rush this type of exercise and do not give the statements it contains sufficient consideration.

It is essential in this type of exercise that you answer the questions truthfully, but it is equally essential that you keep at the front of your mind the context of the question. You are applying for a place at medical school and it is in this context that you are answering the questions. With each question ask yourself: 'As an applicant to medical school, how would I respond in that situation?' Take the first example of the practice questions below: 'I would describe myself as tactful.' You should be able to answer this question positively. You might be able to think up some situation when you would not describe yourself as tactful, perhaps when out with your friends or at home with your family. But this would be the totally wrong response in the context of the question. How you sometimes act with your friends or family is irrelevant to your future role in the medical profession. In such a position tact is essential, and candidates who cannot describe themselves as tactful may not be selected.

Responding truthfully to the questions will sometimes mean that you admit to something that risks counting against you. For example, if you have not undertaken voluntary work and you are asked if you have, be prepared to say so. It is unlikely that a few negative-scoring answers will significantly affect your overall score, and anyway if you lie and it is discovered at a later stage your application may be rejected.

Look out and take extra care if any questions include double negatives. They can be very misleading and you can easily answer them in a way that you did not intend. An example of this sort of question might be: 'Do you agree or disagree with the statement: It is not true that I'm 18 years of age.' This sort of question can be confusing, especially if you are suffering anxiety during the real test. The way to approach this sort of question is to break it down into parts. Begin by answering the factual bit of the question, in this instance 'Are you 18 years of age?' Now add the 'It is not true' part of the question. This in effect changes your answer. If you are 18 then you would disagree that it is not true that you are 18 years of age.

When answering the questions it is best not to give too many responses that imply strongly held views. If you do, you might risk the impression that you are someone too strident in your opinions, with many strongly held views. It is also best not to give too many non-committal responses either, as this might indicate that you find it difficult to make up your mind or commit yourself. It is fine to give some of these strongly held or non-committal responses, but try not to indicate too many.

Be sure that you are confident recognizing the synonyms of key personality attributes desirable in medics. The UKCAT website refers to, for example, 'empathy and robustness' (there are other key attributes, so research them) and you should be entirely familiar with the meaning of these terms and their synonyms ('empathy' suggests sharing someone's feelings, talking the same language, relating to, feeling for, putting yourself in someone else's shoes and sympathizing; 'robustness' includes being practical, hands-on, realistic, pragmatic, matter-of-fact, sensible, unsentimental and down-to-earth and having common sense). You need to be familiar with the synonyms so that despite any nervousness during the UKCAT you can confidently identify the statement as something that you as an applicant medic can agree with or disagree with.

It is important to be consistent in your response. These tests often return to investigate the same issue a number of times (each may be worded differently). You should try to answer these related questions consistently. It can be a bit tricky, because these related questions are spread out through the body of questions. To help you practise spotting and consistently answering related questions we have identified in the explanations a good few but not all the related questions.

In the real non-cognitive analysis test some of the questions require you to read additional information, which is viewed by clicking an 'exhibit' key. Obviously we do not offer this feature, but in these practice questions we have provided a number of background scenarios. When you come across one, you should answer the related questions that follow only in the context of the information contained in the scenario.

Below you will find 100 practice questions. To each you must indicate your personal response. Remember to give honest, considered responses. Be truthful while presenting as many of your positive attributes as possible. Do this by asking yourself in every instance: 'How would I respond to this question as an applicant to medical school?' Use the examples to develop your understanding of yourself and the qualities that you possess that will help make you a great applicant to medical school.

We cannot provide model answers to these questions because in many instances the answers will depend on you. In the answers chapter we have provided an explanation for each of the questions by indicating the likely way in which they will be interpreted and we have indicated the questions that you should have answered consistently. Note that answering questions consistently does not mean that you should have agreed or disagreed with every example of that type but that your approach to the issue is consistent (and a consistent approach might mean you agree with one statement but disagree with another).

Allow yourself 30 seconds for each of the following 100 practice questions.

Q1. I would describe myself as tactful.

Strongly agree ☐

Agree ☐

Neither agree nor disagree ☐

Disagree ☐

Disagree strongly ☐

Q2. I am not more practical than compassionate.

- Strongly agree ☐
- Agree ☐
- Neither agree nor disagree ☐
- Disagree ☐
- Disagree strongly ☐

Additional information for Q3:

Society takes the view that healthcare has to be rationed. As a society we simply cannot afford to treat all conditions.

Q3. Given the fact that healthcare must be rationed I reluctantly conclude that someone who engages in high-risk activities can't expect the same level of medical care as someone who lives life more moderately.

- I agree with this conclusion. ☐
- Generally I agree with this conclusion. ☐
- Generally I would not agree with this conclusion. ☐
- I particularly agree with this conclusion. ☐
- I do not particularly agree with this conclusion. ☐

Q4. I struggle to pay attention to small detail.

I totally disagree with the statement. ☐

I don't agree with the statement. ☐

I partially agree with the statement. ☐

I agree with the statement. ☐

I totally agree with the statement. ☐

Q5. The only reason I do not steal is because I would not want others to steal from me.

Disagree strongly ☐

Disagree ☐

Neither agree nor disagree ☐

Agree ☐

Strongly agree ☐

Q6. People who know me would not describe me as passionate about things.

This is not particularly true about me. ☐

This is particularly true about me. ☐

This is not true about me. ☐

Generally this is true about me. ☐

This is true about me. ☐

Q7. If I was asked to do something critical I would hurry to complete the job I was doing in order to begin the new assignment.

Strongly agree ☐

Agree ☐

Neither agree nor disagree ☐

Disagree ☐

Disagree strongly ☐

Q8. Only those qualified in the field should contribute to a debate.

I totally agree with the statement. ☐

I agree with the statement. ☐

I partially agree with the statement. ☐

I don't agree with the statement. ☐

I totally disagree with the statement. ☐

Q9. I prefer to leave a fast-changing situation for others to deal with.

I totally disagree with the statement. ☐

I don't agree with the statement. ☐

I partially agree with the statement. ☐

I agree with the statement. ☐

I totally agree with the statement. ☐

Q10. I do not find it frustrating to listen to someone who speaks painfully slowly.

This is true about me. ☐

Generally this is true about me. ☐

Generally this is not true about me. ☐

This is particularly true about me. ☐

This is not particularly true about me. ☐

Q11. People have said they find it hard to get to know me.

Strongly agree ☐

Agree ☐

Neither agree nor disagree ☐

Disagree ☐

Disagree strongly ☐

Q12. If after leaving a shop I realized they had given me too much change I would turn around, re-enter the shop and point out their mistake.

Disagree strongly ☐

Disagree ☐

Neither agree nor disagree ☐

Agree ☐

Strongly agree ☐

Additional information for Q13 and Q14:

Mary is an extremely challenging customer. She presented herself at casualty two or three times a week and was usually offensive and sometimes violent. She was prone to self-harm and suffered mental health problems.

Q13. If a colleague was being disrespectful to Mary their behaviour would be excusable so long as it was out of character and they did not take the same attitude with other patients.

This is false. ☐

This is mostly false. ☐

This is mostly true. ☐

This is true. ☐

Q14. After Mary had left, your colleague realized that she had dropped some money, just a few coins to a total value of under a couple of pounds; you decided to put them in the hospital fundraising tin at the main reception.

This was an ok thing to do. ☐

This was not really the best thing to do but understandable in the circumstances. ☐

This was not the best thing to do. ☐

This was the wrong thing to do. ☐

Q15. I am not that interested in hearing about alternative lifestyles.

I totally disagree with the statement. ☐

I don't agree with the statement. ☐

I partially agree with the statement. ☐

I agree with the statement. ☐

I totally agree with the statement. ☐

Q16. I am known for my astuteness.

Strongly agree ☐

Agree ☐

Neither agree nor disagree ☐

Disagree ☐

Disagree strongly ☐

Q17. At some time or another everyone makes a mistake and when I make one I try my hardest to put right the situation and then tell someone in authority what happened and what I did to put it right.

Strongly agree ☐

Agree ☐

Neither agree nor disagree ☐

Disagree ☐

Disagree strongly ☐

Q18. I would prefer others described me as serious rather than lucid.

Strongly agree ☐

Agree ☐

Neither agree nor disagree ☐

Disagree ☐

Disagree strongly ☐

Q19. If someone was really rude to me I might show my disdain but nothing more.

Strongly agree ☐

Agree ☐

Neither agree nor disagree ☐

Disagree ☐

Disagree strongly ☐

Q20. The end justifies the means.

This is false. ☐

This is mostly false. ☐

This is mostly true. ☐

This is true. ☐

Q21. If I were asked to help organize an outing for some people with learning difficulties I would say I am too busy.

I totally disagree with the statement. ☐

I don't agree with the statement. ☐

I partially agree with the statement. ☐

I agree with the statement. ☐

I totally agree with the statement. ☐

Q22. I believe that it is better to help someone you know such as a neighbour rather than a stranger.

This is true about me. ☐

Generally this is true about me. ☐

Generally this is not true about me. ☐

This is particularly true about me. ☐

This is not particularly true about me. ☐

Q23. People may say one thing but they often mean something else.

I totally disagree with the statement. ☐

I don't agree with the statement. ☐

I partially agree with the statement. ☐

I agree with the statement. ☐

I totally agree with the statement. ☐

Q24. I prefer to work independently.

I totally agree with the statement. ☐

I agree with the statement. ☐

I partially agree with the statement. ☐

I don't agree with the statement. ☐

I totally disagree with the statement. ☐

Q25. I like to talk about things that many people find personal.

I totally disagree with the statement. ☐

I don't agree with the statement. ☐

I partially agree with the statement. ☐

I agree with the statement. ☐

I totally agree with the statement. ☐

Q26. If already very busy and you were asked to complete an additional lengthy task, you would take on the new assignment without complaint and complete it only when you got all your other jobs done.

Strongly agree ☐

Agree ☐

Neither agree nor disagree ☐

Disagree ☐

Disagree strongly ☐

Q27. I have never lied in my life.

- Disagree strongly ☐
- Disagree ☐
- Neither agree nor disagree ☐
- Agree ☐
- Strongly agree ☐

Q28. The views of someone with long service are no more important than those of someone who has only been in an organization for a short time.

- I totally agree with the statement. ☐
- I agree with the statement. ☐
- I partially agree with the statement. ☐
- I don't agree with the statement. ☐
- I totally disagree with the statement. ☐

Q29. I believe that a single sincere voice can be louder than a crowd's.

- This is not particularly true about me. ☐
- This is particularly true about me. ☐
- Generally this is not true about me. ☐
- Generally this is true about me. ☐
- This is true about me. ☐

Q30. On the occasions I have felt frustration with others I wished I had not done so.

I totally disagree with the statement. ☐

I don't agree with the statement. ☐

I partially agree with the statement. ☐

I agree with the statement. ☐

I totally agree with the statement. ☐

Q31. People who know me would describe me as sensitive.

This is not particularly true about me. ☐

This is particularly true about me. ☐

This is partially true about me. ☐

Generally this is true about me. ☐

This is not true about me. ☐

Q32. I don't much enjoy social events at which I will not know anyone.

I totally disagree with the statement. ☐

I don't agree with the statement. ☐

I partially agree with the statement. ☐

I agree with the statement. ☐

I totally agree with the statement. ☐

Q33. I am comfortable in providing a justification for the conclusions I have reached.

I totally agree with the statement. ☐

I agree with the statement. ☐

I partially agree with the statement. ☐

I don't agree with the statement. ☐

I totally disagree with the statement. ☐

Q34. It is not true that it is best not to tell someone something they do not want to hear.

Strongly agree ☐

Agree ☐

Neither agree nor disagree ☐

Disagree ☐

Disagree strongly ☐

Q35. In my spare time I would rather pursue my hobby on my own than attend a club with others who share the same interest.

I totally disagree with the statement. ☐

I don't agree with the statement. ☐

I partially agree with the statement. ☐

I agree with the statement. ☐

I totally agree with the statement. ☐

Q36. I best cope with distressing situations by being emotionally detached.

This is not particularly true about me. ☐

This is particularly true about me. ☐

This is not true about me. ☐

Generally this is true about me. ☐

This is true about me. ☐

Q37. I do not steal because I am afraid of getting caught.

Disagree strongly ☐

Disagree ☐

Neither agree nor disagree ☐

Agree ☐

Strongly agree ☐

Q38. In a few very rare circumstances I might make a racist remark.

This is true about me. ☐

Generally this is true about me. ☐

Generally this is not true about me. ☐

This is particularly true about me. ☐

This is not particularly true about me. ☐

Q39. I am prone to vagueness and sometimes lose all track of time.

I totally disagree with the statement. ☐

I don't agree with the statement. ☐

I partially agree with the statement. ☐

I agree with the statement. ☐

I totally agree with the statement. ☐

Q40. Some people want a career in which they might make a difference, others can think of no better reward than a large salary. I agree with the former.

I totally agree with the statement. ☐

I agree with the statement. ☐

I partially agree with the statement. ☐

I don't agree with the statement. ☐

I totally disagree with the statement. ☐

Q41. If I found some money on the street and could not see who it belonged to I might put it in a charity box.

Disagree strongly ☐

Disagree ☐

Neither agree nor disagree ☐

Agree ☐

Strongly agree ☐

Q42. It would be right to say I am thick-skinned.

This is not particularly true about me. ☐

This is particularly true about me. ☐

This is not true about me. ☐

Generally this is true about me. ☐

This is true about me. ☐

Q43. To be non-judgemental is not to be without an ethical code.

Strongly agree ☐

Agree ☐

Neither agree nor disagree ☐

Disagree ☐

Disagree strongly ☐

Q44. Some people believe that nowadays if you still smoke after all the negative press and warnings about the habit and you go on to get a smoking-related illness then you should not expect the National Health Service to treat you at public expense.

This is true about me. ☐

Generally this is true about me. ☐

Generally this is not true about me. ☐

This is particularly true about me. ☐

This is not particularly true about me. ☐

Q45. I find it difficult to get used to people.

Strongly agree ☐

Agree ☐

Neither agree nor disagree ☐

Disagree ☐

Disagree strongly ☐

Q46. In a life-saving situation it may not be possible to deal considerately with people.

Strongly agree ☐

Agree ☐

Neither agree nor disagree ☐

Disagree ☐

Disagree strongly ☐

Q47. Until they give me reason to act otherwise I usually take what people say at face value.

I totally disagree with the statement. ☐

I don't agree with the statement. ☐

I partially agree with the statement. ☐

I agree with the statement. ☐

I totally agree with the statement. ☐

Q48. I prefer to work in a situation where most important decisions are made by (and responsibility rests with) senior management.

I totally agree with the statement. ☐

I agree with the statement. ☐

I partially agree with the statement. ☐

I don't agree with the statement. ☐

I totally disagree with the statement. ☐

Q49. You were late for your shift, and although no one noticed, when you saw your manager at break time you would notify them of your late start.

This is what I would do. ☐

This is what I may do; it would depend on the circumstances. ☐

I may not do this. It would depend on how many times I had been late before. ☐

I would not do this. ☐

Q50. People who know me would describe me as demonstrative rather than reserved.

Strongly agree ☐

Agree ☐

Neither agree nor disagree ☐

Disagree ☐

Disagree strongly ☐

Q51. People may say one thing and from my experience they do not usually mean something else.

I totally disagree with the statement. ☐

I don't agree with the statement. ☐

I partially agree with the statement. ☐

I agree with the statement. ☐

I totally agree with the statement. ☐

Q52. A person who can't speak English can't expect the same level of service as someone who can.

This is true about me. ☐

Generally this is true about me. ☐

Generally this is not true about me. ☐

This is particularly true about me. ☐

This is not particularly true about me. ☐

Q53. It is never necessary to lie.

Disagree strongly ☐

Disagree ☐

Neither agree nor disagree ☐

Agree ☐

Strongly agree ☐

Q54. It would be right to say I am thin-skinned.

This is not particularly true about me. ☐

This is particularly true about me. ☐

This is not true about me. ☐

Generally this is true about me. ☐

This is true about me. ☐

Q55. I am sometimes so distracted by my private thoughts that I make small mistakes.

I totally disagree with the statement. ☐

I don't agree with the statement. ☐

I partially agree with the statement. ☐

I agree with the statement. ☐

I totally agree with the statement. ☐

Q56. If you were sent to find a senior member of staff and deliver an urgent message but when you located the person you found them deep in conversation with a colleague, you would interrupt their conversation immediately even if it appeared rude.

Strongly agree ☐

Agree ☐

Neither agree nor disagree ☐

Disagree ☐

Disagree strongly ☐

Q57. People who know me would say first and foremost I am an enthusiastic person.

This is not particularly true about me. ☐

This is particularly true about me. ☐

This is not true about me. ☐

Generally this is true about me. ☐

This is true about me. ☐

Q58. I would rather be a councillor than a counsellor.

I totally disagree with the statement. ☐

I don't agree with the statement. ☐

I partially agree with the statement. ☐

I agree with the statement. ☐

I totally agree with the statement. ☐

Q59. I would describe my approach to the suffering of others as unfeeling.

This is not particularly true about me. ☐

This is particularly true about me. ☐

This is not true about me. ☐

Generally this is true about me. ☐

This is true about me. ☐

Q60. I often do things spontaneously.

- Strongly agree ☐
- Agree ☐
- Neither agree nor disagree ☐
- Disagree ☐
- Disagree strongly ☐

Q61. I wear my emotions on my sleeve.

- This is not particularly true about me. ☐
- This is particularly true about me. ☐
- Generally this is not true about me. ☐
- Generally this is true about me. ☐
- This is true about me. ☐

Q62. If I was in a national supermarket store and someone in an obvious state of desperation was shoplifting food, I would inform the nearest shop assistant.

- Disagree strongly ☐
- Disagree ☐
- Neither agree nor disagree ☐
- Agree ☐
- Strongly agree ☐

Q63. Working as a part of a team is a more important part of the role of a health professional than keeping abreast of the latest advances in medical knowledge.

I totally agree with the statement. ☐

I agree with the statement. ☐

I partially agree with the statement. ☐

I don't agree with the statement. ☐

I totally disagree with the statement. ☐

Q64. I prefer work that is familiar and routine because it helps with my confidence.

I totally disagree with the statement. ☐

I don't agree with the statement. ☐

I partially agree with the statement. ☐

I agree with the statement. ☐

I totally agree with the statement. ☐

Q65. I would find it slightly irritating if I held out my hand to someone and they declined to shake it.

This is true about me. ☐

Generally this is true about me. ☐

Generally this is not true about me. ☐

This is particularly true about me. ☐

This is not particularly true about me. ☐

Q66. I would not find it irritating if I had to interrupt what I was doing in order to do something else.

- Strongly agree ☐
- Agree ☐
- Neither agree nor disagree ☐
- Disagree ☐
- Disagree strongly ☐

Q67. I have regretted some things I have said and done.

- Strongly agree ☐
- Agree ☐
- Neither agree nor disagree ☐
- Disagree ☐
- Disagree strongly ☐

Q68. Morals are something the well-off can afford but if you are worried where the next meal will come from then they may be a luxury you can't afford.

- This is false. ☐
- This is mostly false. ☐
- This is mostly true. ☐
- This is true. ☐

Q69. Before I say something I often find myself pausing to check that what I am going to say is the correct thing.

I totally disagree with the statement. ☐

I don't agree with the statement. ☐

I partially agree with the statement. ☐

I agree with the statement. ☐

I totally agree with the statement. ☐

Q70. I am known for my shrewd power of judgement.

Strongly agree ☐

Agree ☐

Neither agree nor disagree ☐

Disagree ☐

Disagree strongly ☐

Q71. It would not irritate me if someone would not make eye contact with me when I spoke to them.

This is true about me. ☐

Generally this is true about me. ☐

Generally this is not true about me. ☐

This is particularly true about me. ☐

This is not particularly true about me. ☐

Q72. People who know me would call me unemotional rather than unassuming.

Strongly agree ☐

Agree ☐

Neither agree nor disagree ☐

Disagree ☐

Disagree strongly ☐

Q73. People would describe my approach to people as bold and decisive rather than delicate and diplomatic.

Strongly agree ☐

Agree ☐

Neither agree nor disagree ☐

Disagree ☐

Disagree strongly ☐

Additional information for Q74 and Q75:

It has been a very stressful day and you and your colleagues are finding it hard to cope.

Q74. Under the circumstances it would be acceptable to use bad language in front of patients.

This is false. ☐

This is mainly false. ☐

This is mostly true. ☐

This is true. ☐

Q75. Under the circumstances it would be acceptable to let off steam by using bad language but only in front of your colleagues.

This is false. ☐

This is mainly false. ☐

This is mostly true. ☐

This is true. ☐

Q76. Honesty is always the best policy.

Disagree strongly ☐

Disagree ☐

Neither agree nor disagree ☐

Agree ☐

Strongly agree ☐

Q77. If there is an attractive woman in the team, it is only natural that the men present will try to impress her.

I totally agree with the statement. ☐

I agree with the statement. ☐

I partially agree with the statement. ☐

I don't agree with the statement. ☐

I totally disagree with the statement. ☐

Q78. I prefer to eat familiar food rather than try something new that I have not eaten before.

I totally disagree with the statement. ☐

I don't agree with the statement. ☐

I partially agree with the statement. ☐

I agree with the statement. ☐

I totally agree with the statement. ☐

Q79. If I had to classify myself as either emotional or insensitive then I would choose the former.

This is not particularly true about me. ☐

This is particularly true about me. ☐

This is not true about me. ☐

Generally this is true about me. ☐

This is true about me. ☐

Q80. I believe that charity should begin and largely end at home.

This is true about me. ☐

Generally this is true about me. ☐

Generally this is not true about me. ☐

This is particularly true about me. ☐

This is not particularly true about me. ☐

Q81. I would rather people described me as approachable than polite.

Strongly agree ☐

Agree ☐

Neither agree nor disagree ☐

Disagree ☐

Disagree strongly ☐

Q82. Others may think of me as naïve but not wary.

Strongly agree ☐

Agree ☐

Neither agree nor disagree ☐

Disagree ☐

Disagree strongly ☐

Q83. If you hear one of your colleagues being teased over their sexuality the correct thing to do is to let people know that you don't think it's a fitting way to behave.

This is false. ☐

This would normally be true but if you had only just started in the role then you might ignore it to begin with. ☐

This would only be true if you felt the person being teased objected to the treatment. ☐

This is true. ☐

Q84. Nearly everyone would be OK with taking some paper and the odd pen from work for, for example, a relative's, or the neighbour's, children and no one would really count it as stealing.

Disagree strongly ☐

Disagree ☐

Neither agree nor disagree ☐

Agree ☐

Strongly agree ☐

Q85. Out of youthful exuberance I might be cheeky but I would not be disrespectful and would never be malicious.

Strongly agree ☐

Agree ☐

Neither agree nor disagree ☐

Disagree ☐

Disagree strongly ☐

Q86. There are some sorts of people I know I am not going to get on with.

This is true about me. ☐

Generally this is true about me. ☐

Generally this is not true about me. ☐

This is particularly true about me. ☐

This is not particularly true about me. ☐

Q87. I would rather work in a situation where things go to plan and I find it an effort to deal with a situation if the unexpected occurs.

I totally disagree with the statement. ☐

I don't agree with the statement. ☐

I partially agree with the statement. ☐

I agree with the statement. ☐

I totally agree with the statement. ☐

Q88. When painful choices have to be made I would not commit myself until all the facts are known.

Strongly agree ☐

Agree ☐

Neither agree nor disagree ☐

Disagree ☐

Disagree strongly ☐

Q89. People would say I show greater integrity than a non-judgemental attitude.

Strongly agree ☐

Agree ☐

Neither agree nor disagree ☐

Disagree ☐

Disagree strongly ☐

Q90. A compromise is rarely the right decision.

Strongly agree ☐

I totally agree with the statement. ☐

I agree with the statement. ☐

I partially agree with the statement. ☐

I don't agree with the statement. ☐

I totally disagree with the statement. ☐

Q91. In some very rare circumstances it might be right to steal.

Disagree strongly ☐

Disagree ☐

Neither agree nor disagree ☐

Agree ☐

Strongly agree ☐

Q92. I would still do my best to see the job through if I found it harder to assist in a child's post-mortem, rather than someone who had died in their seventies.

Strongly agree ☐

Agree ☐

Neither agree nor disagree ☐

Disagree ☐

Disagree strongly ☐

Q93. I am prone to be impulsive and regret some of the things I do afterwards.

Strongly agree ☐

Agree ☐

Neither agree nor disagree ☐

Disagree ☐

Disagree strongly ☐

Q94. People who know me would describe my approach to people more as matter-of-fact rather than down-to-earth.

Strongly agree ☐

Agree ☐

Neither agree nor disagree ☐

Disagree ☐

Disagree strongly ☐

Q95. Unlike the vast majority of people, if when you made a cash withdrawal from an ATM (automatic teller machine) the machine dispensed £10 too much you would visit the branch of the bank the next day and hand the overpayment in.

This is false. ☐

This is mostly false. ☐

This is mostly true. ☐

This is true. ☐

Q96. You have to pay attention to people's motives as to why they are saying something.

I totally disagree with the statement. ☐

I don't agree with the statement. ☐

I partially agree with the statement. ☐

I agree with the statement. ☐

I totally agree with the statement. ☐

Q97. My motivation to work to a very high standard might suffer if I were in a role that involved delivering the same procedure over and over again.

Strongly agree ☐

Agree ☐

Neither agree nor disagree ☐

Disagree ☐

Disagree strongly ☐

Q98. I am able to talk about things that many people find personal.

I totally disagree with the statement. ☐

I don't agree with the statement. ☐

I partially agree with the statement. ☐

I agree with the statement. ☐

I totally agree with the statement. ☐

Q99. I expect to take joint responsibility for actions at work.

I totally agree with the statement. ☐

I agree with the statement. ☐

I partially agree with the statement. ☐

I don't agree with the statement. ☐

I totally disagree with the statement. ☐

Q100. It is true that we should all try not to say one thing and do another but in reality it is often acceptable not to do this.

This is false. ☐

This is mostly false. ☐

This is mostly true. ☐

This is true. ☐

7

Answers and explanations

Chapter 2 Verbal reasoning

Warm up questions

Q1. Answer: Cannot tell

Explanation: The passage states that it is now possible to relocate without affecting earning power but the reason for this new development is not given in the passage. It might be because of new technology but we cannot rule out the possibility that there are other causes; for example, the reason might be that it is the introduction of new legislation that allows workers a better work–life balance. Because we cannot establish new technology as the reason we must conclude that we cannot tell if the statement is true or false.

Q2. Answer: False

Explanation: Two reasons for the increase in popularity are mentioned in the passage, and although the passage dwells mainly on one of them, commuter towns, the issue of second-home hotspots is also raised as a reason for the increase in popularity.

Q3. Answer: True

Explanation: This is a tough question, so don't be too hard on yourself if you got it wrong. Although the passage does not mention a traditional high street with local shops, it is reasonable to conclude that this concept might form part of 'an idea of an unspoilt civic centre'. The statement starts with 'an idea' not 'the idea' and states it 'could include' not 'does or should include'. These are weak assertions and allow for many possibilities and for this reason the correct answer is true.

Q4. Answer: Cannot tell

Explanation: The passage states that the most sought-after domesticated varieties prefer a ph of 6.5, but we cannot tell or infer from the information given if other varieties of wild asparagus also share this characteristic.

Q5. Answer: True

Explanation: Inedible means indigestible, unpalatable or poisonous. It is not expressly stated in the passage that the berries are indigestible, unpalatable or poisonous for humans but if we look to the context of the passage then it is clear that we can infer this information. The passage is about asparagus and its edible spears and it is stated that people all over the world enjoy eating them. The context of the passage therefore is asparagus and people growing it or picking it to eat. Given this context we can infer that the berries are inedible for humans. It might be that the berries are inedible for other species too but we cannot infer this from the passage.

Q6. Answer: False

Explanation: The passage states that wild asparagus grows in Europe, northern Africa and central Asia but it also states that cultivated asparagus grows in Canada so we can infer that the statement is false.

Q7. Answer: True

Explanation: The passage states 'when each year an average of 500,000 immigrants entered the country' and we can conclude from the 'when' that the figure is no longer half a million a year. We cannot know if the current figure is higher or lower but it is reasonable to infer that it is no longer 500,000.

Q8. Answer: True

Explanation: This answer depends on how the words 'immigration' and 'inward migration' are used in the passage, and this is an example of a question when what your dictionary says about these terms is beside the point. In the passage 'immigration' is used in a confusing way and can be taken to mean either the inward or outward movement of people. For this reason the term 'inward migration' would better serve the author's intended meaning.

Q9. Answer: False

Explanation: The passage states that 'Some employers stand to gain much from the improved supply of labour and savings made from not having to train young people' and it is reasonable to conclude that such employers are 'winners' in a climate of large-scale inward migration.

Q10. Answer: Cannot tell

Explanation: This is another tough question. The passage states that Jupiter has a rocky core but no information is provided regarding the other gaseous planets and this information cannot be inferred from the passage.

Q11. Answer: False

Explanation: Again this is a tough one and a close call between true and false. False is the preferred answer because a synonym of a word is one that has the same meaning and in the passage the words huge and giant are treated as synonyms in reference to describing the size of the huge/giant gaseous planets Jupiter, Uranus and Neptune. But we cannot conclude that the words moon and satellite are used as synonyms. They occur in the passage in relation to the discoveries of the Voyager probes where it is written 'all were found to have distinctive rings, satellites (or moons)' and there are two possible interpretations here. One is that the words are interchangeable and we can call them either satellites or moons but it is equally possible that the author intended to introduce a difference between the two terms and in some instances it would be correct to use the term moon and in another the term satellite. In this second situation the words would not be synonyms and for this reason it is false to conclude that in the passage the terms moon and satellite are treated as synonyms.

Q12. Answer: Cannot tell

Explanation: Passage 4 is shorter than you might expect in the UKCAT. This is intentional, as we wanted to surprise the reader and provide practice at dealing with questions that seem to have very little direct reference to the passage. The order of the gaseous planets from the sun is not explicitly stated in the passage. Neptune is stated as taking the longest (165 years) to rotate the sun but we cannot infer from this that it is the furthest from the sun. We know that Uranus and Neptune both lie beyond Jupiter in terms of being further from the sun.

Q13. Answer: True

Explanation: It is stated in the passage that the dollar has traded at lower than its historic rate against the Chinese and Indian currencies and that this is bound to continue and has occurred for a reason other than indebtedness of the US economy. For this reason it is true that even if the US economy were free of debt it is probable that the dollar would have weakened and stayed weak against at least some of the world's currencies.

Q14. Answer: False

Explanation: The passage is about the weakness of the US dollar and not about the possibility or otherwise of a US recession. What the author meant by the term inevitable, therefore, is that it was inevitable that the dollar would weaken.

Q15. Answer: Cannot tell

Explanation: It is clear from the opening sentence that people expected the dollar to weaken and that they expected this to happen sooner than it did, but it is not possible to infer the time frame for these predictions. We are told that an economy like that of the United States can live beyond its means for years but not that people were predicting the correction for years.

Q16. Answer: Cannot tell

Explanation: Aside from the benefits of saving on infrastructure investment costs and power loss to resistance in transmission wires, the passage does not describe the motive for the investment in the local generation of the community's energy needs.

Q17. Answer: Cannot tell

Explanation: The energy needs of the community are not quantified and so we are unable to establish whether or even when the wind turbines are turning and the solar panels generating hot water for the hundreds of homes that this amounts to most of the community's energy needs.

Q18. Answer: False

Explanation: The answer to this question is a close call between false and cannot tell. However, while it is a close-run thing, false is the preferred answer because it is stated in the passage that the community's local generation of power has led to savings on the investment cost of additional transmission lines in the national network. In other words, the network has not had to be expanded because of local generation. If the national network were practically non-existent then local generation would do more than save on further expansion – it would help avoid the initial enormous investments in building centralized power plants and transmission lines in the first place. We can infer therefore that it is false to describe that network as practically non-existent.

Q19. Answer: Cannot tell

Explanation: If more than 30 million jobs were lost to India then the case that many skilled jobs will be moved will not be strengthened unless those extra lost jobs were skilled. Moving low-skilled jobs would not strengthen the case and we are not told if the extra jobs involved are skilled or unskilled.

Q20. Answer: True

Explanation: Three reasons why companies are moving jobs to India are identified in the passage: because it is easier to fill highly skilled, English-speaking positions there; because, for the time being, wages for these roles are notably lower there than wages in Europe and America, and because companies want to position their businesses where they believe the future lies.

Q21. Answer: False

Explanation: This claim is not examined in the passage and none of the passage is relevant in terms of either supporting or contradicting it. It is false therefore that the claim can be rebutted by the contents of the passage.

Q22. Answer: False

Explanation: Before we could infer that the sum of the annual running costs of the listed electrical appliances amounted to the average household's net electricity bill we would need to know that the list was exhaustive and listed every item. We do not know this so we cannot infer that the sum of the listed items provides the total net annual bill for the household.

Q23. Answer: False

Explanation: The main point of the passage is not an account of the saving that could be made if we were more frugal with our use of electrical appliances but to provide an illustration of how much we spend using everyday appliances and (secondary point) how much we could save if we were more frugal in using them.

Q24. Answer: Cannot tell

Explanation: The answer is a close call between true and cannot tell. The preferred answer, however, is cannot tell because two examples are provided of the sort of things we would need to do to reduce waste (not leave unnecessary lights on, not leave appliances unnecessarily on standby), and while these examples would not have much of an impact on our daily lives they are only an example of the sort of thing we would need to do in order to make the saving indicated. Before we could determine the extent to which the difference would impact on our daily lives we would need details of all the things we would need to do.

Q25. Answer: False

Explanation: The passage describes beautiful things that we cannot see and if, as instructed, we take the meaning literally then we cannot see all beauty and it is not in the eye of the beholder but in some of the other senses too.

Q26. Answer: Cannot tell

Explanation: The answer to this question is a close call between false and cannot tell. Cannot tell is the preferred answer because the passage states that an idea can be beautiful and lack physical structure while a smell can be beautiful and lack physical appearance (it still has a physical structure). In the context of the opening sentence the term 'form' could mean either appearance or structure and so we cannot tell if by saying a thing of beauty can completely lack physical form it is meant that it lacks physical structure or physical appearance.

Q27. Answer: True

Explanation: Admittedly, this is a difficult question, but the answer is true because the word image confuses the case made in the passage because we see images with our eyes and this implies a contradiction with the claim that we can find a scent beautiful despite it being impossible to see it.

Q28. Answer: True

Explanation: The opening sentence of the passage states that over $50 billion was spent online last year and it is hardly surprising that criminals want a share of the action, and it is reasonable to rephrase this as online shopping offers the criminal the promise of rich pickings.

Q29. Answer: False

Explanation: The passage states that most people do not secure their virtual shops to the same degree as their physical shops, and while the physical shop will be attended and have locks and alarms fitted, their virtual shop will have no more than a firewall, antivirus and anti-spyware software. These virtual securities are therefore not the equivalent of shop assistants, locks and alarms but are inferior in terms of security.

Q30. Answer: Cannot tell

Explanation: While antivirus and anti-spyware software does update automatically and this may well mean that the business owner will believe their security will remain up to date, we cannot establish this from the information contained in the passage so the correct answer is cannot tell.

Q31. Answer: Cannot tell

Explanation: The views of the author cannot be established from the passage. The author is reporting findings rather than stating his or her personal opinions and for this reason we cannot tell if he or she is opposed.

Q32. Answer: False

Explanation: We are told that profits of British pubs have fallen by 20% and many have reported a further worsening of their financial state since the introduction of a new law and a series of tax increases, but it is not possible (or reasonable) to infer from this that some pubs are operating at a loss or not at a profit.

Q33. Answer: Cannot tell

Explanation: We are told that the smoking ban has led to a marked decrease in pub custom but cannot infer from this that pub customers have been encouraged to drink and smoke less because they may simply be drinking and smoking the same amount but at home instead of in the pub.

Q34. Answer: True

Explanation: Even though the passage states that millions of law-abiding people have used recreational drugs, it is clear that users, if found in possession of these drugs, are breaking laws as they face penalties of imprisonment or fines. To be a user unavoidably involves being in possession and so someone who has used recreational drugs can only now be law abiding if they are no longer using them. But if they are using recreational drugs then it is not true that they are law abiding.

Q35. Answer: True

Explanation: The passage offers the opinion that using these drugs in your own home should be no one else's business but your own and this would include the courts and police.

Q36. Answer: Cannot tell

Explanation: This question is made more difficult by the intentionally ambiguous passage. However, it is stated in the passage that dealing in these drugs can result in imprisonment for up to 14 years, but the drugs in question are those classified as class C drugs, the lowest classification. We are not informed of the penalties for dealing in the other categories so we cannot know if the statement is true or false.

Q37. Answer: Cannot tell

Explanation: We are told that 20 years after the eruption only 4,000 of the original population of 12,000 remain. We cannot infer from this that therefore only 4,000 live on the island because it is possible, for example, that people arrived from elsewhere to live on the island, making the population greater than 4,000.

Q38. Answer: False

Explanation: The evacuation averted a greater disaster but the death of 19 people and the irrevocable loss of the way of life that existed before the eruption are still a disaster.

Q39. Answer: False

Explanation: It is true that there must be a mistake but the mistake could lie in either the date 1997 or the figure of 20 years, so it is false that there must be a mistake in the date 1997 as the question states.

Q40. Answer: Cannot tell

Explanation: We are told that the first manned landing was made in 1969 and that probes made soft landings in the 1960s, but we cannot tell from the information given if any landings (unmanned) occurred before that time.

Q41. Answer: Cannot tell

Explanation: The passage states that the later missions visited highlands but we cannot tell from this whether or not the landing occurred in a mountainous region.

Q42. Answer: True

Explanation: The passage is about the manned lunar landings and the search for suitable sites for those landings. The soft landings performed by probes are described in terms of the search for suitable sites for the manned landings. Given the context, reference to a suitable site in the second sentence can be taken to mean suitable for manned missions.

Q43. Answer: False

Explanation: We suffer a suspension of judgement only when we spend money that we intended to use for something essential or unintentionally create an unauthorized overdraft.

Q44. Answer: True

Explanation: The passage states that there is a widely held perception that electronic money and credit are somehow not as real or valuable as notes and coins and that retailers play on this emotional weakness. It is reasonable to take this to mean that electronic money and credit have a lower psychological value than cash in your hand.

Q45. Answer: Cannot tell

Explanation: The passage does not mention a licensing scheme, nor does it indicate if unregulated sites are also unlicensed.

Q46. Answer: True

Explanation: The effects of rising food prices are uneven and for some of the landless poor and, in some places, poor food-importing nations, the burden is greatest.

Q47. Answer: True

Explanation: The subject of the passage is the rise in world food prices and how the effect of this is that some countries and individuals have benefited from this while others are suffering.

Q48. Answer: True

Explanation: The passage states that governments of the poorest food-importing countries are counterbalancing the rapid rises in the prices of staple foods with improved food subsidy programmes. To counterbalance something is not to compensate it nor to stop or bring to an end the rise in food prices.

Q49. Answer: True

Explanation: The term estimate means approximation and does not usually imply a commitment to spend. The passage states that the decision to proceed with the project has still to be made, so it is reasonable to conclude that in this instance the estimated build cost does not include a commitment to spend.

Q50. Answer: False

Explanation: The passage states that the construction work has been priced at a figure higher than the annual gross domestic product of one-quarter of the world's nations, not the sum of the annual gross domestic product of one-quarter of the world's nations.

Q51. Answer: True

Explanation: The plan is described as widening both sides of 240 miles of motorway so it does involve 480 miles of construction – 240 miles of road each side of the motorway.

Q52. Answer: Cannot tell

Explanation: We cannot tell if the current advantages of PFIs will always remain and we cannot infer from the passage that PFIs are used to fund the building of every type of public building (the passage only lists schools, hospitals, social housing and prisons).

Q53. Answer: True

Explanation: The fact that PFIs count as off-balance-sheet expenditure is described as the most important for the government and, for this reason, if the other advantage was no longer to exist, the government might still prefer to use PFIs.

Q54. Answer: False

Explanation: It would in fact be more open to misinterpretation. The private sector bears the cost of building, not the government. The government leases the building and is able to spread out the cost of the lease.

Q55. Answer: False

Explanation: This question is made more difficult by the statement in the passage that 'the same is sadly true' (this statement links the two parts). But a holiday resort that provides a school for local children is an example of a tour operator who is contributing to the local community. The use of an image of a non-existent farmhouse on the product of a meat factory is cynical, while the employment of local people and the provision of social buildings are not.

Q56. Answer: True

Explanation: Historically a bandwagon was literally a wagon carrying a band (playing music) and a metaphor is when a word or phrase is used in a context when it is not literally the case.

Q57. Answer: Cannot tell

Explanation: The passage states only one motive for why tourists prefer to use the services of a tour operator who is contributing to the local community and ecosystem, and that is that they want a guilt-free holiday. We cannot tell if the tourist has other motives.

Q58. Answer: False

Explanation: We are told that the jet stream determines the boundary between Arctic and Atlantic air and we are informed that in north America and northern Europe when the jet stream moves south cold air is experienced and when it moves north warm air is experienced, but this does not allow us to infer that Arctic air is relatively cold and Atlantic air relatively warm.

Q59. Answer: Cannot tell

Explanation: We are unable to identify where this part of the world is from the information given. It could be in northern Europe but it could just as easily be in North America or anywhere on the Atlantic side of the northern hemisphere.

Q60. Answer: False

Explanation: The key qualities of the jet stream on which the explanation of the changeable nature of the weather in the northern hemisphere depends are that it separates the Arctic and Atlantic air and moves around more in the spring and autumn. Neither of these qualities is affected should it in fact not be true that the jet stream is a two-mile-high column of wind.

Mini-test 1

Q1. Answer: False

Explanation: The case for smaller families in the developed world is not dependent on the question of whether or not the population of the developed world is growing or contracting but on the higher carbon dioxide emission lifestyle of people living in the developed world.

Q2. Answer: Cannot tell

Explanation: The passage states that having a child in the developed world has a greater environmental impact than having a child in the developing world. Before we can know that a child not born in the developing world will effect a major cut in a family's future carbon dioxide emissions we would need information about the level of carbon dioxide output produced by the family. If they produced no or very little carbon dioxide then having fewer children would not result in a major cut in their family's future carbon dioxide output.

Q3. Answer: False

Explanation: You are only likely to get this question wrong if you are sacrificing accuracy too much to speed. The passage states that of the 4 million workers who have paid into a pension scheme for the bulk of their working life, only those who have paid into a final salary scheme will enjoy retirement on two-thirds of their final salary and the rest will have to manage on far less because their pension scheme lacked the final salary guarantee.

Q4. Answer: Cannot tell

Explanation: We are told that workers need two-thirds of their final salary to be comfortable in their retirement but we are not told the amount needed to be secure. It is reasonable to infer that the amount needed to be secure (safe) is less than the amount needed to be comfortable. But we cannot infer that 40 per cent of final salary is either sufficient or insufficient to be secure in retirement so the correct answer is cannot tell.

Q5. Answer: False

Explanation: We are told that the population of workers is 15 million (4 million contributing to a pension scheme and a remaining 11 million who have made no or very little contribution to a scheme other than the compulsory state scheme). We can also establish from the passage that the total population of the country to which the passage refers must be greater than 15 million because it also includes some retired people (see the first sentence which reads 'to enjoy a comfortable retirement, many retired people recommend retiring on two-thirds of final salary'). The correct answer therefore is false.

Mini-test 2

Q1. Answer: False

Explanation: The fact that the French national health service is probably the best in the world is left aside so is not a factor attributed to the lower level of heart disease. The passage therefore attributes three factors to the lower level of death caused by heart disease: remaining active, consuming more fruit and vegetables and enjoying more red wine.

Q2. Answer: False

Explanation: It is true that twice as many may still amount to very few but the last sentence of the passage states that 'this allows significant numbers of people to live until their centenary' and just a few people living until their centenary would not be described as a significant number.

Q3. Answer: False

Explanation: The passage states that if extreme weather was occurring more frequently then it is feasible that the forecast might include the prediction that the frequency of these events will continue to be higher than the historic average. It is therefore not a mistake to believe that the exceptional can be forecast in the long term.

Q4. Answer: Cannot tell

Explanation: Neither the date when the passage was written nor the year of the summer to which the passage refers is indicated, so it is not possible to tell from the passage if the summer of 2007 was very wet and windy.

Q5. Answer: Cannot tell

Explanation: It is clear from the passage that the frequency of exceptional events can be predicted, but this is not to predict specific weather events such as an incidence of extreme flooding. While the forecast failed to predict these events last summer, it cannot be established from the passage whether or not it is possible to predict such events as a matter of principle.

Mini-test 3

Q1. Answer: False

Explanation: The passage states that in almost zero gravity and no wind, very large droplets or, in other words, globules of water can form so it is false to say that the passage disproves this.

Q2. Answer: False

Explanation: The passage states that 'in every situation droplets do collide and these combine to form larger droplets that may well survive'.

Q3. Answer: True

Explanation: English is described as a dominant, apparently all-conquering, language and as more and more of the world speak it, it will break up into dialects and then distinct languages.

Q4. Answer: False

Explanation: The passage does answer the question (although the answer is incomplete). It is stated that in the case of a language spoken by a small linguistic community it becomes extinct when there is no one left in that community and it describes how a dominant language might become extinct if it breaks down into dialects which then evolve into new languages.

Q5. Answer: True

Explanation: Ambivalent means in two minds and the passage offers first an account of the theory that English will evolve into dialects and then new languages but also describes this view as controversial because speech is standardized and dialects are prevented from forming.

Mini-test 4

Q1. Answer: Cannot tell

Explanation: We are only informed that there were a total of 23 student volunteers and cannot infer from this how this number was split between the various roles.

Q2. Answer: True

Explanation: All the volunteers were male and the passage provides no indication that women might act differently. For this reason it is true that it is wrong to deduce from the passage that women volunteers would act differently.

Q3. Answer: False

Explanation: Three of Philip Zimbardo's factors are identified in the passage: conformity, anonymity and boredom.

Q4. Answer: True

Explanation: The passage is about how Japan can maintain its competitiveness given the projected fall in its population and the disproportionately elderly character of that population. The proposed answer is through innovation. Although the passage also considers how Japan can remain innovative, unless it engages in new ways of thinking and changes in worldwide values this is a secondary issue and the 'big' question posed is one of competitiveness.

Q5. Answer: False

Explanation: No abilities are attributed to India or China in the passage, nor can you infer from the tone of the passage that the predicted success of these nations is due to their ability to engage in new ways of thinking.

Mini-test 5

Q1. Answer: True

Explanation: The passage states that the S section of the English dictionary is the largest in terms of the number of entries and that 'the longest section in the Italian dictionary and the section that contains the most entries is the S section'.

Q2. Answer: Cannot tell

Explanation: The passage states that the S section contains the largest number of entries but we cannot infer from this that the section is also the longest. It is possible that another section has fewer entries but is longer because of the extent of the definitions.

Q3. Answer: Cannot tell

Explanation: We are told that the Q section of the English dictionary is the shortest but this does not mean that it necessarily has close to the fewest number of entries. The Q section of the Italian dictionary contains close to the shortest number of Italian entries but we are not told how many foreign word entries the J, K, Y and W sections of the Italian dictionary contain (we are told that they are very short as they only contain foreign words used in Italian) and they may be shorter than the Q section.

Q4. Answer: False

Explanation: The list is correct in that the names begin with successive letters of the alphabet and alternate between boy and girl names but there are only eight names and in a typical year nine named storms would occur.

Q5. Answer: Cannot tell

Explanation: We are told that initially only girls' names were used but later this was changed so that the names alternated from boy to girl names. But we cannot establish when this change took place. The question implies that weather forecasts are no longer broadcast over shortwave radio but if this practice stopped there is nothing in the passage to suggest when or whether it stopped before the change to the naming of storms with both boy and girl names.

Mini-test 6

Q1. Answer: False

Explanation: The passage states that their colours hark back to the days when flags were extensively used for identification and communication. So their previous use gave rise to the colours and symbolic designs used today and not the rectangular shape.

Q2. Answer: False

Explanation: You are informed in the passage that the flag of the Republic of Ireland was inspired by the tri-colour of the French revolution and that the tri-colour was blue, white and red. It is possible to infer from the passage that the tri-colour design was the inspiration for the flag of the Republic and that they adopted different colours from those adopted by France.

Q3. Answer: True

Explanation: We can tell that this statement is true because in the passage the use of the symbolic designs and their meanings is mentioned. For example, the crescent moon and cross are referred to as identifying the official religion of a nation.

Q4. Answer: False

Explanation: The passage states that the new threat to personal liberty is how to prevent complete strangers finding out our personal details. While this is quite the opposite problem of the old issue of secrecy, it does not mean that the old problem of finding out the personal details that organizations are holding on us no longer exists. It could be that we now face two threats and for this reason the statement is false.

Q5. Answer: True

Explanation: Penultimate means last but one and the sentence states 'if the person for whom you are searching is active on a social network site or an internet specialist interest forum then you may well be able to identify a database of friends and contacts and by reading recent postings obtain a flavour of their views and preferences'. From this it is clearly the case that the penultimate sentence of the passage illustrates the sort of things that people post on the internet.

Mini-test 7

Q1. Answer: False

Explanation: Satellite images being used to locate a fabled and lost city is not an example of the scientific debunking of popular belief but the scientific confirmation of popular belief (it could be taken as an example of the scientific whittling away of mystery).

Q2. Answer: Cannot tell

Explanation: The passage asks the question 'Do scientific investigations of our past add to our understanding…?' This raises the possibility that science can play a positive role but the passage does not provide an answer to the question raised so we cannot tell from the passage if science can in fact play a positive role,

Q3. Answer: False

Explanation: It is stated that 5 per cent of Canadian land is suitable for the growing of crops while 10 per cent of Russian land is arable and we are also told that Russia is a bigger nation than Canada. But before we can infer from this that Russian arable production is greater than that of Canada we would need to know that the Canadian productivity per hector was not far higher than Russian productivity. Without this information we cannot rule out the possibility that Russian productivity is in fact lower than that of Canada despite Canada having less arable land.

Q4. Answer: Cannot tell

Explanation: This is quite a tough question, which you may well get wrong if you rely on knowledge from outside the passage. Cover means extend over while astride means on both sides. If there is a difference in the meaning of these two phrases then it is one of fact (the extent to which Russia covers the northern parts of the continents of Europe and Asia) and we are not provided with sufficient information to decide which description, covers or sits astride, is the more correct.

Q5. Answer: True

Explanation: Polar means Arctic or Antarctic, cold or freezing, and both countries are described as having a sizable extent of frozen wilderness. The passage states that the majority of Russians live in the temperate part of the country while the bulk of Canadians have settled in the clement conditions found within 400 km of the border. From these statements we can infer that the author of the passage would agree that the polar regions of both countries are relatively sparsely populated.

Mini-test 8

Q1. Answer: Cannot tell

Explanation: The bases of the statements made in the passage are not explained, nor can they be inferred from the contents of the passage.

Q2. Answer: True

Explanation: If the sentence read swell rather than wave it would be consistent with the definition of the difference between waves and swell provided at the start of the passage.

Q3. Answer: False

Explanation: Providing an explanation of what happens after death is attributed to all religions in general and no exception for Buddhism is made.

Q4. Answer: True

Explanation: The passage is not illustrated with details from Hinduism (it is only stated that it is the oldest of the major religions). Details from Buddhism (does not identify a supreme god), Sikhism (its sacred test is called the Adi Granth), Judaism (the synagogue is the place for communal prayer), Christianity (celebrate baptism) and Islam (celebrate important events in the life of the Prophet) do illustrate the passage.

Q5. Answer: False

Explanation: The main theme of the passage is an examination of more than the ceremonies, festivals and observances of the world's major religions and the lives of the prophet or prophets and the lives of the followers. The main theme is an examination of the sense of community, the shared set of values that shape daily life, the definition of the meaning of life and sets of beliefs as to how the world began and what happens after death that religion provides as well as the ceremonies, festivals and observances of the world's major religions and the lives of the prophet or prophets and the lives of the followers.

UKCAT-style verbal reasoning timed test 1

1. True: first paragraph, fourth sentence: family history.
2. False: first paragraph, fifth sentence: usually the doctor's surgery.
3. Can't tell: true but not stated in the text.
4. True: second paragraph, second sentence: psychotherapy encourages a person to talk freely.

5. True: first paragraph, sixth sentence: below 18 °C remain dormant.
6. False: to more than 1,000 at body temperature; not at room temperature.
7. True: second paragraph, second sentence: Campylobacter multiplies rapidly in the body and is responsible for most of the food poisoning in the UK.
8. True: second paragraph, third and fifth sentences.

9. True: second paragraph, third sentence: carbon dioxide not carbon monoxide.
10. Can't tell: third paragraph: not stated either way.
11. False: second paragraph, third sentence: nitrogen oxides also contribute to acid rain.
12. False: last paragraph: methane is not indicated to be a precursor chemical for ozone and acid rain; methane contributes to global warming.

13. False: first paragraph, fifth and sixth sentences: four books.
14. True: compare fifth sentence of first paragraph and third sentence of second paragraph.
15. False: last paragraph, last sentence: float is topped up to original level.
16. Can't tell: second paragraph, fifth sentence: there may or may not be discrepancies because there could be differences.

17. Can't tell: first paragraph: impossible to say; honey was used for medicinal purposes in ancient times, but its use as a foodstuff is not commented on.
18. True: second paragraph, third sentence: UKCAT questions do not require specialist knowledge, but 'bactericidal' clearly means killing bacteria.
19. False: second paragraph, second sentence: states it as a key feature, but this does not identify it as the main aim.
20. True: last paragraph, last sentence: 'no report' does not mean that it has been ruled out.

21. False: first paragraph, second sentence: almost one-quarter.
22. True: second paragraph, second sentence.
23. Can't tell: last paragraph, fourth sentence: 1.1 only indicates a need to lose weight.
24. Can't tell: last paragraph, last sentence: only maximum safe waist measurements stated, with no reference to obesity.

25. True: first paragraph, second sentence: over age 30 (age 29 in the question).
26. True: last paragraph, fourth sentence: for a further 15 years.

27. False: last paragraph, third sentence: non-UK EU citizens are disenfranchised where UK general elections are concerned; their position is clarified further in the last sentence.
28. Can't tell: second paragraph, first sentence: only if resident in the UK.

29. True: first paragraph, third and fourth sentences: state height restriction is 2 metres and the daily rate is punitive.
30. True: last paragraph, first sentence: short stay and long stay (with different tariffs).
31. Can't tell: last paragraph, fifth sentence: insufficient information given on the charges.
32. Can't tell: second paragraph, last sentence: states on the ground floor of car park 3 with no reference to parking on the roof.

33. True: second paragraph: private mint in Birmingham used steam power prior to the Royal Mint.
34. False: last paragraph, second sentence: first phase opened in 1968.
35. Can't tell: last paragraph: insufficient information to establish whether the Tower could also strike special proof coins as well as Llantrisant.
36. True: last paragraph, first sentence: decimalization 1971; last sentence: Tower Hill 1975.

37. Can't tell: the type of fungus that causes wet rot is not mentioned.
38. Can't tell: last paragraph, sixth sentence: impossible to tell, because an intact paint surface can mask fungal penetration.
39. True: last paragraph, second sentence: if the normal water content of wood exceeded 20 per cent then dry rot could never be prevented.
40. False: last paragraph, second sentence: it is only necessary to understand the concept of percentage to recognize that 20 per cent is not high.

UKCAT-style verbal reasoning timed test 2

1. Can't tell: first paragraph, sixth sentence: we are told that Titan is the second-largest satellite and 1.5 times the size of the moon, but there could be several satellites ranging in size between the two.
2. Can't tell: Jupiter has 60 moons, but this is not stated to be the most.
3. Can't tell: The argument is said to be consistent with and not proof of.
4. Can't tell: water on Europa is capable of sustaining life but there is no mention of the atmosphere.

5. True: end of last paragraph: cooking oil fires are Class F.
6. True: three types: water, foam and dry powder.
7. Can't tell: foam is suitable for Classes A and B but not Classes E and F; Class D is not mentioned.
8. Can't tell: no comparison is drawn between the likelihood of flammable liquids and solids reigniting.

9. True: first paragraph, third sentence: more in China than in any other country.
10. Can't tell: last paragraph, first sentence: Latin must have been displaced by another language, but one is not stated.
11. True: last paragraph, fourth sentence: three times as many non-native speakers as native speakers.
12. Can't tell: last paragraph, last sentence: India is ranked above the United States, and Nigeria is ranked above the UK, but the ranking of the United States in relation to Nigeria is not indicated.

13. True: first paragraph, last sentence: the canal network was doomed and investment was redirected into railways.
14. Can't tell: last paragraph, second and third sentences: no direct comparison of leisure and industrial use is made.
15. False: first paragraph, fifth sentence: more quickly than by canal.
16. Can't tell: last paragraph, last sentence: there may be more boats but these are not necessarily all narrowboats.

17. True: last paragraph, sixth sentence: failure of a single system will not affect any other workstations.
18. False: last paragraph, seventh sentence: direct contradiction; only one computer can send and receive data at any one time.
19. True: last paragraph, last-but-one sentence: it is possible to infer that the network might grind to a halt if too many computers are added, because there will be more collisions and each collision slows the system down.
20. True: last paragraph, eighth sentence: when joined to a common ring each computer must have another computer connected either side of it so every node on the loop is connected to two other nodes.

21. Can't tell: first paragraph, fourth sentence: the 154 includes dispensaries as well as hospitals.
22. True: first paragraph, third sentence: Exeter (1741), before Liverpool (1745) but after Bristol (1733) and York (1740).
23. False: last paragraph: Louis Pasteur's work is referred to as a theory and not a method of identifying the germ that is responsible for a disease.
24. False: second paragraph, last-but-one sentence, and last paragraph, first sentence: anaesthetics were not used in surgery prior to 1847, but there is nothing to suggest that the opiates and alcohol referred to in the second paragraph were not administered for pain relief.

25. True: eight hours with breaks at two, four and six hours.
26. False: first paragraph, sixth sentence: temporary measure only.
27. True: last paragraph, fourth sentence: at a time normally spent sleeping, for example in the early hours of the morning.
28. Can't tell: there is no information given on reaction times.

29. True: second paragraph, second sentence: covers old ground.
30. False: second paragraph, last sentence: patients are asked to tick boxes that request information about their sexuality; there is no compulsion to reveal information as suggested by the words 'must declare'.
31. False: third paragraph: the passage states only that the NHS suspended a nurse for offering to pray for an elderly relative. It is the author who has inferred that the equality and diversity policy was breached.
32. False: first paragraph, first sentence: freedom of expression not of thought.

33. False: first paragraph, fourth sentence: about 65 per cent (approximately two-thirds) of those that fail to meet the highest standards go on to be sold as Cripps Pink; the percentage of apples not meeting the Pink Lady™ standard is not specified.
34. Can't tell: no information is provided on the relative prices of Pink Lady™ and Sundowner™.
35. False: the Cripps Red is stated to be equally as popular as the Pink Lady™, in which case sales of its premium grade, the Sundowner™, would be less so.
36. True: colour intensity for Pink Lady™ and colour ratio for Sundowner™.

37. True: British Isles = all land masses (first paragraph), whereas the British Islands = UK + Channel Islands + Isle of Man.
38. False: last paragraph, first and second sentences: Wales is part of Great Britain, so the Isle of Anglesey (Ynys Mon in Welsh) must also be part of Great Britain.
39. True: last paragraph, first sentence.
40. True: first paragraph: British Isles = all land masses; second paragraph, fourth sentence: Channel Islands and Isle of Man are not part of the UK.

Chapter 3 Decision analysis

Twenty questions on synonyms, antonyms, expanded or contracted terms and terms that are similar

Q1. Answer: D self-important

Explanation: Turn around means find the opposite of the term. Humble means, for example, unpretentious, ordinary and modest. It can also mean to belittle or bring someone down. But its antonym is self-important.

Q2. Answer: C excavate

Explanation: Enlarge means increase, so we are looking for a term that means something greater than what is usually meant by deepen. Deepen means make deeper, and synonyms of deepen include dig, hollow or excavate (lessen is its antonym). Of the suggested answers, excavate is used to mean something on quite a big scale and so is in this sense an enlargement of deepen.

Q3. Answer: B corrupting

Explanation: To decrease is to reduce something. Poisonous means venomous, fatal or corrupting; its antonym is cleansing. Of the three suggested answers that have the same or similar meanings, corrupting is the least extreme.

Q4. Answer: A friendly

Explanation: In this context find an equivalent means find a synonym, and from the suggested answers only friendly is a synonym of social.

Q5. Answer: B fool

Explanation: Block can mean a lump, an obstruction and a building (a block of flats); we can suggest someone is a fool by calling them a blockhead but not a block.

Q6. Answer: C offer

Explanation: To request is to ask for, and demand and seek are synonyms; to offer something is the opposite of asking for something.

Q7. Answer: C very good

Explanation: Unsurpassed means the best, and of the suggested answers the lesser term to unsurpassed is very good (not the best but still very good). Even better would be to increase unsurpassed.

Q8. Answer: A scanned

Explanation: Past means in the past tense, to scan something is to copy it, and scanned is the past tense of scan.

Q9. Answer: B superfluous

Explanation: Requirement, obligation and essential are all equivalents of necessity. Superfluous means unnecessary and is the opposite of necessity.

Q10. Answer: D mask

Explanation: Synonyms of display include show, reveal and extend, while to mask something is to cover it up, which is the opposite meaning.

Q11. Answer: A paradox

Explanation: Enigma means mystery, puzzle or paradox. Axiom and platitude are both sayings considered true.

Q12. Answer: B like chalk and cheese

Explanation: Resemble means look alike or be similar. Like, comparable and kindred are synonyms. The saying 'like chalk and cheese' means different and is the opposite of resemble.

Q13. Answer: C chop

Explanation: All the suggested answers are valid ways of saying carve, but to etch or engrave are methods of fine carving, while to chop something is at the extreme of the meaning of carve and so is in a sense an extension.

Q14. Answer: A perimeter

Explanation: Akin means of the same kind or similar and so you must find a word similar in meaning to margin. Both perimeter and margin mean edge.

Q15. Answer: D stroke

Explanation: To shrink is to diminish, and in this context we are looking for a term that diminishes the meaning of slap. Suggested answers whack, knock and punch all have the same or very similar meanings – a slap – while stroke means something much more gentle.

Q16. Answer: B group

Explanation: Analogous means similar or equivalent to, so we are looking for a term with the same or a similar meaning. Assorted, not assort, means mixed, miscellaneous and sundry. Assort means group together, rank or arrange.

Q17. Answer: D dissect

Explanation: To thunder and boom are 'bigger' but related terms to peal, as in a peal of bells; peel means unwrap or skin, and to dissect is to do more than peel or skin something.

Q18. Answer: A sensible

Explanation: Unwise means ill advised or imprudent, and its opposite would be smart or shrewd. Sensible is somewhere in between and so is the correct answer.

Q19. Answer: B weakness

Explanation: Converse means opposite. Might can mean may (we say, for example, I might or may go) and it also means strength, the opposite of which is weakness.

Q20. Answer: C article

Explanation: Analogous means similar or the same, so we are looking for a term with the same or most similar meaning to thing. Belongings are particular things rather than a thing, while an article or object is a thing. Slender is analogous to thin, not thing, and journal is a type of magazine.

Thirty-three warm up questions

Q1. Answer: B

Explanation: The code states reverse delete, wooden flooring. Notice that the comma is after delete, so we can take this to mean that the code 323 refers to delete, and the reverse of delete is add.

Q2. Answer: D

Explanation: The code reads add pasta, cigarettes parallel delete. A and C could be right but for the modifier 32, which means parallel. A parallel is a sort of synonym, and only answer D offers a parallel to delete = remove.

Q3. Answer: A

Explanation: The code reads gasoline, akin add, parallel the basket of goods and services. Akin means similar, and we have already seen that parallel means a synonym. The word 'on' is akin to add ('put in' a synonym) in this context; 'list' and 'inventory' are parallels to basket of goods and services. Only A is correct, because B does not offer a word akin to add but states add.

Q4. Answer: B

Explanation: The code reads append popular, parallel elevated, pasta. Append means 'add', and the phrases 'all the rage' and 'very popular' are phrases with similar but greater meaning to popular. A parallel to elevated is promote. Only suggested answer B offers both something appended to popular and a parallel to elevated.

Q5. Answer: C

Explanation: The code reads reverse commodity, mobile phone contract, landscape gardening. Reverse means the antonym or opposite. A commodity is a useful product that can be bought or sold. Both goods and services can be described as commodities (services are not tangible commodities but they are commodities all the same) so these terms cannot be taken to be the antonym. The reverse of commodity is not commodities, and the best explanation of the code is C; mobile phones and landscape gardening are not commodities.

Q6. Answer: D

Explanation: The code reads banking, append service, akin temperate, inflation. To append service we must add something, and making it plural, services, can be taken to be adding something. In this context, temperate means mild or moderate but not pleasant.

Q7. Answer: A

Explanation: The code reads milk, akin add, inflation, parallel lessen. Only suggested answer A contains a word or phrase akin to add and parallel to lessen.

Q8. Answer: B

Explanation: The code reads unfashionable, mobile phone contracts, pasta, reverse. Of the code words it only makes sense to reverse unfashionable to fashionable or, in other words, popular. A can be questioned because the code makes no reference to a decision to delete mobile phones or pasta from the list. Out of favour and out of date are synonyms, not antonyms, of unfashionable.

Q9. Answer: C

Explanation: The code reads soft furnishings, lessen delete, popular, parallel elevated, inflation. Lessen delete can be to 'think about or consider deleting' (but it can't be 'don't delete'). Parallel elevated can be high or very high. The code for popular is unmodified, so very popular is not the best suggestion. This leaves only suggested answer C as correct and including all the codes.

Q10. Answer: A and D

Explanation: The code reads parallel, add, gasoline; notice the comma, which implies that the modifier parallel could relate to either add or gasoline. Include is a parallel of add, and petrol is a parallel of gasoline, but put on the list is not a parallel of add. B is also questionable, because both gasoline and add have been modified. E is likely to be wrong because neither add nor gasoline has been modified.

Q11. Answer: A, B and C

Explanation: The code reads soft furnishings, delete, refrigerator. The code only provides a single instruction, delete. We should only use this operation once and can use it either to delete (both) soft furnishings and refrigerator or to delete one or the other. D and E are questionable because they imply more than one instruction: to delete one item and keep another.

Q12. Answer: A, B, C and D

Explanation: The code reads parallel delete, append banking. All the suggested answers offer parallels to delete and all but suggested answer E propose appendages to banking. E, however, does not add to banking – it only suggests everything involved in banking.

Q13. Answer: A, B, C, D and E

Explanation: The code reads delete, gasoline, parallel temperate, popular, add, cigarettes. The sequence of codes can be combined differently from the way it is presented in the question, so 607 (delete) may relate to either gasoline or cigarettes, and 321 602 (parallel temperate) can relate to popular, cigarettes or gasoline. All five suggested answers are valid interpretations of the code sequence. If we look to the context there is nothing stated in the situation that suggests we should favour one or more of the suggested answers over any other. This means that all five of the suggested answers are equally valid interpretations of the code.

Q14. Answer: B and D

Explanation: The code reads akin milk, the basket of goods and services, add, reverse tiny. Butter, yogurt, white paint and dairy products are all akin to milk. Suggested answer A does not include the code add, so should be rejected, C should be rejected because minute is a synonym of tiny, not the reverse of it. E can be rejected because cows are not akin to milk (ie similar); also, to ask why they are not in the basket is not to follow the code add.

Q15. Answer: C

Explanation: The code reads octane, alcohol, gasoline, new, high. A does not include gasoline, B uses high twice and D fails to use new.

Q16. Answer: B

Explanation: The code reads gain, turn around contradiction, may. Turn around contradiction means the antonym of contradiction, which is agreement. We can favour suggested answers A and B over C and D because A and B use terms that are either an antonym of contradiction (agreement) or a term related to its antonym (permission). We can favour A over B because it uses the antonym of contradiction (rather than a related term) and because it introduces fewer clauses unsupported by the sequence of codes (in B we have the suggestion that permission may be denied but try). While it is not incorrect to use additional terms not in the sequence of codes, we can favour the suggested answer that does not introduce them over one that does.

Q17. Answer: D

Explanation: The code reads diesel, green, enlarge alternative, similar new, more. Enlarge alternative can be alternatives, and similar new can be innovative or recent. Only D uses all the codes and correctly applies the transformers. A does not include more, B fails to enlarge alternative and C fails to include more.

Q18. Answer: A

Explanation: The code reads investment, new, bio, similar know, fuel. We can reject C because it uses know rather than a word similar to know. Arguably the other three suggested answers all involve words similar to know (no, knows and even now, as there is only one letter missing). They also all include the remaining words in the code. We can, however, question D, because it states bio-fuels not bio-fuel. This leaves A and B, and we can favour A over B because B includes the word high, which features in the matrix but does not occur in the question sequence.

Q19. Answer: A

Explanation: The code reads tell, turn around could. The antonym of could is could not or its abbreviation couldn't. Only suggested answer A offers a correct antonym of could.

Q20. Answer: C

Explanation: The code reads green, turn around may, ethanol. If you turn around may you get may not. Only suggested answer C offers a correct antonym of may.

Q21. Answer: B

Explanation: The code reads enlarge alternative, enlarge more, investment, more. Note that the code 526 occurs twice in this sequence and so we can use it twice (once transformed). A and D are less favourable because they use a synonym of more (additional and extra) rather than its enlargement (most). C can be eliminated because it does not include an enlargement of more.

Q22. Answer: D

Explanation: The code reads gain, similar high, turn around can, tell, new, oil. Soar and gain are similar to high but gains is not. Turn around can is can't. Only D makes use of all the codes and correctly applies the transformations.

Q23. Answer: B and C

Explanation: The code reads similar contradiction, similar investment, bio, fuel. Words or phrases that occur in the suggested answers that are similar to contradiction are inconsistent, disagreement and conflicting evidence. Terms similar to investment include venture, speculation and arguably capital. Suggested answers A and D can be eliminated because they do not make use of the code for similar contradiction. Both B and C make full use of the code.

Q24. Answer: A, B and C

Explanation: The code reads similar few, ethanol, investment, alternative. Answers A, B and C all include terms similar to few: minority, hardly any, small amount. D includes the antonym: many. Suggested answers A, B and C therefore correctly utilize the sequence of code.

Q25. Answer: C and D

Explanation: The code reads turn around gain, diesel, fuel, gasoline, turn around new. If we turn around gain we get decrease, dwindle, decline and fall. If we turn around new we get old, traditional or conventional. Only suggested answers C and D include the meaning of all the codes. Answers A and B both fail to include an antonym of new. (B also uses the term bio, which is in the matrix but does not appear in the question sequence.)

Q26. Answer: B and D

Explanation: The code reads ethanol, gasoline, fuel, octane, high. Suggested answers B and D both use all parts of the sequence; however, suggested answer A does not include gasoline, while answer C fails to utilize the term fuel.

Q27. Answer: D

Explanation: The code reads he or S, information, expand try, online. Tries and trying are both examples of expanded try. Suggested answers A and B fail to use the code for online. B and C do not include an expanded try.

Q28. Answer: A

Explanation: The code reads works, he or S, seems, reverse week. The reverse of week could be many things, including arguably weekend, days and hourly, but it cannot be weekly, which means we can reject suggested answer C. We can also eliminate B and D because the code for seems is not used.

Q29. Answer: C

Explanation: The code reads we, same as ready, online, he or S. Words or phrases the same as ready include, for example, all set and standing by. Suggested answers A and B do not use the code for he so can be rejected. Suggested answer D does not use a term the same as ready.

Q30. Answer: A

Explanation: The code reads staff, similar to no, information, expand ready, he or S, believe, we. Thinking laterally, words similar to no used in the example are on (same letters) and not (one extra letter, also negative). We can favour suggested answer A over B and D because B and D do not make use of the code for expanded ready. We can prefer A over C because C does not use the code for staff and it uses no rather than a word similar to no.

Q31. Answer: B and C

Explanation: The code reads he or S, proves, works. Only answers B and C correctly utilize the three components of the sequence.

Q32. Answer: A and D

Explanation: The code reads we, no, similar to he or S. Similar to he can be him, he's, his and man. Only suggested answers A and D fully comply with the sequence of code. In the case of B we have two terms similar to he, and the code for we is not utilized. In suggested answer C also the code for we is not used.

Q33. Answer: A and B

Explanation: The code reads contract we, same as believe, proves, expand no. Contraction of we is I or my, same as believe can be trust, think or my best judgement, and an expansion of no can be nothing and none. Suggested answer C can be discarded because it does not use the code for expand no. Suggested answer D does not utilize the code for we and uses the term prove not proves.

UKCAT-style decision analysis timed test 1

Q1. Answer: C. We eat breakfast quickly.

Explanation: The code reads: HE, 2, B7(108), 15(6) = personal plural, eat, opposite large (meal), short time. Eliminate answers A and D straight away, as they have no concept of we (I plural); translate short time as quickly (answer C) noting that breakfast could be a small meal (opposite large) and that B has no concept of small and E only a weak concept of short time (morning).

Q2. Answer: D. Equations are hard for many people.

Explanation: The code reads: (106,10) 14, B16(E1) = (number, work), problem, opposite few (plural person). Eliminate answers C and E straight away, as they have no concept of people (plural person); translate opposite few as many (answer D), noting that A and B have no concept of many.

Q3. Answer: D. We should work less and play more.

Explanation: The code reads: EH, 10(BA), B10(A) = plural personal, work (opposite increase), opposite work (increase). Eliminate A, B and C, taking plural personal to mean we; translate opposite work to mean play in answers C and D, noting that only answer D includes the concepts of less (opposite increase = decrease).

Q4. Answer: B. Hard work never hurt anyone.

Explanation: The code reads: 14(10), BF, A110, 1 = problem work, opposite always, increase pain, person. Only answer B correctly translates opposite always as never.

Q5. Answer: A. Others are not as fit as me.

Explanation: The code reads: B(EH), B(C105)H = opposite (personal plural), opposite (similar health) personal. Eliminate B and D because the code does not include concepts of most or many; translate similar health as fit and its opposite as not as fit (answer A) or less healthy (answer C), noting that opposite (personal plural) is opposite (we), which translates better as others rather than no people.

Q6. Answer: C. There is no room in my father's house.

Explanation: The code reads: BD(7,17), H(7,G), 12 = opposite positive (large space), personal (large male), house. Choose B and C as the most likely, translate personal large male to mean husband or father and (opposite positive) large space as negative large space or no large space, meaning no room (answer C).

Q7. Answer: B. I never break the law.

Explanation: The code reads: H(BF), B201, C102 = personal (opposite always), opposite fix, similar rules. Eliminate A and C, which do not code never (opposite always); choose B, which codes for I (personal), noting that break is coded as opposite fix and law as similar rules.

Q8. Answer: C. It's hard to remain on a healthy diet.

Explanation: The code reads: 105, 2(B7),14, A6 = health, eat (opposite large), problem, increase time. All concepts must be coded for; eliminate B and D because I (personal) is not coded; eliminate A and E because hard (problem) is not coded, noting that C codes for remain (increase time).

Q9. Answer: D. I was off work due to illness.

Explanation: The code reads: H, B10, B105 = personal, opposite work, opposite health. Eliminate A, C and E because I is coded for once and not twice; eliminate C because seldom take is not coded.

Q10. Answer: C. There are many buildings and a few open spaces.

Explanation: The code reads: B16, C(E12), 16(7,E17) = opposite few, similar (plural house), few (large, plural space). Opposite few codes many, and similar (plural house) codes buildings, ie answer C, noting that few (large, plural space) codes few open spaces.

Q11. Answer: B. My colleagues and I hold the same view.

Explanation: The code reads: H(10J), A(C3) = personal (work together), increase (similar think). Eliminate D and E because personal codes my; eliminate C because increase similar think translates as same thoughts or same view and work together codes as colleagues.

Q12. Answer: E. We never consume unhealthy food.

Explanation: The code reads: EH, BF, 2, B(105), C2 = plural personal, opposite always, eat, opposite health, similar eat. Eliminate C and D, which do not translate opposite always (never or don't); eliminate B, which does not translate similar eat (food), and eliminate A, which translates as healthy instead of unhealthy, noting that, in E, eat codes for consume.

Q13. Answer: A. We seldom drink alcohol.

Explanation: The code reads: EH, BA(BF), C(11 8) = plural personal, opposite increase (opposite always), similar (fire water). There is no concept of drink in the code so you have to insert it; plural personal translates as we, so B and D can be ruled out; opposite increase is reduce, and opposite always is never, and reduce never translates as seldom, ie A or E; reject E because hot water would code as C(11) 8 and not C(11 8), which could code alcohol.

Q14. Answer: E. Unemployment will rise.

Explanation: The code reads: B10, A(B13)M = opposite work, increase (opposite fall) future. Opposite work translates as jobless or unemployment, ie B, C or E; opposite fall is rise, or will rise in the future.

Q15. Answer: C. People take a ferry across the sea.

Explanation: The code reads: E1, 4K, 18(7 8) = plural person, vehicle specific, travel (large water). Eliminate answers A and D, which have no concept of people (plural person); eliminate E because most is not coded; B mentions no vehicle, whereas C codes ferry as vehicle specific, noting that travel large water translates as across the sea.

Q16. Answer: B. We are all employed at the factory.

Explanation: The code reads: EH, 10(101), C(7 12) = plural personal, work money, similar (large house). Translate work money as paid work or employed and similar large house as factory.

Q17. Answer: B. UK

Explanation: There is no concept of Scotland in the table of code words, whereas the remaining words can be translated from the table's codes: sold codes as money increase (101A); we codes as plural person (E1); home codes as house personal (12H); and moved away codes as travel increase (18A).

Q18. Answer: A. exercise

Explanation: There is no concept of exercise in the table; weight can code as light opposite (202B); diet can code as eat opposite increase (2, BA) or eat meal opposite reduce (2, 108, BA); lose can code as opposite increase (BA); most can code as opposite few (B16).

Q19. Answer: D test and E failed

Explanation: There is no concept of test in the table; there is no concept of passed test in the table, but it can code as opposite (B) failed; my can code as personal (H); old (204) is in the table; car can code as personal vehicle (H4).

Q20. Answer: B city and E live

Explanation: There is no concept of city or live in the table of code words; countryside can code as large space (7,17). Sell can code as money increase.

Q21. Answer: B appetizing and C neither

Explanation: The word appetizing is difficult to code from the table, with eat (2) and meal (108) not sufficient; neither is difficult to code from the table, with together (J) more akin to both than to neither; restaurant can code as similar meal house C(108, 12).

Q22. Answer: A

Explanation: The code reads: ●E1, BD (B●) = happy person plural, opposite positive (opposite happy) or happy people, negative sad. There is no need to translate every code; look for common elements between the answer choices, as these are strong contenders, and anticipate what code you would expect to see, for example E1 rather than 1, not coding as negative (BD), and depressed as the opposite of happy (B●). The remaining answer choices range from close matches to contradictory.

Q23. Answer: C

Explanation: The code reads: 1(BM3), BD(205), 104L = person (opposite future think), opposite seek, danger situation, where opposite future think is taken as the past tense of think or thought and opposite seek is avoid. Code BM3 is at the front of three codes so translate it first; BD(205) is the second code in three codes so translate it second; answer C with both of these codes is the strongest candidate; eliminate the remaining answers if time allows.

Q24. Answer: E

Explanation: The code reads: B(G E1), 10 BA(101), GE1 = opposite (male plural person), work, opposite increase (money), male plural person, ie women, work, reduce money, men. Answers A, C and D code for females and males rather than women and men; answer B is less appropriate than answer E because B fails to include the concept of work, which in conjunction with reduce money translates as earn less, rather than less money.

Q25. Answer: B

Explanation: The code reads: B204(E1), BD109, D(C20) = opposite old people, negative heard, positive similar vision. Answers B and C use opposite old people to convey the word children, which is preferable to opposite large people (A,D) or small people (E). Answers B and C are very similar; however, answer C fails to convey the notion of should be, merely stating similar vision rather than positive similar vision, contrasting with negative heard.

UKCAT-style decision analysis timed test 2

Q1. Answer: A. He was evicted from the house.

Explanation: The code reads: HG, A(C18), 12 = personal male, increase (similar travel), house. Personal male translates as he, as in answers A and D; increase similar travel translates as evicted.

Q2. Answer: B. There are fines for illegally parking your car.

Explanation: The code reads: 101(BA), 102(BD), 18B, K4 = money opposite increase, rules opposite positive, travel opposite, specific vehicle. Specific vehicle must refer to car so rule out answers D and E; money opposite increase could be pay, fines or fined so this does not help, nor does travel opposite, which indicates parking; rules opposite positive suggests negative rules or illegally, ie B.

Q3. Answer: D. The rising tide caused water damage.

Explanation: The code reads: 8(B13), 8(14A) = water (opposite fall), water (problem increase). Water opposite fall translates as rising water, and water problem increase could mean water damage or flooding but not great damage or increased the damage so eliminate A and C; eliminate B because more is not coded. E looks plausible but is rejected on the basis that tide is plural, which is not coded.

Q4. Answer: B. I feel lonely on my own in the evening.

Explanation: The code reads: H■, BJ, B103 6 = personal lonely, opposite together, opposite day time. Personal translates as I so eliminate C, E and also D because it contains we; opposite day time is night-time or evening, ie B, which also codes on my own as opposite together.

Q5. Answer: E. Passive smoking is harmful to health.

Explanation: The code reads: EH17(11 107), 104 105 = plural personal space (fire air), dangerous health. Answer C looks plausible because it translates plural personal as we, fire air as smoke, space as inhalation and dangerous health as unhealthy; however, in C the concept of not (smoke) is not coded so C is eliminated; A does not make use of health, only dangerous, so A is eliminated; B introduces the concept of many, which is not coded, and D introduces the term cigarettes, which is not coded. E combines all the concepts successfully if plural personal space (we space) refers to environment.

Q6. Answer: D. My neighbours are unfriendly people.

Explanation: The code reads: H, J(E1), B♦(E1) = personal, together (plural person), opposite friendly (plural person). Personal refers to I or my; together plural person refers to neighbours in the context of the answer options; the final plural person at the end of the code could refer to people (D) or friends (E) but not me (eliminate A) or my (eliminate B); C is eliminated as it fails to translate plural person; E is eliminated as it includes the concept of not, noting that not friendly people would be coded as opposite (friendly plural person).

Q7. Answer: E. The son stole his father's fortune.

Explanation: The code reads: B7(G), 19(5), H(G7), 7(101) = opposite large (male), take wrong, personal male large, large money. Eliminate B and D, since take wrong codes as stole rather than inherited; personal male codes for his so eliminate A; eliminate C because large is not coded, noting that fortune codes as large money, ie answer E.

Q8. Answer: B. The e-mail was sent from an internet café.

Explanation: The code reads: C(9), 18(MB), BA(12,2) = similar speak, travel future opposite, opposite increase house eat. Eliminate E as he is not coded; eliminate A and C, which fail to include any concept of house eat, which in conjunction with opposite increase (reduce) is coded from internet café; both B and D correctly identify the past tense was coded by future opposite, but only B correctly codes sent as travel.

Q9. Answer: A. The court found him not guilty of the crime.

Explanation: The code reads: C(102 12), H(BD5), (14 102) = similar (rules house), personal (opposite positive, wrong), (problem rules). Eliminate B and C, which fail to code court as similar rules house; eliminate D and E, which fail to code crime as problem rules, noting that personal (opposite positive, wrong) translates as him not guilty, ie answer A.

Q10. Answer: A. Many ill people are depressed.

Explanation: The code reads: B(16), E1, BD(105), 14(B●) = opposite (few), plural person, opposite positive (health), problem (opposite happy). Translate opposite few, plural person as many people, which occurs in A, B or C, but not in E nor D, which state some and all. Eliminate C because there is only enough coding to support two health concepts not all three (depression, illness, sad). Finally, (opposite happy) is the coding for sad (B); however, the inclusion of problem modifies this to depression, ie A.

Q11. Answer: C. Men take home more pay than women.

Explanation: The code reads: G(E1), 19(C12), A(C101), BG(E1) = male (plural person), take (similar house), increase (similar money), opposite male (plural person). The code supports all five answers for men, males, women and females; increase (similar money) is not same money or similar money so eliminate E and D, and also B because increase is linked with money not house; earn more (A) and more pay (C) could both code as increase (similar money) but A lacks the concept of take (similar house).

Q12. Answer: D. A mortgage is a loan paid back over many years.

Explanation: The code reads: 7(12 101), (14 101), A16(7 6) = large (house money) problem money, increase few (large time). Identify straight away that increase few (large time) codes many years, as stated in answer D, noting that large (house money) codes for mortgage and problem money for paid back; A is the second best interpretation of the code, but an instalment is a payment, which should incorporate the concept of money; B is wrong because it does not link the concept of money with house; C is wrong because expensive house would code as house (large money); E fails to include a concept of time.

Q13. Answer: E. Outpatients receive hospital care except at night.

Explanation: The code reads: 1E(B105), C19, C(105 12), BD(B103) = person plural (opposite health), similar take, similar (health house), opposite positive (opposite day). Translate similar (health house) as hospital and eliminate answer B; translate opposite positive (opposite day) as not night and eliminate answer C, noting that E (except at night) is preferred to answers A and D (during the day).

Q14. Answer: C. Children receive weekly pocket money.

Explanation: The code reads: E1(B7), C19, B(7 101), (15 6) = plural person (large opposite), similar take, opposite (large money), short time. Eliminate A and E because there is no coding for school meals or parents, respectively. Eliminate D because it conveys the concept of money but not opposite (large money); eliminate B because the concept of money has been introduced twice, as paid and wage, which leaves answer C, ignoring the word order.

Q15. Answer: E. Married people are the happiest.

Explanation: The code reads: E1, J, A(A●) = plural person, together, increase (increase happy). Take increase happy to be happier and increase (increase happier) to be happiest, ie answers B or E; the concept of people is coded only once so eliminate B.

Q16. Answer: C. Some people ride a motorcycle to work.

Explanation: The code reads: A16(E1), 18(10), B(E)1, 4 = increase few (plural person), travel (work), opposite (plural) person, vehicle. Translate increase few to mean some so eliminate B and D; opposite (plural) person translates as single person; E contains no concept of vehicle, so eliminate it, noting that a motorcycle rather than a car is a single-person vehicle, ie answer C.

Q17. Answer: E. The management stopped the strike.

Explanation: The code reads: 10J, BD(18), B10 = work together, opposite positive (travel), opposite work. Work together is conceptualized in all five answers so ignore this initially; eliminate C and D, which have no concept of travel, and eliminate B, which has no concept of work, noting that stopped (E) can code as negative travel but not went (A); stopped could code as opposite work but this is tenuous, ie answer E not A.

Q18. Answer: C. A child walks before it talks.

Explanation: The code reads: B(7,1) H18, C(MB), 9 = opposite (large person), personal travel, similar (future opposite), speak. Eliminate A, B and D as these refer to people (plural person) not person; similar (future opposite) is similar (past), which translates as before in answer C, noting that personal travel is the code for walks and a child is opposite (large person).

Q19. Answer: B. business and E. successful.

Explanation: Future (C) and people (D) are already coded in the table; optimistic (A) can code as positive or happy; business and successful are very difficult to code from the table codes.

Q20. Answer: C. three and D. points.

Explanation: Three (C) and points (D) cannot be translated from any code in the table; on (B) is not needed to convey the message; your (E) can be coded using personal person (H1); penalty is difficult to code, but problem rules 14(102), pain rules 110(102) or negative money rules BD101(102) could give a notion of it.

Q21. Answer: A. text and D. study.

Explanation: Time (B) is already coded (6); well (C) can code indirectly from positive health (D105); there is little concept of test (A) in the table, with situation rules (L102) being a very tenuous link, so test is one choice; studying could code as similar (work notes); however, this is also tenuous and, as two answers are needed, study is the second choice, noting that spend can code from money (reduce) or expense (increase).

Q22. Answer: A. growth and E. parent.

Explanation: Child's development could code as child's increase; however, this does not indicate the notion of development as well as growth (A), which becomes the first choice; child can code as opposite old person, B204(1), and harm as similar danger, C(104), so hinder can be discounted; parents can code as together male, female, J(G, BG); however, this is convoluted, so parents is the second choice.

Q23. Answer: A

Explanation: The code reads: E1, 12, B(19,7)101 = we, house, opposite (take, large) money. We, house, (give small) money, or we paid a small deposit on the house. Answer B includes the concept of deposit (small money) but not of payment (opposite take); C is erroneous, stating large money; D and E fail to include house.

Q24. Answer: C

Explanation: The code reads: H, 2, BE, 11, 108, B(103) = personal, eat, opposite plural, fire, meal, opposite day. I eat singular hot meal at night; A and D code for day not night; E fails to code meal; B is a close match but does not include opposite plural, which codes for one in answer C.

Q25. Answer: B

Explanation: The code reads: E1(J), BM19, L(B7,17) = plural person (together), opposite future take, situation (opposite large, space). People together taken small space situation. A and E fail to code the concept of meeting (people together); C has no notion of conditions, only of cramped (small space); D is contrary to the sentence.

UKCAT-style decision analysis timed test 3

Q1. Answer: E. Pollution is bad for my breathing.

Explanation: The code reads: (107,14), BD(H107) = air problem, opposite positive (personal air). Eliminate A, C and D, taking personal air to refer to I or my, which are only found in answers B and E; eliminate answer B because the concept of air is only translated once when it should appear twice; opposite positive (personal air) codes for bad for my breathing in answer E, noting that pollution codes as air problem.

Q2. Answer: A. People rest on coach journeys.

Explanation: The code reads: E1, B10, B15(4), 18 = plural person, opposite work, opposite short (vehicle) travel. Eliminate D, which contains no concept of plural person and the word period is not coded; eliminate E, which contains no concept of opposite work nor any strong concept of vehicle; eliminate C, which includes many and the concept of people twice, which are not coded; A and B are the most obvious choices; reject B because the word long in B clearly applies to the journey rather than the length of the train, ie choose answer A, noting that journey codes as travel.

Q3. Answer: D. Fresh food should be eaten soon.

Explanation: The code reads: 2, 15(6), B204(108) = eat, short time, opposite old meal. Eliminate B, which fails to translate opposite in relation to old meal; similarly A and C; both D and E translate opposite old meal as fresh food, but eliminate E as only D translates the concept of short time (soon), noting that the order of the words in the answer is discounted.

Q4. Answer: A. Many young people do voluntary work.

Explanation: The code reads: B16, B7(E1), 10(BD,101) = opposite few, opposite large (plural person), work (opposite positive, money). Eliminate C and E, which do not translate opposite few; eliminate D, which has no concept of work; eliminate B, which has no concept of money, noting that work (opposite positive money) is work negative money or work for nothing, ie voluntary work, answer A.

Q5. Answer: D. Eating barbecued food made them ill.

Explanation: The code reads: BD(105,A), E1, (2,11,108) = opposite positive (health increase), plural person, (eat, fire, meals). Answer A looks plausible but it includes the concept of me rather than people so eliminate it; of the remaining answers only D includes a translation for eat, fire, meals, ie barbecued food, noting that opposite positive (health increase) or negative healthier can mean ill, and that them has been coded as plural person, so D is the correct answer, discounting the order of the words.

Q6. Answer: D. Obese people risk diabetes.

Explanation: The code reads: (108,K,105,14), B(202), E1, C(104) = (meal, specific, health, problem), opposite light plural person, similar danger. Eliminate E, which has no concept of plural person; eliminate A and C, which have no concept of health; eliminate B, which has no concept of large; answer D correctly translates diabetes as meal, specific, health, problem, with obese coded as opposite light.

Q7. Answer: A. After a night out I felt generally unwell.

Explanation: The code reads: C(BK), B105, M, H, B103, 17 = similar (opposite specific), opposite health, future, personal, opposite day, space. Eliminate B, which does not translate personal or health; eliminate E, which does not translate opposite day; eliminate C because diabetes is a specific health problem that is not coded for; eliminate D, which contains no concept of future; answer A reflects the code, with opposite day, space translating as night out, similar (opposite specific), opposite health, future translating as after, and similar (opposite specific), opposite health translating as generally unwell.

Q8. Answer: E. Doctors diagnose illness.

Explanation: The code reads: BD(105), C(BD, 14), E1 = opposite positive (health), similar (opposite problem), plural person. Eliminate A, B and C, which contain no concept of opposite positive health; eliminate answer D, which has no concept of plural person, noting that similar (opposite problem) could translate as similar (solution) or diagnose, as in answer E.

Q9. Answer: B. Diets are easy for poor eaters.

Explanation: The code reads: E108, 202, BD(14), E(1,2)BA = plural meal, light, opposite positive (problem), plural (person, eat), opposite increase. Eliminate A, D and E, which contain no concept of plural (person, eat); C has no concept of opposite positive (problem), ie negative problem or no problem, whereas B translates no problem as easy and plural meal, light as diets, with plural (person, eat), opposite increase translatable as eaters decrease, ie poor eaters.

Q10. Answer: E. People find maths confusing.

Explanation: The code reads: 3, 14, 10, 106, 205, E1 = think, problem, work, numbers, seek, plural person. Eliminate A, C and D, which contain no concept of plural person; eliminate B, which contains no concept of seek, which is translated as find in answer E, noting that maths confusing codes as think, problem, work, numbers.

Q11. Answer: E. Prescriptions are free for unemployed people.

Explanation: The code reads: BD(10)E1, BD(203), 105, 206 = opposite positive (work) plural person, opposite positive (expense), health, notes. Eliminate A, C and D, which have no concept of plural person; eliminate B, which concludes the concept of time, which is not coded, noting that prescriptions are health notes, opposite positive (expense) translates as free and opposite positive (work) translates as unemployed.

Q12. Answer: A. Carrying a weapon is a crime.

Explanation: The code reads: (18, 6) (207, 110) C(B102) = (travel, time), (object, pain), opposite rules. Eliminate E because criminals (ie people) is not coded; eliminate C, which contains no concept of time; eliminate B, which contains no concept of opposite rules; eliminate D because heavy is not coded, noting that, in A, weapon codes as object pain and carrying codes as travel time.

Q13. Answer: C. Showers are forecast for tomorrow.

Explanation: The code reads: M, B7(8), 7(106), M(103) = future, opposite large (water), large number, future day. Eliminate B and D because us and we are not coded; eliminate E because it has no concept of future; eliminate A because future and future day are not expressed, noting that, in C, tomorrow codes as future day, forecast codes as future, and opposite large water, large number codes as showers.

Q14. Answer: C. Friendly people make satisfactory neighbours.

Explanation: The code reads: ♦E1, ♦(BA), 12J = friendly plural person, friendly (opposite increase), house together. Eliminate D and E because I and my are not coded; eliminate B because unfriendly should code as friendly (opposite); eliminate A because excellent is not coded, noting that, in C, friendly (opposite increase) means friendly reduce or satisfactory and neighbours codes as house together.

Q15. Answer: E. I can't breathe without oxygen.

Explanation: The code reads: BD(107A), H, BD(H107) = opposite positive (air increase), personal, opposite positive (personal air). Eliminate A and C, which have no concept of personal; opposite positive (personal air) translates as my breathing rate (B), shortness of breath (D) or I can't breathe (E), in which case opposite positive (air increase) means either exercise increases (B), suffer from (D) or without oxygen (E); eliminate B and D, which have no concept of air, ie only answer E has two concepts of air, noting that oxygen codes as air increase and opposite positive as without (ie without oxygen I can't breathe).

Q16. Answer: D. We crossed the bridge on foot yesterday.

Explanation: The code reads: 17(18), 18E1, H18, BM(103) = space (travel), travel plural person, personal travel, opposite future day. Eliminate B and E, which have no concept of plural person; eliminate A, which has no concept of day; eliminate C, which has only two concepts of travel (ie travelled and car), noting that, in D, on foot codes as personal travel, we crossed codes as travel plural person, bridge codes as space travel, and opposite future day codes as yesterday.

Q17. Answer: A. I envisaged numerous problems.

Explanation: The code reads: H(E14), 20M, 7, 106 = personal (plural problem), vision future, large, number. Eliminate E, which has no concept of personal; eliminate B and D, taking personal (plural problem) to mean I problems, ie answers A or C; eliminate C, which has no concept of vision future, which translates as envisaged in answer A.

Q18. Answer: C. Nobody had considered it risky.

Explanation: The code reads: 104, BM(3), BD1 = danger, opposite future (think), opposite positive person. Eliminate answer E, which contains no concept of person; opposite positive person means negative person or no person so eliminate B and D, which do not include the concept; both A and C look plausible; however, opposite future (think) translates as past think so eliminate answer A, taking had considered as past think, noting that nobody codes as opposite positive person.

Q19. Answer: A. source and D. town.

Explanation: Source (A) cannot be coded from any word in the table and town (D) only indirectly as large number people, space; water (C) is already in the table; reservoir (B) codes as large water vessel, 7(8, 21); fresh (E) codes as new or opposite old (B204).

Q20. Answer: A. possibility and C. deterioration.

Explanation: Possibility (A) cannot be coded from any word in the table; complications (B) can code as plural problem (E14); unconcerned can code as opposite anxious (B♥); deterioration (C) cannot code accurately and is the second choice.

Q21. Answer: B. client and D. store.

Explanation: Store (D) codes for filed away and is the first choice; clients' might code indirectly as specific plural person (KH1); however, client is the second choice because health (C) is already in the table, separate codes as opposite together (BJ) and records codes as similar notes (C206).

Q22. Answer: C. good and E. won.

Explanation: C codes for better, ie good increase; won cannot code from the table; nobody codes as negative plural person (BD, E1); protest is a synonym of object (207); player codes as person opposite work (1 B10).

Q23. Answer: B

Explanation: The code reads: B(G E1), 20A, 202D = opposite (male plural person), vision increase, light positive, ie women, see more, light on. Answers A and E translate as opposite positive man and opposite positive men respectively, ie negative man and negative men, instead of opposite men; answers C and D translate large light and light situation respectively, rather than light on.

Q24. Answer: C

Explanation: The code reads: 11(110), 19, B(15,6), 201(105) = fire pain, take, opposite short time, fix health. Answer A fails to include the concept of health when referring to heal, stating only fix, which is too general; answers D and E also fail to translate heal as fix health, stating only health; B is wrong because it codes long time as opposite few time instead of opposite short time.

Q25. Answer: A

Explanation: The code reads: B204(B G1), 205(BM), L♦, B105, H(7,BG) = opposite old opposite male person, seek opposite future, situation friendly, opposite health, personal large opposite male. Young female person, sought, situation friendly, sick, personal large female. Answer B lacks the concept of opposite future, ie seeks rather than sought, meaning solicits instead of solicited; C translates opposite plural females, ie women rather than woman; in the last set of codes, D translates personal large male rather than female and E translates opposite large male instead of personal large female.

Chapter 4 Quantitative reasoning

1. Answer: D. 29,900. Skill set: Table reading, addition
6,450 + 7,600 + 8,450 + 7,400 = 29,900

2. Answer: D. 25%. Skill set: Table reading, addition, percentages
6,450 + 7,600 + 8,450 + 7,400 + 5,550 = 35,450, (35,450/131,250) = 0.270, therefore approximately 25%.

3. Answer: C. 1/7. Skill set: Table reading, fractions
9,600 + 7,950 = 17,550, (17,550/131,250) = 0.134, approximately 1/7.

4. Answer: A. 4 : 5. Skill set: Table reading, addition, ratios
Schoolchildren: 7,600 + 8,450 + 7,400 = 23,450, retired: 7,450 + 7,100 + 6,450 + 4,500 + 2,750 = 28,250. The ratio 23,450 : 28,250 is about 4 : 5.

5. Answer: E. 81.0. Skill set: Table reading, mean
Add up all the times = 810; then divide by the number of children, 10. 810/10 = 81.0.

6. Answer: B. 81. Skill set: Table reading, median
Put the numbers in numerical order; then take the number in the middle. As there is an even number, split the difference between the two central numbers, 80 and 82, giving 81.

7. Answer: E. Two and a half times greater. Skill set: Table reading, range
Range in east = 95 – 65 = 30, range in west 145 – 70 = 75. 75/30 = 2.5.

8. Answer: C. 121. Skill set: Table reading, mode
Mode is the most frequent. There are two occurrences of 121.

9. Answer: D. Black £20. Skill set: Table reading, multiplication, addition
30 calls for a total of 300 minutes; therefore the charges would be as follows: Green £10: (30 × 10p) + (300 × 0.4p) = 420p; Green £20: (30 × 10p) + (300 × 0.35p) = 405p; Black £10: (30 × 8p) + (300 × 0.5p) = 390p; Black £20: (30 × 6p) + (300 × 0.4p) = 300p.

10. Answer: B. 60%. Skill set: Table reading, multiplication, addition, percentage
The total cost of calls would be £3.90 (see question 9 above), leaving £6.10 unused. (6.10/10.00) = 0.61, or approximately 60% wasted.

11. Answer: B. 10. Skill set: Table reading, mean
The total number of calls was 325 and the total duration 3,243 minutes; therefore the average was (3,243/325) = 10.0.

12. Answer: D. Black £20. Skill set: Table reading, percentages
The price per minute for the Black £20 is now 0.4p + (0.4p × (70/100)) = 0.68p. The cost for 300 minutes is now 300 × 0.68p = 204, and the total cost is (30 × 6p) + 204p = 384p. Still the cheapest (see question 9 above).

13. Answer: B. 4. Skill set: Chart reading
19,000 people in a population of 200,000 is a percentage, (19,000/200,000) = 0.095, 9.5%. Anything bigger than 9.5% will therefore employ more than 19,000 people, ie 12%, 18%, 10% and 14%.

14. Answer: A. 8 times. Skill set: Ratio/proportion
If 12% work in manufacturing and 2% in agriculture, there are 6 times as many in manufacturing and they produce a third more per person, so in total they generate 6 × 1.33 times more, ie 8.

15. Answer: E. 62.5m. Skill set: Fractions, multiplication
Half of £100m is £50m. 50m × 1.25 = 62.5m.

16. Answer: A. 1,000. Skill set: Percentage, division
Number of people in hotels and catering = 10% of 200,000 = 20,000. Number of employers = 20,000/20 = 1,000.

17. Answer: A. 0.55. Skill set: Table reading, percentage
6 out of 11 products have at least 1.5 g of salt, 6/11 = 0.545454, equivalent to 55%.

18. Answer: B. 117%. Skill set: Table reading, fractions/decimals
Each 100 g contains 2 g of salt, so 350 g contains 3.5 × 2 g = 7 g. Divided by the recommended maximum allowance of 6 this gives 7/6 = 116.6666, ie 117%.

19. Answer: D. £3.30. Skill set: Percentage, ratio
The price of the Paella is 1.1 × 1.50 = £1.65. The Fish Curry costs twice as much = £3.30.

20. Answer: C. 66.25 cents. Skill set: Percentage, Venn diagram
1.50 × 2.65 = 3.975, 1.25 × 2.65 = 3.3125. 3.975 – 3.3125 = 66.25 cents.

21. Answer: D. 53%. Skill set: Addition/subtraction, percentage
106 – 50 = 56 people 1.6 m or under; therefore 56/106 = 0.53, ie 53%.

22. Answer: D. 89. Skill set: Venn diagram, addition/subtraction
There are 62 people born in this country, 50 taller than 1.6 m and 14 left-handed, making a total of 126. As there are only 106 people in the survey there are an 'extra' 20 people. As 3 people are in all three groups they have been counted twice more, accounting for 6 of these 'extra' people. This leaves 14 extra who have been counted twice. 14 + 3 = 17 from an original group of 106, leaving 89.

23. Answer: E. Cannot tell. Skill set: Venn diagram
There is no information about how many in the groups overlap.

24. Answer: A. 6. Skill set: Simultaneous equations
This is really a question of simultaneous equations. Let BL equal the number born in England and left-handed, L = number just left-handed. L + BL + 3 + 2 = 14; therefore, BL + L = 9. Also L = 2 × BL; therefore L = 6 and BL = 3.

25. Answer: E. 3X + 2Y = 1285, 2X + 3Y = 1040. Skill set: Simultaneous equations
X is cod, Y is chips and the price is in pence.

26. Answer: B. £5.47. Skill set: Percentage, addition
Cost of cod originally, from the simultaneous equations in question 25, is £3.55 and a portion of chips £1.10. 3.55 + 20% = 4.26, 1.10 + 10% = 1.21; therefore total cost is 4.26 + 1.21 = 5.47.

27. Answer: D. 1 : 1.18. Skill set: Ratio
The new price divided by the old price is 5.47/4.65 = 1.1763, which rounds up to 1.18.

28. Answer: B. €16.74. Skill set: Money, proportion
Cost in euros of cod is 1.20 × 3.55 = 4.26; a portion of chips is 1.20 × 1.10 = 1.32. Therefore the total cost is (3 × 4.26) + (3 × 1.32) = €16.74.

29. Answer: C. 6. Skill set: Square root
The square root of 26 is 5.099, which rounded *up* is 6.

30. Answer: A. 11. Skill set: Mean, table reading
The average is 54.81 and so 11 students have less than this score.

31. Answer: C. 30. Skill set: Percentage, table reading
If three students fail then 23 out of 26 pass, ie 88.5% pass. If the mark is set at 30, three students, those with 26, 28 and 29 points, will fail.

32. Answer: E. 4. Skill set: Table reading, range, percentage
Range is 91 – 26 = 65. 10% of this is 6.5, which when added to the lowest score gives 32.5 as the pass mark. Four students are below this.

33. Answer: E. $(95 \times 87.5 \times 4.75)/30$. Skill set: Formulae, table reading
The number of gallons required would be 95/30 and the price per gallon would be 87.5×4.75. This can be rearranged to give $(95 \times 87.5 \times 4.75)/30$.

34. Answer: C. Belgium, Finland, United Kingdom, Italy. Skill set: Chart reading

35. Answer: D. 22.5%. Skill set: Compound interest
The information about the car and distance is a red herring. The increase is $1.07^3 = 1.225$, ie 22.5%.

36. Answer: B. 342.5. Skill set: Addition/subtraction, multiplication/division
Cost in the Netherlands is $(210/30) \times 4.75 \times 100.3 = 3{,}334.975$. In Germany it is $(210/30) \times 4.75 \times 90 = 2{,}992.5$. $3{,}334.975 - 2{,}992.5 = 342.5$.

37. Answer: A. Nearly twice as much. Skill set: Formulae, proportion
$1.25^3 = 1.953$, ie almost twice.

38. Answer: B. 14.5%. Skill set: Formulae, transposition
$P = Av^3$, rearranged gives $v = {}_3\sqrt{(P/A)}$. If P increases by 50%, v increases by ${}_3\sqrt{(1.5)} = 1.1447$, ie 14.5%, or 15%.

39. Answer: A. $\sqrt{0.4}$. Skill set: Percentage, proportion, formulae
Without the fuel the plane weighs 40% of the original weight, ie a factor of 0.4. If the speed is proportional to the weight the new speed will be $\sqrt{0.4}$ times the original.

40. Answer: D. $2.5^{1.5}$. Skill set: Formulae, proportion
This is a little complicated. The power when full is given by $P_f = Av_f^3$, but $v = B\sqrt{W}$, where B is some constant and W the weight, which can also be written as $v = BW^{0.5}$. So $P_f = A(BW_f^{0.5})^3$. The final weight is equal to 0.4 times the original weight, ie $W_e = 0.4W_f$. Power when empty is $P_e = A(B(0.4W)^{0.5})^3$. Therefore $P_f/P_e = A(BW_f^{0.5})^3/A(B(0.4W)^{0.5})^3 = (1/0.4)^{3\times 0.5} = 2.5^{1.5}$.

41. Answer: E. Cannot tell. Skill set: Table reading
As the number with the substance present in the 780 samples is unknown, it is impossible to tell.

42. Answer: C. About 46. Skill set: Addition, percentage, table reading
500 were identified as having the substance present; 8% of these would be wrong, ie 40. The remaining 280 were identified as having no substance present; of these 2% would be wrong, ie 5.6. 40 + 5.6 is about 46.

43. Answer: D. About 20 more. Skill set: Table reading, percentages
Allcheck: of the 390 positive, 5% would be wrong, giving 19.5; of the 390 negative about 10% would be wrong, giving 39. This makes a total of around 60 wrong. Truespot: of the 390 positive, 8% would be wrong, giving 31.2; of the 390 negative about 2% would be wrong, giving 7.8. This makes a total of around 40 wrong. Therefore there are about 20 more wrong for Allcheck. Hopefully, no one sues.

44. Answer: B. About 465. Skill set: Formulae, table reading, percentage
Let P be the number that actually have the substance present; then 0.95P would be the number identified by Allcheck as positive. Because the result can be only positive or negative, 800 – P are negative, but Allcheck would identify 10% of these as positive, 0.1(800 – P). The total number identified as positive would be 0.95P + 0.1(800 – P) = 475. Rearranging gives 0.85P = 395; therefore P = 395/0.85 = 464.71, about 465.

45. Answer: A. 30. Skill set: Table reading, mean, estimation
The average can be estimated reasonably accurately by saying that, for example, the group of students who play between 10 and 14 hours are 2 students who play 12 hours each (halfway between 10 and 14). This then equates to 2 × 12 = 24 'student hours'. The total number of student hours can then be summed and divided by the number of students to give the average = 6,560/220 = 29.8 or about 30. Or you can just estimate, which is much quicker.

46. Answer: C. 14. Skill set: Table reading, addition
2 + 12 = 14.

47. Answer: E. 5/9. Skill set: Addition, division, proportion
The average, as seen in question 45, is 30. There are 77 + 38 + 8 = 123 students who play more than this. 123 divided by the total number of students gives 123/220 = 0.559. 5/9 = 0.555, which is near enough.

48. Answer: D. 27. Skill set: Percentage, proportion
The heaviest users will have the largest effect on the number of student hours and they reduce their playing by 10%. A large proportion remains unchanged, so a reasonable guess would be about a 10% reduction in average time, ie 30 – 3 = 27. If you choose to calculate, it should come out to 27.2.

49. Answer: C. Skill set: Formulae, table reading
A = 21.5, B = 22.22, C = 22.5, D = 20.5, E = 21.5.

50. Answer: C. Minus 9%. Skill set: Formulae
An increase of 10% is equivalent to multiplying by 1.1, so the increase in BMI would be given by $1.1/1.1^2$, ie 0.909, or a reduction of 9%.

51. Answer: A. 9 kg. Skill set: Transposition, multiplication/division
$B = M/H^2$, so $H = \sqrt{(M/B)} = \sqrt{(80/28)} = 1.69$ m. To have a BMI just within the 'normal' range a value of 24.9 is needed. $M = BH^2 = 24.9 \times 1.69^2 = 71.1$. Person A needs to lose just under 9 kg.

52. Answer: C. 1/5. Skill set: Transposition, fractions
$M = BH^2$, so original weight is $24.9 \times 1.8^2 = 80.7$ kg. Weight at a BMI of 30 is 97.2 kg. The difference is 16.5, which is 16.5/80.7 or 1/5 of the original.

53. Answer: E. Region 2, year 1. Skill set: Table reading
Around 3%.

54. Answer: A. Year 1. Skill set: Percentages, table reading
A 4.4% difference compared to year 3 with 3.5%, for example.

55. Answer: B. £7,000. Skill set: Percentages, table reading
Difference in percentage in year 3 = 3.5%. 3.5 of £200,000 = £7,000.

56. Answer: C. $1.05 \times 1.03 \times 1.075 \times 1.023 \times 0.99$. Skill set: Compound interest
Compound interest and reducing by 0.1% is equivalent to multiplying by 0.99.

57. Answer: E. Cannot tell. Skill set: Venn diagram
Several people may have answered no to all questions.

58. Answer: D. 32. Skill set: Venn diagram, addition
51 buy a paper every day and 32 have been to France, so the maximum number who could have done both would be 32.

59. Answer: A. 20. Skill set: Venn diagram
Yes, sometimes it is that easy. It is the intersection between the two specified groups.

60. Answer: C. 50. Skill set: Venn diagrams, addition/subtraction
The total number of people in the overlapping groups, who have answered yes to *two or more questions*, is 60. However, the 10 people in the centre have answered yes to three questions, so only 50 have answered yes to two.

61. Answer: D. 1/2. Skill set: Graph reading, fractions
Around 32% are intending to vote for one party and 32% for the other, so those' intending to vote are split equally.

62. Answer: A. August. Skill set: Graph reading
This month has the least total number intending to vote and hence the largest number abstaining, 32% and 30%, compared to 34% and 32% in December, for example.

63. Answer: B. 42.5% and 23.5% respectively. Skill set: Graph reading, percentages
A total of 62% are voting, which means that 38% are abstaining. If 10% of these now vote there are an additional 3.8% to distribute among the parties in proportion to their current voting intentions, ie 40/62 × 3.8 to one and 22/62 × 3.8 to the other, an increase respectively of 2.5% and 1.5%, more or less.

64. Answer: E. April to May. Skill set: Graph reading, ratio
The difference in points went from 10 to 0.

65. Answer: D. (200 – 1.20) × 0.97 × 1.20. Skill set: Formulae
You start with £200; then before doing anything you lose £1.20. Then you lose 3%, ie have 0.97 times the original, which is then converted to euros by multiplying by 1.20.

66. Answer: E. Concurrency. Skill set: Multiplication, table reading
For a large enough sum, the fee is irrelevant. You can then calculate the number of euros by subtracting the commission from the exchange rate; thus HH: 1.20 × 0.97 = 1.164; BB: 1.18; XC: 1.22 × 0.98 = 1.1956; FEC: 1.22 × 0.97 = 1.1834; CON: 1.20. Therefore Concurrency will buy you the most euros.

67. Answer: A. 3%. Skill set: Table reading, subtraction, money
The biggest is £177.60 and the smallest £173.20, the difference being £4.40. This is 4.4/150 of the original, or 2.9333%.

68. Answer: C. 1/4. Skill set: Table reading, money, percentage
With no losses, £10 becomes €12.50, but from the table you would receive only €9.60, ie €2.90 less. 2.9/12.5 = 0.232, or nearly a quarter.

69. Answer: E. 5/9. Skill set: Fractions, percentage, chart reading
The total is 32% + 23% = 55%, which is approximately equivalent to 5/9 = 0.555 recurring.

70. Answer: B. Skill set: Chart reading, percentage
PP increases to 20% and 3A decreases to 12%. This is now a ratio of 20 : 12, or 1.67 : 1.

71. Answer: E. 95%. Skill set: Proportion, ratio, chart reading, percentage
It would be theoretically possible for the major brands to have market shares of 0.0032%, 0.0017%, 0.0015% and 0.0023% respectively, thus maintaining the ratios, but for the own brands to have captured the part of the market, 5%, not occupied by the newcomer. This may seem unlikely, but likelihood wasn't the question.

72. Answer: C. 17%. Skill set: Addition, proportion, chart reading, percentage
If the current total sales represent a value of 100, then the current sales of Pepper Pop are 15. Increasing this by 15% gives new sales of 17.25, 2.25 bigger, and new total sales of 102.25. Therefore the new market share of PP is (17.25/102.25) × 100 = 16.9%.

73. Answer: B. $1.1^{0.75}$. Skill set: Formulae, transposition
Factor for the increase in dosage is $D_2/D_1 = (0.5H^{0.5}W_2^{0.75})/(0.5H^{0.5}W_1^{0.75}) = (W_2^{0.75})/(W_1^{0.75}) = (1.1W_1)^{0.75}/W_1^{0.75} = 1.1^{0.75}$.

74. Answer: E. Cannot tell. Skill set: Formulae
No original weight is given, so no proportional increase can be determined.

75. Answer: E. Skill set: Formulae, indices, multiplication
150 ml. 70 in = 177.8 cm, 10 stone = 63.6 kg. $D = 0.5 \times 177.8^{0.5} \times 63.6^{0.75} = 150$.

76. Answer: B. 32%. Skill set: Formulae, indices, proportion
20% more is equivalent to multiplying by 1.2, so the overall increase is given by: $1.2^{0.75} \times 1.15 = 1.318$, or 32%.

77. Answer: C. 10–14.9. Skill set: Table reading, median
473 observations. The 237th value will fall in the 10–14.9 group as this contains the observations from 173 to 327.

78. Answer: A. 12.5 minutes. Skill set: Estimation, mean, table reading
You could check by adding up all the mid-points, ie 2.5, 7.5, 12.5, etc multiplied by the number (5,905.5) and dividing by the total number (473). But, as you only have about 30 seconds per question you just have to judge that the average is in the middle of the 10–14.9 group.

79. Answer: E. Cannot tell. Skill set: Table reading
No information is given about the distribution of the 154 observations within the 10–14.9 group; they could all be before 12.5 minutes or all after.

80. Answer: D. 600 litres. Skill set: Table reading, division, multiplication
473 trips at an average of 12.5 minutes a trip = 5,912.5 minutes. Multiply this by the 0.1 litres per minute to get 600 litres, roughly.

81. Answer: B. 60. Skill set: Speed, division
Velocity is the rate of change of distance with time. You could either determine the formula that relates distance and time, distance, $s = 5t^2$, and differentiate to get $ds/dt = v = 10t$, therefore at 6 seconds v = 60, or you could look at the distance at 7 seconds and 5 seconds and estimate the velocity at 6 seconds as being the difference in distance divided by the difference in time: (245 – 125)/(7 – 5) = 60.

82. Answer: A. 10. Skill set: Estimation, division
The same process as above can be used to determine the velocities at 1, 2 and 3 seconds, 10, 20 and 30 m/s respectively, to give an acceleration of 10 m/s^2.

83. Answer: C. Between 2 and 3 seconds. Skill set: Formulae, table reading
After 2 seconds the first object will have travelled 20 m, and the second, which has now been travelling for 5 seconds, will have travelled 25.4 m. After 3 seconds the first has now reached 45 m and the second, 30.2. Somewhere between these two times the first overtook the second.

84. Answer: E. None of the above. Skill set: Table reading
It has greatest acceleration just after it is released, just after 0 seconds.

85. Answer: B. 0.7. Skill set: Table reading, mode
The mode is 99.9, which subtracting 99.2 leaves 0.7.

86. Answer: D. 25. Skill set: Mean, table reading
There are three numbers greater than 99.9, so the total calculated will be 300 less than it should. The average is determined by dividing the total by 12 in this case. The result will therefore be 300/12 = 25 too small.

87. Answer: C. 5/6. Skill set: Table reading, fractions
With numbers this close to 100 the effect of a 2% increase is to add 2. Thus any number previously above 98 will now exceed 100. Only two numbers are below this threshold; therefore 10 out of 12 or 5/6 will be above 100.

88. Answer: A. Answer + 100. Skill set: Table reading, addition
As all the numbers input are missing 100, the answer will similarly be missing 100.

89. Answer: B. Havanaisday. Skill set: Multiplication, table reading
Multiplying the number of claims by the cost of claim gives the lowest figure for Havanaisday.

90. Answer: E. £163. Skill set: Division/multiplication, table reading
There are 37.7 claims per 100, but this is divided over the 100 cars, so the cost per car is (37.7/100) × 433 = 163.

91. Answer: A. 2/5. Skill set: Multiplication, division, fractions
Original cost = 36.4 × 223 = 8,117. New cost = 25 × 200 = 5,000. Fractional saving = (8,117 – 5,000)/8,117 = 0.384, nearly 0.4 or 2/5.

92. Answer: A. £25. Skill set: Proportion, table reading
1 in 12 cars breaks down at a cost of £250, so the cost per car is 250/12. The company wants to make 20% more than the cost, ie a factor of 1.2, so the premium would be (250/12) × 1.2 = 25.

93. Answer: B. 4.429. Skill set: Table reading, division, money
To get from Robbers to Yangs you have to multiply by 4.429 (104.93/23.69).

94. Answer: A. 56%. Skill set: Percentages, table reading
The first exchange rate drops by 20%, ie 0.8 times the original value; the others increase by 25%, ie 1.25 times the original. Therefore going from one that has dropped to one that has increased the difference is 1.25/0.8 = 1.5625, or 56%.

95. Answer: A. Up 1/4. Skill set: Fractions, proportions
The value of the denominator (the bottom of the fraction) compared to the numerator (top) has dropped to a factor of 0.8. The relative value is therefore 1/0.8 = 1.25, ie up a quarter.

96. Answer: C. 3.09 Dollally. Skill set: Money, division
In the first transaction the tourist loses 3 Dollally (3%). In the second he or she loses 3 Barts or 3/33.15 = 0.09 Dollally.

Mini-test 1

97. Answer: D. 1/40. Skill set: Fractions, Graph reading
The maximum sales were 33,000, the minimum 900. 33,000/900 = 36.67, so the fraction is about 1/40.

98. Answer: A. 500%. Skill set: Proportion, percentage, graph reading
In the same way that a 100% increase is equivalent to doubling, the sales have gone from 1,100 to 6,600, ie 6 times as much or a 500% increase.

99. Answer: E. £45m. Skill set: Addition/subtraction
The total sales over the year add up to £104.7m. The total costs = 12 × £5m = 60m, so the total profits are 104.7 – 60 = 44.7.

100. Answer: A. 1.001^{12}. Skill set: Formulae, compound interest
A 0.1% increase is the same as multiplying by 1.001; do this 12 times (once for each of the 12 months) and you have 1.001^{12}. Compound interest in action.

101. Answer: D. Drug D. Skill set: Table reading, mean
Has the quickest average recovery time at 13.78.

102. Answer: D. Drug D. Skill set: Table reading, median
13.5, apparently.

103. Answer: E. Unchanged. Skill set: Proportion
In effect, if all the values move towards the 'centre' value by the same proportion, this value will remain unchanged.

104. Answer: D. Cannot tell. Skill set: Range, proportion
There is no information on whether other values change, whether the minimum remains unchanged and the maximum is reduced, etc.

(OK, so they were easier, or maybe you're getting better. Well done.)

Mini-test 2

105. Answer: B. A and E. Skill set: Speed, division
As you are not required to give any units, the quickest way to determine speed is probably to calculate in miles per minute. A and E both then give the highest values of 1.0.

106. Answer: C. s = 65/(1 + (11/60)). Skill set: Formulae
There are 60 minutes in one hour, so 11/60 represents the fraction of the hour for 11 minutes, so the total time taken is 1 + (11/60). Speed is distance divided by time, as suggested by the units, miles per hour. Be careful of the right number and position of the brackets.

107. Answer: C. +25%, –17%. Skill set: Percentage, proportion
If you reduce the time by 20% it is now 0.8 times the original value, but because you need to divide by the time to calculate the velocity you get 1/0.8 = 1.25, ie a 25% increase. Similarly, when you increase the time by 20% you get 1/1.2 = 0.8333, a 17% decrease.

108. Answer: A. 26.82 m/s. Skill set: Multiplication, division, speed
There are 95 minutes, 95 × 60 = 5,700 seconds. 95 miles = 95 × 1,609 = 152,855 metres. Speed = 152,855/5,700 = 26.82 m/s.

109. Answer: B. 360. Skill set: Mean, graph reading, estimation
From the graph the average can be seen to be about 15. 15 × 24 = 360.

110. Answer: E. 9/24. Skill set: Fractions, graph reading
Nine of the hours *exceed* 15 TeraBytes.

111. Answer: B. 5 and 6 or 8 and 9. Skill set: Graph reading, proportion
Tricky question. The largest absolute increase was between 8 and 9, going from 10 to 29, but the largest *relative* increase was between 5 and 6, from 2 to 6, a factor of 3 times.

112. Answer: A. 14. Skill set: Graph reading, multiplication, division
The bar chart gives TeraBytes in any particular hour, so to get the transfer rate per second you need to divide by 3,600 (60 × 60). Completing this calculation gives 14 values that are 3 GigaBytes/sec or higher.

Mini-test 3

113. Answer: B. 4/3. Skill set: Proportion
If the pressure changes by 3/4, in order to give the same constant result the volume must correspondingly change by 4/3.

114. Answer: C. +1/5. Skill set: Proportion
To compensate the pressure must increase by 6/5 or increase by 1/ 5.

115. Answer: D. The volume 0.133 should read 0.013. Skill set: Formulae, table reading
All the others when multiplied together (PV = const) give a value of 2.

116. Answer: A. 10%. Skill set: Proportion, formulae
The answer should be 0.0022222, but the experimenter will only read 0.002. This gives a percentage error of ((0.0022222 – 0.002)/0.0022222) × 100 = 10%.

117. Answer: D. 3/20. Skill set: Table reading, proportion
A total of 85% (55 + 30) made some pronouncement, so 15% were undecided. 15/100 = 3/20.

118. Answer: C. 65%. Skill set: Proportion, formulae
Population Y represents two-thirds of the total population and X, 1/3 (2/3 is twice as big as 1/3 and 2/3 + 1/3 = the entire population). The average value, therefore, is (1/3 × 85) + (2/3 × 55) = 65.

119. Answer: A. Population X for juice A. Skill set: Table reading
This has shown a 20-point drop.

120. Answer: C. Around 7% more. Skill set: Percentages, table reading
The preference for the original was 65%, as in question 118. In the second test the preference is 63% (following the same analysis as for question 118 above). However, those 63% generate 10% more revenue, adding around another 6 comparative points, to give a score of about 69.3. (69.3 – 65)/65 = 6.6% higher.

Mini-test 4

121. Answer: E. 5. Skill set: Simultaneous equations, table reading
If you look at team A and team E you can create simultaneous equations: 2W + 2D = 26 and 2W + 1D = 21; therefore D = 5.

122. Answer: A. 9. Skill set: Table reading, multiplication, addition, subtraction
Each of the five teams plays the four others twice, $5 \times 4 \times 2 = 40$, but each match involves two teams, so there are 20 matches; 11 have been played already (there are 22 'results' in the table), so there are 9 to play.

123. Answer: B. 192. Skill set: Multiplication, addition, table reading
There are 102 points so far. The maximum number of points is gained when two teams draw, giving 5 points each, ie 10 points per game. There are 9 remaining games and so 90 more points.

124. Answer: A. 1/5. Skill set: Table reading, proportion
Team C will have 28 points.

125. Answer: A. $y = \sqrt{x}$. Skill set: Graphs, formulae

126. Answer: B. B and C. Skill set: Graph reading, estimation
Slightly sneaky question, but looking at the average height of the line should give you the answer. Integration would give you the exact results; lines B and C have an average value of 3, line D an average of 2.75.

127. Answer: E. 7. Skill set: Formulae
The formula for the curve is $y = 0.5x + 2$, so, when $x = 10$, $y = 7$.

128. Answer: D. 6. Skill set: Transposition
This is asking the value of x for which $x^2/3 = 2x$. Multiply both sides by 3 ($x^2 = 6x$); then divide both sides by x; $x = 6$.

Mini-test 5

129. Answer: B. 87.5. Skill set: Table reading, percentage
Two students have *more* than this.

130. Answer: A. 49. Skill set: Table reading, percentage
If we follow the same process as above then the failure mark should be just above the second lowest, ie 38.5; then the range will be 49.

131. Answer: A. 1. Skill set: Table reading, mode
A mode of 55 in the first set and 56 in the second. Easy, huh?

132. Answer: B. 3. Skill set: Table reading, percentage
The top four marks, rounded to the nearest integer, are now 85, 90, 91, 94, three of which exceed the key, 87.5.

133. Answer: A. 18 m/s. Skill set: Speed, subtraction
$50 - 32 = 18$.

134. Answer: C. 1,620 m. Skill set: Speed, multiplication, subtraction
Every second the car has gone 27 m further than the horse ($50 - 23 = 27$). After 60 seconds it has gone $60 \times 27 = 1{,}620$ m more.

135. Answer: E. 30.43. Skill set: Multiplication, division, subtraction
The horse will complete the 100 m in $100/23 = 4.348$ secs. The bicycle will travel $16 \times 4.348 = 69.57$ m in that time and will therefore need a head start of $100 - 69.57 = 30.43$ m.

136. Answer: B. $s = 100 - 13t$. Skill set: Formulae
The distance between them starts at 100. The horse gains $23 - 10 = 13$ m every second, so the distance between them reduces following the equation $s = 100 - 13t$.

Mini-test 6

137. Answer: C. March, April, May, June. Skill set: Graph reading
The four highest points.

138. Answer: A. 11/20. Skill set: Graph reading, division
2.75/5 = 0.55 or 11/20.

139. Answer: D. £8,500. Skill set: Graph reading, mean, multiplication
The average is 3.4. This gives 0.034 × 250,000 = £8,500.

140. Answer: B. $C = 50{,}000 \times 1.05^{(1/12)}$. Skill set: Compound interest, indices, multiplication
At the end of the year the amount paid with 5% interest will be 1.05 times the loan amount. The interest for each month multiplied together, ie multiplied by itself 12 times, will give this factor. So the factor for the month must be the 12th root of this factor, ie $1.05^{(1/12)}$. Multiply this by the loan amount to give the total due after one month.

141. Answer: A. 300%. Skill set: Chart reading, percentages
The key is how much *more*. The leisure time is 4 times the travel time, so with the 100% you have already you need an *additional 300%* to give the 400% (4 times).

142. Answer: B. 3 : 2. Skill set: Chart reading, proportion
The number of hours spent travelling has gone from 1.5 to 3 and the number of hours' leisure from 6 to 4.5, ie a new ratio of 4.5 : 3, or 3 : 2.

143. Answer: D. 11 minutes. Skill set: Chart reading, multiplication, division
(1.20/6.50) × 60 = 11.07 minutes.

144. Answer: E. 30p/hour. Skill set: Subtraction, division
Travel costs are now 3.00 – 1.20 = £1.80 more expensive. So the student must earn at least £1.80/6 hours, 30p/hour, more than before.

Mini-test 7

145. Answer: B. Equation 2. Skill set: Formulae
The square will generate the largest values at higher values of t.

146. Answer: D. 25%. Skill set: Formulae, percentages
At t = 5, $V_1 = 3(5) + 5 = 20$. $V_2 = (5)^2 = 25$. 25/20 = 1.25, ie 25% larger.

147. Answer: A. $t^3 = 25$. Skill set: Formulae, transposition
They have the same value when the equations are equal, $5\sqrt{t} = t^2$. Squaring both sides gives $25t = t^4$ and then dividing by t gives $25 = t^3$.

148. Answer: A. Equation 1. Skill set: Estimation, graphs
This is a little tricky to answer in 30 seconds, but familiarity with these equations would allow you to sketch quickly and see that equation 1 must have the highest average value. Equation 4 is a close second, starting at 10 and dropping to 1.8 at t = 1.

149. Answer: A. 2001. Skill set: Reading graphs, subtraction
Sometimes it is that easy.

150. Answer: E. None of the above. Skill set: Reading the question carefully!
The graph shows levels of satisfaction, not quality of teaching.

151. Answer: C. 50. Skill set: Formulae
Replacing B by n gives S = 100 (n)/2n = 50.

152. Answer: E. 6. Skill set: Addition, subtraction, division
It is closing the gap at 3 + 3 = 6 points per year and is currently 78 – 44 = 34 points behind. It will therefore take 34/6 = 6 years.

UKCAT-style quantitative reasoning timed test 1

1. Answer: C
   10 out of 12 pupils = 83.3%.

2. Answer: E
   9 out of 10 pupils = 90.0%.

3. Answer: A
   7 out of 12 pupils = 58.3%.

4. Answer: D
   5 out of 7 pupils = 71.4%.

5. Answer: A
   (5,241 ÷ 0.52) × 0.273 = 2,751.

6. Answer: B
   (5,241 × 0.8) ÷ 0.39 × 0.273 = 2,935.

7. Answer: B
   (0.5 × 1,000) × 0.273 = 136.5.

8. Answer: E
   51% carbon dioxide = 0.8 × 1 = 0.8; methane = 0.12 × 22 = 2.64; nitrous oxide = 0.06 × 300 = 18; fluorocarbons = 0.02 × 1,000 = 20; adding these gives 0.8 + 2.64 + 18 + 20 = 41.44; then for fluorocarbons 20 ÷ 41.44 × 100 = 48%.

9. Answer: D
   1,701 = (100 – 83) = 17%; 1,701 ÷ 0.17 = 10,006.

10. Answer: B
    10,006 × (10 + 2)% = 1,201; or 12/17 × 1,701 = 1,201.

11. Answer: C
    0.83 × (3 ÷ 7) × 100 = 35.57%.

12. Answer: A
    35.57% × 10,006 = 3,559; 3,559 × (55 + 5)% = 2,136.

13. Answer: D
    20 × £3,500 + 40 × £4,000 = £70,000 +£160,000 = £230,000.

14. Answer: B
Bar at age 35–44 = 15 staff, of which two-thirds are men (given) = 10 men and 5 women. Sales by females = 5 × £3,000 + 10 × £3,000 + 5 × £3,500 = £62,500.

15. Answer: D
Male total = £230,000 (question 13) + two-thirds × 15 × 3,500 = 265,000; female total = £62,500 (question 14); male + female = 327,500; percentage male = 80.9%.

16. Answer: C
Male total = 265,000; female total = 62,500 × 1.1 = 68,750; male + female = 333,750 × 52 weeks = 17.36 million.

17. Answer: B
90 ml/100 ml × 50 g × 9 kcal/g = 405 kcal.

18. Answer: E
405 kcal from Calogen™ (question 17) and from Ensure Twocal™: 6 × 21 × 2 × 4 + 6 × 8.4 × 2 × 4 + 6 × 8.9 × 2 × 9 = 2,777; 2,777 ÷ 2,550 = 1.09 = 109%.

19. Answer: A
Fat calories (kcal) = 8.9 × 9 = 80.1; total calories, all three nutrients = 80.1 + 21 × 4 + 8.4 × 4 = 197.7; proportion is then 80.1/197.7 = 40.5%.

20. Answer: D
Calogen™: 30 ml/100 ml × 50 × 9 = 135; 1,940 – 135 = 1,805; total calories per 100 ml Ensure Twocal™ = 197.7 (question 19); 1,805 ÷ 197.7 × 100 ml = 913 ml.

21. Answer: E
In pounds: Valu = 2 × 8 × 2 × £10,000 = £320,000; Wilats = 3.5 × 6 × 3 × £10,000 = £630,000; Xsels = 1.5 × 10 × 1 × £10,000 = £150,000; Yamit = 2.5 × 5 × 4 × £10,000 = £500,000; Zonika = 3 × 5 × 6 × £10,000 = £900,000.

22. Answer: A
Cost per copy = 3.5p (Wilats), of which 1p = paper (given); therefore 2.5 p = toner; 2.5 ÷ 3.5 × 100% = 71%.

23. Answer: B
Cost per copy = 1.5p (Xsels) of which 1p = paper (given); double-sided copies cut the paper costs in half, so 0.5 p per copy saving, ie 0.5 p × 10,000 × 1,000 = £50,000.

24. Answer: E
Cost per copy = 2.5 p (Yamit), of which 1p = paper (given). At the normal A4 size, total cost = 2.5p × 4,000 × 5,000 = £500,000 = £200,000 paper + £300,000 toner. At the reduced A5 size, toner consumption = 50% = £125,000.

25. Answer: B
$$\sqrt{\frac{\text{cm} \times \text{kg}}{3{,}600}} = \sqrt{\frac{180 \times 80}{3{,}600}} = \sqrt{4} = 2$$

26. Answer: D
$2 = 1/60 \times \sqrt{170 \times h}$; $120 = \sqrt{170 \times h}$; squaring both sides: 14,400 = 170h, giving h = 84.7 kg.

27. Answer: E
$$\sqrt{\frac{\text{cm} \times \text{kg}}{3{,}600}} = \sqrt{\frac{160 \times 60}{3{,}600}} = \sqrt{\frac{16}{6}} = 4/\sqrt{6}$$

28. Answer: D
$BSA^2 \times 3{,}600$ = cm × kg; 1.73 × 1.73 × 3,600 = 160 × kg, giving new kg = 67.5; increase = 7.5 kg.

29. Answer: A
3 across × (1,100 ÷ 80) = 3 × 13.75, ie 3 × 13 = 39.

30. Answer: D
2 across × (1,100 ÷ 120) = 2 × 9.2, ie 2 × 9 = 18; 18 × £30 = £540.

31. Answer: C
Small = 3 × 13 × £10 = £390; medium = 3 × 18 × £12 = £648; conventional = 3 × 18 × £20 = £1,080; large cube = 2 × 10 × 22 = £440; circular = £540.

32. Answer: E
Most efficient stacking = 3 across × 18 along = 54 bales; least efficient stacking = 1 across × 13 along = 13 bales. Loss of stacking efficiency = (54 – 13)/54 × 100% = 75.9%.

33. Answer: B
35 ml × 0.4% = 14 ml; 14 ml ÷ 10 ml × 8 g = 11.2 g.

34. Answer: D
Maximum safe limit = 3 units = 3 × 10 ml = 30 ml pure alcohol; 30 ÷ 0.17 = 176 ml; 176 ÷ 35 = 5.03.

35. Answer: C
Vodka = 1.5 × 40% = 0.6; Tia Maria = 0.5 × 26.5% = 0.1325; Bailey's = 0.5 × 17% = 0.085. Total = 0.6 + 0.1325 + 0.085 = 0.8175 measures of alcohol in 2.5 measures of drink = 32.7% ABV.

36. Answer: A
Maximum sensible limit is 4 units = 40 ml of pure alcohol; John consumes 150 ml × 1/3 × 0.17 = 8.5 ml + 50 ml × 0.4 = 20 ml; total = 28.5 ml = 71.3%.

37. Answer: E
Clearly not B (Phillip) (Barbara slower) or D (Luke) (Aran slower) so eliminate these two from the calculations. Distance = speed × time and time = distance ÷ speed; Barbara: time = 2/3 hr = 40 minutes (arrives 8.55); Aran: time = 2/10 hr = 12 minutes (arrives 8.52); Katie: time = 2/30 = 4 minutes (arrives 8.59), ie E (Katie).

38. Answer: A
New average speed = 11; new time = 2 ÷ 11 × 60 = 10.9 minutes. Departs at 8.45, arrives at 8.56.

39. Answer: A
Average speed = total distance ÷ total time; first leg: one mile at 3 mph = 0.33 hour; second leg: one mile at 20 mph = 0.05 mph; total distance = 2 miles, total time = 0.38 hour. Average speed = 2 ÷ 0.38 = 5.26 mph.

40. Answer: E
Barbara leaves at 8.15, Katie at 8.45, so Barbara has been walking for 30 minutes before Katie sets off, that is a minimum of 3 mph × 30/60 hr = 1.5 miles, so eliminate answers A, B, C and D, leaving only E. The exact solution is as follows: after 1.5 miles the 'extra' distance (d) walked by Barbara for time 't' to the point where they meet is given by d = 3t (distance = speed × time); so the total distance (D) to the meeting point is: D = 1.5 + 3t; then for Katie we have D = 30t (30 mph × t), so 30t = 1.5 + 3t, giving 27t = 1.5 and then t = 1.5/27; substituting t in D = 30t gives D = 30 × 1.5/27 = 45/27 = 5/3 = 1.67 miles.

Chapter 5 Abstract reasoning

Questions 1–5

Set A has an odd number of shapes and fewer black ones than shaded.
Set B has an even number of shapes and the same number of black as shaded.

1. C.
2. B.
3. A.
4. C. No black shapes.
5. C. Odd, but too many black shapes.

Questions 6–10

Set A: Eight enclosed regions and the rectangles are shaded.
Set B: An odd number of enclosed regions and three-sided regions are shaded.

6. B.
7. C. Shaded three-sided regions, but eight regions in total.
8. A.
9. C. Not all rectangles shaded.
10. C. Even number.

Questions 11–15

Set A: One is a reflection of the other, either horizontally or vertically.
Set B: One is a rotation of the other.

11. A.
12. C.
13. A.
14. B.
15. C.

Questions 16–20

Set A: There is an odd number of shapes. The majority are triangles.
Set B: There is an even number of shapes. Triangles are not the majority.

16. C. Odd number of shapes, not majority triangles.
17. B.
18. A.
19. C. Even number of shapes, majority triangles.
20. C. Odd number of shapes, not majority triangles.

Questions 21–25

Set A: Number of enclosed (overlapping) regions is odd. Overlapping regions with straight sides are shaded.

Set B: Number of enclosed (overlapping) regions is even. Overlapping circles are shaded.

21. A.
22. B.
23. C. Odd number, but straight sides not shaded.
24. A.
25. C. Even number, but circles not shaded.

Questions 26–30

Set A: There are six crossover points. The top or bottom of the space is blank.

Set B: There are four crossover points. The left or right of the space is blank.

26. C. Three crossovers.
27. A.
28. C. Six crossovers, but spaces at left.
29. B.
30. B.

Questions 31–35

Set A: There is at least one internal right angle. The number of circles equals the number of internal right angles. Colour is immaterial.

Set B: The number of circles is greater than the number of internal right angles. Colour is immaterial.

31. B. No right angles, three circles.
32. C. At least one internal right angle (A), but number of circles less than number of right angles.
33. C. At least one internal right angle (A), but number of circles less than number of right angles.
34. A. Two right angles, two circles.
35. B.

Questions 36–40

Set A: At least one triangle means two or more circles will be present. An even number of triangles gives shaded circles.
Set B: The difference between the number of unshaded and shaded triangles gives the number of circles. Circles will be shaded black if a rectangle is present.

36. A.
37. A.
38. C.
39. B.
40. C.

Questions 41–45

Set A: The total number of sides of shaded shapes minus the total number of sides on the unshaded shapes adds up to zero. The largest shape counts double.
Set B: The total number of sides is 20. Shaded shapes count double.

41. C.
42. A.
43. C.
44. C.
45. B.

Questions 46–50

Set A: Odd number of line intersections. Any three-sided enclosed regions are shaded.
Set B: Even number of line intersections. Any four-sided enclosed region is shaded.

46. C. Four-sided shapes would need to be shaded in set B.
47. C. Even number, but three-sided figure shaded.
48. C. Not all four-sided shapes shaded.
49. B.
50. A.

Questions 51–55

Set A: Number of acute angles = number of non-triangular figures. Shading immaterial.
Set B: Number of right angles = number of triangles. Shading immaterial.

51. B. The 'right angles' of the diamond do not count as they are internally divided by lines. There are four right-angle triangles.
52. A.
53. B.
54. B.
55. C.

Questions 56–60

Set A: The angle between the circle, the centre of the large shape and the diamond is always 0°, 90°, 180° or 270°. There are more four-sided shapes than three-sided.
Set B: The angle between the circle, the centre of the large shape and the diamond is always 45°, 135°, 225° or 315°. There is the same number of four-sided shapes as three-sided.

56. C.
57. B.
58. A.
59. C. Not enough triangles for Set B.
60. A. More four-sided than three as there are no triangles at all.

Questions 61–65

Set A: Three similar shapes form a line, as in noughts and crosses.
Set B: Four similar shapes will form a rectangle.

61. B.
62. B.
63. A.
64. C.
65. C.

Questions 66–70

Set A: Pieces put together will form a right angle triangle, five blocks long and five blocks high.
Set B: Pieces put together will form a five by three rectangle.

66. B.
67. B.
68. A.
69. C.
70. B.

Questions 71–75

Set A: The total number of shapes is odd and more shapes are in multiple groups than singularly.
Set B: The total number of shapes is even, same number in multiple groups as singularly.

71. A.
72. A.
73. C.
74. B.
75. C.

Questions 76–80

Set A: Where there are two shapes the same, the smaller one is shaded. All other shading is random.

Set B: Where there are three shapes the same, there are three shaded shapes.

76. B.
77. C. The smaller one should be shaded.
78. A.
79. C.
80. B.

Questions 81–85

Modular arithmetic. The arrow pointing up represents 0, right is 1, down is 2, left is 3. So, 2 + 2 = 0, because four quarter-rotations would bring the arrow back to the top.

Set A: Addition.

Set B: Subtraction. The first minus the second.

81. A. 3 plus 3 quarter-turns = 6 quarter-turns or 2 half-turns. 3 + 3 = 6 (2)
82. B. 3 – 3 = 0.
83. C
84. B. 2 – 3 = –1 (3)
85. B. 0 – 3 = –3 (1)

Questions 86–90

Set A: If the majority of arrows point to the left, the majority of shapes are shaded and vice versa. The top-left shape is white. Arrow shading irrelevant.

Set B: If all arrows point the same way, all shapes are shaded. The top-left shape is shaded. Arrow shading irrelevant.

86. B.
87. A.
88. C.
89. C.
90. C.

Questions 91–95

Sequence of figures to be read clockwise from top left in a spiral towards centre:

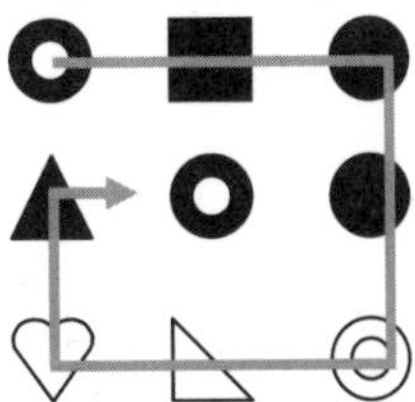

Set A: Same sequence 'A', shading irrelevant.

Set B: Same sequence 'B', figure always shaded the same.

91. B.
92. A.
93. C.
94. C.
95. A.

Questions 96–100

Set A: Moving clockwise around the cells in the hexagon from the top, A – B = C. Negative numbers are shaded black.

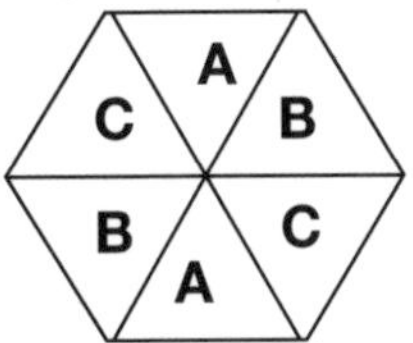

Set B: The total number of spots in the hexagon = 10, using negative numbers shaded black.

96. A.
97. C.
98. B.
99. B.
100. A.

Mini-test 1

Questions 101–105

Set A: The total number of sides is 13, where the shaded figure counts treble (black triangle: $3 \times 3 = 9$). The largest shape is uppermost.
Set B: The total number of sides is 13, where the white figure counts treble (white triangle: $3 \times 3 = 9$). The largest shape is lowermost.

101. C. Upside down for Set B and only a value of 7 for Set A.
102. A.
103. C. Not 13 in either set.
104. C. Score of 13 in Set A, but largest shape lowermost.
105. C. Score of 13 in Set B, no largest shape.

Questions 106–110

Triangle = 1, square = 2, circle = 3. Black shapes have negative values.
Set A: Sum of values in top row plus values in middle row equals values in bottom row.
Set B: Top row minus middle row equals bottom row.

106. A.
107. B.
108. C.
109. A.
110. B.

Mini-test 2

Questions 111–115

Set A: Odd number of bounded regions. Zero or one shaded space.
Set B: Even number of bounded regions. One or two shaded spaces.

111. B.
112. B.
113. A.
114. C.
115. C.

Questions 116–120

Set A: The total number of sides is 15. Striped shapes count double. Shapes are in ascending order of number of sides, reading across and down.
Set B: The total number of sides is 16. Striped shapes count double, black shapes count half. Shapes are in descending order of number of sides, reading across and down.

116. C.
117. C.
118. A.
119. B.
120. B.

Mini-test 3

Questions 121–125

Set A: Moving from top left to bottom right, if there is a circle before a triangle, the last shape will be black. Other shading irrelevant.

Set B: Moving from top left to bottom right, if there is a square before a triangle, the last shape will be black. Other shading irrelevant.

121. C.
122. B.
123. A.
124. B.
125. C.

Questions 126–130

Set A: Biggest shape is the same shape as the smallest. Shading irrelevant.

Set B: Same shapes are also the same size. Shading irrelevant.

126. A.
127. A.
128. C.
129. B.
130. C.

Mini-test 4

Questions 131–135

Set A has 180° rotational symmetry, but no reflective symmetry in vertical axis.
Set B has reflective symmetry in vertical axis, may have 180° rotational symmetry.

131. C.
132. B.
133. A.
134. C.
135. A.

Questions 136–140

Set A: The number of enclosed regions is one larger than the number of line intersections. For example, the second diagram with the two overlapping squares has three regions and two line intersections.
Set B: The number of enclosed regions is the same as the number of line intersections.

136. B.
137. B.
138. C.
139. A.
140. A.

Mini-test 5

Questions 141–145

Set A: Two odd-number-sided figures (circle, triangle, pentagon, etc) means a right arrow. The presence of a square means the arrow is shaded.
Set B: Two odd-number-sided figures (circle, triangle, pentagon, etc) means a left arrow. The presence of a hexagon means the arrow is shaded.

141. A.
142. A.
143. C. Three odd-number-sided figures.
144. C. No hexagon, arrow should not be shaded.
145. B.

Questions 146–150

Circle = 0, rectangle = 1, up arrow = 2, triangle = 3, square = 4, pentangle = 5, hexagon = 6, down arrow = 7, octagon = 8 and right or left arrow = 9.
Set A: Represents addition. The first two plus the second two = the last two. For example, the first cell has the equation: 01 + 03 = 04.
Set B: Represents subtraction.

146. C.
147. A.
148. C.
149. B.
150. B.

Chapter 6 Non-cognitive analysis

Q1. Explanation: Tactful or tact means discretion or diplomatic and these are desirable qualities in applicants to medical school. Check the consistency of your answers with, for example, questions 16, 19, 25, 58 and 69.

Q2. Explanation: To agree with this statement allows you to be both practical and compassionate while to disagree means that you are more practical than compassionate. The role of a medical professional demands both compassion and a practical, ie sensible, realistic approach. For this reason the better response might be to agree.

Q3. Explanation: That healthcare might need to be rationed does not imply that it should be rationed according to people's lifestyle and certain lifestyles should be discriminated against in terms of the level of care they receive.

Q4. Explanation: Your work in the health service will require extensive detail and small differences will make a significant difference to the quality of care that you provide. For these reasons an admission that you struggle to pay attention to small detail is unlikely to support your application.

Q5. Explanation: If you can think of other reasons why you do not steal, like for example the fact that it is wrong, then you should disagree with this statement. Check your answer for consistency with your response to questions 12, 27, 37, 41, 53, 76, 84 and 91.

Q6. Explanation: There is nothing wrong with compassion but too much and you might risk the impression that you may find the stresses and strains of the medical profession a little too much. This question investigates an aspect of how emotional you are; consider, for example, questions 31, 36, 42, 54, 57, 59, 61 and 79 which also investigate aspects of this trait and check your responses for consistency.

Q7. Explanation: You should disagree with this statement because you should first establish if you should stop immediately what you were doing and turn to the critical new task rather than first complete your current assignment. Consider your response to, for example, questions 17, 34, 46 and 88 all of which to some extent investigate your attitude towards aspects of the trait robustness.

Q8. Explanation: The views of someone qualified in the field may carry more weight than someone unqualified but this should not lead you to agree with the suggestion that only the views of those qualified should be allowed to contribute to a debate.

Q9. Explanation: To leave a situation which might well amount to an emergency would not be the kind of response expected from someone who wants to work in the medical profession.

Q10. Explanation: In the medical profession you may well have to take the time to listen to people who are only able to speak slowly; for this reason agreement with this statement would suggest you can empathize with others.

Q11. Explanation: To agree with this statement might suggest that you are reserved, unapproachable and inaccessible in nature and these are not the ideal qualities in someone who wants to work in the medical profession. See questions 45 and 81 for the consistency of your response.

Q12. Explanation: We place medical professionals in very high positions of trust and expect from them exemplary integrity. As a doctor you may well be known in the community in which you shop and for this reason to disagree with this statement might damage your application and your standing in the community that you serve. Check your answer for consistency with your responses to questions 5, 27, 37, 41, 53, 76, 84 and 91.

Q13. Explanation: Despite the fact that Mary is a challenging character she deserves the same treatment and respect as every other patient; such behaviour therefore would never be excusable.

Q14. Explanation: The money was not yours to donate or decide how to spend and so the suggested action would have been the wrong thing to do. If you did not answer that it was the wrong thing to do then you may risk the impression that you lack integrity.

Q15. Explanation: Being identified as a sociable sort of person with a genuine interest in people would support your application to medical school and disagreement with this statement might help give that impression. Check the consistency of your answers with your responses to questions 78 and 87.

Q16. Explanation: Astuteness means intelligence and is a desirable quality in applicants to medical school.

Q17. Explanation: You should be happy to disagree with this statement. If you make a mistake, and we all do from time to time, you should be able to report it immediately and when appropriate work hard to correct it.

Q18. Explanation: You might well disagree with this statement because to be serious not only means taking your role seriously but also is to be solemn, stern or even severe, whereas to be lucid is to be articulate, clear and logical and the latter might be the more valuable quality in a medical professional.

Q19. Explanation: To show disdain is to show contempt or to be condescending and these would be inappropriate responses in work no matter the provocation. A patient might be very uncomfortable or worried and consequently may be rude unintentionally, and in these circumstances one should try to understand and sympathize. Check for consistency with your answers to, for example, questions 1, 16, 25, 58 and 69.

Q20. Explanation: This common saying implies that it matters little how you achieve something so long as it is achieved. Such a pragmatic stance risks you being judged as lacking principle. Would it be right, for example, to achieve departmental targets by forging the results? This question investigates aspects of the trait integrity – consider, for example, questions 13, 14, 29, 49, 68, 74, 75 and 100 for consistency as they too investigate aspects of this trait.

Q21. Explanation: The wish to help others is an important motivation for many in the medical profession and agreement with this statement would suggest a lack of interest in helping others. It may be that on some occasions you are too busy but to say you are busy when your current commitments are unspecified suggests an unwillingness to help as a matter of principle.

Q22. Explanation: To agree with this statement suggests that you would prefer to help only certain sorts of people and that you might treat someone you do not know differently from someone you do. This is unlikely to be the sort of response a medical school would expect of its preferred candidates. Look to question 2 for consistency in your response.

Q23. Explanation: Disagreement with this statement suggests that you do not find it difficult to trust people and are happy to accept at face value what people say.

Q24. Explanation: Health professionals work both independently and as a part of a team. But this does not mean that the ideal candidate should prefer to work independently, because this would suggest that they favour autonomy over interdependence and the role of health professional is dependent on the services of others and teamwork. This question investigates aspects of self-sufficiency. Check that you have responded consistently with, for example, question 8, 28, 48 and 90.

Q25. Explanation: You might recall the earlier statement which asked 'I am able to talk about things that people find personal', a statement that you should have been able to agree with. However, this statement, 'I like to talk about things that many people find personal', is quite a different matter and suggests a certain lack of sympathy. If people find something personal then they are likely to feel uncomfortable and we do not enjoy making people uncomfortable.

Q26. Explanation: You should disagree with this statement because if you were already very busy then you should inform the person who asked you to undertake the additional work that there is a risk that you may not have time to complete anything else. Check question 1 to see if your response is consistent.

Q27. Explanation: You should be honest enough to answer the statement truthfully, which will almost certainly mean that we all disagree with it. Check your answer for consistency with your responses to questions 5, 12, 37, 41, 53, 76, 84 and 91.

Q28. Explanation: On the basis of the information provided it is quite possible that the views of a new member of a team are equal to or more important than those of a long-standing member of the team. This question investigates aspects of self-sufficiency. Check that you have responded consistently with, for example, questions 8, 24, 48 and 90.

Q29. Explanation: To agree with this statement would support the view that you have integrity and are a principled person.

Q30. Explanation: Most people should be prepared to agree with this statement. Agreement does not mean that you lack patience because the most patient person in the world may wish they were even more so. We all feel frustration with others from time to time and it would be a credit to us if we desired that we did not do so.

Q31. Explanation: It is possible to be too sensitive for a role as a medical professional where you will face many stressful and some distressing situations, so it might be best to avoid the suggestion that the statement is particularly true of you. To say that people who know you would not say you are sensitive might also risk the impression that you lack the compassion essential for the role. Perhaps the best answer, if it is true, is that it is partially true that people say you are sensitive.

Q32. Explanation: Feeling at ease with strangers and being able to confidently start a conversation are skills important to the role of a medical professional and agreement with this statement might risk the impression that you do not excel in this aspect of the role.

Q33. Explanation: Agreement with this statement suggests an assured and self-reliant approach to work, qualities that would be valued in a health professional. This question investigates aspects of self-sufficiency. Check that you have responded consistently with, for example, questions 8, 24, 28, 48 and 90.

Q34. Explanation: You should be able to agree with this statement. Your colleagues and managers will want to know all the facts and if you withhold information because you believe they might not want to hear it then problems could arise. Check to see that your response is consistent with question 1.

Q35. Explanation: In the medical profession people work collaboratively and it is a role that suits the naturally gregarious; for this reason, to disagree with this statement might be the preferred response.

Q36. Explanation: Emotional detachment implies an indifference or aloofness so you should only agree with this statement if you are indifferent towards others or aloof. This question investigates an aspect of how emotional you are; consider, for example, questions 31, 42, 54, 57, 59, 61 and 79 which also investigate aspects of this trait and check your responses for consistency.

Q37. Explanation: Only agree with this statement if you would steal in a situation when you could not possibly get caught. Most people, even if they know they could not get caught, would still not steal as a matter of principle. Check your answer for consistency with your responses to questions 5, 12, 27, 41, 53, 76, 84 and 91.

Q38. Explanation: You should have no difficultly in disagreeing with this statement; there are no circumstances when a racist remark is appropriate.

Q39. Explanation: The work of a health professional requires someone's full attention and concentration and to admit to vagueness or losing track of time is something we should guard against and work hard to avoid.

Q40. Explanation: You should only disagree with this statement if it is true that you are primarily motivated by salary. In the health profession salaries can be good but they are not most people's first and foremost motivation.

Q41. Explanation: You should be able to disagree with this statement. The money is not yours and so it is not for you to decide how it should be used. The correct action would be to take it to the police station so that the person who lost it might report it lost and collect it. Check your answer for consistency with your responses to questions 5, 12, 27, 37, 53, 76, 84 and 91.

Q42. Explanation: To be thick-skinned is to be insensitive or indifferent to the feelings of others. To describe yourself in such a way might risk the impression that you lack compassion and empathy, both of which are desirable qualities in health professionals.

Q43. Explanation: To agree with this statement implies that you believe it is possible both to be non-judgemental and to operate according to an ethical code, and this stance is most certainly expected of you in the medical profession. To disagree allows the possibility that you hold an ethical code that requires you to be judgemental. Check your response to question 89 for consistency.

Q44. Explanation: To agree with this statement suggests that you hold that fault and blame might be attributable to people with certain medical conditions and that state-funded medical care should be withdrawn from sufferers in certain circumstances. To criticize people for their lifestyle and to judge them (or even treat them differently if they suffer certain medical conditions) risks being viewed as lacking empathy. Consider your responses to, for example, questions 10, 22, 38, 52 and 65 all of which to some extent investigate your attitude towards aspects of the trait empathy.

Q45. Explanation: Work as a health professional best suits people who are at ease socially and can build and maintain working relationships effectively. To admit that you find it difficult to get used to people does not suggest that you possess these important qualities. Check questions 11 and 81 for consistency of your responses.

Q46. Explanation: To be caring or thoughtful in your approach to others should not get in the way of a life-saving intervention and if you agree with this statement then you risk the impression that you might in some situations be inconsiderate and such an impression is unlikely to support your application to medical school.

Q47. Explanation: To agree with this statement suggests a confident and trusting approach in your dealings with others.

Q48. Explanation: People in senior roles do carry a disproportionate share of responsibility for the actions taken; however, every member of a team should share a sense of ownership for the successful outcome of the team's work and agreement with the statement might suggest a reluctance to share fully that responsibility.

Q49. Explanation: The decent and correct thing to do would be to report the fact that you were late irrespective of the circumstances. This question investigates aspects of the trait integrity; consider, for example, questions 13, 14, 20, 29, 68, 74, 75 and 95 for consistency as they too investigate aspects of this trait.

Q50. Explanation: To be demonstrative is to be warm and open, while someone reserved is formal, reticent or quiet.

Q51. Explanation: Agreement with this statement suggests someone who is secure in their dealings with other people while disagreement might suggest someone distrusting of the motives of others.

Q52. Explanation: Agreement with this statement risks the impression that you find it difficult to share someone's feelings. Imagine yourself having a health problem and living in a community which speaks a language you cannot speak and imagine how difficult that situation might be. You would want the health professionals to assist you as much as is practical and to uphold the principle that they will provide you with the best possible care despite any language barrier.

Q53. Explanation: You should be happy to agree with this statement as there is always the option of telling the truth and a medical professional should never need to lie. Check your answer for consistency with your responses to questions 5, 12, 27, 37, 41, 76, 84 and 91.

Q54. Explanation: To be thin-skinned is to be emotional or to be easily upset. There is a risk that someone who is thin-skinned may find the pressures and daily experiences of a medical professional hard to deal with. This question investigates an aspect of how emotional you are; consider, for example, questions 31, 36, 42, 57, 59, 61 and 79 which also investigate aspects of this trait and check your responses for consistency.

Q55. Explanation: We all make mistakes but to admit that you allow yourself to be distracted to the point where you make them is something different and something we should all work to avoid.

Q56. Explanation: You should agree with this statement; after all, the message is described as urgent and to delay and, for example, wait for a suitable pause in the conversation before you deliver the message may lead to an unaffordable delay.

Q57. Explanation: Enthusiasm is a good thing but like most good things you can have too much of it. The ideal answer might be one that suggests you are enthusiastic but not so enthusiastic as to suggest emotional immaturity. This question investigates an aspect of how emotional you are; consider, for example, questions 31, 36, 42, 54, 59, 61 and 79 which also investigate aspects of this trait and check your responses for consistency.

Q58. Explanation: A councillor is an elected member of a local or city authority; a counsellor is someone qualified to provide support for people with, for example, social or psychological difficulties. The role of a counsellor is very much an aspect of the work of a medical professional and for this reason might be the preferred answer.

Q59. Explanation: It is hard to imagine that agreement with this statement would be desirable in a health professional or would support an application to medical school.

Q60. Explanation: To be spontaneous can mean you are unstructured, unplanned and impulsive. And these may not be great qualities for a medical professional to display. Remember to keep at the forefront of your mind the world of work. You might be spontaneous in your social life or when in the company of friends or family, but would you be in the role of a medical professional at work? I suspect you might be far less spontaneous then, and it is in this context that you should answer the question.

Q61. Explanation: To wear your emotions on your sleeve means that you do not hide your emotions. It implies that you may allow your emotions to interfere with what you are doing and this may not be desirable in the role of a health professional.

Q62. Explanation: The correct thing to do in this situation would be to report the incident.

Q63. Explanation: Both teamwork and keeping abreast of developments are key to the role of a health professional and by not agreeing with the statement you avoid the trap of falsely ranking one above the other.

Q64. Explanation: To agree that you prefer the familiar and routine is fine, but beware the suggestion in this statement that you prefer such work because it helps with your confidence. To agree that you prefer the familiar and routine because otherwise you lack confidence may not support your application to a role in which you must be able to deal with the unexpected.

Q65. Explanation: In the medical profession you are providing a service to people and whether or not they conform to conventions associated with good manners should in no way affect the service you provide or how you feel towards them; see question 2 to check that your response is consistent.

Q66. Explanation: You should be able to readily agree with this statement. Medics and dentists work in a fast-moving environment and when priorities change they have to interrupt what they are doing to do something else. Consider your responses to, for example, questions 17, 34, 46, 88, 92 and 97 all of which to some extent investigate your attitude towards aspects of the trait robustness.

Q67. Explanation: We should all be able to agree with this statement. At some time or another we have all concluded after reflection that we have done or said something that we could have handled better, and to have no regrets suggests an unthinking or unprincipled approach.

Q68. Explanation: Morals, principles, ethical behaviour are not luxuries that we can abandon when things get difficult. Imagine this proposal in a medical context and you will quickly see what is disagreeable about it. For example, imagine a very overworked doctor who decides he will only treat people with minor ailments and not treat the more complex cases.

Q69. Explanation: A considered, reflective approach may be highly desirable amongst applicants to the medical profession, so if this is a quality you possess, have the confidence to disclose it. Check for consistency your answers to, for example, questions 1, 16, 19, 25 and 58.

Q70. Explanation: Shrewd means smart or perceptive and is a desirable quality in applicants to medical school.

Q71. Explanation: In some cultures it is a sign of respect not to make eye contact and it should not trouble you at all if someone does not conform to your expectations of how they should conduct themselves. To agree with this statement might suggest that you were able to put yourself in someone else's shoes. Consider your response to, for example, questions 10, 22, 38, 44, 52 and 65 all of which to some extent investigate your attitude towards aspects of the trait empathy.

Q72. Explanation: Unemotional has a negative connotation of being dispassionate or undemonstrative, while unassuming, which means modest or humble, does not.

Q73. Explanation: In the medical profession, dealing with others in a delicate, diplomatic way might be preferred to a bold, decisive stance. Check for consistency your answers to, for example, questions 1, 16, 19, 25, 58 and 69.

Q74 and Q75. Explanation: You should have found both statements to be false. Bad language in work is simply not acceptable and you must rely on other, more appropriate ways of dealing with a stressful day.

Q76. Explanation: Medical professionals are placed in positions of great trust and their employers expect the very highest levels of honesty from them. You should have no difficulty agreeing with this statement. Check your answer for consistency with your responses to questions 5, 12, 27, 37, 41, 53, 84 and 91.

Q77. Explanation: At work it would be inappropriate to try to impress another member of the team because of their looks or because they belong to the opposite gender. To suggest that such behaviour is natural is incorrect because at work it is neither usual nor acceptable.

Q78. Explanation: Agreement with this statement is unlikely to signify anything that might support or undermine your application but check this answer with those to questions 15 and 87.

Q79. Explanation: To classify yourself as insensitive is unlikely to enhance your application to medical school. It is also true that someone who is emotional might also be the less than perfect applicant. However, of the two adjectives, being emotional might be regarded as preferable to insensitive.

Q80. Explanation: To agree with this statement suggests that you hold the view that you should only help those to whom you are related or with whom you share some common heritage. This implies that you do not sympathize or empathize with people who are not related to you in some way. Consider your response to, for example, questions 10, 22 38, 44, 52 and 65 all of which to some extent investigate your attitude towards aspects of the trait empathy.

Q81. Explanation: To be approachable is to be easy to talk to, which must be a great quality in a medical professional. To be polite is also a desirable quality and means that you are, for example, respectful, but on balance perhaps approachable is the more valuable attribute. Check questions 11 and 45 for consistency of your responses.

Q82. Explanation: Someone who is wary is someone suspicious and distrustful in nature while someone naïve is inexperienced or youthful. Applicants to medical school might be forgiven for being naïve but if they were wary by nature they might find it hard to show the necessary understanding and compassion for the wellbeing of others.

Q83. Explanation: Jokes and humour in the workplace have a value and can help build a team or defuse a stressful situation, but jokes about someone's sexuality would not be appropriate and for this reason an employer would expect you to help discourage such behaviour.

Q84. Explanation: It is really stealing and the fact that a lot of people might do it does not mean it is not still wrong. Check your answer for consistency with your responses to questions 5, 12, 27, 37, 41, 53, 76 and 91.

Q85. Explanation: To be cheeky is to be disrespectful and it would count as inappropriate behaviour at work. Check for consistency your answers to, for example, questions 1, 16, 19, 25, 58 and 69.

Q86. Explanation: To agree with this statement risks the suggestion that you prejudge people according to stereotypes and this is not a desirable personal trait in someone applying to work in healthcare.

Q87. Explanation: Planning is an important part of the work of every medical professional and we would all rather work in a situation where things go to plan. However, dealing well with the unexpected is equally important and someone who finds it an effort to deal with the unexpected might not cope well in the role. Check the consistency of your answers with your responses to questions 15 and 78.

Q88. Explanation: In many practical situations we have to intervene before all the facts are known and this includes situations when painful choices have to be made. While it is more difficult to decide on the best course of action in these circumstances, it is sometimes necessary to do so and for this reason you should be willing to disagree with this statement.

Q89. Explanation: To disagree with this statement does not rule out the possibility that you are equally honest and trustworthy as you are non-judgemental. To agree with the statement might suggest that while you possess the necessary integrity you may lack the necessary tolerance required for the role. Check your response to question 43 for consistency.

Q90. Explanation: Health professionals work collaboratively and often deal with complex matters that include compromises of one type or another. It is mostly wrong, therefore, to say that a compromise is rarely the right decision in healthcare.

Q91. Explanation: There are no circumstances under which it is right to steal. Check your answer for consistency with your responses to questions 5, 12, 27, 37, 41, 53, 76 and 84.

Q92. Explanation: It is normal for people to be affected by the circumstances of their work but the training they receive helps ensure that they are able to demonstrate professionalism and to cope. For this reason it is reasonable to expect you to have agreed with the statement.

Q93. Explanation: To be impulsive is to be reckless, rash or hasty and these are not the best qualities for an applicant to medical school. You might be rash when you are with your friends and you might regret it afterwards, but would you be reckless and rash if you were working as a medical professional?

Q94. Explanation: Matter-of-fact means unemotional or straightforward while down-to-earth means unpretentious, realistic or unassuming. Both are positive attributes but on balance it might be preferable that a medical professional was described as down-to-earth, as being matter-of-fact might mean you lack compassion.

Q95. Explanation: The world of medicine places high expectations of honesty and morality on its professionals and responses that suggest you support or would indulge in dishonest behaviour (even if such behaviour might be widespread) would not enhance your application. This question investigates aspects of the trait integrity; consider, for example, questions 13, 14, 20, 29, 49, 68, 74 and 75 for consistency as they too investigate aspects of this trait.

Q96. Explanation: Agreement with this statement suggests that what people say cannot usually be taken at face value and that you must establish their motive before you can realize what they really mean. Such a view suggests an untrusting, suspicious nature.

Q97. Explanation: Agreement with this statement risks the impression that you might struggle to maintain consistently high standards when involved in the delivery of therapies or treatments for common ailments.

Q98. Explanation: All applicants to medical school should be able to agree with this statement; after all, there will be many occasions when you will have to do just this.

Q99. Explanation: Agreement with this statement would suggest someone self-assured and a team player and such an impression would support most applications to medical school.

Q100. Explanation: To say one thing and do another can be insincere and in some cases deceitful. It is therefore something we should all avoid doing whatever the circumstances.